Turbo Pascal® 6:
The Complete Reference

Turbo Pascal® 6:
The Complete Reference

Stephen K. O'Brien

BORLAND·OSBORNE/McGRAW·HILL

PROGRAMMING   SERIES

Berkeley   New York   St. Louis   San Francisco
Auckland   Bogotá   Hamburg   London   Madrid
Mexico City   Milan   Montreal   New Delhi   Panama City
Paris   São Paulo   Singapore   Sydney
Tokyo   Toronto

Osborne **McGraw-Hill**
2600 Tenth Street
Berkeley, California 94710
U.S.A.

Osborne **McGraw-Hill** offers software for sale. For information on software, translations, or book distributors outside of the U.S.A., please write to Osborne **McGraw-Hill** at the above address.

Turbo Pascal® 6: The Complete Reference

4567890 DOC 9987654321

ISBN 0-07-881703-X

CONTENTS AT A GLANCE

Turbo Pascal has been at the forefront of software innovation for the past seven years. Now Turbo Pascal 6 brings programmers a major breakthrough with Turbo Vision, the first application framework for DOS.

Turbo Pascal 6: The Complete Reference is an indispensable tool for anyone who develops programs in Turbo Pascal. Experienced and novice programmers alike will want this desktop reference at their fingertips while they work. Author Stephen K. O'Brien provides answers to the most frequently asked questions about programming in Turbo Pascal. As a bonus, he presents routines that will be a welcome addition to any programmer's library.

You can rely on this book both for the thoroughness with which it covers the subject and for the lucidity of the explanations. All aspects of Turbo Pascal programming—from accessing DOS services to writing terminate-and-stay-resident programs to the object oriented language features of Turbo Pascal—are included. Special attention is paid to telecommunications, a common use of Turbo Pascal, and to interfacing Turbo Pascal with assembly language. The procedures and functions are well written and extremely useful, and even the most complex processes are accompanied by easy-to-understand examples that users can follow to write their own programs.

Stephen K. O'Brien has been programming in Turbo Pascal since its launch by Borland in 1983. Now he provides you with everything you need to know to develop programs in Turbo Pascal efficiently and productively in one concise, easy-to-use volume.

Philippe Kahn
Chief Executive Officer
Borland International, Inc.

In any book of this size and depth, there are a number of people who contribute. Thanks to the people at Osborne who have done another fine job putting this book together. I would also like to thank the people at Borland, especially Nan Borreson for her help and Amrik Dhillon for catching me whenever I left anything out.

Special thanks are due to author Steven Nameroff for his excellent contributions to the sections on object oriented programming and Turbo Vision. Without his efforts, I'd probably still be writing.

ACKNOWLEDGMENTS

Turbo Pascal has come to dominate the Pascal market. The little compiler that changed the way people program has gone through many changes over the years. Today it is still the best deal in the business. Turbo Pascal combines the benefits of structured programming in Pascal with a whole new array of tools for the professional programmer, including object oriented programming and Turbo Vision. Whether you are just learning about PC programming or are a serious software developer, Turbo Pascal offers every powerful feature you could ask for in one friendly package.

About the Book

This book is intended for all Turbo Pascal programmers, from beginners to experts. It covers all aspects of the compiler, with extensive examples. Both beginners and advanced programmers will find useful information ranging from dynamic allocation to memory-resident programming. Designed primarily as a reference guide, the book provides quick access to concise information on a broad range of topics.

This book includes a brief introduction to object oriented programming with Turbo Pascal and Turbo Vision. With these new extensions to the compiler, Borland has set a new standard. This book should give you a good start in understanding how to use these tools.

How This Book Is Organized

Turbo Pascal beginners will appreciate Chapter 1, "A Quick Start to Programming," which introduces programming basics. Chapters 2 through 9 cover all aspects of the Turbo Pascal system, from the integrated development environment to pointers and dynamic memory allocation. Chapters 10 through 18 offer valuable insights into such important programming topics as DOS and BIOS functions, the use of assembly language, and memory-resident programs. Chapter 19 describes how to use the integrated debugger, which can save you hours of wasted programming time. Chapter 20 is an overview of object oriented programming, and Chapter 21 introduces Borland's newest enhancement, Turbo Vision.

Turbo Pascal is one of the leading programming environments for personal computers. *Turbo Pascal 6: The Complete Reference* is the resource you need to get the most from Borland's premier product.

A Quick Start to Programming

O
N
E

If you are using Turbo Pascal for the first time, this chapter is for you. In it you will discover the fundamentals of the Turbo Pascal system and, at the same time, write and run your first programs. Do not be too concerned about understanding everything presented in this chapter; even simple programming concepts take time to sink in. Just take your time, get comfortable with the system, try the sample programs, and experiment on your own.

A Simple Turbo Pascal Program

The best way to begin learning Turbo Pascal 6 is by writing your first program. To start Turbo Pascal, make sure you are logged in to the drive and directory in which the TURBO.EXE file resides (or specify the Turbo directory in your path). At the DOS prompt, type **TURBO** and press ENTER.

On your screen, you see the Turbo Pascal integrated development environment. At the top of the screen is the main menu, which gives you access to all of Turbo Pascal's features. To begin programming, you must first open an Edit window. Do this by pressing F3. Then type in the name of your new file (call it FIRST.PAS). The Edit window opens immediately, with the cursor positioned in the upper right-hand corner. Now, type in the following program:

```
Program Prog1;

Begin
WriteLn('This is my first program.');
ReadLn;
End.
```

If you make a typing mistake, use the arrow keys on the numeric keypad to position the cursor at the error, press DEL to delete the error, and then type the correct letters.

Once you have typed the complete program, hold down the ALT key and press R to run your program. Turbo Pascal will now execute the program you just wrote—your monitor will show this message:

```
This is my first program.
```

When you are ready to return to the integrated development environment, press ENTER.

While it is small, this program contains elements common to all Turbo Pascal programs. It has a program heading, **Program Prog1**, which identifies the program. It also has a program block that starts with **Begin** and terminates with **End**, as shown in Figure 1-1.

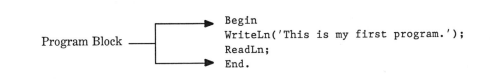

Figure 1-1.   A short program block

A Turbo Pascal program always starts execution at the first **Begin** statement of the main program block and continues until it reaches the final **End** statement. (A program will also stop when it encounters the **Halt** command or a fatal error, but these are exceptions.)

The program block in the example just given contains only two statements.

```
WriteLn('This is my first program.');
ReadLn;
```

The **WriteLn** statement displays the string, and **ReadLn** makes the computer wait until you press ENTER. If you run a program in the integrated development environment (IDE), you can use the **ReadLn** statement to stop a program before the screen switches back to the editor screen. When in the IDE, you can always view the output screen by pressing ALT-F5.

WriteLn is a Turbo Pascal standard procedure that displays numbers and strings of characters to the screen, prints them on a printer, or writes them to a disk file. It also adds two special characters, carriage return and line feed (ASCII codes 13 and 10), to the end of the line. These special characters, often referred to in programming shorthand as CR/LF, signal that the end of a line of text has been reached, and that any additional text should start on the next line.

Inside the parentheses of the **WriteLn** statement are the items to be printed. While in this case the **WriteLn** procedure prints only one line, it is capable of printing more than one item at a time. Figure 1-2 shows an example of a **WriteLn** statement that prints three separate strings.

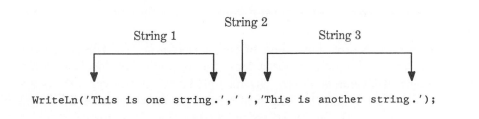

Figure 1-2.   A WriteLn statement with multiple strings

A *string* is any combination of characters that is enclosed in single quotation marks. In the example **WriteLn** procedure, commas separate one string from another. Note that the second string consists of two blank characters, thus creating a space between the first and third strings. When this statement is executed, the result looks like the following.

```
This is one string.   This is another string.
```

Like **WriteLn**, the procedure **Write** also displays strings and numbers; but **Write** does not add CR/LF characters to the end of the line. When you use **Write**, the cursor remains on the same line as the information written, while **WriteLn** moves the cursor to the beginning of the next line.

Adding Variables to a Program

Programs that merely write messages are not very interesting. To be truly useful, a program must process data, and that requires the use of *variables;* places in your computer's memory that hold values, such as numbers or strings.

To define a variable, you must give it a name and a type. You can give a variable almost any name you want, but it is best to choose a name that describes the information the variable holds. For example, you might call a variable that holds the name of a customer **Customer-Name** and define it as follows:

```
Var
  CustomerName : String[50];
```

CustomerName, the name of the variable, is also referred to as the variable identifier because it identifies by name the location in memory where the value is stored. **String [50]** identifies the variable as a string and indicates that the length of this string cannot exceed 50 characters.

Var is a Turbo Pascal *reserved word* that indicates the beginning of variable declarations. There are many other reserved words in Turbo Pascal, such as **Integer, Begin, End,** and so on. (Appendix D contains a complete list of Turbo Pascal reserved words.) Reserved words are central to the Turbo Pascal language, and therefore, you cannot redefine them. These examples illustrate illegal attempts to use reserved words as variable identifiers:

```
Var
  Begin : Integer;
  Real  : String[50];
```

Integer, LongInt, and *Real* variables can hold numbers; *char* variables can hold single characters; *String* variables can hold groups of characters; and *Boolean* variables contain true/false indicators. While they are designed for different purposes, these variable types share one common characteristic—their values can be changed (or varied) in a program by using an *assignment statement.*

Assignment statements set variables to particular values. For example, the statement

```
CustomerName := 'John Doe';
```

takes the group of characters "John Doe" and stores them in the string variable **CustomerName**. Note that the assignment statement uses the := operator, which is known as the *assignment operator.*

Variables and Input

The assignment statement is just one way to set the value of a variable; the **ReadLn** procedure is another. But unlike assignment statements, **ReadLn** gets its value from a source outside the program, such as the person using the program or a disk file. When a program encounters a **ReadLn** statement, it stops and waits until the user types in the data and presses ENTER. **ReadLn** then takes the input and assigns it to a variable named in the **ReadLn** statement. For example, the Pascal input statement **ReadLn(CustomerName)** waits for the user to type in a string of characters, accepts a string, and stores it in the variable **CustomerName**.

The following sample program demonstrates how **ReadLn** obtains input and stores it in variables.

```
Program Prog2;

Uses CRT;

Var
  i : Integer;
  s : String[20];

Begin
ClrScr;

Write('Enter a number: ');
ReadLn(i);
WriteLn('Your number is ',i);

Write('Enter a string: ');
ReadLn(s);
WriteLn('Your string is ',s);

ReadLn;
End.
```

Now, go back into the Turbo Editor and type in the program just listed. You will notice that this program is somewhat more complicated than the first one. For one thing, the program includes the following declaration:

```
Uses CRT;
```

CRT is a Turbo Pascal *standard unit.* Units contain data declarations, procedures, and functions that are designed for specific purposes. The routines in the CRT unit, for example, apply primarily to the use of the video display screen. If you want to use the procedures and functions in a unit, you must include the **Uses** statement at the beginning of your program.

Now that you have typed in the program, start it as you did the first program (select the **Run** option from the Run menu). When the program starts, the **ClrScr** command (from the CRT unit) clears the screen, and the program displays **Enter a number:** on your monitor. Type the number **9** and press ENTER. The program now displays **Your number is 9**, skips one line on the screen, and displays **Enter a string:**. Type in **ABC** and press ENTER. The program now displays **Your string is ABC**. The program used the **ReadLn** statement to obtain a number and a string from the user.

Prog2 uses two variables: **i**, an integer, and **s**, a string. Integers are numerical values with no decimal place and can range in value from 32,767 down to −32,768. The string variable **s** is defined as **String[20]**, which means that it can hold up to 20 characters. (The maximum number of characters a string can hold is 255.)

The example program just given uses a common, if crude, method of getting input from the user. First, the program prompts the user for input by asking for a number. The prompt **Enter a number:** is displayed by using the **Write** procedure, as opposed to **WriteLn**, because **Write** places the cursor directly after the prompt message. This tells the user that the program is waiting for input.

The next statement, **ReadLn(i);**, waits for the user to type a valid integer and press ENTER. The program assigns whatever the user types to the integer variable **i**. The last statement confirms the input by displaying both a message and the contents of **i**.

If the **ReadLn** statement detects an error in the input, it notifies you and halts the program. For example, run **Prog2** again, but when it asks for a number, type **ABC** and press ENTER. Turbo Pascal detects an *input/output error* and displays this message:

```
Runtime error 106 at 0000:008F
```

Error 106 indicates an invalid numeric format. In short, Turbo Pascal was expecting a number, and it got something else, **ABC**, which is not a valid integer. The value 0000:008F is the location in the program at which the error occurred. If you are running the program from within the integrated development environment, Turbo Pascal will automatically locate the error in the source code and bring that part of the program into the editor.

Prog2 also demonstrates the use of the **WriteLn** statement when used with no parameters. When executed, this statement simply writes a CR/LF combination to the computer monitor, which places the cursor on the first position of the next line.

Simple Turbo Pascal Arithmetic

The following example program demonstrates how arithmetic is used in Turbo Pascal programs and introduces another data type called **Real**.

Like **Integer** variables, **Real** variables are numbers; unlike **Integers**, they can have decimal places. They can also be much larger than **Integer**s: the maximum value for an **Integer** variable is 32,767, while for a **Real** variable it is 1.0E38, or a 1 with 38 zeros after it.

```
Program Prog3;
Uses CRT;
Var
  Number1,
  Number2,
  AddResult,
  SubResult,
  MultResult,
  DivResult   : Real;

Begin
ClrScr;

Write('Enter a number: ');
ReadLn(number1);
Write('Enter another number: ');
ReadLn(number2);

AddResult  := Number1 + Number2;
SubResult  := Number1 - Number2;
MultResult := Number1 * Number2;
DivResult  := Number1 / Number2;

WriteLn;
WriteLn('Number1 + Number2 = ',AddResult);
WriteLn('Number1 - Number2 = ',SubResult);
WriteLn('Number1 * Number2 = ',MultResult);
WriteLn('Number1 / Number2 = ',DivResult);

WriteLn;

WriteLn('Number1 + Number2 = ',AddResult:10:3);
WriteLn('Number1 - Number2 = ',SubResult:10:3);
WriteLn('Number1 * Number2 = ',MultResult:10:3);
WriteLn('Number1 / Number2 = ',DivResult:10:3);

WriteLn;
Write('Press ENTER...');
ReadLn;
End.
```

Prog3 asks the user to enter two numbers, which are assigned to **Real** variables **Number1** and **Number2** and then used in four arithmetic operations: addition, subtraction, multiplication, and division. After performing the computations, **Prog3** writes out the results in two different formats: scientific and decimal.

Scientific notation, used only for **Real** variables, is a shorthand way of expressing large values. For example, the result of the following calculation:

5342168903247 × 24729234798734

expressed in scientific notation, would be 1.3210774914E+26. The first part of the number (1.3210774914) contains the significant digits; the second part (E+26) is the power of 10 to which the first part is raised. In other words, the number 1.3210774914E+26 can be expressed as 1.3210774914 times 10 to the 26th power.

Scientific notation is the default format for the value of **Real** variables in Turbo Pascal. You can, however, also write **Real** values in decimal format. For example, in the statement

WriteLn('Number1 + Number2 = ', AddResult:10:3);

the variable **AddResult** is followed by the format specification **:10:3**, which tells Turbo Pascal to print the **Real** variable right-justified in a field that is 10 spaces wide and allows 3 decimal places. If the resulting number were equal to 5, the number would be displayed as shown in Figure 1-3.

If the number printed requires more than the 10 spaces allocated, the program prints the entire number, taking as many spaces as needed.

Repeating Statements with Loops

A loop is a mechanism that allows you to repeat a statement or group of statements. Turbo Pascal provides several ways of creating loops. The

Print position	1	2	3	4	5	6	7	8	9	10
Output						5	.	0	0	0

Figure 1-3.   Formatted numeric output

program shown here demonstrates two of them, the For-Do loop and the Repeat-Until loop.

```
Program Prog4;
Uses CRT;
Var
  NumberArray : Array [1..5] Of Integer;
  Average : Real;
  i : Integer;

Begin
ClrScr;

(*******************)
(* The For-Do Loop *)
(*******************)
For i := 1 To 5 Do
  Begin
  Write('Enter a number: ');
  ReadLn(NumberArray[i]);
  End;

Average := 0;
i := 1;

(************************)
(* The Repeat-Until Loop *)
(************************)

  Repeat
  Average := Average + NumberArray[i];
  i := i + 1;
  Until i > 5;
Average := Average / 5;
WriteLn('The average is: ',Average:0:2);

ReadLn;
End.
```

You need three elements to write a loop: a starting point, an ending point, and an integer variable, which is used as a counter. In the For-Do loop definition

```
For i := 1 To 5 Do
```

i is the counter, 1 is the starting point, and 5 is the ending point. When the loop starts, the program sets i to 1. Each time the loop repeats, the value of i is incremented by one; after the fifth time through the loop, i is equal to 6. Since 6 is greater than the ending point specified in the For-Do loop, the loop ends, and the program proceeds with the first statement that follows the For-Do loop block.

The example program also demonstrates a second type of loop, known as the Repeat-Until loop. Compared with For-Do loops, Repeat-Until loops require a little more work; you, not Turbo Pascal, must initialize the value of the counter, increment its value, and test the value to terminate the loop. For all this work, Repeat-Until loops do have advantages. For one thing, you do not need to know before you write the loop how many times it will execute. Repeat-Until loops repeat until the condition specified in the **Until** line is satisfied. You can also increment the counter by any amount you like. Another advantage is that you can test for more than one condition at the same time, as is shown in this example:

```
Repeat
i := i + 1;
j := j + 1;
Until (i > 100) Or (j = 50);
```

If either of the tests in the **Until** statement is found to be true, the program exits the Repeat-Until loop. Loop structures are fundamental to all aspects of computer programming. You will find many uses for them as your programming skills grow.

Using Disk Files

Eventually, you will write programs that need to store and retrieve data from disk files. Turbo Pascal makes using disk files easy, as this program demonstrates.

```
Program Prog5;
Uses CRT;
Var
  i,j : Integer;
  f : Text;
  r : Real;

Begin
ClrScr;
```

```
Assign(f,'SQUARES.DAT');
Rewrite(f);

For i := 1 To 20 Do
  WriteLn(f,Sqr(i):10);

Reset(f);
For i := 1 To 20 Do
  Begin
  ReadLn(f,j);
  WriteLn(i:4,' squared is ',j:4);
  End;
Close(f);

WriteLn;
Write('Press ENTER...');
ReadLn;
End.
```

Prog5 creates a text file and fills it with the squares of the first 20 positive integers. The program then rereads this file and writes the values to the screen.

Prog5 introduces the Turbo Pascal reserved word **Text**, a type of disk file that holds mainly words and sentences, although a text file can also hold numbers. **Prog5** declares the file identifier **f** to be of type **Text**. This file identifier is then used in the familiar **ReadLn** and **WriteLn** statements to direct input and output to disk files rather than to the screen.

Before you use a file variable, you must first assign it, by name, to a disk file. Do this with the **Assign** command:

```
Assign (f, 'SQUARES.DAT');
Rewrite(f);
```

The **Assign** command links the file variable **f** with the physical file SQUARES.DAT. The **Rewrite** statement prepares the file to accept data. If the physical file SQUARES.DAT does not exist, the **Rewrite** command creates it. If the file does exist, **Rewrite** destroys the contents of the file. Once a file has been rewritten, it is ready to receive output. In **Prog5**, output is written to file **f** with this statement:

```
WriteLn(f,Sqr(i):10);
```

This is the same **WriteLn** procedure used in earlier program examples, but this time the first parameter is the file variable **f**, which tells Turbo Pascal that everything written by this statement goes to this file.

While **Rewrite** prepares a file for writing, **Reset** prepares it for reading. Once the file is reset, the **ReadLn** statement can be used to read data from it, as demonstrated here:

```
ReadLn(f,j);
```

This statement reads an integer from **Text** file **f** and stores that integer in **j**. While Turbo Pascal supports different types of files, **Text** files (like those used in the example just given) are the easiest for beginning programmers because they can be used for input and output in much the same way as the keyboard and monitor are used.

One last note on using files concerns the importance of closing disk files. When a disk file is closed, two things happen. First, if the file is being used for output, any data residing in buffers is flushed to the disk. If your program ends without closing an output file, you risk losing any buffered data that has not yet been written to disk. Second, closing a file frees a file handle. When you start your computer, DOS reserves a fixed number of file handles. The default number of file handles is 8, although you can expand this to up to 20 by adding the line

```
FILES=20
```

to your CONFIG.SYS file. Turbo Pascal always claims the first five file handles for its standard input and output devices. This means that you may have as few as three file handles available to your program. Since every open file uses a file handle, you could be limited to only three open disk files at one time. If your program uses a lot of different disk files, take care to close unused files so that your program will not use up all the available file handles.

As you read through this book, you will find in-depth discussions of the programming concepts introduced in this chapter, as well as information on many advanced topics. Turbo Pascal offers a number of powerful features that may take some time to grasp fully. Read, experiment, have fun, and you will become an accomplished programmer before you know it.

The Integrated Development Environment

Get a Mouse
The Main Menu
The File Menu ALT-F
The Edit Menu ALT-E
The Search Menu ALT-S
The Run Menu ALT-R
The Compile Menu ALT-C
The Debug Menu ALT-D
The Options Menu ALT-O
The Window Menu ALT-W

With Version 6, Borland has completely revamped the Turbo integrated development environment (IDE). The most obvious change is the use of multiple overlapping windows so that you can see several source files at one time. You can even view different parts of the same source file in separate windows, which makes program modification much easier. Other enhancements include a clipboard for copying text from one window to another and terrific mouse support.

Get a Mouse

If you already have a mouse, you will find Turbo Pascal 6 an absolute joy. You can jump from window to window, select menu options, move and resize windows, scroll files, and more with "point and click" simplicity. If you don't have a mouse, it is strongly recommended that you get one. Although the mouse is clearly not required, you will find that the new IDE is much easier to use with one.

Mice generally come with two buttons, and many software packages assign specific functions to each key. In Turbo Pascal 6, you use the left mouse button to select a window, activate a menu option, or position the cursor within a window. The right button, however, is completely programmable. You can use it to set a break point, to call up help, or to perform a number of other functions detailed later in this chapter.

The Main Menu

Turbo Pascal 6 utilizes a pull-down menu system that supports hot-key access to frequently used features. The choices on the main menu are **File**, **Edit**, **Search**, **Run**, **Compile**, **Debug**, **Options**, **Window**, and **Help**, as shown in Figure 2-1. Most of these options will be familiar to

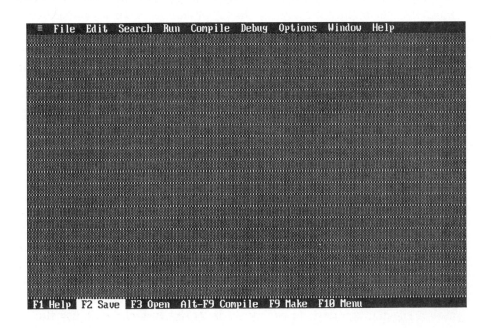

Figure 2-1.   The main menu

users of past versions of Turbo Pascal, but the additions and enhancements are many. For one thing, the **Edit** selection provides options for copying, cutting, and pasting text between windows. Then there is the completely new **Window** option that helps you manage the multi-window Turbo Pascal 6 programming environment.

There are two ways to select a main menu option—using the keyboard or using the mouse. The F10 key activates the main menu, highlighting the currently selected option. You can move the highlight by using the RIGHT ARROW and LEFT ARROW keys on your computer's numeric keypad and then select the option by pressing ENTER. A more direct method is simply to press F10 and the first letter of the desired option (for example, F for **File**, E for **Edit**). Mouse users need only click the mouse on the desired option.

Throughout the IDE, the bottom line of the screen displays a list of the most frequently used hot-key selections for the given context. The hot keys listed will change to match the active window. For example, the Watch window (in which you view variables as you step through a program) has a different set of prompted hot keys than does a text editing window.

Wherever you happen to be, you can select any of the prompted hot-key functions by pressing the desired key (for example, F2 to save the text in the active window), or by clicking the mouse on the displayed option for the same effect.

The File Menu ALT-F

As its name suggests, the File menu contains functions for opening and saving source code files. In addition, you can change the current directory, print a file, get information about the program you are working on, exit to DOS temporarily, or exit from Turbo Pascal 6 entirely.

The File menu is a pull-down menu with options listed vertically. To select an option, use the UP ARROW or DOWN ARROW key to highlight the option and then press ENTER. Some options have hot-key equivalents (for example, F3 for **Open ...**) that can speed things up a bit. As always, mouse users have it easier: you need only point to the option and click. The File menu looks like this:

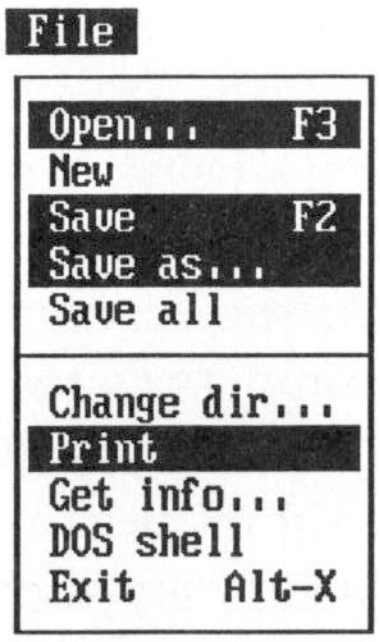

```
 File 
┌─────────────────────┐
│ Open...      F3      │
│ New                 │
│ Save         F2      │
│ Save as...          │
│ Save all            │
│                     │
│ Change dir...       │
│ Print               │
│ Get info...         │
│ DOS shell           │
│ Exit     Alt-X      │
└─────────────────────┘
```

Open . . .   F3

The **Open . . .** option lets you select a file from a list. The file you select is then opened in its own window. When you select **Open . . .**, Turbo Pascal 6 displays the Open a File dialog box, shown in Figure 2-2. At the

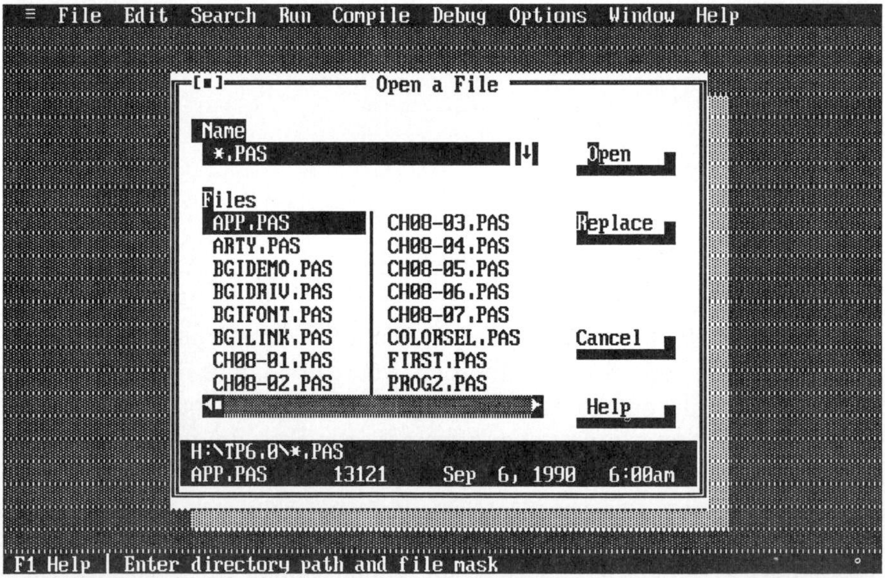

Figure 2-2.   The Open a File dialog box

top of the box is the Name field, in which you can specify a filename or a file specification including the * and ? wildcard symbols. In Figure 2-2, the name field contains *.PAS.

Beneath the Name field is a list of all files that match the file specification you enter. The list contains two columns. You can click the mouse on the desired filename, or you can press the TAB key to move the cursor to the file list and select the desired file by using the arrow keys. If the matching filenames do not fit in the two columns, you can scroll the window by using the scroll bar below the filenames. The scroll bar has arrows at either end and a block selector between the arrows. To use the scroll bar, you can click the mouse on one of the scroll-bar arrows, or you can hold down the left mouse button on the block selector and slide it to the right or left.

On the right-hand side of the Open a File dialog box are four buttons — **Open, Replace, Cancel,** and **Help.** Many windows in Turbo Pascal 6 have similar buttons, which can be selected by clicking the mouse on them, by pressing the highlighted letter (for example, 0 for **Open**), or by tabbing to the key and pressing ENTER. If you select the **Open** button, Turbo Pascal 6 creates a new window containing the file you requested. The **Replace** button loads the selected file into the active edit window, if one exists. The **Cancel** button closes the window without selecting a file, and the **Help** button provides context-sensitive help for the active window.

New

When you select **New** from the File menu, Turbo Pascal 6 opens an empty text window with a default file named NONAME00.PAS. You can open up to a hundred of these temporary edit windows, which will be numbered sequentially up to NONAME99.PAS. If you attempt to save the contents of a new window, Turbo Pascal 6 will ask you to rename the file.

Save F2

The **Save** option writes to disk the contents of the active edit window. If the active edit window was created with the **New** option, Turbo Pascal 6 asks you to enter a new name for the file.

Save as . . .

The **Save as . . .** option saves the contents of the active edit window to disk, but first asks you to enter a filename. The name can be a new filename or the name of an existing file. Once you have selected a filename, all edit windows opened for that file are updated to reflect the new name you have selected.

Save all

The **Save all** option saves the contents of all files currently being edited, but only if the files have been changed in some way.

Change dir . . .

The **Change dir . . .** option lets you change the currently logged directory using the Change Directory dialog box shown in Figure 2-3. You

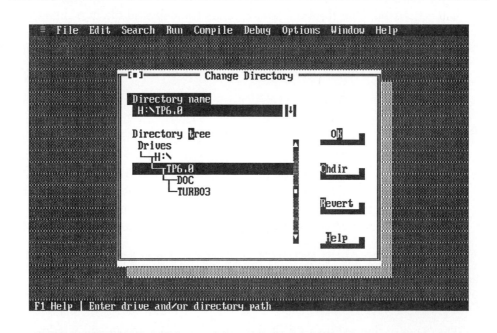

Figure 2-3.   The Change Directory dialog box

can change the directory by entering the desired path or by selecting a directory from the directory tree displayed in the dialog box. Once you select a directory, you can undo the selection by using the **Revert** button.

Print

The **Print** option sends the entire contents of the active edit window to the printer. You cannot print output windows or help windows with this command.

Get info . . .

Once you have compiled a program, the **Get info . . .** option provides information about the program you have just compiled, as shown in Figure 2-4, including the number of lines compiled, the amount of

```
 ≡  File  Edit  Search  Run  Compile  Debug  Options  Window  Help
┌[■]══════════════════════ TEST.PAS ══════════════════════1=[‡]┐
│Program Test;                                                  ▲
│                                                               ▪
│Var    ┌[■]═════════════════ Information ═══════════════┐
│  i,j : Int│                                            │
│           │   ─────── Program ───────     ── Memory ── │
│           │ Source compiled:     23 lines DOS:    234K │
│Procedure A│ Code size:        21648 bytes TURBO:  268K │
│begin      │ Data size:          682 bytes Symbols:  1K │
│end;       │ Stack size:       16384 bytes Program:  0K │
│           │ Minimum heap size:    0 bytes Free:    137K│
│Procedure B│ Maximum heap size:655360 bytes ─── EMS ─── │
│begin      │                               TURBO:  368K │
│A;         │ Status: TEST.PAS compiled.    Other: 2688K │
│end;       │                               Free:    624K│
│           │                                            │
│           │              ┌ OK ┐                        │
│Begin      │              └────┘▜                       │
│i := 1;    └────────────────────────────────────────────┘
│j := 2;
│i := i + j;
│B;                                                             ▼
└ 1:1 ═══◄▐░░░░░░░░░░░░░░░░░░░░░░░░░░░░░░░░░░░░░░░░░░░░░░░░░░▐■┘
F1 Help | Close this dialog box
```

Figure 2-4.   The Information window

memory used for code, data, and the stack, and the maximum and minimum heap requirements. This window also displays system memory usage and expanded memory (EMS) usage.

DOS shell

Selecting the **DOS shell** option temporarily suspends Turbo Pascal 6 and brings you to the DOS prompt, where you can use DOS commands or run other programs. To return to the integrated development environment, enter **EXIT** at the DOS prompt.

Exit ALT-X

The **Exit** option terminates the Turbo Pascal 6 integrated development environment and returns control to DOS. If, when you select **Exit**, a window contains a modified source file, Turbo Pascal 6 asks you if you wish to save the file before exiting.

The Edit Menu ALT-E

Turbo Pascal 6 enables you to have multiple source files open in different windows at the same time. The options on the Edit menu let you transfer blocks of text from one edit window to another via the *clipboard*, a special buffer set up to hold the text that you want to move. For example, to copy a block of text from one window to another, you would first select the block of text and then copy the text to the clipboard. Next, you would move to the position in the other source file where you want the text to appear and use the **Paste** option to copy the text from the clipboard.

You can select text blocks in a number of ways. In all cases, you must first position the cursor at the beginning of the block. To select a single word, press CTRL-KT; to select an entire line, press CTRL-KL. To select a larger block, press CTRL-KB, and then move the cursor to the end of the block and press CTRL-KK.

Selecting a block of text with the mouse is somewhat easier. Simply position the mouse at the beginning of the desired text, hold down the left mouse key, and drag the mouse up or down to the end of the block.

If the text extends beyond the limits of the window, the text will scroll as you drag the mouse. Clicking the mouse twice on any line selects the entire line.

Restore line

Restore line is the first option on the Edit menu, shown here:

You can use it to undo changes made to a single line of text in an edit window. The change will be made only on the most recently edited line of text.

Cut SHIFT-DEL

The **Cut** option removes a selected block of text from the active edit window and moves the block to the clipboard. The removed block of text is now ready to be pasted into another place in the edited file or into a file in another window.

Copy CTRL-INS

The **Copy** option works like the **Cut** option except that it does not remove the selected block from the source file. A copy of the block is placed in the clipboard, from which the block can be pasted elsewhere in the file or in a file in another window.

Paste SHIFT-INS

The **Paste** option copies text from the clipboard into the active edit window, starting at the position of the cursor in the window. Before text can be pasted into a window, it must first be copied or cut from an existing text file. The **Paste** option always uses the block of text that was most recently added to the clipboard.

Copy example

In addition to providing information, the Turbo Pascal 6 help system provides example code that demonstrates how a function or procedure can be used. You can use the **Copy example** option to copy the example code to the clipboard so that you can paste it into your program. Note that example code is preselected; you do not need to select it yourself before copying it.

Show clipboard

The clipboard buffer, which holds all text that has been copied or cut from text files, is actually a special edit window. The **Show clipboard** option opens this window so that you can see its contents. Notice that some of the text in the clipboard is highlighted. This is the text that is waiting to be pasted into an edit window. You can modify this text if you want.

Clear CTRL-DEL

The **Clear** option removes selected text from the active edit window but does not copy it to the clipboard. As a result, the deleted text cannot be retrieved.

The Search Menu ALT-S

Developing a program is largely a task of finding errors and fixing them. The Search menu, shown here, provides a suite of services that can help you in these tasks.

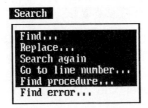

Find . . .   CTRL-QE

The **Find...** option lets you locate a text pattern in a source file. Selecting this option opens up the Find dialog box (Figure 2-5), which lets you specify what to look for and how to perform the search. At the top of the dialog box is a field in which you enter the text that you want to find. Below are options that you can set to control the search.

Options

The following are the options used to control a search:

Case sensitive   Check this option if you want Turbo Pascal 6 to distinguish between lowercase and uppercase letters.

```
  ≡  File  Edit  Search  Run  Compile  Debug  Options  Window  Help
┌[■]══════════════════════════ TEST.PAS ═══════════════════════1═[‡]═┐
│Program Test;                                                       ▲│
│                                                                     │
│Var          ┌[■]════════════════ Find ════════════════┐             │
│  i,j : Int  │                                         │             │
│             │ ┌Text to find┐ Program             │‡│  │             │
│Procedure A  │  Options                 Direction       │             │
│begin        │  [ ] Case sensitive      (•) Forward     │             │
│end;         │  [ ] Whole words only    ( ) Backward    │             │
│             │  [ ] Regular expression                  │             │
│Procedure B  │                                          │             │
│begin        │  Scope                   Origin          │             │
│A;           │  (•) Global              ( ) From cursor │             │
│end;         │  ( ) Selected text       (•) Entire scope│             │
│             │                                          │             │
│Begin        │            OK       Cancel       Help    │             │
│i := 1;      └──────────────────────────────────────────┘             │
│j := 2;                                                               │
│i := i + j;                                                          ▼│
│B;                                                                     │
└═ 1:1 ════◄▓▓▓▓▓▓▓▓▓▓▓▓▓▓▓▓▓▓▓▓▓▓▓▓▓▓▓▓▓▓▓▓▓▓▓▓▓▓▓▓▓▓▓▓▓▓▓▓▓►▼┘
 F1 Help │ Enter literal text or regular expression to search for
```

Figure 2-5.   The Find dialog box

Whole words only   If you check this option, Turbo Pascal will match only those strings that are surrounded by blanks or punctuation marks.

Regular expression   Checking this box enables Turbo Pascal 6's extended expression matching, which provides for the use of the special characters described in Table 2-1. UNIX programmers will recognize these wildcards as those used in the **grep** utility.

Wildcard	Description
^ (Caret)	Match only at the start of a line. ^ABC matches ABC, ABCX, ABCYY, and so on
$ (Dollar sign)	Match only at the end of a line. ABC$ matches ABC, XABC, YYABC, and so on
. (Period)	Match any character. AB. matches ABA, ABB, ABC, and so on
* (Asterisk)	Match any number of occurrences of the specified characters, including no occurrences. ABC* matches AB, ABC, ABCD, ABD, and so on
+ (Plus sign)	Match any number of occurrences of the specified characters, excluding no occurrences. ABC+ matches ABCD, ABCL, and so on
[] (Square brackets)	Match includes any of the characters in the brackets. AB[CD] matches ABC or ABD
[^] (Bracketed caret)	Match excludes any of the characters in the brackets following the caret. AB[^CD] matches ABX, ABF, and so on
[−] (Bracketed minus)	Match includes a range of characters specified by using the minus sign. AB[C−G] matches ABC, ABD . . . ABG
\ (Backslash)	Indicates that the next character is to be treated as part of the string and not as a special character. AB\^ matches AB^

Table 2-1.   Regular Expression Search Wildcards

Scope

The scope of the search can be either global (including the entire file) or limited to the currently selected portion of text.

Direction

The search can proceed backward from the current cursor position (toward the beginning of the file) or forward (toward the end of the file).

Origin

The search can begin from the current cursor position or it can encompass the entire scope of the file.

Replace . . .   CTRL-QA

The **Replace . . .** option works much like the **Find . . .** option but allows you to replace located text with new text. When you select **Replace . . .**, the Replace dialog box appears, as shown in Figure 2-6. This dialog box is almost exactly like the Find dialog box, with two additions. Beneath the field that contains the text to find is another field in which you type the new text that will replace the old. Also, there is a **Prompt on replace** option that, when selected, asks you to confirm each replacement before it is made.

Search again CTRL-L

This option simply repeats the most recent find or search operation. You can select this option from the menu or press CTRL-L.

Go to line number . . .

The **Go to line number . . .** option moves the cursor to the beginning of the line number that you enter.

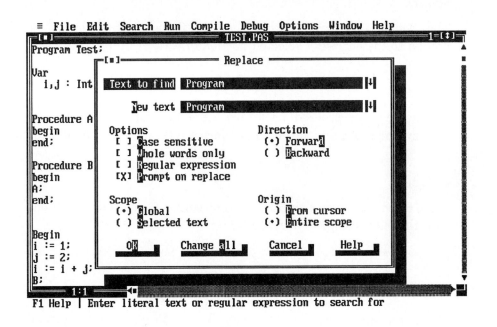

Figure 2-6.   The Replace dialog box

Find procedure . . .

When programming, it is useful to be able to locate procedure or function calls quickly. **Find procedure**... lets you do this by simply entering the name of the desired function or procedure. This option, however, is available only during debugging sessions.

Find error . . .   ALT-F8

When a run-time error occurs, Turbo Pascal 6 will display the location of the error in segment offset format (for example, 0F23:1029). **Find error**... lets you find the location of the error in your source code simply by entering the segment and offset displayed by Turbo Pascal 6. Note, however, that this option works only when the debug information {$D+} option is enabled.

The Run Menu ALT-R

Once you have written your program, you can compile and run it from
the Run menu, shown here:

```
 Run
┌─────────────────────────┐
│ Run              Ctrl-F9 │
│ Program reset    Ctrl-F2 │
│ Go to cursor          F4 │
│ Trace into            F7 │
│ Step over             F8 │
│ Parameters...            │
└─────────────────────────┘
```

You can also use this menu when you are debugging a program.

Run CTRL-F9

The **Run** option compiles and runs your program in one command. If
the file in the active window depends on other files that have been
updated since the last compile, those files will also be compiled. If you
are debugging a program, the **Run** command will execute the program
until a break point or the end of the program.

Program reset CTRL-F2

When debugging, you may wish to start the program over from the
beginning. You can do this by selecting the **Program reset** option.

Go to cursor F4

The **Go to cursor** option is used in debugging. You position the cursor
on the line you are interested in and press F4. Turbo Pascal 6 compiles
the program, if necessary, and executes the program until it reaches the
specified line.

Trace into F7

The **Trace into** option executes a single line of program code. If the
current line is a function or procedure call, pressing F7 takes you into
that function or procedure.

Step over F8

Step over works much like **Trace into,** with one exception—it does not take you into called functions or procedures; it executes them as a single statement.

Parameters . . .

Programs often depend on command-line parameters that are passed to the program when it is executed from the DOS prompt. The **Parameters...** option lets you specify parameters that will be passed to the program when it is run in the integrated development environment.

The Compile Menu ALT-C

The options in the Compile menu, shown here,

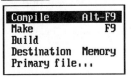

let you compile part or all of your program and specify where the compiled program should be stored.

Compile ALT-F9

Selecting **Compile** tells Turbo Pascal 6 to compile the code in the active edit window. No other code will be compiled from this option.

Make F9

The **Make** option is more powerful than the **Compile** option; it compiles not only the code in the active window, but any source files that the program depends upon that have been changed since the last time the entire program was compiled. The result of the make process is an executable program that can be run and debugged.

Build

The **Build** option operates like **Make**, except that it recompiles all the source files in the program, regardless of whether they have been modified. Usually, you will use the **Build** option when you change global compiler directives.

Destination Memory

By using the **Destination Memory** option, you can specify that the compiled executable program can be stored in memory or to disk. You must store a program to disk if you want to run it from the DOS prompt. Executable programs stored to memory can be run only within the IDE.

Primary file . . .

If your program consists of multiple source files, you should specify the primary source file by using the **Primary file...** option. Specifying a primary file ensures that all units will be compiled properly when the **Make** or **Build** command is issued.

The Debug Menu ALT-D

The integrated debugger built into Turbo Pascal 6 is extremely powerful. With it, you can develop reliable programs much more easily than with other compilers. The Debug menu, shown here,

```
 Debug 
┌─────────────────────────────┐
│ Evaluate/modify...  Ctrl-F4 │
│ Watches                   ▶ │
│ Toggle breakpoint   Ctrl-F8 │
│ Breakpoints...              │
└─────────────────────────────┘
```

gives you access to all the features of the integrated debugger.

Evaluate/modify . . . CTRL-F4

When you debug, it is often useful to alter the value of a variable to understand how different values affect program execution. You can view and alter the value of a variable by using the **Evaluate/modify . . .** option. The Evaluate and Modify dialog box, shown in Figure 2-7, lets you enter an expression to evaluate. The expression can consist of a variable name or a complete expression. Turbo Pascal 6 evaluates the expression and displays its current value in the Result field. If you are viewing a variable and want to change its current value, use the TAB key to move to the New value field, type the desired value, and press ENTER. The new value for the variable now appears in the Result field.

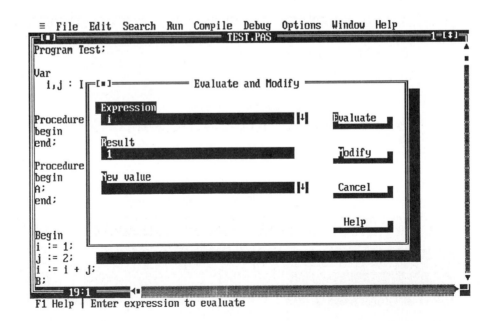

Figure 2-7.   The Evaluate and Modify dialog box

Watches

Perhaps the most important part of debugging is watching how variables change as the program executes. The **Watches** option pops up a menu, shown here,

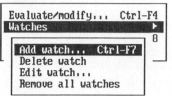

that lets you control what variable you watch. To add a watch variable, press CTRL-F7 and enter the name of the variable you want to watch. Turbo Pascal 6 then opens a Watch window (Figure 2-8) that contains

---

```
 ≡  File  Edit  Search  Run  Compile  Debug  Options  Window  Help
┌─────────────────────────── TEST.PAS ───────────────────────────1─┐
│Program Test;                                                      │
│                                                                   │
│Var                                                                │
│  i,j : Integer;                                                   │
│                                                                   │
│Begin                                                              │
│i := 1;                                                            │
│j := 2;                                                            │
│i := 1 + j;                                                        │
│ReadLn;                                                            │
│End.                                                               │
│                                                                   │
│                                                                   │
│                                                                   │
┌─[■]═══════════════════════ Watches ════════════════════════2=[↑]═┐
│i: 1                                                               │
│                                                                   │
│                                                                   │
│                                                                   │
└──────────────────────────────────────────────────────────────────┘
 F1 Help  F7 Trace  F8 Step  ↵ Edit  Ins Add  Del Delete  F10 Menu
```

Figure 2-8.   The Watch window

the variable you selected. Other options on this menu let you delete a variable from the list being watched, edit the variable specification, or remove all watches with one command.

Toggle breakpoint CTRL-F8

Break points are an important part of debugging a program. Often, you will want to specify break points at critical locations in your code. Break points can be unconditional (always halt program execution) or conditional (halt only when a specified condition is true). To set an unconditional break point, position the cursor on the desired line of code and select **Toggle breakpoint** or press CTRL-F8. Once an unconditional break point has been set, Turbo Pascal 6 halts the program when that line of code is reached.

Breakpoints . . .

Conditional break points allow greater control over your debugging session by letting you specify the conditions that halt program execution. A conditional break point can be any expression that evaluates to a true or false condition (for example, i < = 5). This helps you locate areas where values go beyond an expected range. You can also specify a Pass Count value, which indicates how many times the break point can be triggered before halting program execution. The default is zero times.

The Options Menu ALT-O

The Options menu is the most complex of all Turbo Pascal menus, covering a wide variety of options that control the Turbo Pascal environment. In daily programming, you will need to change only a few of these options, but together they make Turbo Pascal 6 the most comprehensive and powerful Pascal environment available. The Options menu is shown here:

```
Options
┌─────────────────────────┐
│ Compiler...             │
│ Memory sizes...         │
│ Linker...               │
│ Debugger...             │
│ Directories...          │
├─────────────────────────┤
│ Environment           ▶ │
├─────────────────────────┤
│ Save options ...        │
│ Retrieve options...     │
└─────────────────────────┘
```

Compiler . . .

The **Compiler...** option gives you complete control over how Turbo Pascal 6 generates your program code.

Code generation — Force far calls

({$F} compiler directive) When set on, all procedure and function calls are coded as long jumps; when set off, calls made within a unit are coded as near jumps.

Code generation — Overlays allowed

({$O} compiler directive) When set on, Turbo Pascal generates the code needed to support overlays; when set off, this code is not generated.

Code generation — Word align data

({$A} compiler directive) When set on, all noncharacter data are positioned on even addresses for faster operation; when set off, data are positioned contiguously to conserve space.

Code generation — 286 instructions

({$G} compiler directive) When set on, your code will include special instructions that make full use of the 80286 processor, but your program will run only on an 80286 or higher machine; when set off, all code is generated for the standard 8086 processor.

Run-time errors — Range checking

({$R} compiler directive) When set on, code is generated that checks array and string subscripts and out-of-range conditions on scalar data types; when set off, this code is not generated and your program is smaller. These types of errors are difficult to detect, so you should include this directive until your code is debugged.

Run-time errors – Stack checking

({$S} compiler directive) When set on, code is generated to ensure that enough stack space is available for parameters and local variables before a function or procedure is executed; when set off, this code is not generated and your program is smaller.

Run-time errors – I/O checking

({$I} compiler directive) When set on, code is generated that checks for I/O errors after every I/O operation; when set off, Turbo Pascal will not automatically check for I/O errors.

Syntax options – Strict var-strings

({$V} compiler directive) When set on, Turbo Pascal requires that strings passed as variable parameters match the length of the definition of the formal parameter. This avoids the problem of passing a string that is larger than the parameter it is passed to.

Syntax options – Complete Boolean evaluation

({$B} compiler directive) When set on, all Boolean expressions are evaluated completely before continuing. For example, in the Boolean expression (1 > 0) and (2 > 0), both parts of the expression would be fully evaluated, even though either condition is sufficient to know the result. When set off, Boolean expressions are evaluated only to the point where the final result is known with certainty.

Syntax options – Extended syntax

({$X} compiler directive) When set on, Turbo Pascal 6 recognizes the following extended syntax rule: the use of function calls as procedure statements (for example, **Function X : Integer** can be called as **X( );**).

Numeric processing – 8087/80287

({$N} compiler directive) When set on (8087/80287 mode), code is generated to allow the use of the **single, double, extended,** and **comp** data types. When set off, these data types are not available.

Numeric processing — Emulation

({$E} compiler directive) When set on, the program uses the math coprocessor chip if it is available; otherwise, it uses software emulation. When set off, your program requires a math coprocessor only if the 8087/80287 mode has been selected.

Debugging — Debug Information

({$D} compiler directive) When set on, Turbo Pascal generates debugging information that is stored in the .TPU file. This information is used when debugging in the integrated development environment. When set off, debugging information is not stored in the .TPU files.

Debugging — Local symbols

({$L} compiler directive) When set on, debugging information is generated for local symbols (those declared within a procedure, function, or a unit's implementation section). When set off, this information is not generated. This directive is ignored if the Debug directive is off.

Conditional defines

Symbols entered here are used by the compiler when evaluating compiler directives **$IFDEF** and **$IFNDEF**. This is the equivalent of using the **$DEFINE** statement in your code.

Memory sizes . . .

({$M} compiler directive) Here, you can specify the amount of memory to be allocated to your program's stack (default is 64K), and the maximum and minimum sizes of your program's heap (minimum of 0K; maximum of 640K).

Linker . . .

The linker options control the creation of map files, the link buffer, and stand-alone debugging.

Linker—Map file

You can specify whether Turbo Pascal 6 generates no map file, a map file with information on segments only, a map file with segments plus publics (global variables), or a detailed map file that includes information on local symbols.

Linker—Link buffer

For fastest compiling, let Turbo Pascal use memory only for buffering the linking process; if you are short on RAM, select disk buffering.

Debugger—Debugging

You can specify whether you want code generated for integrated debugging (debugging when in Turbo Pascal 6) or stand-alone debugging (for use with Turbo Debugger).

Debugger—Display swapping

When debugging, care must be taken to keep the program's screen output from overwriting the debugging screen. If you select **None**, Turbo Pascal 6 makes no effort to keep the debugging screen free from interference; selecting **Smart** lets Turbo Pascal 6 use its judgment to keep display swapping to a minimum; selecting **Always** instructs Turbo Pascal 6 to take every precaution to keep the debugging screen free from interference.

Directories . . .

In order to operate properly, Turbo Pascal needs to know where to look for .TPU files, include files, unit source files, and object code. Although the default is always the current directory, you can specify other directories for Turbo Pascal to search if the files are not located in the current directory.

Environment

The Environment dialog box lets you control how Turbo Pascal 6 works with your computer equipment, including your mouse, and what information should be saved at the end of each session.

Preferences

If your PC has an EGA or VGA display adapter, you can display 43 or 50 lines on the screen instead of the standard 25. You can also control whether or not new windows are opened when stepping through a debugging session. Selecting **New window** ensures that a new source window will be opened every time a new source file is required; selecting **Current window** tells Turbo Pascal 6 to replace the contents of the active window when a new source file is required.

The selection you make for the Auto Save mode determines what gets stored to disk when you exit Turbo Pascal or run a program within the integrated development environment. You can specify automatic saving of editor files, the Turbo environment, the "desktop" (the configuration of windows on your screen), or any combination of the three.

Editor

Turbo Pascal 6 lets you control certain aspects of the editor such as tabbing, autoindent, and Insert mode.

Mouse

The right button on your mouse can be programmed to perform the function you want. You can have it do nothing at all, or you can use it to get help (select **Topic search**), move to the position of the cursor in the text file, set a break point, evaluate an expression, or add a selected variable to the watch list. Choose the option that you expect to use most and you will save a lot of time.

Startup

The options contained in the Startup options dialog box control the way Turbo Pascal sets up its operating environment. This includes memory allocation, video interface preferences, and use of expanded memory.

Colors

The Colors dialog box lets you specify the foreground and background colors for every aspect of the integrated development environment. Colors are set by group (e.g., Desktop, Menus, Dialogs) and item (e.g., normal text, selected text). Use the mouse or the cursor keys to select the colors you want for each item. When done, select the **OK** button to save your changes.

Save options . . .

Once you have made changes to the Turbo Pascal options, you can save your selections by using **Save options . . .** . Turbo Pascal saves your current settings in a file you specify. The default filename is TURBO.TP.

Retrieve options . . .

If you saved Turbo Pascal options in a disk file (such as TURBO .TP), you can retrieve them using this selection. By having different sets of options stored in different files, you can customize Turbo Pascal to suit your needs.

The Window Menu ALT-W

Turbo Pascal 6's overlapping window environment is the most visible improvement over earlier versions of the compiler. The Window menu, shown here,

```
 Window
┌─────────────────────────┐
│ Size/Move    Ctrl-F5    │
│ Zoom            F5      │
│ Tile                    │
│ Cascade                 │
│ Next            F6      │
│ Previous     Shift-F6   │
│ Close        Alt-F3     │
├─────────────────────────┤
│ Watch                   │
│ Register                │
│ Output                  │
│ Call stack   Ctrl-F3    │
│ User screen  Alt-F5     │
├─────────────────────────┤
│ List...      Alt-0      │
└─────────────────────────┘
```

gives you complete control over all aspects of window management.

Size/Move CTRL-F5

When you select the **Size/Move** option, you can move the active window around the screen by using the arrow keys. To shrink or expand the size of the window, hold down the SHIFT key and use the arrow keys until the window is the size you desire.

Zoom F5

Selecting **Zoom** expands the active window to the size of the full screen. Selecting it again returns the window to its previous size and position.

Tile

When you have many windows open at once, things can get a bit confusing. Use the **Tile** command to shrink all windows down to a size where they all fit on the screen at once. Then you can select the window you want by holding down the ALT key and pressing the number of the desired window.

Cascade

This option is another way to order your windows. Instead of shrinking them, it cascades them in a way that causes the top line of each window to be visible.

Next F6

Pressing the F6 key is a quick way of moving to the next numbered window.

Previous SHIFT-F6

Pressing the SHIFT and F6 keys is a quick way of moving to the previous numbered window.

Close ALT-F3

The **Close** option removes the active window from the screen. If the window contains a file that has been modified, you will be asked if you want to save the file before the window closes.

Watch

Select this option to open or view the Watch window.

Register

Select this option to open or view the Register window. This window shows you the status of all the CPU's registers and can be very helpful in tracking down difficult bugs in a program.

Output

This option opens a window that displays a portion of the screen "outside of Turbo Pascal." It will contain the contents of the screen at the time Turbo Pascal 6 was loaded and any screen output created by your programs.

Call stack CTRL-F3

The Call Stack window is available only when debugging and is a great help in keeping track of your location in the program. The window shows the hierarchy of procedure and function calls that have been made.

User screen ALT-F5

When debugging a program, you might want to know what the user would be seeing at any point in time. Selecting the **User screen** option switches to the full output screen used by your program; press ESC to return to the Turbo Pascal 6 integrated environment.

List . . .   ALT-0

An easy way to select a desired window is to use the **List...** option. This option displays a list of all files currently viewable in open windows. The list also contains files of windows that have been closed recently. Selecting a file makes that window the active window.

Fundamental Concepts of Turbo Pascal Programming

Pascal Control Structures and Goto-less Programming
Turbo Pascal and Standard Pascal
Strong Typing of Variables in Pascal
Type Casting
Procedures and Functions
Functions Versus Procedures

Two of the most widely used programming languages today, Pascal and BASIC, started out as teaching tools. There the similarity between the two languages ends. Comparing the two will help you understand what Pascal is all about.

In the early 1970s, a major movement in programming began. Known as *structured programming,* this approach stressed breaking a program down into manageable pieces and then assembling those pieces into a program with a coherent, logical flow.

Pascal, developed by Niklaus Wirth, was designed to teach structured programming skills to future programmers. By enforcing a strict set of rules regarding the declaration of variables, program structure, and flow of control, Pascal steered the aspiring programmers toward good programming habits. In addition, Pascal provided a wide range of programming tools that made writing good, clear code much easier than was possible with COBOL or FORTRAN.

BASIC, on the other hand, was developed as an easy-to-learn language for nonprogrammers. It lets nontechnical people quickly learn to write simple programs. Unfortunately, BASIC encourages poor programming habits and unreadable code. It is significant that many new versions of BASIC resemble Pascal.

Pascal Control Structures and Goto-less Programming

Contemporary students of programming, who are generally taught structured programming from the outset, might be surprised at just how pervasive the **Goto** command was and, to a great extent, still is. This simple command allows programmers to jump anywhere within a program regardless of consistency in the program flow. Debugging and maintaining programs full of **Goto**s is very difficult.

Structured programming, sometimes known as "**Goto**-less programming," sought to eliminate the **Goto** command by providing a rich set of program control structures. Pascal, a direct result of the structured programming philosophy, provided these control structures, which both increased program readability and helped eliminate unforeseen errors created by unstructured program flow. As a result, by learning to program in Pascal, students were almost forced into learning good programming habits.

Turbo Pascal and Standard Pascal

While standard Pascal had many strong points, it was never fully developed for use in commercial applications. It lacked useful input and output functions and sorely needed string types. Nonetheless, this version of Pascal was considered the standard for the world.

Borland recognized both the strengths and the weaknesses of standard Pascal and updated the language substantially. The result is a rich language that provides the programmer with the logical structure of standard Pascal plus an extensive set of tools.

In making these additions, Borland broke away from the Pascal standard, a move that prompted criticism from some quarters. Despite this, Turbo Pascal and its extensions have become the standard international microcomputer Pascal.

Strong Typing of Variables in Pascal

Pascal is often called a *strong-typed language*. This means that you cannot mix different types of variables. In assignment statements, the values on the right must be compatible in type with the corresponding variable on the left. For example, if the variable **i** is defined as an integer, the following statement would be illegal:

    i := 1.0 + 2;

The value **1.0** is a real value and cannot be used in an assignment statement for an integer because using a real value to evaluate an integer variable goes against the properties of a strong-typed language. Observing the strong-typing rules helps avoid errors in programming. Turbo Pascal is less picky about strong typing than standard Pascal, but you still have to follow these rules:

- A **Real** cannot be used directly in an assignment statement for an **Integer** or **Byte**. The **Real** must first be converted to an **Integer** by using the **Trunc** or **Round** standard functions.

- An array can be assigned to another array only when the two have the same range and type.

- A variable that is passed to a procedure (or function) must be defined as the same type as the variable defined in the procedure heading. This rule can be relaxed for **String** variables by using the {**$V−**} compiler directive.

Strong typing as implemented in Turbo Pascal is relatively unrestrictive, yet it still helps programmers avoid unnecessary errors.

Type Casting

While strong typing has its advantages, there are times when a programming problem can be solved best by relaxing type checking. This can be done with type casting, a technique in which a variable of one type is temporarily treated as another type. For example, you cannot normally assign a character variable to an integer variable because the types are incompatible. You can, however, use the following type cast to achieve the same result,

```
i := Integer(c);
```

where **i** is an integer variable and **c** is a character variable. This statement treats the binary value of **c** as if it were an integer value. The program below demonstrates more ways to use the type cast technique:

```
Program TestTypeCast;
Uses CRT;
Var
  i : Integer;
  w : Word;
  c : Char;
  b : Boolean;
  p : Pointer;
  r : Real;
  s : String;

Begin
ClrScr;

c := 'A';
WriteLn('c = ',c);

(* Convert character to integer *)
i := Integer(c);
WriteLn('i = ',i);

(* Convert integer to boolean *)
b := Boolean(i);
WriteLn('b = ',b);

(* Convert pointer value to real *)
p := @c;
r := Real(p^);
WriteLn('r = ',r);

(* Convert pointer value to a string *)
s := String(p^);
Writeln('s = ',s);

ReadLn;
End.
```

Note how the pointer variable is interpreted as both a **Real** variable and a **String** variable. When used with type casts, pointers are particularly powerful, since they can take on any data type.

Procedures and Functions

The logic of modular programming states that it is easier to write a good program if you break it down into small chunks. In Pascal, these chunks are called *procedures* or *functions*. Modular programs are easier to write and maintain because each procedure and function can be written and tested independently of the main program. Once you are sure it is functioning correctly, you can integrate it into the main program with confidence. In addition, Pascal allows you to pass variables into the function or procedure, further increasing the modularity of the program.

Defining Procedures in Pascal

To define a procedure in Pascal, you need at least two things: a name for the procedure and a block of code. The example shown here presents a simple procedure definition that provides both ingredients.

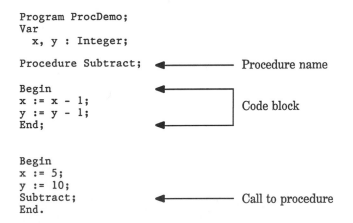

```
Program ProcDemo;
Var
  x, y : Integer;

Procedure Subtract;          ◄─────────── Procedure name

Begin                        ◄──────────┐
x := x - 1;                             │ Code block
y := y - 1;                             │
End;                         ◄──────────┘


Begin
x := 5;
y := 10;
Subtract;                    ◄─────────── Call to procedure
End.
```

The Pascal reserved word **Procedure** tells the compiler that a procedure is about to be defined. The next identifier is the name of the procedure, **Subtract**. When you want to execute a procedure in your program, you will call it by the name you gave it in the procedure definition.

The procedure **Subtract** decrements the value of variables **x** and **y** by 1. In the example, **x** and **y** are initialized to 5 and 10, respectively. Upon returning from **Subtract**, **x** is equal to 4 and **y** is equal to 9. Note that **Subtract** can use variables **x** and **y** because they are *global variables*—variables that are declared at the main program level and can be used by any procedure in the program.

Passing Parameters to a Procedure

The preceding example works for global variables **x** and **y** only. If you want to decrement any other pair of variables, you are out of luck. You can expand the usefulness of this procedure by defining parameters. Then you can use the same procedure for any two-integer variables. The following example shows the revised procedure with the **Subtract** parameters.

```
Program ProcDemo2;
Var
  q, w, x, y : Integer;

(************************************************)

Procedure Subtract(a : Integer; Var b : Integer);
Begin
a := a - 1;
b := b - 1;
End;

(************************************************)

Begin
x := 5;
y := 10;
q := 1;
w := 4;
Subtract(x,y);
Subtract(q,w);
End.
```

Note that the procedure name is now followed by a list of two parameters—**a** and **b**—both of which are integers. When **Subtract** is called, the program passes two integer values to the procedure. In the statement **Subtract(x,y)**, **x** supplies the value for parameter **a**, and **y** supplies the value for parameter **b**. Thus, **x** and **y** are the parameters being passed to the procedure. Once inside the procedure, **a** takes the value of **x**, and **b** takes the value of **y**. The same logic applies to the second call to **Subtract**, where **q** and **w** are passed as parameters.

While the procedure **Subtract** decrements each parameter by one, the effect on **x** will be different than on **y**. In the procedure definition, parameter **b** is preceded by the Pascal reserved word **Var**, while **a** is not. Parameters preceded by **Var** are called *reference parameters;* those without it are called *value parameters*.

Reference Parameters

When a variable is passed to a procedure as a reference parameter, changes made to that variable within the procedure remain even after the procedure has ended. Changes to reference parameters are permanent because Turbo Pascal passes to the procedure not the variable's value, but the variable's address in memory. In other words, the variable inside the procedure and the variable passed to the procedure as a reference parameter share the same address. Therefore, a change in the former is reflected in the latter.

In the preceding example, the global variable **y**, with a value of 10, is passed to the procedure as parameter **b**. The procedure subtracts 1 from **b**, giving a value of 9. When the procedure ends, **y** is passed back to the main program, where it retains the value of 9.

In short, the reference parameter and the actual variable passed to the procedure are the same; that is, they share the same position in memory. Therefore, any change made to the reference parameter is stored as a permanent change in the actual variable.

Value Parameters

Value parameters are different from reference parameters. When a value parameter is passed to a procedure, a temporary copy of the variable is placed in memory. Within the procedure, only the copy is used. When the value of the parameter is changed, it only affects the temporary storage; the actual variable outside the procedure is never touched.

In the preceding illustration, **a** is a value parameter because it is not preceded by the reserved word **Var**. When the program starts, it initializes **x** to 5. Upon calling **Subtract**, the program makes a copy of **x** in temporary storage and passes the copy to the procedure. Within **Subtract**, parameter **a** refers to the temporary storage location, not to the actual location of **x**. Therefore, when **a** is decremented, only the value in temporary storage is affected. At the end of the procedure, the value in temporary storage is discarded, and the global variable **x** retains the original value of 5.

Functions Versus Procedures

Both procedures and functions provide modularity to your programs. Both are self-contained blocks of code and both can accept data through parameters. The difference between functions and procedures, illustrated by the following examples, is in how they return values.

```
Procedure Square(x : Real; Var x2 : Real);
Begin
x2 := x * x;
End;

Function Square(x : Real) : Real;
Begin
Square := x * x;
End;
```

The procedure **Square** passes two parameters. The first parameter, **x**, is the number to be squared, and the second, **x2**, is the result. The procedure multiplies parameter **x** by itself and assigns the result to the parameter **x2**. Because **x2** is a reference parameter, its new value is retained when the procedure ends.

The function **Square** produces basically the same result as the procedure. However, the function does not store the result in a parameter, but passes it back through the function itself. To clarify the difference, examine how the two would be used in a program.

Using the Procedure **Square**,

Square(x, x2);
or
Square(x, x2);
if x2 > 100 then . . .

Using the Function **Square**,

```
x2 := Square(x);
or
if Square(x) > 100 then . . .
```

A function can (and must) be used in an assignment, comparison, or arithmetic expression. Another way of looking at it is that functions are like variables whose value depends on the parameters you pass to them.

Procedures, on the other hand, cannot be used in assignment, comparison, or arithmetic expressions. At most, a procedure can return a variable that can be used in expressions.

Both functions and procedures have their strong points. Functions are generally preferred when one clearly identifiable result is desired. In the preceding example, a function makes more sense than a procedure since obtaining the squared value is the objective. A procedure, rather than implying a specific result, performs an operation that may return many or no results. In the end, experience is the best guide in deciding between functions and procedures.

Passing Parameters of Different Types

The variables that you pass to a procedure or function must match the type declaration of their respective parameters. If, for example, a parameter is declared to be an **Integer**, you cannot pass a **Real** type through it. A procedure declaration that includes the standard Turbo Pascal scalars follows.

```
Procedure Example (i : Integer;
                   r : Real;
                   b : Boolean;
                   x : Byte);
```

User-defined types, such as **String**s, can also be used to define parameters, as follows.

```
Program ProcDemo3;
Type
  Str255 = String[255];
  Str80 = String[80];

Var
  St1 : Str255;
  St2 : Str80;

(************************************************)

Procedure Blank(Var s : Str255);
Begin
s := '';
End;

(************************************************)

Begin
Blank(St1); (* legal *)
{
Blank(St2); (* not legal *)
}
End.
```

Note that the parameter **s** is defined by using the type definition supplied by the user. Note also that you can pass strings to the procedure as reference parameters only if the parameter and the variable have been defined as the same string type. In the example just given, variable **St2** cannot be passed as a parameter because it is defined as **String[80]**, while the procedure heading defines the parameter as **String[255]**. This is an example of Pascal's strong typing.

You can override Turbo Pascal's strict checking on string reference parameters by using the **{$V−}** compiler directive, which turns off string-type checking. With the **{$V−}** compiler directive disabled, Turbo Pascal allows you to pass any type of string variable through any type of string parameter. Compiler directives are discussed in detail in Chapter 4.

Passing Set Parameters

Sets, another type of user-defined type, follow the same rules that apply to strings. An example of a set used as a parameter is shown in the following illustration:

```
Program ProcDemo4;
Type
  CharSet = Set Of Char;

Var
  Ch : Char;
  UpCaseChar : CharSet;

(************************************************)

Function TestChar(Ch : Char; TestSet : CharSet) : Boolean;
Begin
TestChar := Ch In TestSet;
End;

(************************************************)

Begin
Ch := 'A';
UpCaseChar := ['A'..'Z'];
If TestChar(Ch,UpCaseChar) Then WriteLn(Ch);
End.
```

The user-defined type **CharSet** is used to define a parameter in **TestChar**. When the function is called, the variable **UpCaseChar** is passed to the function as parameter **TestSet**.

Passing Untyped Parameters

Parameters defined using a data type (such as **Real, Integer,** and so on) are appropriately called *typed parameters.* Turbo Pascal also allows you to use *untyped parameters.* The advantage of untyped parameters is that you can pass variables of any type of data into them—**String**s, **Real**s, **Integer**s, **Boolean**s, and any other data type are all legal.

How is it that an untyped parameter can accept any data type? To understand this, think about typed parameters. When you define a typed parameter, you tell Turbo Pascal what type of data to expect. Thus, Turbo Pascal can easily determine if a mismatch exists between the variable type and the parameter type. When you use untyped parameters, however, the procedure or function has no idea what it is you are passing to it. The procedure accepts whatever is passed to it and expects the programmer to know how to handle it. Because of this, untyped parameters must be used carefully. Consider the example shown here:

```
Procedure Example(Var x);
Var
  y : Integer Absolute x;
Begin
WriteLn(y);   (* Legal: y is of type Integer *)
WriteLn(x);   (* Illegal: x has no type *)
End;
```

Parameter **x** (a reference parameter) has no type associated with it. Therefore, **x** is an untyped parameter. The reserved word **Var** is necessary because all untyped parameters must be reference parameters.

While **x** is clearly a parameter, it cannot be used directly by the procedure. Why not? The procedure does not know what **x** is, so it cannot handle the parameter.

Instead of using **x**, you must declare a variable in the procedure that is *Absolute* at **x**. This means that the variable you declare will reside at exactly the same address as **x**. In the example, **y** is defined as an **Integer** variable that is located at the same place in memory as **x**. Now you can use variable **y** in place of **x**.

When this procedure is called, any type of variable can be passed to this procedure, and the procedure will treat the variable as an integer. What does that mean? Suppose you pass a string into the procedure. Since **y** is an integer, and an integer is two bytes long, the procedure will take the first two bytes of the string and treat them as an integer value. Of course, the integer value will have absolutely no relation to the value of the string. If you pass a string with the value "TEXT" into the procedure, the integer value will be 21,500—a totally arbitrary value.

So why use untyped parameters? In certain and very few instances, untyped parameters are useful. One example, a procedure that compares two variables to see if they are equal, is shown in the following illustration:

```
{$V-}
Program CompareData;
Var
  i1,i2 : Integer;
  r1,r2 : Real;
  s1,s2 : String;

(*************************************************)

Function Compare(Var x,y; kind : Char) : Integer;
Var
  aString : String[255] Absolute x;
  bString : String[255] Absolute y;
```

```pascal
      aReal : Real Absolute x;
      bReal : Real Absolute y;

      aInteger : Integer Absolute x;
      bInteger : Integer Absolute y;

  Begin
    Case kind Of

    'R' : (* Real *)
      Begin
      If aReal > bReal Then
        Compare := 1
      Else If aReal < bReal Then
        Compare := -1
      Else
        Compare := 0;
      End;

    'I' : (* Integer *)
      Begin
      If aInteger > bInteger Then
        Compare := 1
      Else If aInteger < bInteger Then
        Compare := -1
      Else
        Compare := 0;
      End;

    'S' : (* String *)
      Begin
      If aString > bString Then
        Compare := 1
      Else If aString < bString Then
        Compare := -1
      Else
        Compare := 0;
      End;

    End; (* of case *)
  End;

  (***********************************************)

  Begin
  r1 := 10000.0;
  r2 := -33.0;
  WriteLn(Compare(r1,r2,'R'));

  i1 := 100;
  i2 := 200;
  WriteLn(Compare(i1,i2,'I'));

  s1 := 'Xavier';
  s2 := 'Smith';
  WriteLn(Compare(s1,s2,'S'));

  End.
```

This example passes two variables at a time into the function **Compare**. The variables are passed as untyped parameters and are subsequently redefined as **Real, Integer,** and **String** variables. The third parameter, **kind,** is a character denoting the type of the first two parameters. An **S** indicates **String, R** indicates **Real,** and **I** indicates **Integer.**

By checking the value of **kind,** the procedure knows whether to compare **String**s, **Real**s, or **Integer**s. The final result, then, is a generalized procedure that can compare any two variables of type **Integer, Real,** or **String.** The only restriction is that you must tell the procedure what type of variable you are comparing.

Passing Literal Values

In the examples so far, only variables have been passed as parameters to functions. You can also pass literal values, such as a number or a string, to a procedure, but only as value parameters. The example here shows how the numeric literal 3.0 is passed to the function **Square.** The function performs just as it would if a variable had been passed to it.

```
Function Square(x : Real) : Real;
Begin
Square := x * x;
End;

Begin
WriteLn(Square(3.0));
End.
```

String literals are groups of characters enclosed in single quotation marks. The following example illustrates how a string literal is passed to a procedure:

```
Program StringTest;

(*********************************************)

Procedure WriteUpCase(st : String);
Var
  i : Integer;
Begin
For i := 1 To Length(st) Do
  st[i] := UpCase(st[i]);
```

```
WriteLn(st);
End;

(*********************************************)

Begin
WriteUpCase('This is a string literal');
End.
```

This procedure takes the string passed to it, converts it to all uppercase characters, and writes it out. In the preceding example, the string passed is a literal, but the procedure would accept a string variable as well. Note, however, that you can pass literal values and string literals to value parameters only, not to reference parameters.

Procedures and the Scope of Variables

In BASIC and some other programming languages, all variables are *global*, that is, all variables can be referred to at any point throughout the program. Pascal supports global variables, but also provides local variables. These are variables that exist within a limited portion of the program, also known as the *scope of a variable.* By limiting the scope of variables, unwanted side effects are eliminated.

The scope of a variable is determined by the block in which it is declared, as illustrated in Figure 3-1. Because it is defined within the program block, variable **x** is global in scope, meaning it can be accessed throughout the program. The variable **y**, defined within **Procedure A**, is limited in scope and can only be referred to within the scope of **Procedure A**.

Finally, variable **z**, defined within **Procedure B**, is even more limited in scope: it can only be referred to within the scope of **Procedure B**. Therefore, **Procedure B** can use variables **x**, **y**, and **z**; and **Procedure A** can use both variable **x** and variable **y**, but not variable **z**. The main program, the most limited of all, can refer only to variable **x**.

Variables at different levels can share the same name. However, giving variables the same name limits the scope of one of the two. This is demonstrated in the program listed here:

```
Program DoubleName;
Var
  x : Integer;
```

```
Procedure Proc1;
Var
  x : String[20];

  Procedure Proc2;
  Begin
  x := 'Bill';
  End;

Begin
x := 'Jones';
End;

Begin
x := 1;
End.
```

This program contains two variables named **x**. In the program block, **x** is an integer variable, while in **Proc1** it is a string variable. **Proc1** cannot access the global variable **x** because it has already defined its own variable with the same name. When **Proc2** refers to **x**, it uses the variable defined in **Proc1** because **Proc2** is declared within **Proc1**.

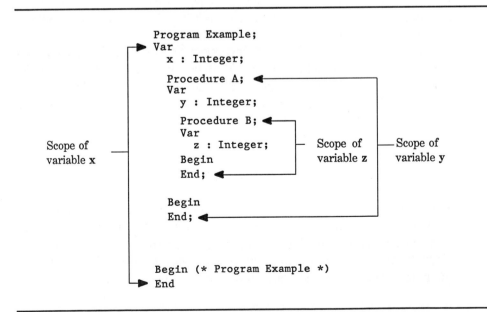

Figure 3-1.   Determining the scope of a variable

Turbo Pascal Program Structure

The Program Heading
The Data Section
The Code Section
More on Program Blocks
Include Files
Overlays

A place for everything and everything in its place. This saying accurately describes Pascal, an orderly language consisting of well-defined sections, each of which serves a specific purpose. The major sections of a Pascal program are the *program heading,* the *data section,* and the *code section,* whose components are shown in Figure 4-1.

The Program Heading

The first two lines in a Turbo Pascal program generally consist of the *program name* and the *compiler directives.* Both are optional, but for the sake of program documentation, it is preferable to include them.

As the first line in the program, the *program heading* does no more than identify the name of the program and whether it will be using input, output, or both. A typical program heading follows.

```
Program ProgName(Input,Output);
```

Note that Turbo Pascal allows you to add a parameter list after the program name. This is a holdover from standard Pascal, in which such parameters were required, and is ignored by Turbo Pascal.

The second line of the program contains the *compiler directives,* which can play an active and vital role in Turbo Pascal programs,

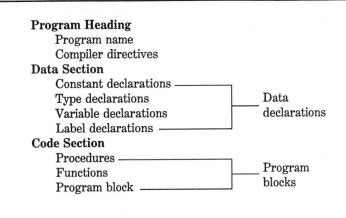

Figure 4-1.   The structure of a Turbo Pascal program

controlling various types of error checking and input/output control. Although beginners can often ignore compiler directives entirely, more advanced programmers must understand how to use these options to get the most out of Turbo Pascal.

Compiler Directives

The Turbo Pascal compiler offers many options that you can use to make programming and debugging easier. These options, which perform tasks such as error checking, are called compiler directives because they direct the compiler in its work. Compiler directives can be broadly classified into three groups: *switch directives*, *parameter directives*, and *conditional directives*.

Switch Directives

Switch directives turn on or off Turbo Pascal's special features, such as input/output error checking, stack checking, and data alignment. They are called switch directives because they can have only two conditions: on or off.

Switch directives are identified by single letters (uppercase or lowercase). For example, the **S** directive controls stack checking, **R** sets up range checking, **I** specifies input/output error checking, and so on. The format for enabling or disabling a compiler directive is a dollar sign followed by the directive and either a plus sign (to enable) or a minus sign (to disable); these characters are enclosed in comment delimiters (either parentheses with asterisks or braces). The following are examples of valid compiler directive statements:

```
(*$I-*)
```

```
{$i-}
```

```
{$s+,v-,r+,a+}
```

The first two statements are the same; both disable input/output error checking. As you can see from the examples, either type of comment delimiter (braces or parentheses with asterisks) can be used; the case of the directive (upper or lower) is unimportant. The third example specifies four compiler directives at once. It enables **Stack-Overflow Checking**, disables **Var-String Checking**, and enables **Range Checking** and **Align Data by Word**. Note that in this statement, the dollar sign appears before the first directive only.

Turbo Pascal lets you set compiler directives in two ways. The easiest way is to set the directives from the Options/Compiler menu. The directive settings in this menu become the global default values for all programs and units. In other words, Turbo Pascal will use the settings in the Options/Compiler menu for all compiler directives not specified in the source code.

Switch directives are of two types: global and local. Global directives, as the name implies, affect the compilation of an entire program, from beginning to end, and must be declared at the very beginning of your program or unit (before the first **Uses**, **Label**, **Const**, **Type**, **Procedure**, **Function**, or **Begin** keyword). Local directives can appear at any point in a program and only affect that portion of the program which follows the directive. For example, you can turn on range checking, a local directive, at the beginning of a procedure and then turn it off at the end of the procedure.

Align Data (Global)

The 8086 family of microprocessors can access memory faster when data are aligned on even-numbered addresses, also known as *word boundaries*. When the **Align Data** compiler directive is active ({$A+}, Turbo

Pascal makes sure that every variable and typed constant larger than one byte begins at an even address. Aligning data on word boundaries makes data access faster, but also increases the amount of memory required for data storage because "dead" bytes are inserted where necessary to make sure that variables begin on word boundaries. If you are concerned about the amount of memory your program requires, you may want to disable this directive ({$A−}).

Boolean Evaluation (Local)

Turbo Pascal supports two types of Boolean evaluation—complete and short-circuit. To understand the difference between the two, consider the following example:

```
If (a < b) And (b > c) Then
  Begin
  .
  .
  .
  End;
```

The preceding Boolean statement consists of two separate tests connected with **And**. Under complete Boolean evaluation, Turbo Pascal will test both comparisons before branching. But, if **a** is greater than or equal to **b**, there is really no need to test if **b** is greater than **c**. Under short-circuit evaluation, Turbo Pascal will only test so far as is necessary to determine the result of the entire expression. Under certain circumstances, short-circuit evaluation can speed up a program appreciably. To turn on short-circuit evaluation, use **{$B−}**; to select complete evaluation, use **{$B+}**.

Debug Information (Global)

Enabling the **Debug Information** directive (**{$D+}**), instructs Turbo Pascal to generate information needed to match executable instructions to locations in source files. This is the information that allows you to step through a program one line at a time or to locate the source of a run-time error when it occurs. Turbo Pascal adds debugging information to the end of .TPU files, making the files larger than they otherwise would be. This does not, however, affect the speed of the executable code.

Disabling this directive will gain you very little (for example, a little extra disk space, slightly shorter compile time) at the cost of not being able to step through a program. Generally speaking, **Debug Information** should always be enabled.

Emulation (Global)

The 8087 math coprocessor chip offers significant computational advantages over the 8088/8086. Unfortunately, not every computer has the 8087 installed. When enabled, the **Emulation** compiler directive gives you access to the 8087's data types whether or not the math chip is present.

Let's say you are distributing a statistics program that requires the mathematical precision of the 8087. But you also want to sell the program to people without the coprocessor installed. When **Emulation** is enabled, Turbo Pascal checks to see if the 8087 chip is installed. If it is, your program will use the power of the math chip; if not, your program will perform all the 8087 computations using the main microprocessor. Naturally, your computations will take much longer without the 8087 chip. Even so, it is better to have one program that everyone can use than to have separate versions for 8087 and non-8087 machines. Unless you are going to need extremely precise mathematical results, you are better off leaving **Emulation** disabled.

Force Far Calls (Local)

Turbo Pascal supports multiple code segments—one code segment for each unit and an additional one for the main program. Function and procedure calls that take place within a unit or program file are known as *intrasegment* or *near* calls because the code that executes the call and the called procedure both reside in the same code segment. When, however, a statement in one unit calls a procedure in another unit, this is an *intersegment* or *far* call because the call crosses code segment boundaries.

Near calls require less work than far calls because the code segment does not change. Far calls, by virtue of the fact that more than one code segment is involved, require more work and execute more slowly. Fortunately, Turbo Pascal is smart enough to know when to use a near call and when to use a far call. There are, however, times when you will want to override Turbo's judgment and force a procedure to be called as a far call, even though it would normally be considered a near call.

The circumstances under which you would need to force a far call are generally very advanced and uncommon. Suffice it to say that when necessary, you can force a procedure to be a far call by enabling the **F** compiler directive as demonstrated here:

```
Program TestFarCall;

(*****************************************)

{$F+}Procedure FarCall;{$F-}
Begin
End;

(*****************************************)

Begin
FarCall; { This would normally be a near call }
End.
```

The procedure **FarCall** is clearly in the same code segment as the call made at the end of the program, which means that the procedure would be executed as a near call. The **F** compiler directive alters the situation by forcing the procedure to be a far call.

Input/Output Checking (Local)

The **I** compiler directive, which is used to check for I/O errors in your program, is enabled with the statement **{$I+}**. Perhaps the most common type of Turbo Pascal error, I/O errors are also among the most dangerous. Undetected, they can produce unpredictable results in a program that appears to be operating normally.

When **Input/Output Checking** is enabled, an I/O error produces a run-time error and halts your program. However, enabling the **I** compiler directive is not the best way to handle I/O errors. A more effective method is to disable the **I** directive with the statement **{$I−}** and trap I/O errors yourself.

Local Symbol Information (Global)

Local Symbol Information refers to information about variables and constants that are local to a unit or procedure. Normally, Turbo Pascal does not save information about these symbols, making it impossible to view or change their values in a debugging session. By enabling the **Local Symbol Information** compiler directive, **{$L+}**, Turbo Pascal generates and saves information about all local variables so that you can use them as you debug your program.

The Local Symbol Information compiler directive works with the Debug Information directive in the following ways. When **Debug Information** is disabled (**{$D−,L−}** or **{$D−,L+}**), Turbo Pascal saves no information for debugging purposes and the **L** compiler directive has no effect. When **D** is enabled but **L** is disabled (**{$D+,L−}**), Turbo Pascal stores debugging information only for global variables and constants. When both **D** and **L** are enabled (**{$D+,L+}**), Turbo Pascal saves debugging information for both global and local symbols.

Numeric Processing (Global)

Turbo Pascal offers two types of floating-point numeric processing: Normal mode and 8087 mode. The Normal mode supports the 6-byte **Real** data type and does not use the 8087 match coprocessor, even if it is available. The 8087 mode offers four additional floating-point data types as well as access to the power of the 8087 math chip. Use the **{$N−}** compiler directive to select the Normal mode and **{$N+}** to select the 8087 mode.

The **N** compiler directive is used in conjuction with the **E** (Emulation) compiler directive. When both are enabled (**{$N+,E+}**), your program can use the 8087 mode even when the math chip is not installed. If the chip is installed, your program will use it for floating-point operations; if not, your program will use emulation routines that provide the same level of precision, but at a lower speed. When **Emulation** is not enabled in the 8087 mode, (**{$N+,E−}**), your program will run only on machines with the math chip installed.

Overlay Code Generation (Global)

If you want to include a unit in an overlay file, you must enable the **Overlay Code Generation** compiler directive (**{$O+}**). This tells Turbo Pascal to generate the code necessary to manage this unit as an overlay. Note, however, that enabling the **O** compiler directive does not require you to overlay the unit, it only makes overlaying possible. On the other hand, you cannot overlay a unit unless you have enabled the **O** compiler directive.

Range Checking (Local)

Most data types in Turbo Pascal have limitations. For example, a byte cannot hold a value greater than 255. An array of five elements cannot hold a sixth element. A string defined as **String[20]** cannot hold 21 characters. Any attempt to violate these limitations creates a range error—a value or condition that does not fit within the limits of the variable.

When **Range Checking** is enabled ({$R+}), Turbo Pascal generates code that checks that all indexing and assignments are within proper range. When a range error is found, Turbo Pascal generates a run-time error and halts the program. If, on the other hand, **Range Checking** is disabled, all out-of-bounds assignments and indexing operations go unreported. The results could be disastrous.

Range errors never occur in a properly functioning program, but they can be common during early stages of program development. To protect yourself against them, always enable the **R** compiler directive while developing a program and then disable it when compiling the final version.

One final point about **Range Checking**: when enabled, it significantly increases the size of your compiled program and slows its execution. If you find your program poking along where it should be flying, make sure that you did not inadvertently leave **Range Checking** enabled somewhere in your program.

Stack-Overflow Checking (Local)

When your program calls a procedure or function, Turbo Pascal allocates memory from the stack for local variables. Enabling the **Stack-Overflow Checking** compiler directive ({$S+}) tells Turbo Pascal to generate the code needed to make sure that enough memory is available on the stack to hold these local variables. If there is not enough memory, your program will terminate with a run-time error. If the S compiler directive is disabled ({$S−}), no checking will be done, and your computer will probably crash when it runs out of stack memory. Stack checking takes time and increases your program's executable code, so you should only enable the **S** directive when you are developing and debugging your program.

Var-String Checking (Local)

When **Var-String Checking** is enabled, Turbo Pascal performs strict type checking on string parameters passed to procedures and functions. To understand how **Var-String Checking** works and why it is important, consider the following program:

```
Program TestVarStr;
Type
  Str30 = String[30];
Var
  S : String[20];

(************************************************)

Procedure ChangeS(Var S : Str30);
Var
  i : Integer;
Begin
For i := 1 To 30 Do
  s[i] := Chr(Ord(s[i]) + 1);
End;

(************************************************)

Begin
s := 'abc';
ChangeS(s);
WriteLn(s);
ReadLn;
End.
```

In this program, S, a variable declared to be **String[20]**, is passed to procedure **ChangeS** whose parameter type is **String[30]**. If **Var-String Checking** were enabled ({$V+}), this program would not compile because the variable type and the parameter type do not match. You might think that forcing string variables to match procedure parameters is unnecessary, but consider what could happen.

In the preceding program, procedure **ChangeS** alters each character in a 30-character string. The variable S, however, is declared to be only 20 characters long. What happens when **ChangeS** tries to modify 30 characters when the variable has only 20? The answer is that the program will alter memory beyond the limit of string S. In short, you will be trashing memory and not know it. By now you should realize just how important **Var-String Checking** is and how insidious **Var-string** errors can be if they go undetected. If you do decide to disable **Var-String Checking**, make certain that there is no chance that your program will create undesired havoc.

Parameter Directives

Unlike switch directives, parameter directives do not have clearly defined on/off states. Instead, these directives indicate names of files that are to be used during compilation and the size of memory to be allocated to the program.

Include File (Local)

An *include file* is a source file that is compiled as part of another source file. The **I** directive is used followed by the name of the file with the source code. If you do not specify a file extension for the **I** directive, Turbo Pascal will assume the .PAS extension.

To understand how this works, look at the following listing. The procedure **ProcA** is contained in a file named MAININC.PAS. The main program file uses the Include compiler directive to insert the code in MAININC.PAS into the program. Include files are normally used when a program becomes too large to fit into the Turbo Pascal editor in one piece or when you wish to make changes to a program as a whole by changing values in the include file.

```
(* Contents of file MAININC.PAS *)
Procedure ProcA;
Begin
WriteLn('ProcA');
End;

(* Program using MAININC.PAS *)
Program Main;
{$I MainInc}
Begin
ProcA;
ReadLn;
End.
```

Link Object File (Local)

If you write routines in assembler for use in your Pascal programs, you will need to link the assembler object files with your Pascal program. This is done with the Link Object File compiler directive (**L**) followed by the name of the object file.

Memory Allocation Sizes (Global)

The Memory Allocation Sizes (**M**) compiler directive gives you complete control over the amount of memory your program uses for its stack and heap. The directive is followed by three numbers, separated by commas, representing the amount of memory for the stack, and the minimum and maximum memory sizes for the heap. For example, the directive {$M 30000,1000,5000} allocates 30,000 bytes to the stack and a minimum of 1000 and a maximum of 5000 to the heap. The amount of memory you allocate to the stack must be from 1024 to 65520. The heap can have from 0 to 655360 bytes allocated to it.

Overlay Unit Name (Local)

The Overlay Unit Name compiler directive (**O**) is followed by the name of a unit and instructs Turbo Pascal to include that unit in the overlay file. The unit named in this directive must be compiled with the **{$O+}** compiler directive to allow it to be overlaid. The Overlay Unit Name compiler directive must be placed after the program **Uses** clause, as shown here:

```
Program OvrTest;
Uses
  Unit1,
  Unit2,
  Unit3;

{$O Unit1}
{$O Unit2}
```

In this program's declaration section, **Unit1** and **Unit2** are named to be included in the overlay file; **Unit3** will not be overlaid.

Conditional Compilation

Turbo Pascal's conditional compilation directives allow you to maintain different versions of a program in the same source file. By changing certain definitions, you can compile some sections of code and hide others. At the heart of conditional compilation is the *condition symbol*, a symbol defined by you to control the conditional compilation process. The program listed here demonstrates how the conditional symbol is defined and used to control compilation.

```
Program ConditionExample;

{$DEFINE TEST} (* Define symbol *)

{$IFDEF TEST}   (* If symbol defined, do this... *)
{$R+,S+}

{$ELSE}         (* If symbol not defined, do this... *)
{$R-,S-}

{$ENDIF}        (* End of conditional compilation. *)

Begin
{$UNDEF TEST}   (* Undefine the symbol *)

{$IFDEF TEST}   (* If symbol defined, do this... *)

WriteLn('TEST DEFINED');

{$ELSE}         (* If symbol not defined, do this... *)

WriteLn('TEST NOT DEFINED');

{$ENDIF}        (* End of conditional compilation. *)

ReadLn;
End.
```

The program begins by defining the symbol TEST. The first use of TEST enables the **R** and **S** compiler directives if TEST is defined (as it is in this case) and disables them if TEST is not defined. After the **Begin** keyword, TEST is undefined, a process that nullifies the previous **{$DEFINE TEST}** directive. Since TEST is no longer defined, the line **WriteLn('TEST NOT DEFINED');** is compiled. The conditional compilation directives offered by Turbo Pascal are described next.

DEFINE

Use this directive to define a conditional symbol. Any code that depends on the symbol defined will be compiled, *but only in the file in which the DEFINE directive appears*. Consider the case of a program that uses a main source file, an include file, and a unit file. In each file, conditional compilation directives are used. If you use the **DEFINE** directive in the main source file, and not in the include and unit files, only the main source file will be affected; the other files will compile without the **DEFINE** directive. The only way to globally define a compilation symbol is to use the **Conditional defines** feature on the Options/Compiler menu.

UNDEF

This directive negates the **DEFINE** directive. Once a symbol has been used with **UNDEF**, any code that depends on that symbol will not be compiled.

IFDEF

This directive instructs Turbo Pascal to compile code if a named conditional symbol is defined.

IFNDEF

This directive instructs Turbo Pascal to compile code if a named conditional symbol is *not* defined.

IFOPT

You can also control compilation based on another compilation directive. For example, you can compile code only when the **R** compile directive is enabled by writing **{IFOPT R+}**.

ELSE

Use this directive after any of the IF. . . directives (**IFDEF, IFNDEF, IFOPT**) as a branch when the first condition is untrue.

ENDIF

This directive marks the end of a conditional compilation sequence. All code appearing after the **ENDIF** statement will be compiled regardless of conditional symbols.

Using compiler directives effectively is an important step in becoming a productive programmer. You must understand how to use these directives to get the most out of Turbo Pascal.

The Data Section

In Turbo Pascal global variables, constants, labels, and user-defined data types are declared directly following the program heading and global compiler directives. Local variables are declared within procedures and functions, but follow the same basic rules.

Constant Definitions

Many programs have certain values that never change, such as the number of days in a week, or if they do change, they change for the program as a whole. Using constant identifiers for these constant values simplifies your programs and makes them easier to maintain; for a change to be reflected throughout a program, you need only change the value of the constant.

The Turbo Pascal reserved word **Const** signals the beginning of a constant-definition block. (Reserved words are those used solely by Turbo Pascal; they cannot be defined by users as identifiers.)

You have two choices of constants in Turbo Pascal: *untyped* and *typed*. An untyped constant is declared with the following syntax: an identifier followed by an equal sign, a literal value (numeric or text), and a semicolon, as shown in this example:

```
CONST
      DaysPerWeek = 7;
      HoursPerDay = 24;
      Message = 'Good Morning';
```

These constants are called untyped because you do not specify their type definition.

Typed constants are defined similarly, except that the type definition is inserted between the identifier and the equal sign, as shown in the following example.

```
CONST
      DaysPerWeek : Integer = 7;
      Message : String[20] = 'Good Morning';
      Interest : Real = 0.14;
```

If you are concerned about code space, you should use typed constants rather than untyped constants. Untyped constants take up more space because the constant identifier is replaced by the literal value when the program is compiled. In the preceding example of untyped constants, Turbo Pascal would replace every identifier **Message** with the string literal 'Good Morning'.

Typed constants, on the other hand, are defined in the data segment one time and take up only as much space as the data type requires. Anytime your program uses a typed constant, it refers to that single copy.

Another characteristic of typed constants is that you can change their values. In a sense, typed constants are not constants at all, but are initialized variables. If you want to be absolutely certain that a constant's value remains the same throughout a program, use an untyped constant.

Type Definitions

In the type-definition block, denoted by the Turbo Pascal reserved word **Type,** you can define your own data types and later use them to declare variables. The general form for type definitions is an identifier followed by an equal sign, the data type, and a semicolon, as shown here:

```
Type
 PayType = (Salary,HourlyRate);
 Customer = Record
   Name : String[30];
   Age : Integer;
   Income : Real;
   End;
 MaxString = String[80];
 NameList = Array [1..100] Of String[30];
```

The first data type, **PayType,** is an enumerated scalar with two legal values. The second, **Customer,** is a **Record** data type containing three fields. **MaxString** denotes a string variable with 80 characters, and **NameList** is an array of 100 strings, each 30 characters long. The ability to create customized data types is one of Pascal's most powerful features and is discussed throughout this book.

Variable Declarations

Variables are areas in memory that you name. To begin a variable-declaration block, type the reserved word **Var** followed by the variable identifier (the name you give the variable), a colon, and the data type (for example, **Var i : Integer;**).

You can declare variables by using standard Turbo Pascal data types (for example, **Boolean, Real, Integer**) or user-defined data types created in the **Type** section. The format for variable declarations is nearly the same as that used for **Type** definitions, but the identifier is followed by a colon rather than an equal sign.

```
Var
   i, j, k : Integer;
   x, y, z : Real;
   BeyondLimit : Boolean;
   Ad : AdType;

Book : Record
   Title : String[20];
   TotPages : Integer;
   Text : Array [1..10000] Of String[20];
   End;
```

The declaration of the variable **Book** uses the **Record** type that allows you to group more than one data element into a single variable.

Label Declarations

Labels are used to mark points in a program. By using the **Goto** statement together with a label, you can force the program flow to jump from place to place. Many programmers consider the use of the **Goto** statement bad programming technique because it leads to messy, unstructured programs. To keep you from abusing the **Goto** statement, Turbo Pascal limits the scope of a label to a single procedure block.

The label-declaration block begins with the reserved word **Label**. The declarations themselves consist simply of identifiers that are separated by commas and terminate with a semicolon, as shown next:

Label
   EndOfProgram, NextStep;

When used in your program, the label is followed by a colon (for example, **EndOfProgram:**). Statements following the label are executed whenever a **Goto** statement branches to that label. The following program demonstrates a valid use of a label and **Goto** statement.

```
Program GoToTest;
Var
  i,j : Integer;
  a : Array [1..100,1..100] Of Integer;

(********************************************************)

Function Found : Boolean;
Label JumpOut;
Begin
For i := 1 To 100 Do
  Begin
  For j := 1 To 100 Do
    Begin
    If a[i,j] < 0 Then
      Begin
      Found := True;
      Goto JumpOut;
      End;
    End;
  End;
Found := False;

JumpOut:
End;

(********************************************************)

Begin
FillChar(a,sizeof(a),0);
a[50,50] := -1;
WriteLn(Found);
ReadLn;
End.
```

The function **Found** searches through a matrix of integers looking for a negative value. If a negative value is found, the function should return TRUE, if not, FALSE. In cases where you need to break out of a nested loop, the **Goto** command is a good choice because avoiding **Goto** would significantly increase the complexity of the routine.

The Code Section

The third major part of a Turbo Pascal program is the code section. It is the largest portion of the program and contains the step-by-step instructions that make the program work.

The code section always contains a program block and often contains procedures and functions. Blocks, delimited by the Turbo Pascal reserved words **Begin** and **End**, contain the instructions that assign values to variables, create logical branching, call other procedures and functions, and so on. In Turbo Pascal, the part of the program that executes first, the program block, is defined at the end of the program, as shown in Figure 4-2.

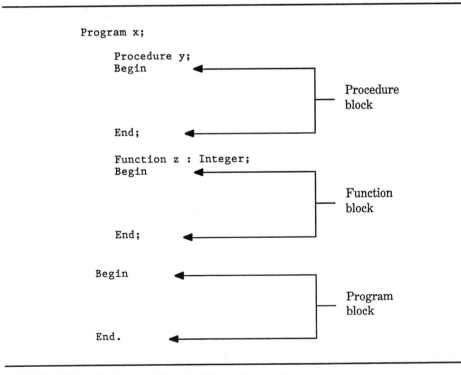

Figure 4-2.   Organization of the code section

The program in Figure 4-3, which computes the weekly pay for a group of employees, demonstrates all the fundamental characteristics of a Turbo Pascal program. The program heading and the compiler directives are at the top. The data section defines constants and data types and declares variables and labels. Procedures and functions are defined in the code section.

At the heart of this program is the user-defined record type **EmployeeType**. This record, containing basic information about an employee, defines the array **Employee**. This array contains 60 elements,

```
Program Payroll;          ◄─────────────────  Program heading
(*$v-,r-,s-*)             ◄─────────────────  Compiler directives

Const  ◄────────────────────────────────  Definition of constants

  BonusRate = 0.07;
  Employees = 60;


Type  ◄─────────────────────────────────  Definition of user-defined types

  EmployeeType = Record
    Name : String[30];
    Id : Integer;
    HourlyRate : Real;
    HoursWorked : Integer;
    GetsBonus : Boolean;
    TotalPay : Real;
    End;

  MaxStr = String[255];




Var  ◄──────────────────────────────────  Declaration of variables

  Employee : Array [1..Employees] of EmployeeType;
  i : Integer;
  s : MaxStr;

Label  ◄────────────────────────────────  Declaration of label

  EndOfProgram;

(**********************************************)
```

(Left margin vertical label: Data Section)

Figure 4-3.   A typical Turbo Pascal program

```
Procedure CalcPay(Var Employee : EmployeeType)

  Function CalcBonus(Pay : Real) : Real;
  Begin
  CalcBonus := Pay + (Pay * BonusRate);
  End;
Begin
Employee.TotalPay := Employee.HoursWorked *
                     Employee.HourlyRate;

If Employee.GetsBonus then
  Employee.TotalPay := CalcBonus(Employee.TotalPay);
End;

(************************************************)

  Procedure WriteReport (Employee : EmployeeType);
  Begin
  Writeln('Name:        ',Employee.name)
  Writeln('Total Pay: ',Employee.TotalPay:0:2);
  Writeln;
  End;

(************************************************)


Begin
For i := 1 To Employees Do
  Begin
  CalcPay(Employee[i];
  If Employee[i].TotalPay < 0 then
    Begin
    Writeln('Error: Total pay less than zero');
    Goto EndOfProgram;
    End;
  WriteReport(Employee[i]);
  End;


EndOfProgram:
End.
```

Code Section

Main program block

Figure 4-3. A typical Turbo Pascal program (*continued*)

each of which is a record of type **EmployeeType**. A customized data type (the constant **Employees**) defines the array. If the number of employees changes, all you need to do is change the definition of this constant.

The main program block in Figure 4-3 consists of a loop that executes once for every employee. Each iteration, or execution, of the loop calls the procedure **CalcPay**, which calculates the pay for the employee. When the procedure ends, the main program block tests to make sure that the result, **TotalPay**, is not less than zero, since clearly no one should (or could) be paid a negative amount. If the result is less than zero, the program jumps to the **EndOfProgram** label and terminates. If, however, the amount of **TotalPay** is in the correct range, the program calls the procedure **WriteReport**, which writes the employee's name and the total amount paid.

More on Program Blocks

Pascal is known as a block-structured language, that is, a language in which every statement in a program belongs to a specific block of code. A simple program can consist of only one block, as shown here:

```
Program Sample;
Begin
WriteLn('Hello');
End.
```

The program block is the lowest level in the program: it is the foundation upon which you can build more layers. In the preceding example, the entire program exists at the program-block level. When you add procedures and functions to a program, you add more levels, as shown in Figure 4-4. This program consists of three blocks—one program block and two procedure blocks—but has only two levels. Because both procedures are nested within the program block, they are both level-2 procedures, as the indentation suggests.

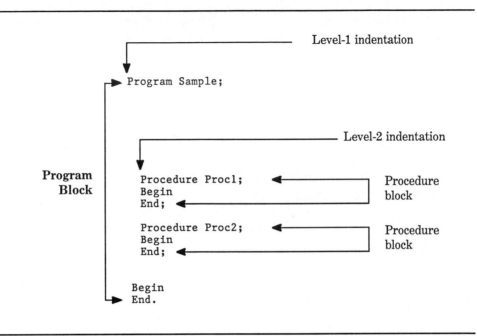

Figure 4-4.   Adding levels to a Turbo Pascal program

By nesting procedures within other procedures, you can add even more levels to the program. In Figure 4-5, for example, procedure **Proc1A** is nested inside procedure **Proc1** to form a third level in the program.

Nesting procedures creates "privacy" among procedures. A procedure that is nested inside another is private to that procedure. Keeping procedures private can decrease programming errors by limiting the use of a procedure to a specific section of your program.

Procedural Scope

Note that Figure 4-5 contains three procedures named **Proc1A:** the first is at level 2; the other two are at level 3, nested within the procedures **Proc1** and **Proc2**.

Although these three procedures have the same name, each is treated as a distinct entity. A call to **Proc1A** in the program block executes the level-2 procedure, while calls made within **Proc1** and **Proc2** refer to their respective nested procedures.

Two rules govern the scope of procedures:

```
Program Sample;          ◄──────────────────── Level 1

    Procedure Proc1A;    ◄──────────────── Level 2
    begin
    end;

    Procedure Proc1;     ◄──────────────── Level 2

        Procedure Proc1A;   ◄──────────── Level 3
        begin
        end;

    begin
    end;

    Procedure Proc2;     ◄──────────────── Level 2

        Procedure Proc1A;   ◄──────────── Level 3
        begin
        end;

    begin
    end;

begin
end.
```

Figure 4-5.   Nesting procedures within procedures

• A program may call a procedure within the block where it is declared and within any subblock nested in that block.

• The exception to Rule 1 occurs when the program declares another procedure of the same name in a higher-level subblock.

In Figure 4-5, the level-2 procedure **Proc1A** would normally extend its scope into **Proc1** and **Proc2**. But because the program declares the same procedure name in **Proc1** and **Proc2**, the scope of the level-2 procedure is limited to the first level.

Procedural Precedence

In some languages (notably C), the order in which you declare procedures makes no difference. In Turbo Pascal, a language far more orderly than C, you cannot call procedures until you have declared them. (The only exception to this is when you use **FORWARD** declarations, which are discussed in the next section.) For example, in Figure 4-5, **Proc2** can call **Proc1**, but **Proc1** cannot call **Proc2**.

The rule of procedural precedence is based on the logic that a complex idea is best built from simple ideas. In other words, a program should be built from small, simple procedures that are combined to form increasingly complex procedures. A programmer should see a continual evolution from the beginning to the end of a Turbo Pascal program, culminating in the program block, which may well consist of only a few procedure calls.

Forward Declarations

While procedural precedence enforces a desirable order in a program, there are times when you simply need to refer to a procedure before you declare it. For these cases, Turbo Pascal provides the *FORWARD declaration*, which informs the compiler that a procedure exists before it specifies what the procedure does. A **FORWARD** declaration consists of the normal procedure heading followed by the word **FORWARD** and a semicolon. The body of the procedure is declared later, at which point only the name of the procedure, and not the entire program heading, is declared. The following listing shows an example of a **FORWARD**-declared procedure.

```
Program Endless_Loop;
Var
  i : Integer;

  Procedure Step2(i : Integer); FORWARD;

  Procedure Step1(i : Integer);
  Begin
  i := i + 1;
  WriteLn(i);
  Step2(i);
  End;

  Procedure Step2;
  Begin
  i := i + 1;
  WriteLn(i);
  If i > 100 Then Halt;
  Step1(i);
  End;

Begin
```

```
i := 1;
Step1(i);
End.
```

In this case, **Step2** and **Step1** both call each other — something not allowed by procedure precedence, but overcome by the **FORWARD** declaration of **Step2**.

Include Files

The Turbo Pascal editor cannot hold more than 62K of text at any time. If your program exceeds this limit, you have to break it into pieces by storing it in multiple files. When you compile the program, the Include File directive pulls all the pieces together from these multiple files. The Include File directive is also useful when you have standard libraries of frequently used routines.

To include a file in a Pascal program, type a left parenthesis or brace followed by an asterisk, $I, the name of the file to be used, another asterisk, and a right parenthesis or brace. For example, the sample directive (*$I PROCS.INC*) tells Turbo Pascal to read the include file PROCS.INC as if the text were written in the program. Another example of how to include a file is shown in Figure 4-6.

Include file is PROCS.INC

```
Procedure ListFiles;
Var
  i : Integer;
Begin
End;
```

Main program file is MAIN.PAS

```
Program Main;
(*$I Procs.Inc*)
Begin
ListFiles;
End.
```

Figure 4-6.   Using an include file

Here, the main program file (MAIN.PAS) makes a call to the procedure **ListFiles**, yet **ListFiles** is defined not in the file MAIN.PAS but in the file PROCS.INC. The include statement in MAIN.PAS tells the compiler to read in PROCS.INC at that point and use its code as part of the program.

Overlays

To support overlays, Turbo Pascal supplies a standard unit aptly named **OVERLAY**. By including this unit in your program's **Uses** clause, you can overlay your program's units to minimize the amount of memory your program requires. Using overlays is quite easy as long as you follow some simple rules.

- Enable the Force Far Calls compiler directive for the program and all units.

- Name the **OVERLAY** unit first in your program's **Uses** clause.

- Compile overlaid units with the **{$O+}** compiler directive.

- List the overlaid units using the **{$O *filename*}** compiler directive.

- Make sure that your program initializes the overlay before any statements execute, including initialization sections of overlaid units.

The use of overlays is best described by example. The following listing includes the code for two units (**Ovr1** and **Ovr2**) and a main program **TestOvr**. Both the units are to be overlaid and, therefore, include the **{$O+,F+}** compiler directive.

```
{$O+,F+}
Unit Ovr1;
Interface
Procedure Message1;
Implementation

Procedure Message1;
Begin
WriteLn('Message 1');
End;

End.
```

```
(**********************************)

{$O+,F+}
Unit Ovr2;
Interface

Procedure Message2;

Implementation

Procedure Message2;
Begin
WriteLn('Message 2');
End;

End.

(**********************************)

{$O+,F+}
Program TestOvr;
Uses Overlay,
     Ovr1,
     Ovr2;

{$O Ovr1}
{$O Ovr2}

Begin
OvrInit('TESTOVR.OVR');
Message1;
Message2;
ReadLn;
End.
```

The program declares the **OVERLAY** unit as the first unit in the **Uses** clause and also declares the units to be overlaid using the **{$O *filename*}** directive. The first line of the program performs the necessary initialization of the overlay.

As you can see, the overlay process is extremely simple. Complications arise, however, when the overlaid units contain initialization code. Consider the following listings, which are similar to the previous unit, except that initialization code has been added to the units to be overlaid. Turbo Pascal always executes initialization code before it executes the first statement in the main program. This means that the overlaid units will execute before the overlay manager is initialized. How can you overcome this problem?

```
{$O+,F+}
Unit Ovr1;
Interface
```

```
Procedure Message1;

Implementation
Var
  s : String;

Procedure Message1;
Begin
WriteLn(s);
End;

Begin
s := 'Message 1';
End.

(**********************************)

{$O+,F+}
Unit Ovr2;

Interface

Procedure Message2;

Implementation
Var
  s : String;

Procedure Message2;
Begin
WriteLn(s);
End;

Begin
s := 'Message 2';
End.

(**********************************)

{$O+,F+}
Unit OvrStart;
Interface
Uses Overlay;

Implementation

Begin
OvrInit('TESTOVR.OVR');
If OvrResult = OvrNotFound Then
  Begin
  WriteLn('File TESTOVR.OVR not found.');
  Halt;
  End;
End.

(**********************************)
```

```
{$O+,F+}
Program TestOvr;
Uses Overlay,
     OvrStart,
     Ovr1,
     Ovr2;

{$O Ovr1}
{$O Ovr2}

Begin
Message1;
Message2;
ReadLn;
End.
```

Fortunately, the answer is not so difficult. Instead of initializing the overlay manager in your main program, place the initialization code in a unit and include this unit in the **Uses** clause *before* any of the overlaid units. This ensures that the overlay manager will be installed before any of the overlaid files execute.

The Turbo Pascal overlay system includes five routines for initializing the overlay manager and controlling the program's use of memory. When they execute, these routines set the global variable **OvrResult** to indicate if any problems occurred. The Overlay unit defines the following constants to help you interpret the value of **OvrResult**:

```
Const
  OvrOk          =  0; (* No error *)
  OvrError       = -1; (* Nonspecific error *)
  OvrNotFound    = -2; (* Overlay file not found *)
  OvrNoMemory    = -3; (* Not enough memory *)
  OvrIOError     = -4; (* Error reading .OVR file *)
  OvrNoEMSDriver = -5; (* EMS driver not loaded *)
  OvrNoEMSMemory = -6; (* Insufficient EMS memory *)
```

Your program should take care to test the value of **OvrResult** every time you use one of the five overlay routines.

OvrInit

This procedure initializes the overlay manager and prepares overlaid units for use. **OvrInit** takes a single string parameter containing the name of the overlay file, which is usually the name of the main program file with the .OVR suffix. This procedure is called only once and must be called before any of the overlaid units.

OvrInitEMS

While overlays save memory, they slow down your program due to frequent disk reads. The Turbo Pascal overlay manager is capable of loading the entire overlay file into expanded memory, which greatly reduces access time to overlaid procedures. To load an overlay into expanded memory, simply execute the procedure **OvrInitEMS**. If the computer has enough expanded memory available, the overlay file will be loaded into it; if not, the overlay will execute from disk as it normally would.

OvrSetBuf

When you initiate **OvrInit**, the overlay manager captures the minimum amount of memory needed to run the overlaid procedures. You can expand this amount of memory with **OvrSetBuf**, a procedure that takes a **LongInt** parameter which represents the size, in bytes, of the overlay buffer you wish to use. For example, the statement **OvrSetBuf(100000)** reserves 100,000 bytes for use as an overlay buffer. The size of the buffer must be at least as large as the minimum buffer size and less than **MemAvail**. Also, **OvrSetBuf** must be called only when the heap is clear of dynamic variables.

OvrGetBuf

This function returns a **LongInt** representing the current size of the overlay buffer. You can use this value as a guide when increasing the size of the buffer with **OvrSetBuf**.

OvrClearBuf

This procedure removes all overlaid units from the overlay buffer. Doing this ensures that any subsequent call to an overlaid procedure will require a disk read. You will normally never need to clear the overlay buffer. One circumstance where you might is when you want to reclaim, for other purposes, the memory used by the overlay buffer.

Turbo Pascal's program structure is straightforward and logical, but requires the programmer to understand the concepts of structured programming. Some programmers see this imposition of structure as a limitation, an unnecessary attempt to tell them how to program. In time, however, you will come to appreciate the strict nature of Turbo Pascal and will learn from it good programming habits that apply to any language.

Turbo Pascal Data Types

Standard Data Types
Constants in Turbo Pascal
Sets
User-Defined Data Types

Turbo Pascal provides programmers with a rich set of data types, each of which serves a specific purpose. **Byte** and **ShortInt** variables are used for small, unsigned, and signed numbers, respectively; **Integer** and **LongInt** for numbers without decimal places; **Real** for numbers with decimal places; **Boolean** for true and false conditions; **char** for characters; and **String** for concatenated characters. This chapter discusses the standard data types offered by Turbo Pascal and how they can be used.

Standard Data Types

A variable of type **Byte** occupies one byte. A **Byte** is an unsigned numeric value that can range from 0 to 255. In arithmetic expressions, a **Byte** variable can be assigned a value from an **Integer** or **LongInt** variable as long as the value does not exceed the byte's numeric range.

Like **Byte** variables, **Integer** variables hold numerical values that have no decimal places. Because they are two bytes (16 bits) long, **Integers** can range in value from −32,768 to 32,767. The **Word** data type is two bytes long, like **Integer**, but is unsigned, giving it a range of 0 to 65,535. **LongInt** variables occupy four bytes in memory and have a range of −2,147,483,648 to 2,147,483,647.

For numbers with fractional portions, or with magnitudes that exceed 2,147,483,647 (the maximum value of **LongInt**), Turbo Pascal provides the **Real** data type, also known as the **floating-point** type. A

Real variable requires six bytes of storage and can range in value from 2.9 × 10E−39 to 1.7 × 10E38. Because of their complex structure, arithmetic operations involving **Real**s take far longer to execute than do operations on **Integer**s or **Byte**s, which are stored in their binary numerical equivalents.

A common problem encountered with **Real** variables is the overflow condition. This occurs when you try to assign too large a number to a **Real** variable and causes a run-time error in the program. You will find, however, that this is not always true. For example, if 1 is added to a **Real** variable with the maximum value of 1.7 × 10E38, the value remains unchanged and no execution error is detected. Even though an overflow condition logically should exist, the program does not detect one. This is because a **Real** can store only 11 to 12 significant digits. That means that adding small numbers to a large **Real** value will not change the value of the **Real**.

On the other hand, an overflow condition can occur unexpectedly. If a **Real** variable with the maximum value of 1.7 × 10E38 is multiplied by 1.0, the value should not change and there should be no overflow error. Even so, Turbo Pascal detects an overflow condition and halts execution.

Admittedly, you are unlikely to encounter such extreme conditions regularly; in most cases you will never come close to the limit of **Real**s in Turbo Pascal.

Char

Like the **Byte** type, the **char** (character) data type occupies one byte of storage in memory. Unlike the **Byte** variable, however, a **char** variable cannot be used directly in arithmetic expressions. It is used instead for manipulating and comparing text, as well as in string-assignment statements.

String

The **String** data type stores text information. A **String** variable can be from 1 to 255 characters long, but it occupies one byte more than its defined length. For example, if a **String** variable is declared to be 10 characters long (**S : String[10];**), the variable occupies 11 bytes in memory. This is because the first byte in every **String** variable keeps track of the length of the string currently stored in the variable (and so is called the *length byte*). If a 10-character **String** variable contains the word "HELLO", the first byte in memory holds the binary value 5, indicating that the variable contains five characters. In this case, the last five bytes of the variable are ignored by Turbo Pascal's string-manipulation procedures. The memory allocated to the **String** variable would look like this:

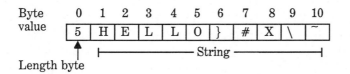

Note that the first byte is not the character "5" but the number 5 in binary (00000101) and that the last five bytes contain random data.

Maintaining a length byte requires quite a bit of overhead. As a result, string-manipulation statements tend to be among the slowest in Turbo Pascal. Yet the alternative implementation of strings, such as in C, is even less efficient. In C, the character array (the equivalent of the Pascal **String** type) has no length byte. Consequently, any time a program needs to know the length of a string, it has to calculate it by counting every character until a delimiter is reached.

Turbo Pascal allows you to define variables as type **String** without any specified length. In this case, the **String** will be given the maximum length of 255 characters.

8087 Data Types

In addition to the **Byte, Integer, Word, LongInt,** and **Real** data types, Turbo Pascal supports four other numerical data types: **Single, Double, Extended,** and **Comp.** The **Single** data type is a "short **Real**" in the sense that it requires only 4 bytes of storage and has only 7 to 8 significant digits. The **Double** data type is a "long **Real**," requiring 8 bytes and giving 15 to 16 significant digits. And for those who need the ultimate in precision, there is the "really, really long **Real**," the **Extended** data type, which uses 10 bytes and provides 19 to 20 significant digits with a range in value of $3.4 \times 10E-4932$ to $1.1 \times 10E4932$.

The 8087 data types also include the **Comp** type, which is not floating-point. This data type uses 8 bytes, contains 19 to 20 significant digits, and ranges from $-(2 \times 10E63) + 1$ to $(2 \times 10E63) -1$. This data type can be useful for calculations requiring large integer values.

With Turbo Pascal's range of numerical data types, you should be able to select the one that precisely fits your needs. And best of all, Turbo Pascal's Emulation mode gives you access to them whether or not your computer has the 8087 math coprocessor installed.

Constants in Turbo Pascal

Turbo Pascal does not initialize variables when a program starts up. As a result, there is no way of telling what value a variable has until you assign one.

Constants, on the other hand, are assigned values specified by the programmer when the program starts. To illustrate the importance of constants, consider the example of a program that computes interest on loans. The program uses a fixed interest rate of 7%, which appears about 100 times within the program. At the same time, a variable interest rate of 7% also appears frequently in the program. To change all the fixed-rate values from 7% to 8% would require checking each occurrence of the number 7, deciding if the number is a fixed or a variable rate, and changing the value manually.

If, on the other hand, a constant named **FixedRate** (or some other appropriate name) is declared, changing the value throughout the program would be accomplished simply by changing the declaration.

Untyped and Typed Constants

Turbo Pascal provides two types of constants, untyped and typed. Untyped constants are true constants in that Turbo Pascal does not allow their value to be altered. Typed constants, on the other hand, can change in value (just as variables can).

To understand how typed constants got their name, consider the sample declarations shown here.

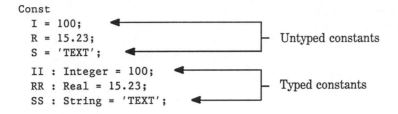

```
Const
  I = 100;
  R = 15.23;
  S = 'TEXT';
  II : Integer = 100;
  RR : Real = 15.23;
  SS : String = 'TEXT';
```

A definition of a typed constant contains the type declaration (for example, **Integer**, **Real**, **String**) and can be used in assignment statements. Untyped constants cannot be used in assignment statements, as is shown here.

```
Const
  S : String[4] = 'TEXT';
Begin                          Correct
S := 'AAAA';
End.

Const
  S = 'TEXT';
Begin                          Incorrect
S := 'AAAA';
End.
```

Since Turbo Pascal provides both constants and variables, what is the intrinsic value of a typed constant? Some programmers prefer to initialize all variables to specific values when a program starts. This avoids the unpredictable results that can occur when a variable is not properly assigned.

One difference between typed and untyped constants concerns their use as parameters to a procedure. Either constant can be passed as a value parameter without any difficulty; however, only a typed constant can be passed by reference.

Sets

In Turbo Pascal, a *set* is a group of related numbers or characters. Sets are primarily used to see if a character or number belongs to the set. For example, you might define a set that consists of the capital letters from A to Z and then use the set to check if other characters in the program are included in it. If a character is included in the set, you know it is uppercase. A discussion of numeric and character sets follows.

Numeric Sets

Numeric sets can consist only of integers (actually byte values). The sets include any integers from 0 to 255; such numbers as −1 and 256 exceed the range established by Turbo Pascal. Here are two examples of numeric set definitions.

Zero _ Through _ Nine : Set of 0 . . 9;

FullRange : Set of Byte;

In the first line, Zero _ Through _ Nine can include any combination of integers (byte values) from 0 to 9, but the number 10 cannot be included because it is outside the range of the set.

In the second line, no range is specified for the set FullRange; the definition specifies only that the set consists of bytes. Later in the program, the programmer can define FullRange to be any numeric subset with a statement such as this:

FullRange := [0 . . 9];

Now, the set FullRange has the same elements as

Zero _ Through _ Nine.

Character Sets

Character sets can consist only of characters. Like numeric sets, the maximum range of character sets is from 0 (00h) to 255 (FFh). The major difference between numeric sets and character sets is that character sets can be directly compared with character variables. Here are two examples of character-set definitions:

UpperCase : Set of 'A' . . 'Z';
AllChars : Set of Char;

The set UpperCase can include any combination of uppercase characters from "A" (ASCII code 65) to "Z" (ASCII code 90). Thus, the character "a" (ASCII code 97) could not be included in this set.

The second set, AllChars, is defined as a "Set of Char." This means that this set can include any combination of characters from 0 to 255.

Sets of User-Defined Elements

Finally, a set can consist of elements defined by the user. These elements are neither numeric nor character and must be listed individually. The maximum number of elements allowed is 255. Here is an example of a user-defined set:

Ingredients : Set of (eggs, milk, butter, flour);

All operations on sets of user-defined elements follow the same rules as all other sets.

Sets and Memory Allocation

Sets can use a maximum of 32 bytes of storage—the equivalent of 256 individual bits. This is what limits the scope of a set to the range 0 to 255. If your set has only a few elements, it uses only a few bytes, and allocating the full 32 bytes would be wasteful.

Therefore, sets are automatically reduced in size. For example, a set defined as

X : 1 .. 5;

needs only one byte, so Turbo Pascal allocates just one byte for the set. The values in the byte are allocated as follows:

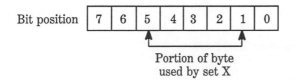

Bit position | 7 | 6 | 5 | 4 | 3 | 2 | 1 | 0 |

Portion of byte
used by set X

The arrows indicate the part of the byte used to store the set. When an element is present in a set, the appropriate bit is turned on (that is, set to 1). To illustrate how the memory would represent the presence of elements in a set, consider the following set assignment:

X := [1 .. 3,5];

This statement assigns the elements 1, 2, 3, and 5 to set X. In memory, this assignment creates the following bit pattern:

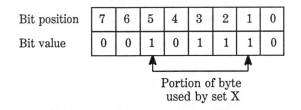

Portion of byte
used by set X

The ones in the bit value portion of this illustration indicate the presence of an element in the set. They are found in the 1, 2, 3, and 5 positions of the byte, which correspond precisely to the assignment statement.

Since Turbo Pascal needs only one byte to store set X, the remaining 31 bytes are used for other purposes. Only three bits of memory (the 0, 6, and 7 positions) are wasted. To further illustrate the storage of sets, consider the following set definition:

X : Set of 7..8;

This set comprises only two elements, but requires two bytes of storage. Why? Because the set straddles a byte boundary, as shown in this illustration:

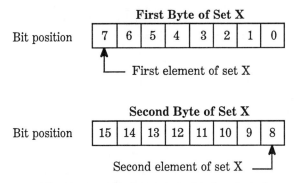

The first element (7) is in the first byte, while the second element (8) is in the second byte. Two bytes are used (but 14 of the 16 bits are ignored), and 30 bytes are used for other purposes.

It is possible to create a compiler that eliminates this kind of wasted memory, but such a compiler would increase the size of the compiled programs and slow down execution. Wisely, Borland decided to accept a minimal amount of waste in return for faster execution and smaller code.

User-Defined Data Types

One of the most powerful aspects of Turbo Pascal is its ability to define customized data types. By tailoring data structures to a program's specific algorithms, you can increase your program's readability and simplify its maintenance. User-defined data types fall into one of three categories: user-defined scalars, records, and arrays.

User-Defined Scalar Type

A user-defined scalar (or enumerated scalar) requires one byte of memory and can have up to 256 elements. The power of user-defined scalars is that the programmer names the values, allowing easier programming and debugging. The following are examples of enumerated scalars:

```
Income : (High, Moderate, Low);
Sex : (Male, Female);
Occupation : (Doctor, Teacher, Other);
```

The following code excerpt demonstrates the readability of user-defined scalars:

```
If Occupation = Doctor Then
    Income := High
Else If Occupation = Teacher Then
Income := Moderate
Else
Income := Low;
```

Without user-defined scalars, the programmer must develop coding schemes to represent the values (for example, 1 = Doctor, 2 = Teacher, 3 = Other). When the number of coded variables is large, it is difficult to keep track of the meanings of different values.

Each element of a user-defined scalar equates to a byte value according to its position in the enumerated set, with the first element having a value of 0. In the preceding examples of enumerated sets, the high income has the value 0, while low income has the value 2. To determine the current value of **Income**, use the Turbo Pascal standard function **Ord**. If **Income** is currently High, then the statement **Ord(Income)** returns the value 0; if it is Low, it returns 2. If you wish, you can assign this value to a numeric variable, as is done next, where the variable **i** will be equal to 1 after the assignment statement:

```
Var
  i : Integer;
  Color : (Black, Brown, Blue, Green, Red, Yellow, White);
Begin
Color := Brown;
i := Ord(Color);
End.
```

While transforming a user-defined scalar to a numeric value is easy, the opposite is untrue. In the following example, the statement **Color := i** is illegal:

```
Var
  i : Integer;
  Color : (Black, Brown, Blue, Green, Red, Yellow, White);
Begin
i := 1;
Color := i;
End.
```

To resolve this illegal statement simply, you can use the Turbo Pascal standard function **Fillchar**, which is discussed in greater detail in Appendix E. The following example shows one way to assign a numeric value (**Integer** or **Byte**, not **Real**) to an enumerated set.

```
Var
  i : Integer;
  Color : (Black, Brown, Blue, Green, Red, Yellow, White);
Begin
i := 1;
FillChar(color,1,i);
End.
```

Records

A record is a combination of other data types into a new data type. This example exhibits a typical record definition:

```
Var
  Customer : Record
    Name : String[30];
    Address : String[60];
    Age : Integer;
    Income : Real;
    Married : Boolean;
    End;
```

Using records has two advantages. First, all data elements for a single record are logically connected to each other. This makes it easier to keep track of things. Second, some operations, such as assignments and file operations, can be performed on an entire record, eliminating the need to refer to each element in the record.

Using records in assignment statements is straightforward. You can access elements in a record in two ways: by explicit reference or implicit reference using the reserved word **With**, as shown in Figure 5-1. The statement

Rec1.b := 1;

is an example of explicit reference because both the record name and the element name, separated by a period, appear in the assignment. In an implicit reference, using the reserved word **With**, you do not need to repeat the record name in each assignment statement. The assignment statement

Rec2 := Rec1;

assigns every element in Rec1 to the corresponding element in Rec2.

Implicit references can be nested so that one **With** statement refers to more than one record, as shown in Figure 5-2. The statement

With Rec2, Rec1 Do

allows the programmer to reference elements in both records implicitly. Problems can arise, however. In Figure 5-2, Rec1 and Rec2 both have an element "a". This ambiguous reference does not tell Turbo Pascal which record element is being referred to. Thus, the compiler assumes that the ambiguous element belongs to the last record that contains that element. In Figure 5-2, the assignment statement

a := a;

```
Program X;
Uses CRT;
Var
  Rec1, Rec2. : Record
    a : String[20];
    B : Integer;
    c : Real;
    End;

Begin
ClrScr;

Rec1.a := 'sss';
Rec1.b := 1;
Rec1.c := 123.23;

With Rec1 Do
  Begin
  a := 'sss';
  b := 1;
  c := 123.23;
  End;

Rec2 := Rec1;

With Rec2 Do
  Begin
  WriteLn(a);
  WriteLn(b);
  WriteLn(c);
  End;

WriteLn;
Write('Press ENTER ...');
ReadLn;
End.
```

These segments do exactly the same thing

Record-to-record block assignment

Output using the **With** option

Figure 5-1. Using the With statement with records

assumes that both elements are from Rec1. In short, it assumes that the statement means

Rec1.a := Rec1.a;

Variant Records

Turbo Pascal allows programmers to produce what are known as *variant records*. Variant records are records that permit different types of

```
Program X;
Uses CRT;
Var
  Rec1 : Record
    a : String[20];
    b : Integer;
    c : Real;
    End;

  Rec2 : Record
    a : String[20];
    r1, r2 : Real;
    End;

Begin
ClrScr;

With Rec1 Do
  a := 'sss';
  b := 1;
  c := 123.23;
  End;

With Rec2 Do
  Begin
  a := 'xxx';
  r1 := 20.0;
  r2 := 10.0;
  End;

With Rec2, Rec1 Do
  Begin
  a := a;
  c := r1 * r2;
  End;

With Rec2 Do
With Rec1 Do
  Begin
  a := a;
  c := r1 * r2;
  End;

With Rec1 Do
  Begin
  WriteLn(a);
  WriteLn(b);
  WriteLn(c);
  End;

WriteLn;
Write('Press ENTER ...');
ReadLn;
End.
```

These segments do exactly the same thing

Figure 5-2.   Nested With statements

data to be stored in the same memory location; they are a combination of a record type and the Turbo Pascal logical operator **Case**. Variant records are explored more fully in Chapter 6 under the general discussion of the **Case** operator.

Arrays

Any data type, whether standard or user defined, can be extended into an *array*. An array is a variable that repeats a data type a specified number of times. To define an array, follow this general format:

Variable Name :
          Array [lower limit .. upper limit] of Data Type;

The lower limit and the upper limit are any legal integer values in which the upper limit is greater than the lower limit.

Arrays are usually used when a program includes a list of recurring elements. For example, to hold a year's worth of stock prices, define the array as follows:

Price : Array [1 .. 365] of Real;

To refer to a specific price, indicate which element in the array you want. For example, to set the price on the tenth day in the year, you would use

Price[10] := 34.50;

The lower limit on an array does not have to be 1. It makes more sense to start the array at a value that corresponds to the context of your data. If you were measuring the conductivity of a metal with a temperature range of $-100°$ to $+100°$ C, you would define the array as

Conductivity : Array [-100 .. 100] of Real;

The range of the array now matches the functional range of temperatures (assuming that the measurements will be taken at whole-number intervals).

Another example of an array that matches its data is one that stores the average income of people age 35 to 65. An array defined as

Average Income : Array [35 .. 65] of Real;

would do the trick.

Multidimensional Arrays

Any arrays defined to have more than one dimension are considered to be *multidimensional arrays*, although they rarely exceed three dimensions. Two-dimensional arrays, sometimes called *matrices*, are quite common, especially in multivariate statistics. For example, when measuring the conductivity of a metal, the following two-dimensional arrays could be used, assuming that the temperature intervals are not whole numbers:

Temp _ Conductivity : Array [1 .. 200,1 .. 2] of Real;

The best way to think about this array is to visualize a table of columns and rows: the first dimension in the array (1 .. 200) provides the rows, and the second dimension (1 .. 2) provides the columns. Going row by row, all you need to do is put the temperatures in one column and the matching conductivity ratings in another, as shown in Table 5-1.

	1 Temperature	2 Conductivity
1	− 99.34	12.3
2	− 97.76	12.2
3	− 96.01	11.9
.		
.		
.		
200	99.01	2.9

Table 5-1.   Sample Temperature and Conductivity Readings

To assign a value in a multidimensional array, specify both dimensions, as shown in the following two statements:

```
Temp_Conductivity[1,1] := -99.34;
Temp_Conductivity[1,2] := 12.3;
```

To refer to the first pair of observations, specify both the row and the column. In this example, the first temperature reading is "Temp_Conductivity[1,1]," while the corresponding conductivity rating is "Temp_Conductivity[1,2]."

Substitute for Multidimensional Arrays

The examples of multidimensional arrays should make one thing clear—it is hard to keep track of what values are in which column. There is simply no clue given in the array itself. Because it is preferable to deal with variables that have meaningful names, Turbo Pascal provides an alternative to multidimensional arrays: arrays of records. The following example shows why these arrays are better than the multidimensional ones:

```
Observation : Array [1..200] Of Record
  Temperature : Real;
  Conductivity : Real;
  End;
```

Arrays of records create clear definitions; it is immediately apparent that the **Record** definition in the preceding illustration defines a series of observations consisting of temperatures and conductivities. These can be referred to by name in the following manner:

```
Observation[1].Temperature
Observation[1].Conductivity
```

Whenever you use multidimensional arrays, consider the possibility that you may be able to substitute an array of a record type that does the job, yet improves program clarity.

Arithmetic and Logic in Turbo Pascal

Arithmetic in Turbo Pascal
Logical Operators

Intelligence and number-crunching power are characteristics long associated with computers, an association reinforced by the names of such computer languages as FORTRAN (from Formula Translator) and ALGOL (from Algorithmic Logic). Pascal continues in this vein: it is named after Blaise Pascal, a 17th-century mathematician, and provides powerful arithmetic functions and extensive logic commands.

Arithmetic in Turbo Pascal

Turbo Pascal arithmetic is based on the concept of an expression or equation. An expression consists of a combination of identifiers, numeric values and functions, and operators, all of which result in a specific numeric value. If that sounds too complicated, consider this well-known expression:

    2 + 2

This has all the elements of a mathematical expression—numeric values and an operator (the plus sign)—but it is not a Pascal statement. In Pascal, a mathematical expression must be part of either an assignment statement or a logical statement. A numerical assignment statement computes a value from an expression and stores the value in a numeric variable. An example of an arithmetic assignment statement is

Result := 2 + 2;

When this statement is executed, Turbo Pascal calculates the right-hand side of the statement and assigns the result in the variable **Result**.

An arithmetic expression in a logical statement is similar, except that the expression does not result in a numerical value but in a TRUE or FALSE condition. For example, the logical statement

If Result = (2 + 2) Then . . .

does not change the value in the variable **Result**. Rather, Turbo Pascal adds the two numbers and compares them to the value that is already in **Result**. In this case, if **Result** is equal to 4, then the expression is TRUE; if NOT, it is FALSE. Logical structures are discussed more fully later in this chapter.

Note that the assignment operator in Pascal is :=, while the logical operator is =. This might seem to be a trivial distinction, but there is a rationale behind it: an assignment statement does not imply equality. In arithmetic, a statement such as X = X + 1 is simply incorrect. In Pascal, however, the statement **X := X + 1** is perfectly legal. Remember, this assignment statement does not say, "X is equal to X + 1"; it says, "Take the value of X + 1 and assign it to the variable X."

Integer and Real Expressions

In Turbo Pascal, arithmetic expressions result in either an **Integer** value or a **Real** value. For an expression to yield an **Integer** result, two conditions must be met. First, all the operands in the expression must be integers (or floating-point variables converted to integers with the **Trunc** or **Round** function). Second, if division is performed, the **Div** operator must be used instead of the / character.

Any expression that is not an **Integer** expression is, by default, a **Real** expression. Even if an expression has 50 **Integer** operands and only 1 **Real** operand, the expression results in a **Real** value. The following illustration shows examples of both **Integer** and **Real** expressions:

```
Program Math1;
Var
  i,j,k : Integer;
  x,y,z : Real;

Begin

j := 2;

i := 1 + j;
j := 3 Div i;
k := (i + j) Div (3 * j);

WriteLn(i,' ',j,' ',k);

j := 2;

x := 1.0 + j;
y := 3 / i;
z := (i + j) Div (3 * j);

WriteLn(x:2:2,' ',y:2:2,' ',z:2:2);
WriteLn;
Write('Press ENTER...');
ReadLn;
End.
```

Integer expressions

Real expressions

Hierarchy of Arithmetic Operators

The order of precedence dictates that multiplication and division are performed before addition and subtraction and that any operation in parentheses is done first. Turbo Pascal follows these rules: it has four hierarchical levels of arithmetic operators, as shown here:

Level 1: Unary Minus, Unary Plus   ← Highest priority
Level 2: Parentheses
Level 3: Multiplication, Division
Level 4: Addition, Subtraction   ← Lowest priority

A *unary minus* is the sign that directly precedes a number and indicates that the number is negative. For example, the minus sign in the number −3 is a unary minus. When used in arithmetic expressions, the unary minus can lead to statements such as

Result := 1 − −3

in which case, **Result** is equal to 4.

Turbo Pascal also supports the unary plus. While the unary plus has absolutely no impact on the value of the number, the fact that it is supported means that a statement such as

Result := 1 − +2

is perfectly legal. Please note, however, that the unary plus operator is not an indicator of absolute value (the absolute value of a negative number is its positive equivalent). If a unary plus precedes a variable with a negative value, the variable remains negative.

The second level in the hierarchy of Turbo Pascal arithmetic operators is parentheses. Following the order of precedence, operations within parentheses are executed before operations outside parentheses. To clarify this rule, consider the following two expressions:

A := 3 * 4 + 5;
A := 3 * (4 + 5);

In the first case, the multiplication operator takes precedence, so that 3 * 4 is evaluated first, yielding 12, and 5 is added to 12 for a final result of 17. In the second case, the operation within the parentheses takes precedence over the multiplication operator, so that 4 + 5 is evaluated first, yielding 9, and 9 is multiplied by 3 for a final result of 27.

You should use parentheses to increase clarity, even when they are not strictly necessary. For example, the following two expressions yield the same result, yet the parentheses in the latter make it more readable.

r := a + b * c * d + x + y / r;
r := a + (b * c * d) + x + (y / r);

Integer Versus Real Arithmetic

The last two levels in the hierarchy of arithmetic operators are multiplication and division (level 3) and addition and subtraction (level 4). Here Turbo Pascal's strong typing forces a separation between integer arithmetic and real arithmetic.

Integer Arithmetic

The rules of integer arithmetic apply when an expression is assigned to an **Integer** variable. All operators in an integer expression must be either **Integer**s or **Real**s converted to **Integer**s using the Turbo Pascal standard functions **Round** or **Trunc**. The program shown next provides examples of both legal and illegal integer arithmetic statements.

```
Program IntegerMath;
Var
  i,j,k : Integer;
  x,y,z : Real;

Begin

(* Legal Statements*)

i := 10 + j;
j := i Div k;
k := j + Round(x) + Trunc(y/z);
WriteLn('i = ',i);
WriteLn('j = ',j);
WriteLn('k = ',k);
WriteLn;
Write('Press ENTER...');
ReadLn;

(* Illegal Statements*)

{
i := 10.0 + j;
j := i / k;
k := j + x + y / z;
}

End.
```

Note that numeric literals are not allowed to have decimal places in integer expressions.

Round and **Trunc** are Turbo Pascal standard functions that convert real values into integer values, but in slightly different ways. The **Round** function rounds a real value to the nearest integer. If the decimal portion is below 0.5, the real value is rounded down; otherwise, it is rounded up. For example, the result of **Round(10.49)** is the integer value **10**, while **Round(10.5)** returns the value **11**.

The **Trunc** standard function truncates a real value, chopping off any decimal places. Therefore, the result of **Trunc(10.99)** is 10. With the **Round** and **Trunc** standard functions, you can freely mix **Real**s within

Integer expressions. However, it is important that the value of the **Real** does not exceed the limits of an **Integer**.

Special Integer Operators

The integer-division operator **Div** is replaced by the slash character for floating-point arithmetic. The following integer operators, however, have no counterpart for floating-point operations: **Mod, And, Or, Xor, Shl,** and **Shr.**

The **Mod** operator returns the remainder of integer division. For example, 7 **Div** 2 yields 3; the remainder of 1 is lost. The **Mod** operator, however, discards the dividend and returns the remainder. Therefore, 7 **Mod** 2 returns 1.

The remaining integer operators—**And, Or, Xor, Shl,** and **Shr**—are familiar to anyone who has used Assembler. These are also known as *bit-manipulation operators* since they are usually used not for arithmetic but to alter the values of specific bits in a byte or integer variable. To understand how these operators work, it is necessary to know what a byte and integer look like in memory.

A byte consists of eight bits, each bit capable of storing one of two values: 0 and 1. Because bits can store only two numbers, they are base-two numbers. Consider the equivalent binary and decimal numerical values in Table 6-1. (Binary numbers are typically indicated by a lowercase "b" appended to the digits.) Note that the highest value a byte can hold is 255.

Decimal	Binary
0	00000000b
1	00000001b
2	00000010b
3	00000011b
10	00001010b
100	01100100b
255	11111111b

Table 6-1. Binary and Decimal Equivalents

Integers consist of two bytes. As a result, their numerical range extends far beyond the limit of 255 that a single byte can hold. The largest possible two-byte integer value is 65,535, or 11111111 11111111b. In Turbo Pascal, however, the left-most bit in an integer determines the sign of the number; 0 indicates a positive number, 1 a negative number. As a result, the largest integer value in Turbo Pascal is 32,767, or 01111111 11111111b, and the smallest integer value is −32,768, or 11111111 11111111b. For simplicity, the bit-manipulation operators are illustrated with byte values rather than integers; the general concepts apply equally to both.

The And, Or, and Xor Operators

The **And, Or,** and **Xor** operators compare each bit in two different byte variables and return a third byte variable as the result. The value of the resulting byte depends on the type of the comparison.

The **And** operator compares each bit in two bytes one by one and stores the result in a third byte. If the comparison finds both bits are on, the corresponding bit in the third byte is also turned on (that is, set to a value of 1). If the bits compared are not both on, the corresponding bit in the third byte is turned off.

Figure 6-1 gives an example of the **And** command. Byte1 is **AND**ed with Byte2, yielding Byte3. Bit 0 in Byte1 is on, but it is off in Byte2. Because only one, and not both, of these bits is on, bit 0 in Byte3 is turned off. Bit position 2 is different in that it is on in both Byte1 and Byte2. Therefore, bit 2 in Byte3 is turned on.

Like the **And** operator, the **Or** operator compares each bit in two bytes and stores the result in a third byte. However, the bit in the third byte is turned on if the comparison finds either bit or both bits in Byte1 and Byte2 are on. The corresponding bit in the third byte is turned off only if both of the bits compared are off.

In Figure 6-2, Byte1 is **OR**ed with Byte2, yielding Byte3. Bit 0 in Byte1 is on, but in Byte2 it is off. Because the **Or** operator requires only one of the bits to be on, bit 0 in Byte3 is turned on. In this example, the only bit position that fails the **Or** test is bit 7. Because bit 7 is off in both Byte1 and Byte2, bit 7 in Byte3 is also turned off.

The **Xor** comparison is TRUE if one bit, and only one bit, is on between two bytes. If both bits are on or both bits are off, the comparison fails and the corresponding bit in the third byte is turned off.

```
PROGRAM AndOperator;
VAR
   Byte1, Byte2, Byte3 : BYTE;
BEGIN
Byte1 := 77;
Byte2 := 62;
Byte3 := Byte1 AND Byte2;
WriteLn (Byte3);
END.
```

Bit position	7	6	5	4	3	2	1	0
Byte1	0	1	0	0	1	1	0	1
And	↓	↓	↓	↓	↓	↓	↓	↓
Byte2	0	0	1	1	1	1	1	0
Gives	↓	↓	↓	↓	↓	↓	↓	↓
Byte3	0	0	0	0	1	1	0	0

Figure 6-1.   Bit manipulation using the And operator

In Figure 6-3, Byte1 is **XOR**ed with Byte2. Bit 0 is on in Byte1 and off in Byte2. Because only one of the bits is on, the comparison is TRUE, and bit 0 in Byte3 is turned on. On the other hand, bits 2 and 7 are turned off in Byte3 because bit 2 is on in both Byte1 and Byte2 and bit 7 is off in both bytes.

The Shl and Shr Operators

As their names suggest, the operators **Shift-left (Shl)** and **Shift-right (Shr)** shift the bits in a byte left or right. A byte can be shifted left or right a maximum of eight times, at which point all the bits are set to zero. When a byte is shifted left by 1, each bit in the byte moves one position to the left. The left-most bit is lost, and a zero appears in the right-most position, as follows:

```
{$R-}
Program ShiftLeft;
Var
  i : Byte;
```

```
Begin
i := 255;       (* i equals 11111111b *)
WriteLn('i = ',i);
i := i Shl 1;  (* i equals 11111110b *)
WriteLn('i = ',i);
i := i Shl 1;  (* i equals 11111100b *)
WriteLn('i = ',i);
i := i Shl 1;  (* i equals 11111000b *)
WriteLn('i = ',i);
i := i Shl 1;  (* i equals 11110000b *)
WriteLn('i = ',i);
i := i Shl 1;  (* i equals 11100000b *)
WriteLn('i = ',i);
i := i Shl 1;  (* i equals 11000000b *)
WriteLn('i = ',i);
i := i Shl 1;  (* i equals 10000000b *)
WriteLn('i = ',i);
i := i Shl 1;  (* i equals 00000000b *)
WriteLn('i = ',i);

WriteLn;
Write('Press ENTER...');
ReadLn;
End.
```

```
PROGRAM OrOperator;
VAR
   Byte1, Byte2, Byte3 : BYTE;
BEGIN
Byte1 := 77;
Byte2 := 62;
Byte3 := Byte1 OR Byte2;
WriteLn (Byte3);
END.
```

Bit position	7	6	5	4	3	2	1	0
Byte1	0	1	0	0	1	1	0	1
Or	↓	↓	↓	↓	↓	↓	↓	↓
Byte2	0	0	1	1	1	1	1	0
Gives	↓	↓	↓	↓	↓	↓	↓	↓
Byte3	0	1	1	1	1	1	1	1

Figure 6-2.   Bit manipulation using the Or operator

```
PROGRAM XorOperator;
VAR
  Byte1, Byte2, Byte3 : BYTE;
BEGIN
Byte1 := 77;
Byte2 := 62;
Byte3 := Byte1 XOR Byte2;
WriteLn (Byte3);
END.
```

Bit position	7	6	5	4	3	2	1	0
Byte1	0	1	0	0	1	1	0	1
Xor	↓	↓	↓	↓	↓	↓	↓	↓
Byte2	0	0	1	1	1	1	1	0
Gives	↓	↓	↓	↓	↓	↓	↓	↓
Byte3	0	1	1	1	0	0	1	1

Figure 6-3.   Bit manipulation using the Xor operator

Shift-right (**Shr**) operates in the same way as **Shift-left,** but it works in the opposite direction. When a byte is shifted to the right, the right-most bit is lost and the left-most bit is set to zero.

While they are considered arithmetic in nature, bit-manipulation operators are not often used for computations. More often, they test or set specific bit values. The following listing contains several procedures that use these bit-manipulation operators.

```
Program BinaryDemo;
Uses CRT;
Type
  Binstr = String[8];
Var
  i : Integer;
  b : Byte;

(******************************************************)

Function Binary(b : Byte) : Binstr;
{
```

```
This function accepts a byte parameter and returns
a string of eight ones and zeros indicating the binary
form of the byte.
}
Var
  i : Integer;
  bt : Byte;
  s : Binstr;
Begin
bt := $01;
s := '';
For i := 1 To 8 Do
  Begin
  If (b And bt) > 0 Then
    s := '1' + s
  Else
    s := '0' + s;
  {$R-}
  bt := bt Shl 1;
  {$R+}
  End;
Binary := s;
End;


(******************************************************)


Procedure SetBit(Position, Value : Byte;
                 Var ChangeByte : Byte);
{
This procedure sets a particular bit in the byte ChangeByte
to either 1 or 0. The bit is specified by Position, which
can range from 0 to 7.
}
Var
  bt : Byte;
Begin
bt := $01;
bt := bt Shl Position;
If Value = 1 Then
  ChangeByte := ChangeByte Or bt
Else
  Begin
  bt := bt Xor $FF;
  ChangeByte := ChangeByte And bt;
  End;
End;


(******************************************************)


Function BitOn(Position, TestByte : Byte) : Boolean;
{
This function tests if a bit in TestByte is turned on
(equal to one). The bit to test is indicated by the parameter
Position, which can range from 0 (right-most bit) to 7
```

```
(left-most bit). If the bit indicated by Position is
turned on, then BitOn returns TRUE.
}
Var
  bt : byte;
Begin
bt := $01;
bt := bt Shl Position;
BitOn := (bt And TestByte) > 0;
End;

(****************************************************)

Begin
ClrScr;
WriteLn;
WriteLn('Demonstrate binary conversion.');
Write('Enter a number (0 - 255): ');
ReadLn(b);
WriteLn('Binary equivalent is: ',binary(b));
WriteLn;
Write('Press ENTER...');
ReadLn;

ClrScr;
WriteLn;
WriteLn('Demonstrate SetBit procedure.');
WriteLn;
b := 0;
For i := 0 To 7 Do
  Begin
  SetBit(i,1,b);
  WriteLn(binary(b));
  End;

For i := 0 To 7 Do
  Begin
  SetBit(i,0,b);
  WriteLn(binary(b));
  End;
WriteLn;
Write('Press ENTER...');
ReadLn;

ClrScr;
WriteLn;
Write('Enter a number (0 - 255): ');
ReadLn(b);
WriteLn('Binary value is ',binary(b));
If BitOn(0,b) Then
  WriteLn('Bit 0 is on.')
Else
  WriteLn('Bit 0 is off.');
WriteLn;
Write('Press ENTER...');
ReadLn;
End.
```

Procedure **Binary** converts a byte value into a string of ones and zeros that represent the bits. Procedure **SetBit** turns on or off any individual bit in a byte. The last procedure, the Boolean function **BitOn**, tests whether a particular bit in a byte is turned on.

Real Arithmetic

An arithmetic expression yields a floating-point result under two conditions: when the expression contains any floating-point operands and when division is executed with the slash (/) operator. Floating-point operands are any identifiers defined as **Real** or any numeric literal with decimal places (for example, 10.2). The following program, which comprises examples of both integer and floating-point expressions, highlights the small differences between the two expression types.

```
{$N-,E-}
Program Math1;
Uses CRT;
Var
   i,j,k : Integer;
   x,y,z : Real;

Begin
ClrScr;
i := 1;
k := 3;
z := 3.324;

j := i Div k; (* integer expression *)
x := i / k;   (* floating-point expression *)
WriteLn('Integer math.  i Div k = ',j);
WriteLn('Real math.     i / k   = ',x:0:4);
WriteLn;

j := i + 3;   (* integer expression *)
x := i + 3.0; (* floating-point expression *)
WriteLn('Integer math.  i + 3 = ',j);
WriteLn('Real math.     i + 3.0 = ',x:0:4);
WriteLn;

j := i + k;   (* integer expression *)
x := i + z;   (* floating-point expression *)
WriteLn('Integer math.  i + k = ',j);
WriteLn('Real math.     i + z = ',x:0:4);
WriteLn;
WriteLn;


x := 10 * 10;
WriteLn('Valid conversion to real.  10 * 10 =   ',x:0:2);
WriteLn;
```

```
i := 10000;
j := 10000;
x := i * j;
WriteLn('i = 10000');
WriteLn('j = 10000');
WriteLn('Invalid conversion to real.  i * j = ',x:0:2);
WriteLn;

i := 10000;
j := 10000;
x := 1.0 * i * j;
WriteLn('i = 10000');
WriteLn('j = 10000');
WriteLn('Valid conversion to real.  1.0 * i * j = ',x:0:2);
WriteLn;
Write('Press ENTER...');
ReadLn;
End.
```

The preceding listing points out a potential source of error in programs. Consider the assignment statement

$$x := 10 * 10;$$

The right side of the statement, which is an integer expression, is evaluated as an integer before being converted into a floating-point value.

A problem arises when the result of the integer expression exceeds the maximum integer value of 32,767. In the following statements

```
i := 10000;
j := 10000;
x := i * j;
```

the integer expression overflows the maximum integer value before being converted to a **Real**. As a result, **x** is incorrectly assigned the value -7936. To eliminate this error, include a floating-point operand in the expression. The expression is then evaluated as a floating-point expression.

In the preceding program listing, the solution is to multiply the expression by 1.0. This forces the expression to be evaluated as a floating-point value, thereby producing the correct result.

Arithmetic Functions

Turbo Pascal provides a rich set of standard arithmetic functions that give easy access to complex computations. These are as follows:

Abs(num)   Returns the absolute value of the number passed as a parameter. The value passed can be either **Integer** or **Real,** and the value returned will match the type of the parameter: If **num** is an **Integer,** then **Abs** returns an **Integer.**

Arctan(num)   Returns the arctangent of **num. Num** can be either **Real** or **Integer,** but the result is **Real.**

Cos(num)   Returns the cosine of **num,** where **num** is either **Real** or **Integer,** and the result is **Real.**

Exp(num)   Computes the exponential of **num. Num** is **Real** or **Integer;** the result is **Real.** When using standard **Real**s (no emulation or 8087), **Exp** produces an overflow error when **num** is greater than 88 or less than −88.

Frac(num)   This is the fractional part of **num. Num** can be **Real** or **Integer,** although **Integer**s always return a value of zero. The result is **Real.** When using standard **Real**s (no emulation or 8087), **Frac** returns zero for any number raised to 1.0E10 power.

Hi(num)   Returns an **Integer** whose high-order byte is zero and whose low-order byte contains the high-order byte of **num. Num** must be of type **Integer.**

Int(num)   Returns the nonfractional portion of **num. Num** may be either **Real** or **Integer.** If **num** is **Integer,** the function does not change the value, but it does produce a **Real.**

Ln(num)   Calculates the natural logarithm of **num. Num** can be either **Real** or **Integer,** but it must be greater than zero.

Lo(num)   Returns an **Integer** whose high-order byte is zero and whose low-order byte contains the low-order byte of **num. Num** must be of type **Integer.**

Ord(var)   Returns the relative value of any scalar, including type **Char**. The result is of type **Integer**.

Pred(num)   Returns the value of the **Integer**-type **num** decremented by one. The result is of type **Integer**.

Random   Returns a random value than one but greater than or equal to zero. The result is of type **Real**.

Random(num)   Computes a random number from an **Integer**-type **num**. The random number will be of type **Integer**, and its value will be greater than or equal to zero but less than **num**.

Round(num)   Returns the value of **num**, rounded to the nearest whole number. **Num** is **Real**, while the result is of type **Integer**.

Sin(num)   Computes the sine of **num**. **Num** can be **Real** or **Integer**; the result is **Real**.

Sqr(num)   Returns the square of **num**. **Num** can be **Real** or **Integer**; the result is **Real**. When using standard **Real**s (no emulation or 8087), an overflow error will occur when **num** exceeds 1.0E18.

Sqrt(num)   Computes the square root of **num**. **Num** can be **Real** or **Integer**; the result is **Real**.

Succ(num)   Returns the value of the **Integer**-type **num** incremented by one. The result is of type **Integer**.

Trunc(num)   Returns the value of **num** with the decimal portion removed. **Num** is **Real**, and the result is **Integer**.

You can also write your own numeric functions. The following listing contains two valuable numerical functions; the first computes the cumulative normal probability density function of a number and the second raises a number to a power.

```
{$N+,E+}

Program NumberFunctions;
Uses CRT;
```

```
{$IFOPT N+}
Type
  Float = Double;
{$ELSE}
  Float = Real;
{$ENDIF}

(**********************************************)

Function n(x : Float) : Float;
(* Computes the Cumulative Normal *)
(* Probability Density Function   *)
Var
  x2, t, y1, y2, y3, y4, y5, z, R : Float;

Begin
y1 := 1.0/(1.0+(0.2316419*Abs(x)));
y2 := y1*y1;
y3 := y2*y1;
y4 := y3*y1;
y5 := y4*y1;
x2 := x*x;

z := 0.3989423 * Exp(-x2/2.0);

R := (1.330274*y5) -
     (1.821256*y4) +
     (1.781478*y3) -
     (0.356538*y2) +
     (0.3193815*y1);

t := 1.0 - (z*R);

If x > 0 Then
  n := t
Else
  n := 1-t;
End;

(****************************************************)

Function X_To_Y(x, y : Float) : Float;
Var
  r : Float;

Begin
r := y*Ln(x);
X_To_Y := Exp(r);
End;

(****************************************************)

Begin
ClrScr;
WriteLn('3 to power of 2 is: ',X_To_Y(3, 2):0:4);
WriteLn;
WriteLn('Cumulative normal probability of 1.96 = ',
        n(1.96):0:4);
```

```
WriteLn;
Write('Press ENTER...');
ReadLn;
End.
```

Notice the use of conditional compilation in this example program. If the {N+} directive is present (activating the 8087 mode), the data type **Float** represents a **Double** data type. If, however, the {$N+} is not present, the **Float** type is declared to be a standard **Real**. This use of conditional compilation lets you choose the degree of numerical precision throughout a program simply by changing a compiler directive.

Logical Operators

Turbo Pascal supports the following logical operators:

=	Equal to
< >	Not equal to
<	Less than
>	Greater than
< =	Less than or equal to
> =	Greater than or equal to
Not	Negation of condition
Case	Multiple comparison

Strictly speaking, **Case** is a statement and not an operator. Yet it is so closely allied with the logical operators discussed in this section that it makes sense to include it here.

Logical operators are generally used in **If-Then** statements, which test to determine whether adjacent statements should be executed. This is an example of an **If-Then** statement:

```
If a > b Then
  WriteLn('A is greater than B');
```

In this example, **a** and **b** are **Integer** variables. If **a** equals 5 and **b** equals 2, then the test **a > b** will be TRUE, and the line following the statement will execute.

The **Not** operator negates the result of a logical test. For example, if **a > b** is evaluated as TRUE, then **Not a > b** will be FALSE. For any test using the **Not** operator, there is an equivalent test without it. For example, **Not a > b** is the same as **a < = b**.

An **If-Then** statement can control the execution of more than one statement by using **Begin** and **End** to create a block of code. In the following example, if **a** is greater than **b**, all the statements between the **Begin** and **End** statements will execute:

```
If a > b Then
  Begin
  WriteLn('A is greater than B');
  b := a;
  End;
```

The **If-Then** statement can be extended with the Turbo Pascal reserved word **Else**. If the condition tested fails, the program executes the code following the **Else** clause, as shown in this example:

```
If a > b Then
  Begin
  WriteLn('A is greater than B');
  b := a;
  End
Else
  Begin
  WriteLn('A is not greater than B');
  a := b;
  End;
```

Note that the statement preceding the **Else** clause is not terminated with a semicolon. Turbo Pascal considers the **Else** clause to be a continuation of one long statement, so a semicolon indicating the end of a statement is inappropriate.

To create *multiple-condition branching*, you can give an **If-Then** statement more than one **Else** clause. This is useful when you test a variable against many possible values.

```
If a = 1 Then
  Begin
  WriteLn('A equals 1');
  End
Else If a = 2 Then
```

```
   Begin
   WriteLn('A equals 2');
   End
Else If a = 3 Then
   Begin
   WriteLn('A equals 3');
   End
Else If a = 4 Then
   Begin
   WriteLn('A equals 4');
   End;
```

Case Operator

An alternative to multiple **Else-If** statements is the **Case** statement, which is specifically designed to handle tests that require multiple conditions. A typical **Case** statement looks like this:

```
Case a of

1 :    WriteLn('a equals 1');

2..4 : Begin
         WriteLn('a is between 2 and 4');
         WriteLn('Case statements can specify ranges.');
         End;

5 :    WriteLn('a equals 5');

Else Begin
         WriteLn('a is not between 1 and 5');
         WriteLn('The case statement supports the Else clause');
         End;

End;
```

Case statements are easier to read than extended **If-Then-Else** statements and are more flexible because they allow you to specify a range of values, such as **2 .. 4**.

Note, however, that because it uses only simple data types, the **Case** statement is more restrictive than the **If-Then** statement. Therefore, you cannot use **Real** or **String** data types with the **Case** statement.

Using the Case Operator in Variant Records

Declaring **Record** data types is discussed in Chapter 5. This section discusses how the **Case** operator can be used within the **Record** data type to create what is called a *variant record.*

Variant records are intended to conserve space as well as create data structures that more precisely reflect the entities they represent. For example, consider the use of the variant record in the following listing:

```
Program VariantRecord;
Uses CRT;
Type
  VehicleType = (Car, Boat, Plane);
  VehicleRec = Record
    IDnumber : Integer;
    Price    : Real;
    Weight   : Real;

      Case Kind : VehicleType Of
      Car : (MilesPerGallon : Integer;
             Odometer : Real);

      Boat : (Displacement : Real;
              Length : Integer);

      Plane : (Engines : Integer;
               Seats : Integer);

    End;

Var
  Vehicle : VehicleRec;

Begin
ClrScr;

Vehicle.IDnumber := 123;
Vehicle.Price := 12000;
Vehicle.Weight := 1200;
Vehicle.Kind := Car;
Vehicle.MilesPerGallon := 21;
Vehicle.Odometer := 75000.0;

With Vehicle Do
  Begin
    Case Kind Of

    Car:
      Begin
      WriteLn('Kind = Car');
      WriteLn('Miles per gallon = ',MilesPerGallon);
      WriteLn('Odometer = ',Odometer:0:1);
      End;

    Boat:
      Begin
      WriteLn('Kind = Boat');
      WriteLn('Displacement = ',Displacement);
```

```
      WriteLn('Length = ',Length);
      End;

  Plane:
    Begin
    WriteLn('Kind = Plane');
    WriteLn('Engines = ',Engines);
    WriteLn('Seats = ',Seats);
    End;

  End;
  End;
WriteLn;
Write('Press ENTER...');
ReadLn;
End.
```

Notice how the record contains separate sections pertaining to different types of transportation. Because of this flexibility, variant records can cover broad classes of categorical data, yet still retain specific detailed information.

The fields under Car, Boat, and Plane comprise a total of four **Integer**s and two **Real**s—20 bytes in total. But the variant portions of the records share the same memory. Since the largest single block of memory used by a variant portion of the record is eight bytes (a **Real** and an **Integer**), only eight bytes are allocated to the variant part of the record.

The field named Kind is known as the *tag field*. The tag field helps keep track of which part of the variant record is in use. When a tag field is used, the variant record is known as a *discriminated union* because the tag field can discriminate which portion of the variant record should be used.

Another type of variant record is the *free union*, or a variant record that does not have a tag field. COBOL programmers will feel at home with free unions because they resemble COBOL's redefined fields.

The following program example presents an example of a free-union variant record.

```
Program FreeUnion;
Uses CRT;
Type
  CharByte = Record
    Case Integer Of
    1 : (Characters : Array [1..10] Of Char);
    2 : (Numbers : Array [1..10] Of Byte);
    End;
```

```
Var
  CB : CharByte;
Begin
ClrScr;
With CB Do Characters[1] := 'A';
With CB Do
  WriteLn('Numeric value of character A is: ',Numbers[1]);
WriteLn;
Write('Press ENTER...');
ReadLn;
End.
```

Notice that the variant record definition has no tag field; only a data type, **Integer,** is specified. The lack of a tag field means no tag value is stored and that you can refer to any of the variant elements without restriction.

This example program is special because the variant record defines one array in two different ways. The 10-byte array in one line is defined as an array of characters, while in the next line it is defined as an array of bytes. Since these arrays share the same memory (because they are the variant part of the record), you can refer to the elements in the arrays as either characters or numbers. This is demonstrated in the program block. Notice where a character is assigned to the first element in the array using the identifier **Characters,** and then the element is written out as a number using the identifier **Numbers.**

Program Control Structures

**S
E
V
E
N**

This chapter discusses the various control structures Pascal provides, the ways they are used, and their good and bad points.

The least complicated Turbo Pascal program starts at the first **Begin** statement of the program block, executes each statement in order, and stops when it hits the final **End** statement. This straightforward program structure is illustrated in the following program:

```
Program PayRoll;
Uses CRT;
Var
  TotalPay,
  HourlyRate,
  HoursWorked : Real;

Begin
ClrScr;
Write('Enter your hourly rate: ');
ReadLn(HourlyRate);
Write('Enter the number of hours you worked: ');
ReadLn(HoursWorked);
TotalPay := HourlyRate * HoursWorked;
WriteLn('Your total pay is: $',TotalPay:0:2);
WriteLn;
Write('Press ENTER...');
ReadLn;
End.
```

Programming tasks can rarely be expressed in such simple terms, however. The preceding program, for example, does not take into account that people often work more than 40 hours per week, entitling them to overtime pay.

You can express additional complexity by using *control structures.* Control structures give programs the ability to act differently under different situations. Adding a control structure (in this case, the **If-Then** statement) to the preceding program gives it the ability to compute overtime pay:

```
Program PayRoll2;
Uses CRT;
Var
  TotalPay,
  HourlyRate,
  HoursWorked,
  OvertimeHours : Real;

Begin
ClrScr;
Write('Enter your hourly rate: ');
ReadLn(HourlyRate);
Write('Enter the number of hours you worked: ');
ReadLn(HoursWorked);

OvertimeHours := 0.0;
If (HoursWorked > 40.0) Then
  Begin
  OvertimeHours := HoursWorked - 40.0;
  HoursWorked := 40.0;
  End;

TotalPay := (HourlyRate * HoursWorked) +
            (1.5 * HourlyRate * OvertimeHours);

WriteLn('Your total pay is: $',TotalPay:0:2);
WriteLn;
Write('Press ENTER...');
ReadLn;
End.
```

Here, the **If-Then** statement tests whether an individual put in any overtime by comparing the number of hours worked to 40. If the number of hours is greater than 40, overtime pay is clearly due. The expanded equation includes the calculation of overtime pay at 1.5 times the standard rate.

Condition Statements

All Turbo Pascal control structures, with the major exception of the **Goto** statement, have one thing in common: they do something based on the evaluation of a *condition statement*. A condition statement, also known as a *Boolean statement*, is any expression that results in either a true or false condition. In **For-Do** statements, explained later in this chapter, the condition is implied, but for all other control structures (**If-Then, While-Do, Repeat-Until**), the condition statement is explicitly defined.

Condition statements can consist of direct comparisons:

```
age > 12
name = 'Jones'
x < y
```

or they can include calculations:

```
x > (y * 12)
(x−15) < > (y * 12) + Sqr(z)
```

or they might have multiple conditions:

```
(age > 12) And (name = 'Jones');
```

All Boolean expressions have a common element: they have a left side that is compared with a right side using a logical operator. Logical operators were discussed briefly in Chapter 6, but are presented here again:

>	Greater than
<	Less than
> =	Greater than or equal to
< =	Less than or equal to
=	Equal to
< >	Not equal to

These operators can be used to compare any two expressions when the operands are compatible. For example, it is illegal to compare a **Real** with a **String**, or a **String** with an **Integer**. You can, however, mix **Reals**, **Integers**, and **Bytes** in Boolean expressions because they are all numeric types.

Simple Boolean expressions, those that use only one operator, are easy to understand. For example, the Boolean expression ($i > 0$) is clearly understood to mean "**i** is greater than 0." Complications arise, however, when you combine multiple expressions with the **And** or **Or** operator. The following program illustrates the kind of unexpected results that can occur:

```
Program IntegerOr;
Uses CRT;
Var
  i,j : Integer;

Begin
ClrScr;
i := 9;
j := -47;
WriteLn('i Or j > 0  = ',i Or j > 0);
WriteLn;
WriteLn('(i > 0) Or (j > 0)  = ',(i > 0) Or (j > 0));
WriteLn;
Write('Press ENTER...');
ReadLn;
End.
```

This program writes out the result of two Boolean expressions. Both expressions are legal and appear to test if either **i** or **j** is greater than zero. Since **i** is assigned a value greater than zero, you might expect both expressions to be true. Appearances can be deceiving, however: the result of the first Boolean expression is false.

To understand why the first expression is false, you must understand Turbo Pascal's hierarchy of operators. Arithmetic operators (**+**, **−**, *****, **/**, **Div**) are always executed before logical operators (**And, Or, Xor**). The **And** and **Or** operators, however, can serve as either arithmetic or logical operators, depending on how they are used. In the preceding example, the **Or** operator is positioned between two integers, which tells Turbo Pascal to treat it as an arithmetic **Or**. When **i** equals 9 and **j** equals −47, the arithmetic result of **i Or j** is −39. Since −39 is less than 0, the result of the Boolean expression is false.

The program's second Boolean expression, on the other hand, separates the tests of **i** and **j** into two distinct Boolean expressions and clarifies the separation with parentheses. (In general, parentheses make Boolean expressions more readable and less prone to error.) In this case, the **Or** operator is treated as a logical operator. First **i** is compared with 0, which results in TRUE. Then **j** is compared with 0, resulting in FALSE. Finally, the two results are combined with the **Or** operator, giving an overall true result.

The Not Operator

The **Not** operator negates a Boolean expression. If the result is TRUE, the **Not** operator reverses the result to FALSE. For example, (10 > 0) is TRUE, but **Not** (10 > 0) is FALSE.

While the **Not** operator can be useful, it is never required. For every Boolean expression that uses the **Not** operator, there is an equivalent expression that does not. For example, the expression **Not (age >** 65) can be replaced by the expression (**age** < = 65). The **Not** operator sometimes increases the readability of a Boolean expression, but it is better to avoid it because it unnecessarily complicates a Boolean expression and thus increases the possibility of introducing errors in your program.

Boolean Functions in Control Structures

If a control statement requires an especially complex Boolean expression or if the same Boolean expression is used in many control statements throughout your program, you should create a Boolean function that contains the expression. Using the Boolean function in place of the expression decreases your coding and reduces errors. For example, the following program uses the Boolean function **Qualifies** to determine whether a potential site for a store is a good candidate.

```
Program SiteEvaluation;
Uses CRT;
Var
  CarsPerHour,
  PopulationDensity,
  TaxRate,
  LandCostPerSquareFoot,
  LaborCostPerHour : Real;

(**************************************************)

Function Qualifies : Boolean;
Begin
Qualifies := (CarsPerHour > 1000) And
             (PopulationDensity > 5000) And
             (TaxRate < 0.10) And
```

```
                  (LandCostPerSquareFoot < 150) And
                  (LaborCostPerHour < 6.50)
End;

(**************************************************)

Begin
ClrScr;
Write('Enter number of cars per hour: ');
ReadLn(CarsPerHour);
Write('Enter population density per square mile: ');
ReadLn(PopulationDensity);
Write('Enter Tax Rate: ');
ReadLn(TaxRate);
Write('Enter land cost per square foot: ');
ReadLn(LandCostPerSquareFoot);
Write('Enter labor cost per hour: ');
ReadLn(LaborCostPerHour);
WriteLn;
If Qualifies Then
  WriteLn('Good site!')
Else
  WriteLn('Forget it.');
WriteLn;
Write('Press ENTER...');
ReadLn;
End.
```

The following Boolean expression is complex:

```
(CarsPerHour > 1000) And
(PopulationDensity > 5000) And
(TaxRate < 0.10) And
(LandCostPerSquareFoot < 150) And
(LaborCostPerHour < 6.50)
```

By isolating it in a function, you can substitute the identifier **Qualifies** wherever the full Boolean statement would normally go. This reduces the possibility of error (and the amount of typing) and makes it easier to modify the program since all changes can be done in the function itself; these modifications are automatically reflected throughout the program.

Decision Making and Conditional Branching

Based on information it receives, a program can choose between different courses of action. However, if you want your program to make decisions, you must specifically tell it what information it will use, how to evaluate the information, and what course of action to follow. This type of programming is often called *conditional branching* because programs that use this method branch in different directions based on a condition (that is, the evaluation of data).

The If-Then Statement

The simplest form of conditional branching is the **If-Then** statement, which causes a program to execute a block of code if a condition is true. This process is described schematically in Figure 7-1.

The first thing an **If-Then** statement does is to evaluate the information provided to it in the form of a Boolean statement. If, for example, the Boolean statement is (**Age** > 21), the information is contained in the variable **Age**, which is compared with the test value 21.

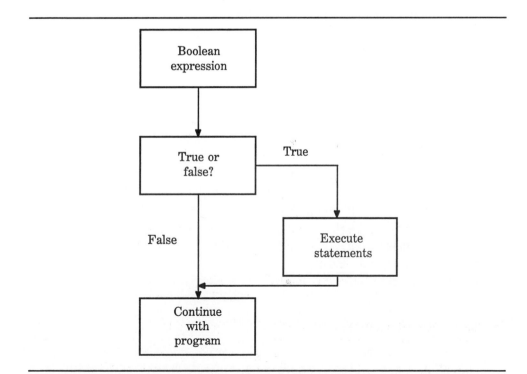

Figure 7-1.   Flowchart of If-Then statement

The evaluation produces one of two possible results—true or false. If the statement is true, the program executes the block of code that immediately follows the **If-Then** statement. If the result is false, the program skips the block. Consider the following example.

```
Program TestAge;
Uses CRT;
Var
  Age : Integer;

Begin
ClrScr;
Write('Enter Age: ');
ReadLn(Age);
If (Age >= 21) Then
  WriteLn('This person is not a minor.');
WriteLn;
Write('Press ENTER...');
ReadLn;
End.
```

The program asks the user to enter a number (an age), and then the **If-Then** statement tests to see if **Age** is greater than or equal to 21. If the result of the test is true, the program executes the statement

WriteLn('This person is not a minor');

The program executes the second **WriteLn** statement regardless of the result of the **If-Then** statement. In this example, only one statement follows the **If-Then** test. If you want to conditionally execute more than one statement, use **Begin** and **End** to indicate what statements are included. For example, the expanded version of **TestAge**, shown here, writes two lines when **Age** is greater than or equal to 21:

```
Program TestAge;
Uses CRT;
Var
  Age : Integer;

Begin
ClrScr;
Write('Enter Age: ');
ReadLn(Age);
If (Age >= 21) Then
  Begin
  WriteLn('This person is not a minor.');
  WriteLn('This person is ',Age,' years old.');
```

```
   End;
WriteLn;
Write('Press ENTER...');
ReadLn;
End.
```

The **Begin** and **End** statements tell Turbo Pascal to execute both of the enclosed **WriteLn** statements when **Age** is greater than or equal to 21. Although the **Begin** and **End** statements are not required when only one statement is to be executed conditionally, you might want to include them for the sake of program clarity and consistency.

The If-Then-Else Statement

The **If-Then** statement provides just one branch, which executes when the Boolean statement is true. Many times, a program requires two branches: one that executes if true, the other if false. This situation is shown in Figure 7-2, where a program executes different blocks of code depending on the outcome of an evaluation.

To express this situation in Turbo Pascal code, you must use the control structure of an **If-Then-Else** statement. This statement works as follows: if an evaluation is true, the block of code that follows the **Then** statement executes; if false, the block of code that follows the **Else** statement executes. In either case, when the selected block of code terminates, program control skips to the end of the **If-Then-Else** statement, as depicted here:

```
Program TestAge;
Uses CRT;
Var
  Age : Integer;

Begin
ClrScr;
Write('Enter Age: ');
ReadLn(Age);
If (Age >= 21) Then
  Begin
  WriteLn('This person is not a minor.');
  WriteLn('This person is ',Age,' years old.');
  End
Else
  Begin
  WriteLn('This person is a minor.');
```

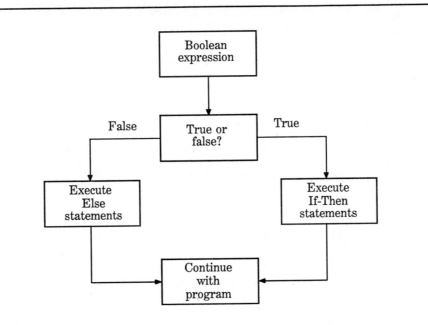

Figure 7-2. Flowchart of If-Then-Else statement

```
  WriteLn('This minor is ',Age,' years old.');
  End;
WriteLn;
Write('Press ENTER...');
ReadLn;
End.
```

As in the earlier examples, the following statements are executed when **age** is greater than or equal to 21:

```
WriteLn('This person is not a minor');
WriteLn('This person is ',Age,' years old');
```

If **age** is less than 21, the program executes these two statements:

```
WriteLn('This person is a minor');
WriteLn('This minor is ',age,' years old');
```

When writing code that uses **If-Then-Else** statements, do not terminate the **End** that precedes the **Else** with a semicolon. Turbo Pascal considers the entire **If-Then-Else** structure to be one continuous statement, and semicolons appear only at the end of a statement.

Extending the If-Then-Else Statement

The **If-Then** structure provides one branch, and the **If-Then-Else** structure provides two. But what happens when you need to express a series of conditions? In such cases, you can extend **If-Then-Else** with the **Else-If** statement. **Else-If** statements allow you to chain Boolean statements, giving your program the ability to multiple branch (see Figure 7-3). The key element of this figure is the path that the program takes when it finds the first Boolean expression to be false. Instead of executing a block of code, the program evaluates a second Boolean expression; it is here that the **Else-If** statement comes into play. If this expression is also false, the program executes the final block of code.

The following sample program demonstrates how **Else-If** can create multiple branches:

```
Program PrintGradeMessage;
Uses CRT;
Var
  Grade : Char;

Begin
ClrScr;
Write('Enter your Grade: ');
ReadLn(Grade);
Grade := UpCase(Grade);

If Grade = 'A' then
  WriteLn('Excellent.')
Else If Grade = 'B' Then
  WriteLn('Getting there.')
Else If Grade = 'C' Then
  WriteLn('Not too bad.')
Else If Grade = 'D' Then
  WriteLn('Just made it.')
Else If Grade = 'F' Then
  WriteLn('Summer school!')
Else
  WriteLn('That''s not a Grade.');
WriteLn;
Write('Press ENTER...');
ReadLn;
End.
```

This program asks the user to enter a grade (A, B, C, D, or F) and prints a message that comments on the grade entered. The program's five Boolean expressions result in a total of six branches. (The sixth branch is the statement that follows the final **Else**.)

As you can see by now, the **If-Then-Else** structure is extremely powerful, allowing you to build a tremendous amount of intelligence into your programs.

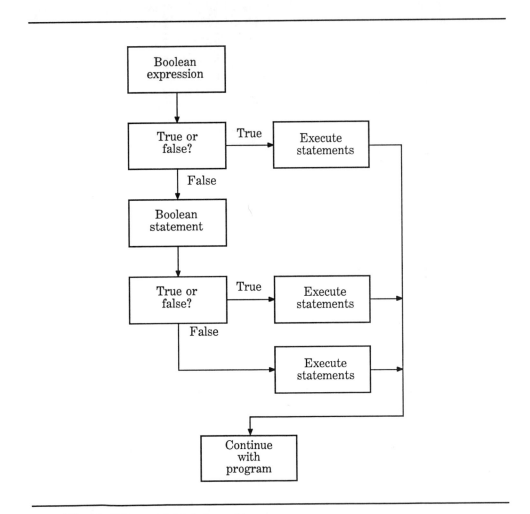

Figure 7-3. Multiple branching

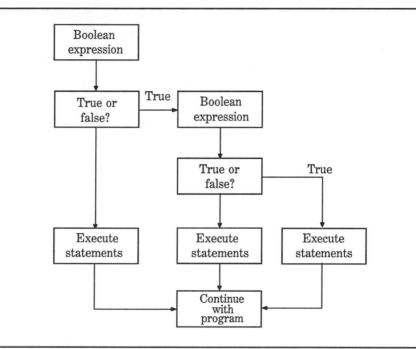

Figure 7-4.   Nested If-Then statements

Nested If-Then Statements

One way to allow your program to consider two or more separate conditions before embarking on a course of action is to nest the **If-Then** statements. Figure 7-4 depicts the flow of a nested **If-Then** statement.

A nested **If-Then** statement can produce very complex branching schemes. Consider this problem: you are running a game of chance using a box full of black and white marbles. A player takes two marbles from the box at random, and, depending on the combination of colors chosen, he or she is paid at the following rate:

First Marble	Second Marble	Payoff
White	White	0:1
White	Black	2:3
Black	White	1:1
Black	Black	2:1

If the first marble is white and the second is white, the gambler loses everything. If white is first and black is second, he or she loses two-thirds of the bet. If black is followed by white, the gambler breaks even. Two black marbles doubles the bet.

To code this game in Turbo Pascal, use the **If-Then-Else** statement, as shown here:

```
Program BetTest;
Uses CRT;
Var
  FirstMarble,
  SecondMarble : (black,white);
  i   : Integer;
  Bet : Real;

Begin
ClrScr;
  Repeat

  i := Random(2);
  FillChar(FirstMarble,1,i);

  i := Random(2);
  FillChar(SecondMarble,1,i);

  Write('Enter amount of bet (zero to quit): ');
  ReadLn(Bet);
  If Bet = 0 Then Halt;

  If (FirstMarble = white) And (SecondMarble = white) Then
    Begin
    Bet := Bet * 0.0;
    WriteLn('First Marble is White; Second Marble is White');
    End
  Else If (FirstMarble = white) And (SecondMarble = black) Then
    Begin
    Bet := Bet * (2 / 3);
    WriteLn('First Marble is White; Second Marble is Black');
    End
  Else If (FirstMarble = black) And (SecondMarble = white) Then
    Begin    Bet := Bet * 1.0;
    WriteLn('First Marble is Black; Second Marble is White');
    End
  Else (* (FirstMarble = black) And (SecondMarble = black) *)
    Begin
    Bet := Bet * 2.0;
    WriteLn('First Marble is Black; Second Marble is Black');
    End;
  WriteLn('You get $',Bet:0:2,' back.');
  WriteLn;
  WriteLn;
  Until i > 100;
End.
```

The program explicitly refers to each of the four possible combinations of black and white marbles. It will work just fine, but it could be coded more efficiently in this format:

```
If (FirstMarble = white) Then
  Begin

  (****************************************)
  (* Beginning of nested If-Then statement. *)
  (****************************************)

  If (SecondMarble = white) Then
    Begin
    Bet := Bet * 0.0;
    WriteLn('First Marble is White; Second Marble is White');
    End
  Else (* SecondMarble = black *)
    Begin
    Bet := Bet * (2 / 3);
    WriteLn('First Marble is White; Second Marble is Black');
    End
  End
Else (* FirstMarble = black *)
  Begin

  (****************************************)
  (* Beginning of nested If-Then statement. *)
  (****************************************)

  If SecondMarble = white) Then
    Begin
    Bet := Bet * 1.0;
    WriteLn('First Marble is Black; Second Marble is White');
    End
  Else (* SecondMarble = black *)
    Begin
    Bet := Bet * 2.0;
    WriteLn('First Marble is Black; Second Marble is Black');
    End;
  End;
End;
```

The preceding program's first-level **If-Then** statement tests for the color of the first marble, and its second-level, or nested, statement tests for the color of the second marble. Rather than testing both marbles in each **If-Then** statement, the nested **If-Then** structure separates the tests.

The first example evaluates up to three Boolean statements before it finds the correct branch. Since each Boolean statement contains two comparisons, the program may execute as many as six comparisons before coming to a result.

If you use nested **If-Then** statements, however, you do not need to test more than two comparisons at any time. Thus, your program does less work and gives results more quickly than it would otherwise. While the time saved by the sample program is too small to be noticeable, it can be significant in programs with nested **If-Then** statements that are repeated many times.

Conditional Branching with the Case Statement

If you often use simple data types (that is, no **Real** or **String**) in your programs, you can use the Turbo Pascal **Case** statement in place of the **If-Then** statement. **Case** provides a logical and clear structure for multiple branching. Here is a typical use of the **Case** statement:

```
Program CaseExample;
Uses CRT;
Var
  Number1,
  Number2  : Real;
  Operator : Char;
  St,St1,St2 : String[80];
  p,
  Code : Integer;

(****************************************************)

Procedure Compute;
Begin
St1 := '';
St2 := '';
p := 1;

Write('Enter a formula with two numbers (e.g. 1+2): ');
ReadLn(St);

(* Pick up the first number *)

While (St[p] = ' ') And (p <= Length(St)) Do
  p := p + 1;
While (St[p] in ['1'..'9','.']) And (p <= length(St)) Do
  Begin
  St1 := St1 + St[p];
  p := p + 1;
  End;

(* Pick up the Operator *)
```

```
While (St[p] = ' ') And (p <= Length(St)) Do
  p := p + 1;
Operator := St[p];
  p := p + 1;

(* Pick up the second number *)

While (St[p] = ' ') And (p <= Length(St)) Do
  p := p + 1;
While (St[p] in ['1'..'9','.']) And (p <= Length(St)) Do
  Begin
  St2 := St2 + St[p];
  p := p + 1;
  End;

(* Convert number strings to reals *)

Val(St1,Number1,Code);
Val(St2,Number2,Code);

(* Perform computations *)

  Case Operator Of
  '+' : WriteLn('Answer is: ',Number1 + Number2:0:3);
  '-' : WriteLn('Answer is: ',Number1 - Number2:0:3);
  '*' : WriteLn('Answer is: ',Number1 * Number2:0:3);
  '/' : WriteLn('Answer is: ',Number1 / Number2:0:3);
  End;

End;

(*****************************************************)

Begin
ClrScr;

  Repeat
  Compute;
  Until St = '';

End.
```

This program asks for a string that contains a simple formula (for example, 1 + 2). It extracts the numbers and the operator from the string, converts the extracted strings into **Real** values, and then uses the **Case** statement to perform the correct calculation.

An especially powerful feature of the **Case** statement is its ability to interpret ranges, as shown here:

```
Program CaseWithRanges;
Uses CRT;
Var
  Key : Char;
```

```
Begin
ClrScr;
  Repeat
  WriteLn;
  Write('Press a Key (q to quit): ');
  Key := ReadKey;
  WriteLn;
  If Key = 'q' then halt;

    Case Key of

    'A'..'Z' :
      WriteLn('You pressed an uppercase letter');

    'a'..'z' :
      WriteLn('You pressed a lowercase letter');

    '0'..'9' :
      WriteLn('You pressed a numeric key');

    Else
      Begin
      WriteLn('You pressed an unknown key');
      WriteLn('Try again');
      End;

    End;
  Until False;
End.
```

When the user of this program presses a key, the **Char** variable **Key** stores the character. The **Case** statement then evaluates the character according to the ranges specified; if the character falls between "A" and "Z," the program knows it must be an uppercase letter. The last statement in the **Case** structure is preceded by **Else**, which provides a default branch for variables that do not fit into any of the specified categories. Any time a character is not in one of the ranges A . . Z, a . . z, or 0 . . 9, the program executes the statement that follows **Else**.

Repetitive Control Structures

Most programs require a method of repeating a block of code. One way is simply to write as many statements as you need, as in the program in Figure 7-5, which reads in five numbers and writes out the sum.

```
Program NoLoop;
Uses CRT;
Var
  Numbers : Array [1..5] OfReal;
  Sum : Real;

Begin
ClrScr;
Write('Enter a number: ');
ReadLn(Numbers[1]);
Write('Enter a number: ');
ReadLn(Numbers[2]);
Write('Enter a number: ');
ReadLn(Numbers[3]);
Write('Enter a number: ');
ReadLn(Numbers[4]);
Write('Enter a number: ');
ReadLn(Numbers[5]);

Sum := Numbers[1] + Numbers[2] + Numbers[3] +
       Numbers[4] + Numbers[5];

WriteLn('The sum is: ',Sum:0:2);
WriteLn;
Write('Press ENTER...');
ReadLn;
End.
```

Figure 7-5.   A program without looping structures

All those **ReadLn** statements are not only inefficient, but they also produce a very limited program, one that must have five numbers entered, no more, no less. To improve this program, you can use one of Turbo Pascal's three looping control structures.

For-Do Loop

The For-Do loop is a particularly powerful looping structure. Nearly every programming language provides some form of this structure, but Turbo Pascal's implementation of it is superior to that of most other languages.

When coding a For-Do loop, you must specify a starting point, an ending point, and a **scalar** variable to be used as a counter. A typical For-Do loop statement might look like the following.

```
For i := 1 To 100 Do
  Begin
  {
  Statements
  }
  End;
```

The first time Turbo Pascal executes this For-Do loop, it sets **i** equal to 1 and executes the block of code following the loop statement. When it has executed the last statement in the block, it increases **i** by one. When **i** exceeds the upper limit (in this case, 100), the loop terminates, and control passes to the next line in the program. But as long as **i** is less than or equal to 100, Turbo Pascal continues to execute the block of code.

Figure 7-6 shows an updated version of the program in Figure 7-5. Adding For-Do loops to a program substantially reduces the amount of code needed.

```
Program ForDoLoop;
Uses CRT;
Var
  i : Integer;
  Numbers : Array [1..5] Of Real;
  Sum : Real;

Begin
ClrScr;
For i := 1 To 5 Do
  Begin
  Write('Enter a number: ');
  ReadLn(Numbers[i]);
  End;

Sum := 0;
For i := 1 To 5 Do
  Sum := Sum + Numbers[i];

WriteLn('The sum is: ',Sum:0:2);
WriteLn;
Write('Press ENTER...');
ReadLn;
End.
```

Figure 7-6. A program with For-Do loops

Repeat-Until Loop

While the For-Do loop clearly improves the program, it still must read five numbers, and no more or no less than five numbers, to run properly. You can eliminate this restriction by using the Repeat-Until loop.

Following is the general format for the Repeat-Until loop.

```
Repeat
{
Statements
}
Until (Boolean condition);
```

The word **Repeat** tells Turbo Pascal to execute statements until it reaches the **Until** instruction. Turbo Pascal then evaluates the Boolean expression or function in the **Until** instruction, and if it is not true, the program goes back to the **Repeat** instruction and continues executing the block of code.

The main advantage of the Repeat-Until loop is that it does not require you to specify a set number of iterations in advance: it continues to repeat until the Boolean expression is true.

The following sample program is a refined version of the previous example. This program allows you to enter from zero to five numbers, which are then summed:

```
Program RepeatUntilLoop;
Uses CRT;
Var
  i : Integer;
  Numbers : Array [1..5] Of Real;
  Sum : Real;

Begin
ClrScr;
Sum := 0;
i := 0;

  Repeat
  Write('Enter a Number: ');
  i := i + 1;
  ReadLn(Numbers[i]);
  Until (i = 5) Or (Numbers[i] = 0);

For i := 1 To i Do
  Sum := Sum + Numbers[i];
```

```
WriteLn('The sum is: ',sum:0:2);
WriteLn;
Write('Press ENTER...');
ReadLn;

End.
```

In this example, the Repeat-Until loop terminates under two conditions: when **i** equals five or the number entered is zero. For example, if you enter the numbers 1, 3, and 0, the program exits from the Repeat-Until loop without asking for the fourth and fifth numbers. The For-Do loop that calculates the sum is the same as the one in the previous program, but in this program the upper limit is set to the **Integer** variable **i**, which counts the number values the user enters. Therefore, the For-Do loop executes once for each number entered.

While-Do Loop

The While-Do loop is similar to the Repeat-Until loop, except the While-Do loop tests a Boolean condition *before* it executes any statements in a block. The following code shows the sample program with a While-Do loop:

```
Program WhileDoLoop;
Uses CRT;
Var
  i : Integer;
  Numbers : Array [1..5] Of Real;
  Sum : Real;

Begin
ClrScr;
Sum := 0;
i := 1;
Write('Enter a Number: ');
ReadLn(Numbers[i]);

While (Numbers[i] <> 0) And (i < 5) Do
  Begin
  Write('Enter a Number: ');
  i := i + 1;
  ReadLn(Numbers[i]);
  End;

For i := 1 To i Do
  Sum := Sum + Numbers[i];
```

```
WriteLn('The sum is: ',sum:0:2);
WriteLn;
Write('Press ENTER...');
ReadLn;
End.
```

If the While-Do loop finds that the Boolean expression is not true, Turbo Pascal does not execute the block of code that follows the While-Do block.

Unstructured Branching

The term *unstructured branching* describes what happens when a program jumps directly from one point to another. This process is also known as *direct transfer* or *unconditional branching*. The latter term is misleading because unstructured branching can and usually is used with a Boolean condition statement. Turbo Pascal allows unstructured branching through the **Goto** statement, which is used with a *label identifier*. The label identifier marks the position in the program to which control is to be transferred.

Labels are declared with the Turbo Pascal reserved word **Label**, followed by the label identifiers, which are separated by commas and terminated with a semicolon.

```
Label
    Point1,
    Point2;
```

You can place the label identifiers in the program at locations to which you wish to transfer control. To do this, simply type the label identifier followed by a colon, as shown here:

```
i := 1;
WriteLn(i);
Point1:
b := j / 3;
```

To execute a **Goto** statement, simply specify the label to which the code is to branch. For example, the instruction

Goto Point1;

tells Turbo Pascal to skip directly to the point in the program where the label Point1 is located. The following program shows an example of unstructured branching:

```
Program GoToExample;
Uses CRT;
Var
  i : Integer;
  ch : Char;

Label
  Retry,
  Stop,
  DoLoop,
  Next,
  Male,
  Female;
Begin
ClrScr;
Retry:
Write('What is your sex: ');
ReadLn(ch);
ch :=UpCase(ch);
If Not (ch In ['F', 'M']) Then
  GoTo Retry;

If ch = 'M' Then
  GoTo Male
Else
  GoTo Female;

Male:
  WriteLn('Sex is Male');
  GoTo DoLoop;

Female:
  WriteLn ('Sex is Female');

DoLoop:
i := 1;

Next:
i := i + 1;
If I > 10 Then
  GoTo Stop;
WriteLn('i = ',i);
GoTo Next;
```

```
Stop:
WriteLn;
Write('Press ENTER...');
ReadLn;
End.
```

As discussed earlier, the Pascal language was developed to do away with the **Goto** statement. Turbo Pascal supports the **Goto** statement, but with one major restriction that keeps it from being misused: Turbo Pascal will not let you transfer control to a label that is outside the current program block. In other words, you can jump to a point within a program or procedure block, but you cannot jump from one procedure into another. With this restriction, you can learn to use the **Goto** statement fairly safely.

While the **Goto** statement is never strictly necessary, there are a number of situations where it can yield a more elegant solution to a problem than using other control structures. Consider the following program. In it, a three-dimensional array is searched until an element with the value of 1 is found. The first approach uses the **Goto** statement, while the second uses the **While-Do** statement. The former is easier to understand and executes more efficiently.

```
Program TestGoTo;
Uses CRT;
Label Found;
Var
  i,j,k : Integer;
  m : Array [1..25, 1..25, 1..25] Of Byte;

Begin
ClrScr;
FillChar(m,SizeOf(m),0);
m[20,20,20] := 1;

(* Using GoTo *)

For i := 1 To 25 Do
For j := 1 To 25 Do
For k := 1 To 25 Do
If m[i,j,k] = 1 Then
  GoTo Found;
Found:
  WriteLn('Found at: ',i,',',j,',',k);

(* Avoiding GoTo *)
```

```
i := 1;
j := 1;
k := 1;
While (i <= 25) And (m[i,j,k] <> 1) Do
  Begin
  While (j <= 25) And (m[i,j,k] <> 1) Do
    Begin
    While (k <= 25) And (m[i,j,k] <> 1) Do
      k := k + 1;
    If (m[i,j,k] <> 1) Then
      Begin
      k := 1;
      j := j + 1;
      End;
    End;
  If (m[i,j,k] <> 1) Then
    Begin
    j := 1;
    i := i + 1;
    End;
  End;
WriteLn('Found at: ',i,',',j,',',k);
WriteLn;
Write('Press ENTER...');
ReadLn;
End.
```

Given the **Goto** command's drawbacks, when does it make sense to use it? One rule is to use **Goto** when the point to which the program jumps is close to the **Goto** statement that branches to it. Here is an example of a program with a valid use of a **Goto** statement:

```
Program MathError;
Uses CRT;
Var
  Numbers1,
  Numbers2,
  Numbers3 : Array [1..3] Of Real;

(**********************************************)

Procedure Divide;
Var
  i : Integer;
Label
  DivideEnd;

Begin
For i := 1 To 3 Do
  Begin
  If Numbers2[i] = 0 Then
    Begin
    WriteLn('Error: Division by zero');
    GoTo DivideEnd;
```

```
    End;
  Numbers3[i] := Numbers1[i] / Numbers2[i];
  WriteLn(Numbers3[i]:0:2);
  End;
DivideEnd:
End;

(**********************************************)

Begin
ClrScr;
Numbers1[1] := 1;
Numbers1[2] := 2;
Numbers1[3] := 3;

Numbers2[1] := 5;
Numbers2[2] := 2;
Numbers2[3] := 0;
Divide;
WriteLn;
Write('Press ENTER...');
ReadLn;
End.
```

This program relies on three arrays of integers. The procedure **Divide** divides the elements in one array by the elements in another and assigns the result to an element in a third array. Whenever you divide in Turbo Pascal, you risk a run-time error if the divisor is zero, so the program first tests the divisor to see if it is zero, in which case the **Goto** statement is used to branch to the end of the procedure. This is a valid use of the **Goto** statement because not only is the distance between the **Goto** statement and the label small, but also the logic behind the statement is clear. Nonetheless, the following structure is an example of more elegant and precise code:

```
i := 0;
  Repeat
  i := i + 1;
  If (Numbers2[i] <> 0) Then
    Numbers3[i] := Numbers1[i] Div Numbers2[i]
  Else
    WriteLn('Error: Division by zero');
  Until (i = 100) Or (Numbers2[i] = 0);

For i := 1 To 100 Do
  Begin
  If (Numbers2[i] = 0) Then
    Begin
    WriteLn('Error: Division by zero');
```

```
   Exit;
  End;
Numbers3[i] := Numbers1[i] Div Numbers2[i];
End;
```

The first routine uses the Repeat-Until loop to provide both a means to increment **i** and to exit if the divisor is found to be zero. The second routine uses **Exit**, a standard Turbo Pascal function. Strictly speaking, **Exit** is an unconditional branching statement because it ignores the normal path of execution for the block of code.

Turbo Pascal offers both structured and unstructured methods for creating clear, concise applications. This variety of tools makes programming in Turbo Pascal especially rewarding, allowing you to develop a personal programming style while encouraging you to learn good programming habits.

Pointers and Dynamic Memory Allocation

Turbo Pascal Memory Allocation
The Heap and Pointers
Using Pointers with Complex Data Types
Using the @ Operator

Turbo Pascal uses different parts, or segments, of your computer's memory for different purposes. Some segments hold the instructions your computer executes, while the others store data. Each of these segments performs a specific role, and you must understand these roles and how the segments work before you can master advanced programming concepts.

Turbo Pascal Memory Allocation

Turbo Pascal divides your computer's memory into four parts—the code segment, the data segment, the stack segment, and the heap. Programs that use units have a code segment for each unit as well as for the main program. All programs, however, have only one data segment, which contains typed constants and global variables.

Although the data segment is clearly dedicated to data storage, data also can be stored in other locations. The stack and heap hold dynamic data, allocating memory as it is needed. While the stack is critically important, its operation is controlled automatically by Turbo Pascal—you can't do much with the stack yourself. The heap, on the other hand, is especially important for advanced programming techniques. This chapter discusses the role of the heap and how you can use *dynamic allocation* in your programs.

159

DOS Memory Mapping Conventions

The first step in understanding how Turbo Pascal manages memory is to learn something about the internal workings of your microcomputer. A computer has a certain amount of RAM (random access memory). Let's say yours has 640 kilobytes. A kilobyte represents 1024 bytes, so your 640K computer really has a total of 655,360 bytes of RAM.

When your program first starts, it sets up a segment that holds the program's instructions (the code segment or segments), a segment to hold the program's data (the data segment), and a segment to hold temporary data (the stack segment). As the instructions in the code segment execute, they manipulate data in both the data segment and the stack segment.

How does the program know at which byte these three segments begin? For that matter, how does a program locate any particular byte in memory? By using addresses. Every byte has an *address,* a 20-bit value that uniquely identifies that location. When a program needs to access a particular byte, it uses the address to find the byte's location in memory.

If a computer's address consisted of a single word (two bytes), it could not address more than 64K (65,536 bytes) of RAM. This was the case for the early 8-bit microprocessors.

The advent of 16-bit processors, particularly the Intel 8086/88 family, ushered in a new memory-addressing scheme, known as *segmented addressing.* Segmented addressing combines two word values—a segment and an offset—to form a 20-bit address. Think of segments as blocks on a street and offsets as the houses on each block.

Each segment holds 64K of RAM. The 8086/88 processors have 16 segments, resulting in 1,048,560 bytes (1 *megabyte*) of addressable memory. However, DOS limits the amount of memory your computer can use to 640K.

Segments and Offsets

Turbo Pascal provides two standard functions, **Seg** and **Ofs**, that make it easy to explore memory addressing on your PC. **Seg** provides the segment in which a variable resides, and **Ofs** provides its offset. The following program uses these functions to display the addresses of four variables:

```
Program Addresses;
Uses CRT;
Type
  StType = String[10];
Var
  i : Word;
  s : String[5];
  r : Real;
  c : Char;


Type
  St4 = String[4];


(********************************************)


Function IntToHex(i : Word) : St4;
Var
 HexStr : String[8];
 b : Array [1..2] Of Byte Absolute i;
 bt : Byte;


(********************************************)


Function Translate(b : Byte) : Char;
Begin
If b < 10 Then
  Translate := Chr(b + 48)
Else
  Translate := Chr(b + 55);
End;


(********************************************)


Begin
HexStr := '';
HexStr := HexStr + Translate(b[2] Shr 4);
HexStr := HexStr + Translate(b[2] And 15);
HexStr := HexStr + Translate(b[1] Shr 4);
HexStr := HexStr + Translate(b[1] And 15);
IntToHex := HexStr;
End;


(********************************************)


Begin
ClrScr;
WriteLn('Word:    ',IntToHex(Seg(i)),':',IntToHex(Ofs(i)));
WriteLn('String:  ',IntToHex(Seg(s)),':',IntToHex(Ofs(s)));
WriteLn('Real:    ',IntToHex(Seg(r)),':',IntToHex(Ofs(r)));
WriteLn('Char:    ',IntToHex(Seg(c)),':',IntToHex(Ofs(c)));
WriteLn;
Write('Press ENTER...');
ReadLn;
End.
```

This program defines four variables of different types and then displays the addresses of each of the variables. For example, the statement **Seg(i)** finds the segment of variable **i**, while **Ofs(i)** returns the offset.

The function **IntToHex** accepts a word parameter and returns the hexadecimal value as a string of four characters. Segments and offsets are customarily shown in hexadecimal format.

When you run the previous program, your screen will show the following messages, though you will see different numbers because your computer may be configured differently.

```
Word:   68BB:003C
String: 68BB:003E
Real:   68BB:0044
Char:   68BB:004A
```

As you can see, all the variables, which are global, have the same segment. (Global variables all reside in the data segment.) Furthermore, the distance between offsets exactly matches the number of bytes needed to store each variable type. For example, a word starts at offset 3Ch and requires two bytes of storage; the next variable in line (a **String**) starts at offset 3Eh.

Turbo Pascal typed constants are stored in the data segment, while untyped constants exist in the code segment. Actually, untyped constants simply become part of the computer code. For this reason, untyped constants do not have addresses.

Variables that are declared in procedures and functions are stored on the stack, a dynamic data storage area. When a program calls a procedure, Turbo Pascal allocates space on the stack for the procedure's local variables. As Turbo Pascal adds variables to the stack, the stack grows downward in memory. When the procedure ends, Turbo Pascal discards these variables and frees the memory to be used again.

The fourth segment in Turbo Pascal memory, the heap, is a dynamic data area that you control. The heap allows efficient use of memory because it eliminates the need to preserve all the data structures throughout a program; instead, you can create a variable on the heap at one point, remove it from the heap at another, and then reuse the space for another variable at still another place.

The following program demonstrates how data can exist in any of the four Turbo Pascal segments:

```pascal
Program Segments;
Uses CRT;
Type
  StType = String[80];
Var
  r1,r2 : Real;
  x : Word;
  p : ^Word;
Type
  St4 = String[4];

(*********************************************)

Function IntToHex(i : Word): St4;
Var
  HexStr : String[8];
  b : Array [1..2] Of Byte Absolute i;
  bt : Byte;

(*********************************************)

Function Translate(b : byte) : Char;
Begin
If b < 10 Then
  Translate := Chr(b + 48)
Else
  Translate := Chr(b + 55);
End;

(*********************************************)

Begin
HexStr := '';
HexStr := HexStr + Translate(b[2] Shr 4);
HexStr := HexStr + Translate(b[2] And 15);
HexStr := HexStr + Translate(b[1] Shr 4);
HexStr := HexStr + Translate(b[1] And 15);
IntToHex := HexStr;
End;

(*********************************************)

Procedure ShowCodeSegment;
Begin
WriteLn;
WriteLn('The code segment is ',IntToHex(cseg));
End;

(*********************************************)

Procedure ShowDataVariable;
Begin
WriteLn;
WriteLn('The location of global variable x is ',
        IntToHex(seg(x)),':',
        IntToHex(ofs(x)));
```

```
WriteLn('This is in the data segment.');
End;

(*******************************************)

Procedure ShowStackVariable;
Var
  i : Word;
Begin
WriteLn;
WriteLn('The location of variable i is ',
        IntToHex(seg(i)),':',
        IntToHex(ofs(i)));

Writeln('This is in the stack segment.');
End;

(*******************************************)

Procedure ShowHeapVariable;
Begin
WriteLn;
WriteLn('The location of pointer variable p is ',
        IntToHex(seg(p^)),':',
        IntToHex(ofs(p^)));

WriteLn('This is on the heap.');
End;

(*******************************************)

Begin
ClrScr;
WriteLn('Addresses are shown in the format Segment:Offset.');
New(p);
ShowCodeSegment;
ShowDataVariable;
ShowHeapVariable;
ShowStackVariable;
WriteLn;
Write('Press ENTER...');
ReadLn;
End.
```

When you run this program, your terminal will display output that looks something like this:

Addresses are shown in the format Segment:Offset.

The code segment is 67A9

The location of global variable x is 691E:0048
This is in the data segment.

The location of pointer variable p is 709C:0000
This is on the heap.

The location of variable i is 6949:7524
This is in the stack segment.

Each of the four variables in this example resides in a different segment. The first location, that of the code segment, is 67A9h. The variable **x** is located in the data segment (691Eh). Pointer variable **p**, placed on the heap with the statement **New(p)**, is located in segment 709Ch.

The last variable listed is a local variable declared within a procedure. All local variables get stored on the stack, and in this example the stack segment begins at 6949h.

Figure 8-1 provides a schematic diagram of Turbo Pascal's memory. The lines separating the segments are matched with the hexadecimal values from the sample program. The code segment occupies lowest memory followed by the data and stack segments. The heap occupies all the high memory that is left over, up to the maximum you set with the **M** compiler directive. The diagram also demonstrates that the stack grows downward and the heap grows upward.

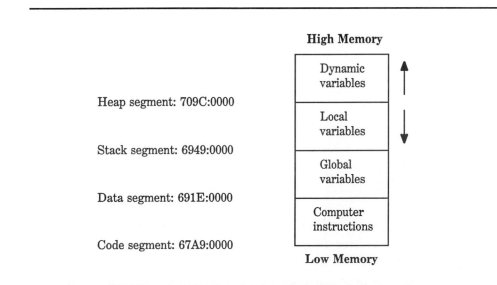

Figure 8-1.   Turbo Pascal memory allocation

The Heap and Pointers

Most variables you declare in Turbo Pascal are static, that is, memory is allocated to them from the time the program starts until it ends. The heap, on the other hand, uses dynamic data types known as *pointers.* Pointer variables are dynamic because you can create them and dispose of them while a program is running. In short, different pointer variables can use and reuse memory on the heap.

Using pointer variables on the heap offers two main advantages. First, it expands the total amount of data space available to a program. The data segment is limited to 64 kilobytes, but the heap is limited only by the amount of RAM in your computer.

The second advantage of using pointer variables on the heap is that it allows your program to run with less memory. For example, a program might have two very large data structures, but only one of them is used at a time. If these data structures are declared globally, they reside in the data segment and occupy memory at all times. However, if these data structures are defined as pointers, they can be put on the heap and taken off as needed, thus reducing your program's memory requirements.

The Pointer Variable

A pointer variable does not hold data in the same way that other variables do. Instead, it holds the address that points to a variable located on the heap. Suppose you have a pointer variable named **px** that holds the address of an **Integer**. Now, you can use **px** to point to the **Integer**, but **px** itself is not the **Integer**. If you are confused, this example, which demonstrates the simple use of a pointer variable, may help. The following program listing demonstrates the simple use of a pointer variable:

```
Program PointerDemo;
Uses CRT;
Var
  i : ^Integer;
  j : Integer Absolute i;

(**********************************************)

Type
  St4 = String[4];
```

```pascal
Function IntToHex(i : Word) : St4;
Var
 HexStr : String[8];
 b : Array [1..2] Of Byte Absolute i;
 bt : Byte;

(*********************************************)

Function Translate(b : Byte) : Char;
Begin
If b < 10 Then
  Translate := Chr(b + 48)
Else
  Translate := Chr(b + 55);
End;

(*********************************************)

Begin
HexStr := '';
HexStr := HexStr + Translate(b[2] Shr 4);
HexStr := HexStr + Translate(b[2] And 15);
HexStr := HexStr + Translate(b[1] Shr 4);
HexStr := HexStr + Translate(b[1] And 15);
IntToHex := HexStr;
End;

(*********************************************)

Begin
ClrScr;
New(i);
i^ := 100;
WriteLn('The value of i is: ',IntToHex(j));
WriteLn('The value that i points to is: ',i^);
Dispose(i);
WriteLn;
Write('Press ENTER...');
ReadLn;
End.
```

The ^ placed before the data type in the definition tells Turbo Pascal to define **i** as a pointer variable:

    i : ^Integer;

When the program starts, the heap is a blank slate. Before you can use pointer **i**, you must use the statement **New(i)** to tell Turbo Pascal to assign an address on the heap to the pointer **i**. **Dispose(i)**, which appears near the end of the program, is the opposite of **New(i)**. **Dispose** effectively takes a variable off the heap, allowing memory to be used for other variables.

Once you place it on the heap, you can use the variable in **Assign** and **Arithmetic** statements by adding the ^ symbol to the identifier:

i^ := 100;

The ^ tells Turbo Pascal that you are referring to the variable on the heap and not to the pointer itself. What would happen if the statement were i := 100? This statement changes the value of the pointer, not the value of the variable on the heap. Now, i points to memory location 100 rather than to its proper location.

When you run the preceding program, your terminal displays the following messages:

The value of i is: 0000
The value that i points to is: 100

The first line displays the address that the pointer is holding. In this case the address is 0000, indicating that this variable is the first to be placed on the heap. The second line is the value of i^, the variable at address 0000 on the heap.

New and Dispose

When you allocate and dispose of dynamic variables, what actually happens in the heap? Figure 8-2 describes the process of allocation and deallocation. In the figure, Turbo Pascal declares four pointer variables: one **Integer,** one **Real,** and two **Strings,** one 5 and the other 10 bytes long. The columns represent memory on the heap. Turbo Pascal always allocates memory on the heap in exact amounts. Thus, when the program executes the statement **New(i),** the heap provides 2 bytes, just enough to store the **Integer** variable.

In the second column, Turbo Pascal allocates a string of 10 characters to the heap. Because this string requires 11 bytes of storage (10 characters plus the length byte), Turbo Pascal allocates 11 bytes on the heap. In short, the heap always provides as many bytes of memory as are necessary to contain the data structure put on the heap.

The third column in Figure 8-2 shows the additional allocation of a **Real** variable, requiring 5 bytes of memory. The next column demonstrates the impact of the **Dispose** statement. When Turbo Pascal disposes i, the 2-byte chunk that i was using is released for use by other dynamic variables. This creates a "hole" in the heap. To use this portion

```
Type
  St10 = String[10];
Var
  i : ^Integer;
  r : ^Real;
  s10 : ^St10;
  w : ^Word;
```

New(i)   New(s10)   New(r)   Dispose(i)   New(w)

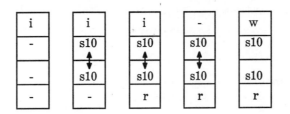

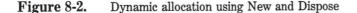

Figure 8-2.   Dynamic allocation using New and Dispose

of memory again, the data structure must fit into this hole. If not, Turbo Pascal must allocate memory elsewhere on the heap.

In the fifth column, Turbo Pascal allocates a **word** variable to the heap. Because this variable fits into the hole left by **i**, Turbo Pascal reuses that memory.

Using **New** and **Dispose** requires careful planning and rigorous testing. One common error is to reallocate the same variable on the heap. For example, the two following statements

New(i);
New(i);

both allocate an **Integer** on the heap, but only one of the **Integers** can be accessed as a variable. You not only cannot access the first **Integer**, you cannot even get rid of it. Since the **i** pointer points to the second **Integer**, it cannot be used to **Dispose** the first variable. Always make sure that each **New** is matched by a **Dispose**.

Mark and Release

Turbo Pascal offers an alternative to using **New** and **Dispose** to dynamically allocate memory: **Mark** and **Release**. Instead of leaving holes in the heap the way **New** and **Dispose** do, **Mark** and **Release** lop off an entire end of the heap from a particular point onward. This process is demonstrated in the following program:

```
Program HeapRelease;
Uses CRT;
Type
  Atype = Array [1..100] Of Char;
Var
  HeapTop : ^Word;
  a1,a2,a3 : ^Atype;

Begin
ClrScr;
Mark(HeapTop);

WriteLn('Initial free memory: ',MemAvail);
WriteLn;
WriteLn('--------------');
WriteLn;

New(a1);
WriteLn('Free memory after allocating a1: ',MemAvail);
New(a2);
WriteLn('Free memory after allocating a2: ',MemAvail);
New(a3);
WriteLn('Free memory after allocating a3: ',MemAvail);
WriteLn;
WriteLn('--------------');
WriteLn;

Release(HeapTop);
WriteLn('Free memory after release: ',MemAvail);
WriteLn;
Write('Press ENTER...');
ReadLn;
End.
```

This program allocates three pointer variables—**a1**, **a2**, and **a3**—and uses the **MemAvail** standard function to display the amount of free memory left over. **MemAvail** returns the total amount of memory in bytes available on the heap returns. For example, if **MemAvail** returns a value of 20, that means there are 20 bytes of memory left on the heap for use in dynamic allocation.

The previous program uses a pointer variable named **HeapTop** to keep track of the point from which you release memory. The statement **Mark(HeapTop)** stores the current address of the top of the heap to the pointer **HeapTop**. The program calls **Mark(HeapTop)** prior to placing any variables on the heap. As a result, when it calls **Release-(HeapTop)**, it deallocates all the variables on the heap, freeing the memory for another use. Running the program results in the following messages:

```
Initial free memory: 195632

--------------

Free memory after allocating a1: 195532
Free memory after allocating a2: 195432
Free memory after allocating a3: 195332

--------------

Free memory after release: 195632
```

As you can see, each time a variable is placed on the heap, the amount of available memory decreases. When **Release(HeapTop)** is called at the end of the program, the amount of free memory reverts to the initial amount. If you had marked the **HeapTop** pointer after **a1** was allocated, only the memory for **a2** and **a3** would be released.

Note that **Dispose** and **Release** are incompatible methods of recovering memory. You can choose to use one or the other, but never use both in the same program.

GetMem and FreeMem

A third method of dynamic memory allocation is **GetMem** and **FreeMem**. These are much like **New** and **Dispose** in that they allocate and deallocate memory one variable at a time. The special value of **GetMem** and **FreeMem** is that you can specify how much memory you want to allocate regardless of the type of variable you are using. For example, you can allocate 100 bytes to an **Integer** with the statement

```
GetMem(i,100);
```

Variables allocated with **GetMem** are deallocated with **FreeMem**, as shown by the following:

```
GetMem(i,20);
i := x + y;
WriteLn(i);
FreeMem(i,20);
```

The number of bytes specified in the **FreeMem** statement must match that in the **GetMem** statement. Do not use **Dispose** in place of **FreeMem**; if you do, the heap will become hopelessly unsynchronized.

Using Pointers with Complex Data Types

Since the heap is generally used to access large data spaces, pointer variables are generally used with large, complex data structures. Defining a complex data structure as a pointer is a two-step process.

```
Type

   CustPtr = ^CustRec;

   CustRec = Record
     Name : String[25];
     Address : String[30];
     City: String[30];
     State: String[2];
     Zip: String[5];
     End;

Var

   Cust : CustPtr;
```

Here, the statement **CustPtr = ^CustRec;** defines **CustPtr** as a pointer to **CustRec**. Note that **CustRec** has not yet been defined. Declaring pointers is the one case in which Turbo Pascal allows you to refer to a data structure before it is defined. The variable **Cust** is then defined as type **CustPtr**.

Linked Lists

The easy way to manage a list is to define an array. One problem with arrays, however, is that you always have to allocate enough space for the maximum possible number of elements. As a result, you either define very large arrays and waste memory or define small arrays and limit the power of your program. Pointers provide an alternative to arrays— *linked lists*.

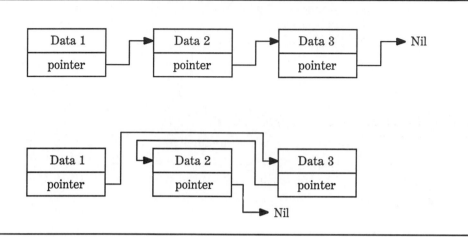

Figure 8-3.   A singly linked list

Data items in a linked list have pointers that keep track of the order of the list. *Singly linked lists* use one pointer that points to the record that comes next. *Doubly linked lists* have pointers in both directions, so that each data item is linked to the one before it and the one after it.

Figure 8-3 shows the structure of a singly linked list. Each record contains data and a pointer. The pointers indicate which record comes next in the list. The pointer of the last record is set to Nil, indicating there are no more records in the list.

To change the order of the list, only the pointer values need to be changed. In Figure 8-3, the pointer in Data 1 is changed to point to Data 3, and Data 3 is made to point to Data 2. Now, the pointer in Data 2 points to Nil, indicating that this is the last record in the list.

Building a linked list in a Turbo Pascal program requires considerable effort. Even so, it is a skill worth learning since many advanced sorting and searching routines use linked lists to increase their speed and maximize memory usage.

A data item in a singly linked list must have a *forward-referencing pointer* that tells Turbo Pascal where it can find the next data item in the list. The following record definition includes a forward-referencing pointer named **Next:**

```
CustPtr = ^CustRec;
CustRec = Record
  Name    : String[20];
```

```
Address : String[40];
City    : String[20];
State   : String[2];
Next    : CustPtr;
End;
```

CustPtr points to the record **CustRec**. The record **CustRec**, in turn, contains a field named Next, which is defined as **CustPtr**.

You, not Turbo Pascal, are responsible for maintaining pointers correctly, and this takes a bit of doing. First, you must keep track of where your list begins and ends. You must also know where the program currently is in the list and where the next data record is located.

A typical singly linked list requires at least three pointers: one to point to the beginning of the list, one to point to the current record, and one to point to the previous record. The following definition shows how these pointers might be defined:

```
Var
FirstCust,
PrevCust,
CurrentCust : CustPtr;
```

If you want to process the list sequentially from beginning to end, you must know the location of the first link in the list. **PrevCust**, which points to the link preceding the current link, makes the pointer called **Next** point to the next record.

A new link in a linked list must be connected to the previous link. The very first link, however, has no previous link and is, therefore, an exception. How does a program know if it is creating the first link or some other link? When the program begins, you must initialize the pointer **FirstCust** to Nil:

```
FirstCust := Nil;
```

The procedure that creates new links tests **FirstCust** to see if it is equal to Nil. If it is, the program knows this is the first link in a linked list and processes it appropriately. The following program segment demonstrates how these pointers create a linked list.

```
If FirstCust = Nil Then
  Begin
  New(CurrentCust);
```

```
   FirstCust := CurrentCust;
   CurrentCust^.Next := Nil;
   End
Else
  Begin
  PrevCust := CurrentCust;
  New(CurrentCust);
  PrevCust^.Next := CurrentCust;
  CurrentCust^.Next := Nil;
  End;
```

The **If-Then-Else** statement checks to see if this is the first link in the list (**FirstCust = Nil**). If so, the program creates a **CurrentCust** record and sets **FirstCust** equal to **CurrentCust**. It sets the Next field in **CurrentCust** equal to Nil because there is no next link in the chain at this time.

The second time through, **FirstCust** is not equal to Nil since it was previously set equal to **CurrentCust**. Therefore, the program skips to the **Else** branch, where it sets the pointer **PrevCust** equal to **Current-Cust** and creates a new **CurrentCust**. At this time, the program is using all three position pointers: **CurrentCust** points to the newly created link, **PrevCust** points to the preceding link, and **FirstCust** points to the first link in the list. After it creates the new **CurrentCust**, the program sets the Next field in **PrevCust** to point to the new link. The elements of these lists are linked by the connection of one record to another with a pointer field.

The following program shows how a singly linked list creates and manipulates a list of customer names and addresses:

```
Program SimpleLink;
Uses CRT;
Type
  CustPtr = ^CustRec;
  CustRec = Record
    Name : String[20];
    Address : String[40];
    City : String[20];
    State : String[2];
    Next : CustPtr;
    End;
Var
  FirstCust,
  PrevCust,
  CurrentCust : CustPtr;
  ch : Char;

(************************************)
```

```pascal
Procedure AddRecord;

(***********************************)

Procedure EnterData;
Begin
With CurrentCust^ Do
  Begin
  Write('Enter customer name: ');
  ReadLn(Name);
  Write('Enter address: ');
  ReadLn(Address);
  Write('Enter city: ');
  ReadLn(City);
  Write('Enter state: ');
  ReadLn(State);
  End;
End;

(***********************************)

Begin
ClrScr;
If FirstCust = Nil Then
  Begin
  New(CurrentCust);
  EnterData;
  FirstCust := CurrentCust;
  CurrentCust^.Next := Nil;
  End
Else
  Begin
  PrevCust := CurrentCust;
  New(CurrentCust);
  EnterData;
  PrevCust^.Next := CurrentCust;
  CurrentCust^.Next := Nil;
  End;
End;

(***********************************)

Procedure ListRecords;
Var
  Cust : CustPtr;
Begin
Cust := FirstCust;
While Cust <> Nil Do
  Begin
  With Cust^ Do
    WriteLn(Name,', ',Address,', ',City,', ',State);
  Cust := Cust^.Next;
  End;
WriteLn;
Write('Press ENTER...');
ReadLn;
End;
```

```
(************************************)
Begin
FirstCust := Nil;

  Repeat
  ClrScr;
    Repeat
    Write('A)dd a customer, L)ist customers, Q)uit: ');
    ch := ReadKey;
    If ch = #0 Then
      ch := ReadKey;
    WriteLn;
    ch := Upcase(ch);
    Until ch In ['A','L','Q'];

  If ch = 'A' Then
    AddRecord
  Else If ch = 'L' Then
    ListRecords;

  Until ch = 'Q';
End.
```

The procedure **ListRecords** demonstrates how to process a linked list sequentially. The essential parts of the code are as follows:

```
CurrentCust := FirstCust;
While CurrentCust <> Nil Do
  Begin
  (* Statements *)
  CurrentCust := CurrentCust^.Next;
  End;
```

The procedure sets pointer **CurrentCust** equal to **FirstCust**, the first item in the list. Next, a While-Do loop repeats a block of code until the pointer **CurrentCust** is Nil, indicating that the program has reached the end of the list. Within the block of code, the last statement

```
CurrentCust := CurrentCust^.Next;
```

causes **CurrentCust** to point to the next item in the list.

Even a cursory review of the previous program illustrates the added complexity of using a linked list instead of a standard array.

Every time the program needs a new record, it must create it and set up all the appropriate links. And if you want to move backward through a singly linked list, you simply cannot do it.

Doubly Linked Lists

Doubly linked lists maintain links in both directions, allowing you to process the list backward or forward. This requires another pointer field (**Prev**) in the record definition, as follows:

```
CustRec = Record
  Name : String[20];
  Address : String[40];
  City : String[20];
  State : String[2];
  Prev,
  Next : CustPtr;
  End;
```

The **Prev** pointer keeps track of the link preceding the current one, while the **Next** pointer keeps track of the next link.

While they are more powerful than singly linked lists, doubly linked lists require you to write even more code. Compare the doubly linked list in Figure 8-4 with the singly linked list in Figure 8-3. Adding the *backward-referencing pointer* doubles the number of linkages to maintain.

Doubly linked lists require position pointers to keep track of both the beginning and the end of the list. When a new link is created, you must keep track of the location of the first record, the last record, the

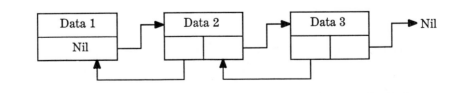

Figure 8-4.   A doubly linked list

current record, and the record prior to the current record. The following program segment illustrates this process:

```
If FirstCust = Nil Then
  Begin
  New(CurrentCust);
  CurrentCust^.Next := Nil;
  CurrentCust^.Prev := Nil;
  FirstCust := CurrentCust;
  LastCust := CurrentCust;
  End
Else
  Begin
  PrevCust := LastCust;
  New(CurrentCust);
  EnterData;
  PrevCust^.Next := CurrentCust;
  CurrentCust^.Next := Nil;
  CurrentCust^.Prev := PrevCust;
  LastCust := CurrentCust;
  End;
```

When **FirstCust** is equal to Nil, the program creates the first element in the linked list and sets its pointers, **Prev** and **Next**, to Nil. The other position pointers, **FirstCust**, **LastCust**, and **PrevCust**, are set equal to **CurrentCust**.

The next time through, the program branches to the **Else**, where it sets **PrevCust** equal to **LastCust** before creating the new link. When it creates the new link, the program sets the **Prev** pointer to **PrevCust** and the **Next** pointer in **PrevCust** to **CurrentCust**. This establishes the double link that allows processing in either direction.

The following program uses doubly linked lists to manage a list of names and addresses. Two features to pay attention to are the ability to sort the list and to write out the list in reverse order.

```
Program DoubleLink;
Uses CRT;
Type
  CustPtr = ^CustRec;
  CustRec = Record
    Name : String[20];
    Address : String[40];
    City : String[20];
    State : String[2];
    Prev,
    Next : CustPtr;
    End;
```

```
Var
  FirstCust,
  LastCust,
  PrevCust,
  CurrentCust : CustPtr;
  ch : Char;

(************************************)

Procedure AddRecord;

(************************************)

Procedure EnterData;
Begin
With CurrentCust^ Do
  Begin
  Write('Enter customer name: ');
  ReadLn(Name);
  Write('Enter address: ');
  ReadLn(Address);
  Write('Enter city: ');
  ReadLn(City);
  Write('Enter state: ');
  ReadLn(State);
  End;
End;

(************************************)

Begin
ClrScr;
If FirstCust = Nil Then
  Begin
  New(CurrentCust);
  EnterData;
  CurrentCust^.Next := Nil;
  CurrentCust^.Prev := Nil;
  FirstCust := CurrentCust;
  LastCust := CurrentCust;
  End
Else
  Begin
  PrevCust := LastCust;
  New(CurrentCust);
  EnterData;
  PrevCust^.Next := CurrentCust;
  CurrentCust^.Next := Nil;
  CurrentCust^.Prev := PrevCust;
  LastCust := CurrentCust;
  End;
End;

(************************************)
Procedure ListRecords;
Var
  ch : Char;

(************************************)
```

```
Procedure ListForwards;
Begin
CurrentCust := FirstCust;
While CurrentCust <> Nil Do
  Begin
  With CurrentCust^ Do
    WriteLn(Name,', ',Address,', ',City,', ',State);
  CurrentCust := CurrentCust^.Next;
  End;
End;

(************************************)

Procedure ListBackwards;
Begin
CurrentCust := LastCust;
While CurrentCust <> Nil Do
  Begin
  With CurrentCust^ Do
    WriteLn(Name,', ',Address,', ',City,', ',State);
  CurrentCust := CurrentCust^.Prev;
  End;
End;

(************************************)

Begin
  Repeat
  Write('F)orwards or B)ackwards, Q)uit: ');
  ch := ReadKey;
  If ch = #0 Then
    ch := ReadKey;
  WriteLn;
  ch := upcase(ch);
  Until (ch In ['F','B','Q']);

If ch = 'F' Then
  ListForwards
Else If ch = 'B' Then
  ListBackwards;
WriteLn;
Write('Press ENTER...');
ReadLn;
End;

(************************************)

Procedure SortRecords;
Var
  NextRec,FarCust : CustPtr;
  SortDone : Boolean;

Begin

  Repeat
  CurrentCust := FirstCust;
  PrevCust := Nil;
  SortDone := True;
```

```pascal
While CurrentCust^.Next <> Nil Do
  Begin
  NextRec := CurrentCust^.Next;

  If CurrentCust^.Name > NextRec^.Name Then
    Begin
    SortDone := False;

    If NextRec^.Next <> Nil Then
      Begin
      FarCust := NextRec^.Next;
      FarCust^.Prev := CurrentCust;
      End
    Else
      FarCust := Nil;

    If CurrentCust^.Prev = Nil Then
      Begin
      FirstCust := NextRec;
      PrevCust := Nil;
      End
    Else
      Begin
      PrevCust := CurrentCust^.Prev;
      PrevCust^.Next := NextRec;
      End;

    CurrentCust^.Next := FarCust;
    CurrentCust^.Prev := NextRec;

    NextRec^.Next := CurrentCust;
    NextRec^.Prev := PrevCust;

    CurrentCust := FirstCust;
    End
  Else
    CurrentCust := CurrentCust^.Next;
  End;

Until SortDone;

LastCust := CurrentCust;
WriteLn;
Write(Sort completed. Press ENTER...');
ReadLn;
End;

(*************************************)

Begin
FirstCust := Nil;

Repeat
ClrScr;
  Repeat
  Write('A)dd a customer, L)ist customers, S)ort, Q)uit: ');
```

```
   ch := ReadKey;
   If ch = #0 Then
     ch := ReadKey;
   WriteLn;
   ch := Upcase(ch);
   Until ch In ['A','L','S','Q'];

  If ch = 'A' Then
    AddRecord
  Else If ch = 'L' Then
    ListRecords
  Else If ch = 'S' Then
    SortRecords;

  Until ch = 'Q';
End.
```

Dynamic memory allocation is a powerful tool. It allows you to expand your program's data space while opening the door to linked lists and other dynamic data structures. But there is a price to pay. Linked lists maximize the efficient use of memory, but impose considerable overhead and require much more time to develop. In the end, dynamic data structures are best used when the benefits they provide are certain to outweigh the costs of developing and using them. Such programs include database applications that benefit from using as much memory as possible, but must be able to run on computers that have small amounts of memory.

Using the @ Operator

When performing address operations, it is often necessary to assign the address of a variable or procedure to a pointer. This is accomplished with the @ operator, which returns the address of the identifier that follows it. For example, if **A** is an **Integer**, then @A is the memory address of the **Integer** variable. The following code demonstrates how you might use the @ operator with a pointer variable:

```
Program AddressTest;
Type  B_Type = Array [1..2] Of Byte;
Var
  i : Word;
  b : ^B_Type;
```

```
Begin
i := $FFFF;
b := @i;
WriteLn(b^[1],' ',b^[2]);
WriteLn;
Write('Press ENTER...');
ReadLn;
End.
```

In this example, **b** is a pointer to an array of two bytes, and **i** is a word variable. The program initializes **i** to FFFFh and then assigns the address of **i** to pointer **b**. Now, using the pointer variable, it is possible to treat the two bytes in the word variable as separate entities. This chapter gives only a hint at the usefulness of pointers and dynamic allocation. While it is a difficult topic to master, the rewards can be great in terms of program efficiency and flexibility.

Turbo Pascal Files

File Handling Concepts
Turbo Pascal Text Files
Disk Files and Buffers
Typed Files
Untyped Files
Erasing and Renaming Files

A computer that does not store programs and data is little more than a powerful calculator. People who bought early microcomputers without disk drives soon found this out—when they turned their computers off, their work disappeared. Of course, your computer does have at least a floppy disk drive and possibly a hard disk drive. This allows you to take advantage of Turbo Pascal's powerful disk file operations. Learning to use disk files is vital to producing useful programs, and Turbo Pascal helps by supporting three basic types of disk files: *text*, *typed*, and *untyped*. This chapter discusses how you create and use these kinds of files.

File Handling Concepts

All Turbo Pascal files, regardless of type, share common characteristics. First, all files are used for either input or output. Input is when a program takes data from a file and uses it in the program; output stores the results of a program in a file or sends the results to a *device* such as a terminal or printer. As you will see, it is also possible for a file to be used for both input and output.

Files can be stored on floppy disks and hard disk drives. There are, of course, other storage media (tape, optical disks, RAM disks, and so on), but they are less common. DOS requires that every file have a name of one to eight characters. Filenames can also include a three-letter *extension* that usually helps describe the contents of a file. For example, the Turbo Pascal program file is named TURBO.EXE. The .EXE file-name extension tells DOS that this is a program file that can be executed from the DOS prompt. Turbo Pascal source files (the files you create with the Turbo Pascal editor) generally have the .PAS filename extension (for example, PROG1.PAS).

If a file is stored in a DOS directory, the directory path is also part of the filename. If, for example, the file PROG1.PAS is in the Turbo directory on drive C:, the full description or *pathname* of the filename is C:\TURBO\PROG1.PAS. DOS filename conventions are discussed in detail in the DOS user's manual. You should be thoroughly familiar with these conventions before using Turbo Pascal files.

Turbo Pascal Text Files

Text files consist of lines that are terminated by a carriage return and linefeed (CR/LF) and which contain characters, words, and sentences, as shown in Figure 9-1. The CR/LF combination (ASCII codes 10 and 13) is known as a delimiter. A delimiter marks the end of some element, such as a field, record, or in this case, the end of a line.

You can tell if a file consists of text by using the DOS **Type** command. For example, your Turbo Pascal disk comes with a text file called README. If you enter **TYPE README** at the DOS prompt and press ENTER, the file is displayed on the screen in a readable form. If, however, you try to display a nontext file (such as TURBO.EXE) in the same way, you will see only gibberish.

File Name: TEXT.DAT

Line 1	→	This is an example of a line of text.[CR/LF]
Line 2	→	Every line in a text file ends with a[CR/LF]
Line 3	→	carriage return and linefeed.[CR/LF]
Line 4	→	[CR/LF]
Line 5	→	Even empty lines, like the one above.[CR/LF]
Line 6	→	50 12.23 0.23 40343 332324[CR/LF]

Figure 9-1.   A typical text file

Text-File Identifiers

Before you work with text files, you must declare a *text-file identifier* in your program. Text-file identifiers are declared just like variable identifiers, except that the Turbo Pascal reserved word **Text** is used. An example of a text-file declaration is as follows:

```
Program TextFile;
Var
      TxtFile : Text;
```

In this illustration, **TxtFile** is a variable identifier of type **Text**. Before using **TxtFile** for input or output, you must assign it to a disk file. A typical **Assign** statement looks like this:

```
Assign(TxtFile,'TEXT.DAT');
```

Once **TxtFile** is assigned to TEXT.DAT, the disk file is never referred to by name again: all file operations refer to the identifier **TxtFile**.

After you assign a file identifier to a disk file, prepare the disk file with one of three Turbo Pascal commands—**Reset**, **Rewrite**, or **Append**. **Reset** opens the disk file and prepares it as an input file. Only input commands can be used on a file that has been reset. Any attempt to write to a **Reset** text file generates an I/O (input/output) error.

The **Reset** command also positions the *file pointer*, a counter that keeps track of a program's position in a file, at the beginning of the file. This causes all input to start at the very beginning of the file and move forward from there.

An attempt to *Reset* a file that does not exist generates an I/O error. You can override the I/O error, if desired, by disabling the **I** compiler directive with the statement **{$I −}**.

Rewrite and **Append** both prepare a text file for output, but they function in different ways. When an existing file is prepared with **Rewrite**, its contents are erased and the file pointer is placed at the beginning of the file. If the file identifier is assigned to a nonexisting file, the **Rewrite** command creates a file with the name given in the **Assign** statement. The **Append** command, on the other hand, preserves the contents of a file and positions the file pointer at the very end of the file.

As a result, any data added to the file is appended to what is already there.

As with the **Reset** statement, should you attempt to use **Append** on a file that does not exist, Turbo Pascal generates an I/O error.

When you are finished using a file for either input or output, you must close the file. The **Close** command performs this task and performs several other tasks in the process. **Close** makes sure that all data in temporary buffers is stored to disk. This is known as *flushing the buffer* and is discussed in detail later in this chapter.

The **Close** command also frees up a DOS *file handle*. A file handle is a mechanism that DOS provides to programs that helps manage file operations. When you **Reset** or **Rewrite** a file, DOS allocates a file handle to Turbo Pascal. Because DOS limits the number of file handles, you cannot have more than 15 Turbo Pascal files open at one time. Closing files keeps the supply of file handles plentiful. Finally, the **Close** command updates the DOS file directory to reflect the file's size, time, and date.

Once closed, a file cannot be used for input or output until it is opened again with **Reset, Rewrite**, or **Append**. The link between the file identifier and the disk file, however, remains in force even after the file is closed. Therefore, to reopen a file, it is not necessary to repeat the **Assign** command. This process is illustrated in Figure 9-2.

Reading Strings from Text Files

Once a text file is reset, you can extract information from it with the **Read** and **ReadLn** procedures. Examples of text-file input can be seen in the following program, in which the disk file TEXT.DAT is linked to the file identifier **TxtFile**.

```
Program Text1;
Var
  TxtFile : Text;
  s : String[80];

Begin
Assign(TxtFile,'TEXT.DAT');
Reset(TxtFile);

ReadLn(TxtFile,s);
WriteLn(s);

Read(TxtFile,s);
WriteLn(s);
Close(TxtFile);
End.
```

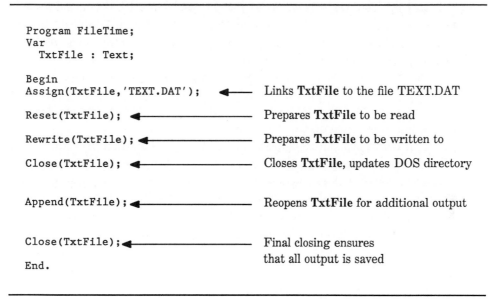

```
Program FileTime;
Var
  TxtFile : Text;

Begin
Assign(TxtFile,'TEXT.DAT');  ◄—— Links TxtFile to the file TEXT.DAT

Reset(TxtFile); ◄——————— Prepares TxtFile to be read

Rewrite(TxtFile); ◄————— Prepares TxtFile to be written to

Close(TxtFile); ◄———————— Closes TxtFile, updates DOS directory


Append(TxtFile); ◄——————— Reopens TxtFile for additional output


Close(TxtFile); ◄———————— Final closing ensures
                          that all output is saved
End.
```

Figure 9-2.   Opening text files

Subsequently, **TxtFile** is prepared for reading with the **Reset** command. The first input operation in this program example is the statement

ReadLn(TxtFile,s);

which tells Turbo Pascal to read characters from the current line in the file and place them into the string variable **s**. After the characters are read, the file pointer skips any remaining characters on the line and moves to the beginning of the next line in the file.

When reading in a string from a text file with the **ReadLn** procedure, three possible situations can occur:

• There are exactly enough characters left in the line to fill the string to its maximum length.

• There are not enough characters left in the line to fill the string to its maximum length.

• There are more characters left in the line than are needed to fill the string to its maximum length.

In the first two cases, Turbo Pascal reads in all the characters left in the line, assigns them to **s**, and then moves the file pointer to the beginning of the next line. The string length is set equal to the number of characters read.

In the third case, Turbo Pascal reads in as many characters as necessary to fill the **String** variable and then moves the file pointer to the next line. Any characters between the end of the string and the end of the line are discarded.

The **Read** procedure operates much like the **ReadLn** procedure, but after it reads in a string, **Read** places the file pointer just after the last character read; it does not move the file pointer to the beginning of the next line. If the **Read** procedure encounters a CR/LF (or just a simple carriage return), indicating the end of the line has been reached, it stops reading characters and also does not advance the file pointer until a **ReadLn** procedure is used.

Reading Multiple Strings per Line

A single **ReadLn** procedure can read in several strings at one time. For example, the statement

ReadLn(TxtFile,s1,s2,s3)

reads characters from the current line and fills the **String** variables **s1**, **s2**, and **s3** in order. If the line being read is

This is a line of characters

and the **String** variables are all of type **String[5]**, the **Strings** would be assigned values as follows:

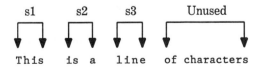

Reading Numbers from Text Files

Text files can store not only words and sentences, but also numeric data. Numbers, however, are not stored in their binary form but as characters. For example, in RAM, the **Integer** value 20,545 is stored as two

11	27.53	6.4144900000E+02
21	50.83	1.1843390000E+03
31	74.13	1.7272290000E+03
41	97.43	2.2701190000E+03
51	120.73	2.8130090000E+03
61	144.03	3.3558990000E+03
71	167.33	3.8987890000E+03
81	190.63	4.4416790000E+03
91	213.93	4.9845690000E+03
101	237.23	5.5274590000E+03

Figure 9-3.   TEST.DAT, a numeric text file

bytes with a binary value of 0101000001000001. But in a text file, the number is stored as the characters 2, 0, 5, 4, 5, requiring a total of five bytes. When reading the number 20,545 from a text file, Turbo Pascal translates the number from a string of characters into binary integer format.

As it reads a number from a text file, Turbo Pascal skips the blank characters in a line until it finds a nonblank character. It then reads in characters until it encounters either another nonblank character or a CR/LF. When the characters are read in, Turbo Pascal combines the characters into an alphanumeric string and converts the string into either an **Integer** or a **Real** value, depending on the type of variable being used. If the conversion is successful, the number is assigned to the variable; if it is not successful, Turbo Pascal generates an I/O error.

To learn how numbers are read from text files, examine the numeric text file TEST.DAT in Figure 9-3. This file contains three columns of numbers. The first column is **Integer**s, the second **Real** numbers in decimal format, and the third **Real** numbers in scientific notation. You can read the three numbers on each line of the file by employing the following statements:

```
Read(TxtFile,i);
Read(TxtFile,r1);
ReadLn(TxtFile,r2);
```

or by using the equivalent single statement:

ReadLn(TxtFile,i,r1,r2);

Turbo Pascal assigns the first number found in a line to the **Integer** variable **i** and the next two numbers to **Real** variables **r1** and **r2**.

The following program contains a routine that reads the numerical file TEST.DAT and calculates the average of each column of figures.

```pascal
Program ComputeAverages;
Var
  f : Text;

  i,count : Integer;

  imean,
  r1,r2,
  r1mean,
  r2mean : Real;

Begin
Assign(f,'TEST.DAT');
Reset(f);

count := 0;
imean := 0;
r1mean := 0;
r2mean := 0;

While Not Eof(f) Do
  Begin
  ReadLn(f,i,r1,r2);
  WriteLn(i:10,' ',r1:10:3,' ',r2:10:3);

  count := count + 1;
  imean := imean + i;
  r1mean := r1mean + r1;
  r2mean := r2mean + r2;
  End;

imean := imean / count;
r1mean := r1mean / count;
r2mean := r2mean / count;

WriteLn;
WriteLn(imean:10:3,' ',r1mean:10:3,' ',r2mean:10:3);
Close(f);
WriteLn;
Write('Press ENTER...');
ReadLn;
End.
```

This program introduces the Turbo Pascal standard function **Eof**, which stands for end-of-file. **Eof** is a Boolean function that is true only when the file pointer is at the end of your file. It can be used to repeat input commands so that an entire file is processed from beginning to end. In the previous example, the statement

While Not Eof(f) Do

tells Turbo Pascal to execute the next block of code until **Eof(f)** returns TRUE, that is, until the last character in the file is read.

The function **Eoln** tests for the end of a line. **Eoln** is true under two conditions: when the file pointer encounters a carriage return and when the file pointer reaches the end of a file. You can use **Eoln** to read each character in a line one by one, as is shown in Figure 9-4. **Eoln** reads the characters in a line and writes them out on separate lines.

```
Program ReadChar;

Var
  f : Text;
  i : Integer;
  c : Array [1..1000] Of Char;

Begin
Assign(f,'TEST.TXT');
Reset(f);

While Not Eof(f) Do          ◄──── Continue for the entire file
  Begin
    While Not Eoln(f) Do     ◄──── Continue until next carriage return
      Begin
      Read(f,Ch);
      WriteLn(Ch);
      End;
    ReadLn(f);               ◄──── Skip past the carriage return,
    End;                            to beginning of the next line

Close(f);
End.
```

Figure 9-4.   Reading characters from a text file

SeekEof and SeekEoln

To give you even more control over text files, Turbo Pascal offers **SeekEof** and **SeekEoln**. Like their counterparts **Eof** and **Eoln**, **SeekEof** returns TRUE at the end of a file and **SeekEoln** returns TRUE at the end of a line. These functions have a unique capability to skip over ASCII characters in the range 0 to 32 when testing for end-of-file or end-of-line. This range includes the standard ASCII control characters as well as the blank character. Consequently, **SeekEof** returns TRUE even when there are characters left in the file, so long as those characters are blank or control codes.

Errors In Numeric Input

If the format of a number read from a text file is incorrect, the program produces an I/O error. For example, reading the number 50,000 into an **Integer** variable would cause an error because the largest **Integer** allowable is 32,767. Similarly, reading the number 32.1 into an **Integer** variable would cause an error because of the decimal place, which is illegal for **Integers**. **Real** variables pose fewer restrictions since numbers can be read with or without a decimal place or in scientific notation.

Writing Text Files

A text file can be used for output after being prepared with the **Rewrite** or **Append** procedures, as discussed earlier in this chapter. Once prepared, the **Write** or **WriteLn** procedures output the file. The first parameter in these procedures, the text-file identifier, tells Turbo Pascal where to send the data. It is followed by any number of variable identifiers or literal values to be output. For example, the following statements write the line "Jones 21" to the text file identified as **TxtFile**.

```
Name := 'Jones';
i := 21;
WriteLn(TxtFile,name,' ',i);
```

Write and **WriteLn** normally output values without any special formatting. Adding a colon and a number after the parameter, however, specifies that the value is to be right-justified in a space defined by the number. For example, these statements

```
Name := 'Johnson';
WriteLn(Name)
WriteLn(Name:20);
WriteLn(Name:4);
```

result in the following output:

```
Johnson
            Johnson
Johnson
```

The first **WriteLn** statement is unformatted, so the value is written left-justified. The second statement tells Turbo Pascal to create a field 20 characters wide and to right-justify the value within this field. Since the name "Johnson" is seven characters long, Turbo Pascal right-justifies the name by preceding it with 13 blanks. The third statement is also formatted, but the field width of 4 is less than the length of the value itself. When this occurs, the formatting has no effect. **Integer**s follow the same output formatting as **String**s: a single colon followed by the number of spaces to right-justify the number. **Real**s, however, can be formatted with either one or two parameters. The first parameter determines the width of the field in which the number will be right justified, and the second determines the number of decimal places. The following program demonstrates various formats for **Real** numbers and shows their results:

```
Program RealFormat;
Var
  r : Real;
Begin
r := 123.23;
WriteLn(r);            (* Result: ' 1.2323000000E+02'  *)
WriteLn(r:0);          (* Result: ' 1.2E+02'           *)
WriteLn(r:10);         (* Result: ' 1.2323E+02'        *)
WriteLn(r:10:2);       (* Result: '    123.23'         *)
WriteLn(r:0:0);        (* Result: ' 123'               *)
WriteLn;
Write('Press ENTER...');
ReadLn;
End.
```

Disk Files and Buffers

Reading from and writing to a disk file are two of the slowest operations a computer performs. The time it takes for a disk drive to locate data seems like years to a microprocessor. Small chunks of memory called *buffers* are set aside for data to be used in disk operations. Buffers speed up processing by reducing the number of disk reads and writes. For example, suppose a program reads five characters from a text file with the following statements:

```
Read(TxtFile,Ch1);
Read(TxtFile,Ch2);
Read(TxtFile,Ch3);
Read(TxtFile,Ch4);
Read(TxtFile,Ch5);
```

If the input is not buffered, the program must go to the disk for each character read. If, however, the program picks up all five characters with the first **Read** statement and stores them in a buffer, the buffer can distribute the characters to the next four **Read** statements without having to access the disk.

Turbo Pascal provides text files with a standard 128-byte buffer. Every time a program reads data from a text file, the buffer is filled with 128 bytes, even if you only ask for 10. Of course, you will never know the extra bytes are in memory since Turbo Pascal takes care of all that for you.

When you process large text files, the standard 128-byte buffer is inadequate. Turbo Pascal allows you to expand a text file's buffer with the **SetTextBuf** procedure, in which you specify a variable to use as the buffer, for example:

```
Var
  f : Text;
  Buffer : Array [1..512] of Byte;
Begin
Assign(f,'TEST.DAT');
SetTextBuf(f, Buffer);
Reset(f);
```

This code assigns a buffer of 512 bytes to text file F, though you could have made the buffer larger. Be careful, however, not to call **SetTextBuf** once you have opened a file, or you will probably lose some data.

Also, make sure that the buffer is declared globally; if you use a local buffer, you might lose data if the local variable is discarded.

Flushing a File

When writing to a buffered file, Turbo Pascal actually sends the data to an output buffer. When the buffer is filled, the entire contents are written to the disk at one time.

To force Turbo Pascal to empty an output buffer before it is filled, use the **Flush** procedure. The statement **Flush(f)** forces any data in the **f** buffer to be saved to disk immediately, thus eliminating any possibility that the data will be lost. Closing an output file automatically flushes the output buffer.

Typed Files

Typed files are files that contain data of a particular type, such as **Integer**s, **Real**s, **Record**s, and so on. These valuable files can make your programming easier and more efficient. In fact, typed files provide far faster input and output than do text files.

Unlike text files, which are unstructured, typed files have a rigid structure that is dependent on, and defined by, the type of data they hold. In the following example, the file identifier **f** is declared as a typed file called File of Real.

```
Program TypedFile;
Var
     f : File Of Real;
```

This declaration tells Turbo Pascal that this file will be used to store only **Real** numbers. In fact, this file will store **Real** numbers in the same format in which they are stored in RAM. Herein lies the reason that typed files are fast: because they bypass all the translation and conversion processes that data undergoes within text files, they can transfer the data directly to memory.

For example, a file that is declared to be of type **Integer** knows that it is to store only **Integer**s; the data within it does not have to be converted into **Integer**s before it can be processed.

Records and Untyped Files

Because they are not made up of lines, as are text files, typed files cannot use the **ReadLn** and **WriteLn** statements. But if typed files are not organized into lines, how are they organized? Untyped files are organized into records, each data item representing one record. The length of a record corresponds to the number of bytes required to store the data type. In the previous example, the file stores numbers of type **Real**. Since a **Real** number requires six bytes in Turbo Pascal, the record length for the file is six bytes: the first six bytes of the file contain the first record (**Real** number), the next six contain the second record, and so on. For **Integer**s, numbers that require just two bytes, an untyped file is organized into two-byte records.

The following program shows how a typed file is declared, used for output, and then used for input:

```
Program RealFile;
Uses CRT;
Var
  r : Real;
  f : File Of Real;
Begin
ClrScr;
Assign(f,'REAL.DAT');
Rewrite(f);

r := 100.234;
Write(f,r);

r := 32.23;
Write(f,r);

r := 9894.40;
Write(f,r);

Reset(f);

While Not Eof(f) Do
  Begin
  Read(f,r);
  WriteLn(r:0:3);
  End;
```

```
WriteLn;
Write('Press ENTER...');
ReadLn;
End.
```

This program writes out three **Real** numbers. Since each **Real** number requires six bytes, the size of the file is 18 bytes. You can confirm this with the **Dir** command at the DOS prompt.

Strings and Typed Files

Typed files can also be of a **String** type, but this is very different from a text file. Even though both are designed to hold strings, the way they store strings is what separates them. Consider the following example:

```
Program OutputCompare;
Type
  Str10 = String[10];
Var
  TxtFile : Text;
  StringFile : File Of Str10;
  s : Str10;

Begin
WriteLn('Rewriting OUTPUT.TXT');
Assign(TxtFile,'OUTPUT.TXT');
Rewrite(TxtFile);

WriteLn('Rewriting OUTPUT.STR');
Assign(StringFile,'OUTPUT.STR');
Rewrite(StringFile);

s := 'ABCD';

WriteLn('Writing to OUTPUT.TXT');
Write(TxtFile,s);
WriteLn('Writing to OUTPUT.STR');
Write(StringFile,s);
WriteLn('Closing files.');
Close(TxtFile);
Close(StringFile);
WriteLn;
Write('Press ENTER...');
ReadLn;
End.
```

The program declares two files, one Text and the other type File Of Str[10]. Both files are prepared for output, and the string 'ABCD' is written to both. This is where the similarity ends.

In the case of the Text file, Turbo Pascal writes the letters A, B, C, and D and nothing more, as shown here:

A	B	C	D

In the typed file, however, Turbo Pascal stores the string in its full form: the length byte, the legitimate characters in the string (ABCD), and any garbage characters that fill out the remaining six bytes of storage, as shown here:

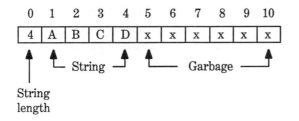

This example demonstrates that **String** files require more space than text files because the **Record** includes the string length byte as well as any garbage bytes.

Typed Files and Speed

The data stored in a typed file has exactly the same form that it has when it is stored in RAM. This fact leads to a tremendous increase in input/output performance when compared to text-file processing. Why? Because every time Turbo Pascal uses a text file, some time is wasted while numbers are converted into characters and back again and strings are stripped of their length byte and any unused bytes. Data from typed files, on the other hand, can be read directly into RAM without any transformation. That means less work for the computer and, as a result, faster processing.

More Complex Typed Files

Just as you can define your own data types, you can also define a file to hold these data types. For example, a record of data type **Customer** with fields Name, Address, and Telephone could be stored in a file as defined in the following program:

```
Program RecordFile;
Uses CRT;
Type
  CustomerRec = Record
    Name : String[30];
    Address : String[40];
    Telephone : String[15];
    End;

Var
  Customer : CustomerRec;
  CustFile : File Of CustomerRec;

(***************************************************)

Procedure CreateFile;
Var
  i : Integer;
Begin
Assign(CustFile,'CUST.DAT');
Rewrite(CustFile);

With Customer Do
  Begin
  Name      := 'L. M. Quibble';
  Address   := 'New York City';
  Telephone := '(123) 456-7890';
  End;
Write(CustFile,Customer);

With Customer Do
  Begin
  Name      := 'Berlina Flopp';
  Address   := 'Miami';
  Telephone := '(098) 765-4321';
  End;
Write(CustFile,Customer);

With Customer Do
  Begin
  Name      := 'Arthur Brainer';
  Address   := 'Hollywood';
  Telephone := '(111) 222-3333';
  End;
Write(CustFile,Customer);

Close(CustFile);
End;

(***************************************************)
```

```
Begin
ClrScr;
CreateFile;

Assign(CustFile,'CUST.DAT');
Reset(CustFile);

While Not Eof(CustFile) Do
  Begin
  Read(CustFile,Customer);
  With Customer Do
    Begin
    WriteLn(Name,'  ',Address,' ',Telephone);
    End;
  End;
Close(CustFile);
WriteLn;
Write('Press ENTER...');
ReadLn;
End.
```

Because the file is declared to be of the same type as the record **Customer,** it is possible to read and write a complete record at a time. This increases speed because you do not have to read or write each item of the record separately.

Untyped Files

Untyped files are an especially powerful tool provided by Turbo Pascal. While text files assume that a file consists of lines terminated with CR/LF, and typed files assume that a file consists of a particular type of data structure, untyped files make no assumptions about the structure of the data in a file. You can read data from an untyped file into any data type you want.

Because Turbo Pascal makes no assumptions about the format of the data, the transfer from disk to your data structure is immediate. This is why untyped files are used for applications requiring high-speed input and output.

The following example, which copies the contents of one file to another, demonstrates a typical use of untyped files. As you can see, two file identifiers, **SourceFile** and **DestFile**, are declared to be of type **File**.

Untyped files get their name from the fact that the reserved word **File** is not followed by a type specification, as is the case with typed files.

```
Program CopyFile;
Uses CRT;
Var
  SourceFile,
  DestFile    : File;
  RecordsRead : Integer;
  Buffer : Array [1..1000] Of Byte;

Begin
ClrScr;
If ParamCount <> 2 Then
  Begin
  WriteLn('CopyFile [FromFile] [ToFile]');
  Halt;
  End;

Assign(SourceFile,ParamStr(1));
{$I-}
Reset(SourceFile,1);
If IOresult <> 0 Then
  Begin
  WriteLn(ParamStr(1),' not found.');
  Halt;
  End;

Assign(DestFile,ParamStr(2));
Rewrite(DestFile,1);

WriteLn('. = 1,000 bytes copied.');

BlockRead(SourceFile,Buffer,SizeOf(Buffer),RecordsRead);

While RecordsRead > 0 Do
  Begin
  Write('.');
  BlockWrite(DestFile,Buffer,RecordsRead);
  BlockRead(SourceFile,Buffer,SizeOf(Buffer),RecordsRead);
  End;

Close(SourceFile);
Close(DestFile);
WriteLn;
Write('Press ENTER...');
ReadLn;
End.
```

Unlike text and typed files, the **Reset** and **Rewrite** statements for untyped files can take a second parameter, the record size. For example, the statement

    Reset(SourceFile,1);

prepares the file to be read and specifies that the record length is 1 byte. This makes sense since the data structure is an array of **Byte**s. If the data structure were an array of **Integer**s, you could set the record length to 2. While Turbo Pascal does not require you to match the record length to the size of the data type you are using, doing so makes programming easier. Note that if you do not specify a record length in the **Reset** or **Rewrite** statements, Turbo Pascal assigns a default record length of 128 bytes. Reading and writing to untyped files requires two special Turbo Pascal standard procedures, **BlockRead** and **BlockWrite**. In the previous example, the statement

BlockRead(SourceFile,Buffer,SizeOf(Buffer),RecordsRead);

takes four parameters. The file identifier **SourceFile** is first. The second parameter specifies the data structure into which the data will be placed. In the example, the data structure is the array of bytes **Buffer**.

The third parameter specifies the number of records to read. In the example, the record size was set to 1 byte by the **Reset** statement. The data structure **Buffer**, however, is 10,000 bytes in length. To completely fill **Buffer**, then, you have to read in 10,000 records. You could simply write in the number 10,000 as the third parameter, but the Turbo Pascal standard function **SizeOf** offers a better alternative. **SizeOf** returns the number of bytes used by a specific data structure. For example, if **i** is an **Integer**, then **SizeOf(i)** returns the value 2 because **Integer**s require two bytes of storage. In the example, the statement **SizeOf(Buffer)** returns 10,000 because that is the number of bytes **Buffer** uses. By using the **SizeOf** function, you can change the size of the buffer without having to change **BlockRead** statements.

The fourth and last parameter in the **BlockRead** statement is the **Integer** variable **RecordsRead**. When the **BlockRead** statement executes, it attempts to read in the number of records specified (10,000 in the example). However, if the file pointer is close to the end of the file, you may actually read fewer than 10,000 records. **RecordsRead** tells you exactly how many records were read by the **BlockRead** statement. When **RecordsRead** equals zero, the end of the file has been reached.

BlockWrite operates much the same as **BlockRead**, except that there are only three parameters. The file identifier comes first, followed by the data structure used for the output. The third parameter is the number of records to write to the file. In the example program **Copy-File, RecordsRead** specifies the number of records to write because you want to write out exactly what was read in.

Procedures for Typed and Untyped Files

Nontext files (that is, typed and untyped files) are also known as *random access files,* meaning that records in a file can be accessed in nonsequential order. If you want to, you can read the third record first, then the tenth record, and the first record after that. This is done in a two-step process: first position the file pointer at the correct record, and then read the record. This is demonstrated in the following program, which creates a typed data file and then reads the records back in nonsequential order.

```
Program DataBaseFile;
(*$v-*)
Uses CRT;
Type
  MaxStr  = String[255];
  CustRec = Record
    Name : String[30];
    Age  : Integer;
    Income : Real;
    End;

Var
  Cust : CustRec;
  CustFile : File Of CustRec;

(**********)

Procedure AddRec(NameIn : MaxStr;
                 AgeIn : Integer;
                 IncomeIn : Real);
Begin
With Cust Do
  Begin
  Name := NameIn;
  Age := AgeIn;
  Income := IncomeIn;
  Write(CustFile,Cust);
  End;
End;

(**********)
```

```
Procedure DumpRec;
Begin
WriteLn;
With Cust Do
  Begin
  WriteLn('Name:    ',Name);
  WriteLn('Age:     ',Age);
  WriteLn('Income: ',Income:0:0);
  End;
End;

(**********)

Begin
ClrScr;
Assign(CustFile,'CUSTFILE.DAT');
Rewrite(CustFile);

AddRec('Jones',30,23000.0);
AddRec('Adams',65,34000.0);
AddRec('Smith',21,18000.0);

Reset(CustFile);

WriteLn('The number of records in the file is: ',
        FileSize(CustFile));
WriteLn;
Write('Press ENTER...');
ReadLn;

(***********************************************************)
(* Write out the contents of the third record in the file.   *)
(* Because the first record in a file is number 0, the third *)
(* record is number 2.                                       *)
(***********************************************************)

Seek(CustFile,2);
WriteLn;
WriteLn;
WriteLn('This is record number: ',FilePos(CustFile)+1);
Read(CustFile,Cust);
DumpRec;
WriteLn;
Write('Press ENTER...');
ReadLn;

(***********************************************************)
(* Write out the contents of the first record in the file. *)
(***********************************************************)

Seek(CustFile,0);
WriteLn;
WriteLn;
WriteLn('This is record number: ',FilePos(CustFile)+1);
Read(CustFile,Cust);
DumpRec;
WriteLn;
```

```
Write('Press ENTER...');
ReadLn;

(**************************************************************)
(* Write out the contents of the second record in the file. *)
(**************************************************************)

Seek(CustFile,1);
WriteLn;
WriteLn;
WriteLn('This is record number: ',FilePos(CustFile)+1);
Read(CustFile,Cust);
DumpRec;
WriteLn;
Write('Press ENTER...');
ReadLn;

(*******************************************)
(* Change the contents of the first record *)
(*******************************************)

Seek(CustFile,0);
AddRec('Arnold',32,43000.0);

Seek(CustFile,0);
WriteLn;
WriteLn;

WriteLn('This is record number: ',FilePos(CustFile)+1);
Read(CustFile,Cust);
DumpRec;
WriteLn;
Write('Press ENTER...');
ReadLn;

Close(CustFile);
End.
```

The **Seek** statement moves the file pointer to the beginning of the third record. Note that the third record is referred to as number 2 in the **Seek** statement because Turbo Pascal typed files begin with record 0. When the file pointer is in place, you can read the record as you normally would. After the **Read** is executed, the file pointer is automatically moved to the beginning of the next record. In this case, the third record is the last record in the file. Any attempt to read beyond the end of the file results in an I/O error.

An example of a nonsequential **Read** is shown by the following two statements:

```
Seek(CustFile,2);
Read(CustFile,Cust);
```

Two other standard functions, **FileSize** and **FilePos**, are also used. **FileSize** returns the total number of records in the file; **FilePos** returns the current position of the file pointer.

An especially powerful feature of random access files is the ability to update records at any point in the file. This is demonstrated at the end of the previous example program (titled **DataBaseFile**), where the information in the first record is changed and then displayed. What is particularly noteworthy is that the **Write** procedure is used without a preceding **Rewrite** statement. This seems to go against the rule that a file must be prepared with **Rewrite** before you can add data to it. For nontext files, the **Rewrite** command is only necessary to create the file. Once the file exists, the **Reset** command allows you to both read and write to the file.

Erasing and Renaming Files

Sophisticated file management requires the ability to rename and erase files without going back to the DOS prompt. Turbo Pascal provides two procedures to do just that. To rename a file, first assign a file to a file variable, then call the **Rename** procedure with the new name specified:

```
Assign(f,'FILE.OLD');
Rename(f,'FILE.NEW');
```

The **Erase** procedure works essentially the same way. Assign the disk file to a file identifier and then call the **Erase** procedure.

```
Assign(f,'FILE.OLD');
Erase(f);
```

The following program provides a simple method for renaming and erasing files. When you start the program, three choices are presented: rename a file, erase a file, or quit.

```
Program FileControl;
Uses CRT;
Var
  File1 : File;
```

```
    Name1,
    Name2 : String[255];
    Choice : Char;

Begin
ClrScr;
  Repeat
    Write('R)ename, E)rase, Q)uit: ');
    ReadLn(Choice);

      Case Upcase(Choice) Of
      'R':
        Begin
        Write('Name of file to rename: ');
        ReadLn(Name1);
        Write('New name for the file: ');
        ReadLn(Name2);
        Assign(File1,Name1);
        Rename(File1,Name2);
        End;
      'E':
        Begin
        Write('Name of file to erase: ');
        ReadLn(Name1);
        Assign(File1,Name1);
        Erase(File1);
        End;
      End; (* of case *)

  Until Upcase(Choice) = 'Q';
End.
```

Make a selection by typing **R**, **E**, or **Q** and pressing ENTER. When renaming a file, enter the name of the existing file as well as the new name for the file. Erasing a file requires only that you enter the name of the file to be erased.

General Programming Techniques: Strings, Recursion, and Files

Using Strings in Turbo Pascal
Using Recursion in Turbo Pascal
DOS Devices

A carpenter can build many houses of different shapes and sizes using the same tools and techniques. Like carpenters, programmers use the same tools over and over to perform common programming tasks. A well-stocked programming toolbox is a sure sign of an experienced programmer. This chapter introduces several useful tools that can make your programming easier and better.

Using Strings in Turbo Pascal

The Turbo Pascal **String** data type (which is described in Chapter 5) is a powerful and frequently used data structure. While it is most commonly used to hold words and messages, a string can perform far more interesting tasks.

As you may recall, a string consists of a length byte followed by as many bytes as are defined in the string declaration. For example, **String[4]** declares a 5-byte data type: one length byte followed by four character bytes.

One of the reasons that the **String** type is so powerful is that it can be processed in two different ways: by directly manipulating its individual elements or by using one of the Turbo Pascal standard functions and procedures for strings. Both methods (each of which are discussed in this chapter) have advantages, depending on the circumstances.

Standard Procedures and Functions for Strings

Because they require a great many character manipulations, string-handling procedures are sometimes difficult to write. Turbo Pascal eliminates the need to write these character-by- character manipulations by providing powerful standard functions, making string manipulation an easy job.

Chr

The standard function **Chr** accepts an **Integer** parameter and returns its equivalent ASCII value. For example, because ASCII code 65 represents the character "A," the statement **Chr(65)** returns **A**.

While it is not a **String** procedure, the **Chr** function is frequently used with **String** statements, especially those with unusual characters. For example, the following program writes out a string with a double exclamation point, a character represented by ASCII code 19.

```
Program DoubleExclamation;
Uses CRT;
Var
   s : String[20];
Begin
ClrScr;
s := 'Wow' + Chr(19);
WriteLn(s);
WriteLn;
Write('Press ENTER...');
ReadLn;
End.
```

Upcase

Upcase, another character-level function, accepts a single lowercase alphabetic character from a to z and returns its uppercase equivalent. If the character is not lowercase and alphabetic, **Upcase** returns the character unchanged.

Concat

Concatenation is the combination of several strings into a single string. Turbo Pascal offers two ways to concatenate strings: **Concat** and the **Plus** (+) operator.

The standard function **Concat** accepts any number of strings as parameters and returns them as one string. This program shows how to use this function:

```
Program Concatenate;
Uses CRT;
Var
   s1,s2,s3 : String[80];
Begin
ClrScr;
s1 := 'This is the beginning -';
s2 := '- This is the end.';
s3 := Concat(s1,s2);
WriteLn(s3);
WriteLn;
Write('Press ENTER...');
ReadLn;
End.
```

In this example, strings **s1** and **s2** are passed into **Concat**, where they are combined and assigned to **s3**. When **s3** is written out, the message displayed is

This is the beginning -- This is the end.

Most programmers prefer to use the + operator to concatenate their strings, primarily because it is simpler to use and produces more readable code, as shown here:

```
Program Concat;
Uses CRT;
Var
   s1,s2,s3,s4: String[80];
Begin
ClrScr;
s1 := 'This is ';
s2 := 'all one ';
s3 := 'sentence.';

s4 := s1 + s2 + s3;
WriteLn(s4);
WriteLn;
Write('Press ENTER...');
ReadLn;
End.
```

The statement

```
s4 := s1 + s2 + s3;
```

produces the same result as

```
s4 := Concat(s1,s2,s3);
```

but the **+** operator is cleaner looking and easier to type.

With both **Concat** and the **+** operator, the concatenated string is truncated when the total length of the concatenated strings exceeds the maximum length of the receiving string.

Copy

The standard function **Copy** extracts a substring from a larger string. To use **Copy**, you must know where in the larger string you want to start copying and how many characters you want to copy. For example, the statement **Copy(s,12,3)** tells Turbo Pascal to return three characters from string **s** starting with character 12.

The following program uses the **Copy** function to write a long string as a column ten characters wide.

```
Program DoCopy;
Uses CRT;
Var
  s : String[80];
  i : Integer;

Begin
ClrScr;
s :=
'This is a long line that will be written out in a column.';
i := 1;
While i < Length(s) Do
  Begin
  WriteLn(Copy(s,i,10));
  i := i + 10;
  End;
WriteLn;
Write('Press ENTER...');
ReadLn;
End.
```

When you run this program, the output looks like this:

```
This is a
long line
that will
be written
 out in a
column.
```

Each line in the output, except the last line, contains ten characters, including blank characters. The last line contains only seven characters because this is all that remained at the end of the sentence. If you attempt to copy beyond the end of the string, you get either a partial result or no characters at all, but Turbo Pascal does not generate an error.

Delete

The **Delete** procedure removes characters from a string. As with **Copy**, you must specify the starting point in the string and the number of characters to delete. For example, the statement **Delete(s,5,3)** tells Turbo Pascal to delete three characters from string **s** starting at the fifth character.

Insert

The **Insert** procedure inserts a substring into another string. Three parameters are passed into **Insert**: the substring to insert, the string into which the substring will be inserted, and the position of the insertion. For example, the statement **Insert(s1,s2,4)** tells Turbo Pascal to insert string **s1** into **s2** starting at the fourth character. This sample program illustrates both **Delete** and **Insert**:

```
Program TestInsert;
Uses CRT;
Var
  s1,s2 : String[80];

Begin
ClrScr;
s1 := 'A';
s2 := '1234567890';
WriteLn('Insert ',s1,' into ',s2);
Insert(s1,s2,3);
WriteLn(s2);
WriteLn('Remove ',s1,' from ',s2);
Delete(s2,3,1);
```

```
WriteLn(s2);
WriteLn;
Write('Press ENTER...');
ReadLn;
End.
```

This program displays the string '12A34567890', showing that "A" has been inserted into the third character in the string. The statement **Delete(s2,3,1)** then removes the "A" from the string and displays it once again.

Length

The standard function **Length** returns the number of characters currently held in a **String** variable. Thus, if a string **s** is equal to 'This is a string.   ', then **Length(s)** will be equal to 20. The blanks at the end of the string are counted as part of the string.

Pos

When you want to know if one string is contained in another, Turbo Pascal can tell you this with the standard function **Pos**. Consider the following example.

```
Program TestPos;
Uses CRT;
Var
  s : String[80];
Begin
ClrScr;
s := 'This is a test string';
WriteLn('The position of ''test'' in "',s,'" is: ',
        pos('test',s));
WriteLn('The position of ''TEST'' in "',s,'" is: ',
        pos('TEST',s));
WriteLn;
Write('Press ENTER...');
ReadLn;
End.
```

This program displays the following messages:

> The position of 'test' in "s" is: 11
> The position of 'TEST' in "s" is: 0

```
Var
   s : String[20];
```

Statement	Result
Str(10,s);	'10'
Str(10:4,s);	' 10'
Str(3.2,s);	' 3.2000000000E + 00'
Str(3.2:0,s);	'3.2E + 00'
Str(3.2:15:3,s);	' 3.200'

Figure 10-1.   Results of the Str procedure

The first message confirms that the word "test" is located at the 11th character of the larger string. The second message simply shows that **Pos** returns zero when a match is not found.

Str and Val

Str and **Val**, two closely related standard procedures, are frequently used in programs that process numerical input and output. **Str** converts a number into a string, and **Val** converts a string into a number.

Str makes two parameters: a number (**Integer** or **Real**) and a **String** variable. The number can be formatted according to Turbo Pascal conventions. Examples of **Str** statements and their results are shown in Figure 10-1.

The first **Str** statement—**Str(10,s)**—converts an **Integer** to a **String** with no formatting. The statement **Str(10:4,s)**, on the other hand, is formatted as right-justified in a field four spaces wide. The resulting string, therefore, consists of two blank characters before the number 10.

Formatting **Real** numbers is a bit more complicated. When a **Real** number is unformatted, **Str** produces a string inscientific notation. For example, the statement **Str(3.2,s)** sets **s** equal to ' 3.2000000000E + 00'. Note that a string begins with a blank character and contains all significant digits. If the number is negative, the leading blank is replaced with a minus sign.

If the **Real** is formatted to a field width of 0— **Str(3.2:0,s)**—the result is '3.2E + 00'. Only the essential digits are present, and no blanks are added to the string. The final example, **Str(3.2:15:3,s)**, creates a 15-character string with three decimal places: '   3.200'.

The **Val** procedure accepts three parameters: the string to convert into a number, the numeric variable to receive the value, and an **Integer** variable used to flag errors. The following sample program shows how to use the **Val** procedure:

```
Program StringToNumber;
Uses CRT;
Type
  MaxStr = String[20];
Var
  r : Real;
  code : Integer;

(*****************************************)

Procedure WriteNumber(s : MaxStr);
Begin
Val(s,r,code);
If code = 0 Then
  WriteLn(r:0:3)
Else
  WriteLn('Error in numeric conversion');
End;

(*****************************************)

Begin
ClrScr;
WriteLn('Below is the conversion of 123.23');
WriteNumber('123.23');
WriteLn;
WriteLn('Below is the conversion of s123.23');
WriteLn;
WriteNumber('s123.23');
WriteLn;
Write('Press ENTER...');
ReadLn;
End.
```

At the heart of the sample program is the statement **Val(s,r,code)**, which attempts to convert string **s** into a valid **Real** number. If **s** contains a valid number in the correct format, the conversion will be successful and **code** will set to zero; if **s** contains a nonnumeric character, **code** will be set to a nonzero value.

To be valid for numeric conversions, a string must meet these conditions:

1. It must contain a number in **Integer, Real,** or scientific notation.

Valid	Invalid	Reason
'12'	'1×2'	String contains nonnumeric character
'3.2E+100'	'3.2E+00 '	String contains a trailing blank character

Table 10-1.   Valid and Invalid Strings for Numeric Conversion

2. It must not contain any alphabetic or other characters not used in numeric representation. The "E" used in scientific notation is an exception.

3. It must not contain any trailing blanks—leading blanks are acceptable.

Table 10-1 shows examples of both valid and invalid strings for numeric conversion. As you can see, a string must be in a proper form before it can be converted.

A final point on converting strings to numbers: if you try to convert a string that contains a valid **Real** number (for example, 1.32) into an **Integer**, Turbo Pascal generates an error. The safest approach in such cases is to convert all numeric strings into **Real**s and then convert the **Real** to an **Integer** with the **Round** or **Trunc** functions.

Direct Manipulation of Characters

While the Turbo Pascal string procedures are powerful, they do have limitations. For example, to change a string to all uppercase characters, you must process the string yourself. This is not a difficult task; a string, after all, is nothing more than an array of characters with a length byte in position zero. The following program shows how you can process strings. It contains the function **UpCaseStr**, which accepts a string parameter, changes all lowercase letters to uppercase, and then returns the string.

```
Program UpperCase;
Uses CRT;
Type
  MaxStr = String[255];
Var
  s : MaxStr;

(*******************)

Function UpCaseStr(s : MaxStr) : MaxStr;
Var
  i,j : Integer;
Begin
j := ord(s[0]);
For i := 1 To j Do
  s[i] := Upcase(s[i]);
UpCaseStr := s;
End;

(*******************)

Begin
ClrScr;
s := 'abc';
WriteLn(s);
WriteLn('Change to upper case.');
WriteLn(UpCaseStr(s));
WriteLn;
Write('Press ENTER...');
ReadLn;
End.
```

The first statement in the function **UpCaseStr** is

```
j := ord(s[0]);
```

where **s** is defined as **String[255]**. But **s[0]** appears to be outside the range 1 .. 255. How can this be? Whatever their length, all strings have a character at position zero that contains the length of the string. The statement **ord(s[0])** converts that character into its equivalent byte value so that it can be assigned to the **Integer j**. The same thing could have been accomplished with the statement **j := Length(s)**.

The next part of the procedure processes the string from the first character to the last. A character that is referred to individually in a string (for example, **s[2]**) can be substituted for a variable of type **Char** in any expression. Thus, the **Upcase** procedure, which takes a parameter of type **Char**, can accept individual characters from a string.

```
For i := 1 to j Do
  s[i] := Upcase(s[i]);
```

When all characters in the string are uppercase, the function passes the altered string back to the program.

Manipulating the Length Byte

You can play some tricks with strings by altering the value of the length byte. This lets you lengthen or shorten a string without assigning a new value. For example, consider this block of code:

```
s := 'ABCDEFG';
s[0] := Chr(3);
WriteLn(s);
```

When the string 'ABCDEFG' is assigned to variable **s**, Turbo Pascal sets the length to ASCII code 7. The next line, however, changes the length byte to ASCII code 3. The **Chr** function is used because Turbo Pascal considers the length byte to be a character. Thus, when the statement **WriteLn(s)** is executed, the output is **ABC**. In Turbo Pascal, changing the length byte changes the string.

On the other hand, changing characters in the string directly does not change the length byte, as illustrated by this code segment:

```
s := 'ABC';
s[4] := 'D';
s[5] := 'E';
WriteLn(s);
```

The first statement assigns the string 'ABC' to the variable and sets the length byte to ASCII code 3. The next two statements change the value in positions 4 and 5 of the string, but this does not affect the length byte. Therefore, the statement **WriteLn(s)** displays **ABC**, not **ABCDE**.

Direct manipulation of strings has many practical uses, such as the creation of strings for special text displays. For example, the following program uses an 80-character string that contains the double horizontal line character (ASCII code 205) to split the screen in half:

```
Program SplitScreen;
Uses CRT;
Type
  MaxStr = String[255];
Var
  Divider : MaxStr;
```

```
Begin
ClrScr;
FillChar(Divider,Sizeof(Divider),205);
Divider[0] := Chr(80);

Gotoxy(1,14);
Write(Divider);

Gotoxy(1,7);
Write('This is the upper portion of the screen.');

Gotoxy(1,21);
Write('This is the lower portion of the screen.');
WriteLn;
Write('Press ENTER...');
ReadLn;
End.
```

The first statement in the procedure,

    FillChar(Divider,SizeOf(Divider),205);

fills the entire string, from position 0 to position 255, with the ASCII value 205. To make the string fill one line of the screen, however, the length byte must be 80. Therefore, the length byte is set to 80 with the statement

    Divider[0] := Chr(80);

Now the string can be written to the screen, providing an attractive divider. In other places in the program, you might want to use the same string, but in shorter lengths, perhaps only 10 or 20 characters. Just change the length byte according to your needs; you do not have to change the characters because they are already set properly.

Resolving Programming Problems with Strings

Now that you understand how to manipulate **String** variables, you can put them to use. The rest of this section is devoted to some of the more common programming problems that can be resolved by creatively using strings.

A Search and Replace Procedure

From their earliest days, microcomputers have been associated with word processing and text editing. It is not surprising, therefore, that

Turbo Pascal provides string procedures that closely resemble the features of a word processor. These procedures allow you to locate a combination of letters in a string, delete that combination, and replace it with another, as shown in the following example.

```
Program SearchAndReplace;
Uses CRT;
Var
  BigString : String[255];
  FindString,
  ReplaceString : String[20];
  i : Integer;

Begin
ClrScr;
FindString := 'Steve';
ReplaceString := 'John';
BigString :=
'Tell Steve to pay me the five dollars he owes me.';

WriteLn(BigString);
i := Pos(FindString,BigString);
Delete(BigString,i,Length(FindString));
Insert(ReplaceString,BigString,i);
WriteLn(BigString);
WriteLn;
Write('Press ENTER...');
ReadLn;
End.
```

This program uses four string procedures: **Pos**, **Delete**, **Insert**, and **Length**. The substring 'Steve' is contained in the larger string starting at the sixth character. Therefore, the statement

i := Pos(FindString,BigString);

assigns the value 6 to **i**.

Now that you know where in the larger string the substring is located, you can remove it with **Delete**. This is accomplished with the following statement:

Delete(BigString,i,Length(FindString));

Here the substring is the **String** variable **FindString**, which holds the value 'Steve'. The first parameter, **BigString**, contains **FindString**;

the second parameter, **i**, indicates the position of **FindString** in **Big-String**. **Length(FindString)**, the third parameter, uses the standard function **Length** to tell the program how many characters to delete.

Because **FindString** is equal to 'Steve', **Length(FindString)** is equal to 5. Thus, the **Delete** statement tells Turbo Pascal to delete five characters from **BigString**, starting with the sixth character.

Finally, the following statement inserts the second substring (**ReplaceString**) in **BigString** at exactly the same position as the other string.

```
Insert(ReplaceString,BigString,i);
```

This tells Turbo Pascal to insert **ReplaceString** into the **BigString** at position **i**.

Now that you know how the program works, you should be able to guess how it will look when it runs. The program first writes out **BigString** in its original form. It then substitutes 'John' for 'Steve' and writes **BigString** out again, as shown here:

```
Tell Steve to pay me the five dollars he owes me.
Tell John to pay me the five dollars he owes me.
```

Thus, by combining four of the string-processing procedures, you are able to perform a rather complex piece of programming with only a few lines of code.

Personalizing Messages

Obviously you cannot write a complete word processing program with these few functions. You can, however, put the search-and-replace principle to some clever uses. For example, suppose you want to add a personal touch to a program by inserting the user's name into some of the messages your computer displays. To do this, you need to know the user's name, in what strings it is to be inserted, and where it goes in those strings.

First, set a general rule: the @ character in a string indicates where the user's name should be placed. If the name is "John," the string 'Hello, @' would become 'Hello, John'. You can place the @

character anywhere you want the name to appear. The following sample program demonstrates how to do this:

```
Program InsertName;
Uses CRT;
Type
  Str255 = String[255];
Var
  Message1,
  Message2,
  Message3 : String[255];
  Name : String[20];

Function WriteMessage(s,Name : Str255) : Str255;
Var
  i : Integer;
Begin
i := Pos('@',s);
If i > 0 Then
  Begin
  Delete(s,i,1);
  Insert(Name,s,i);
  End;
WriteMessage := s;
End;

Begin
Message1 := 'Hello, @';
Message2 := 'This message is unchanged.';
Message3 := 'This message, @, has been changed.';

ClrScr;
Write('Enter your Name: ');
ReadLn(Name);

WriteLn(WriteMessage(Message1,Name));
WriteLn(WriteMessage(Message2,Name));
WriteLn(WriteMessage(Message3,Name));

WriteLn;
Write('Press ENTER...');
ReadLn;
End.
```

One problem with this program is that every time it encounters the @ character in a message, it replaces it with the user's name. For example, in the message 'This is the @ character, @.', you want the first @ to print as is and the second @ to change the individual's name. Unfortunately, **WriteMessage** will change the first @ and leave the second unchanged. Therefore, you should choose a character that will not be used in its literal form in messages.

Error-free Data Entry

Converting strings to numbers has one very important application: checking for errors in numbers entered by a user. For example, the code for a program that asks a user to enter his or her age may look like this:

```
Var
   Age : Integer;
Begin
Write('Enter age: ');
ReadLn(age);
End.
```

The problem with this code is that if a user enters invalid numbers or numbers with spaces, Turbo Pascal generates a run-time error and aborts the program. Avoid this situation by having the user enter the number into a string and then convert the string into a number. If the conversion fails, the user entered an invalid number, and you can ask for input again. The following program illustrates this method:

```
Program EnterNumber;
Uses CRT;
Var
  Age,Code : Integer;
  AgeString : String[10];
Begin
ClrScr;
  Repeat
  Write('Enter your age: ');
  ReadLn(AgeString);
  Val(AgeString,Age,Code);
  If Code <> 0 Then
    Write(^g);          (* Make the computer beep *)
  Until Code = 0;
WriteLn('Your age is : ',Age);
WriteLn;
Write('Press ENTER...');
ReadLn;
End.
```

In this example, when the user enters his or her age into the **String** variable **AgeString**, the program attempts to convert **AgeString** into the **Integer Age**. If the conversion fails, the **Integer** variable **Code** is set to a value other than zero. When this occurs, the program writes the character ^g, which makes the terminal beep, and continues the loop until the user enters a valid number.

Removing Blanks

As mentioned previously, blank characters at the end of a numeric string cause a numeric conversion to fail. The string ' 10 ', for example, cannot be converted to a numeric value unless the blank character at the end is removed. This can be accomplished with the procedure **Strip-Blanks,** as shown here:

```
Program NoBlanks;
Uses CRT;
Type
  MaxStr = String[255];
Var
  s : MaxStr;
  i,code : Integer;

(********************************)

Procedure StripBlanks(Var s: MaxStr);
Begin
While (s[Length(s)] = ' ') Do
  Delete(s,Length(s),1);
End;

(********************************)

Begin
ClrScr;

(* Note: Leading blanks do not *)
(* cause conversion problems.  *)

s := '    20    ';
WriteLn('String = <',s,'>');
StripBlanks(s);
WriteLn('String = <',s,'>');
Val(s,i,code);
WriteLn('Value is: ',i);
WriteLn;
Write('Press ENTER...');
ReadLn;
End.
```

This program passes a string into **StripBlanks** as a reference parameter, so whatever changes are made to the string are retained after the procedure ends. **StripBlanks** consists of a While-Do loop that controls a **Delete** statement:

```
While (s[Length(s)] = ' ') Do
    Delete(s,Length(s),1);
```

This loop removes blanks from the end of a string by repeatedly deleting the last character from the string: the statement **s[Length(s)]** points to the last character in the string, 's'. If the last character is blank, that character is removed with the **Delete** procedure.

These are just a few examples of how strings can be used to solve tricky programming problems. As you program, you will discover many more.

Using Recursion in Turbo Pascal

Recursion is a technique wherein a procedure, in the process of performing its tasks, makes calls to itself. How can a procedure make calls to itself? It is a difficult concept to grasp, even for experienced programmers. Recursion can best be described by the classic example, the *factorial function*. The factorial of **Integer n** is the cumulative product of all **Integer**s from 1 to **n**. For example, the factorial of 2 is 1 * 2, while the factorial of 3 is 1 * 2 * 3. The nonrecursive factorial function would be coded as follows:

```
Function Factorial(n : Integer) : Real;
Var
  r : Real;
  i : Integer;
Begin
r := 1;
For i := 2 To n Do
  r := r * i;
Factorial := r;
End;
```

The calculation in this nonrecursive example is straightforward: **r**, originally set equal to 1, is repeatedly multiplied by successive **Integer** values up to and including **n**. Compare this to this recursive version:

```
Function Factorial(n : Integer) : Real;
Begin
If n = 0 Then
  Factorial := 1
Else
  Factorial := n * Factorial(n-1);
End;
```

The recursive version works by repeatedly multiplying **n** by the factorial of the number just preceding it. While the recursive version is more elegant and intellectually appealing, most programmers find the nonrecursive version easier to understand and code. Which is better? That depends on several things.

On the negative side, recursive procedures have a major weak point: each time a procedure calls itself, Turbo Pascal must set up space on the stack for temporary storage. This not only slows a procedure's execution, but also increases the danger of using up the program's stack space, which could cause the program to crash.

On the other hand, some algorithms are so naturally adapted to a recursive structure that forcing them into a non-recursive form just does not make sense. A good example of such an algorithm is a function that evaluates a mathematical expression stored in a string. The following program shows how the recursive process follows the flow of the underlying algorithm. Study it carefully.

```
Program Calculator;
Uses CRT;
Type
  MaxCompStr = String[255];
Var
  i : Integer;
  Formula : String[80];
  p : Integer;
  Result : Real;
  Error : Boolean;

(********************)

Function Compute_Formula(Var p : Integer;
                            Strg : MaxCompStr;
                            Var Error : Boolean) : Real;

Var
  r : Real;
  i,
  BreakPoint : Integer;
  Ch : Char;

(*******************)

Procedure Eval(Var Formula : MaxCompStr;
                  Var Value : Real;
                  Var BreakPoint : Integer);
Const
  Numbers : Set Of Char = ['0'..'9','.'];
Var
  p,i : Integer;
  Ch : Char;
```

```
(********************)

Procedure NextP;
Begin
  Repeat
  p := p+1;
  If p <= Length(Formula) Then
    Ch := Formula[p]
  Else
    Ch := #13;
  Until (Ch <> ' ');
End;

(****************************************)

Function Expr : Real;
Var
  E : Real;
  Operator : Char;

(****************************************)

Function SmplExpr : Real;
Var
  S : Real;
  Operator : Char;

(****************************************)

Function Term : Real;
Var
  T : Real;

(****************************************)

Function S_Fact : Real;

(****************************************)

Function Fct : Real;
Var
  fn : String[20];
  l,start: Integer;
  F : Real;

(****************************************)

Procedure process_as_number;
Var
  code : Integer;
Begin
Start := p;
  Repeat
  NextP
  Until Not(Ch In Numbers);
If Ch = '.' Then
```

```
   Repeat
   NextP
   Until Not(Ch In Numbers);
If Ch = 'E' Then
   Begin
   NextP;
     Repeat
     NextP
     Until Not(Ch In Numbers);
   End;
Val(Copy(Formula, Start, p-Start), F, code);
End;

(****************************************)

Procedure process_as_new_Expr;
Begin
NextP;
F := Expr;
If Ch = ')' Then
   NextP
Else
   BreakPoint := p;
End;

(****************************************)

Procedure process_as_standard_Function;

(****************************************)

Function Fact(I : Integer) : Real;
Begin
If I > 0 Then
   Fact := I*Fact(I-1)
Else
   Fact := 1;
End;

(****************************************)

Begin
If Copy(Formula, p, 3) = 'ABS' Then
   Begin
   p := p + 2;
   NextP;
   F := Fct;
   f := Abs(f);
   End
Else If Copy(Formula, p, 4) = 'SQRT' Then
   Begin
   p := p + 3;
   NextP;
   F := Fct;
   f := Sqrt(f);
   End
Else If Copy(Formula, p, 3) = 'SQR' Then
```

```
       Begin
       p := p + 2;
       NextP;
       F := Fct;
       f := Sqr(f);
       End
     Else If Copy(Formula, p, 3) = 'SIN' Then
       Begin
       p := p + 2;
       NextP;
       F := Fct;
       f := Sin(f);
       End
     Else If Copy(Formula, p, 3) = 'COS' Then
       Begin
       p := p + 2;
       NextP;
       F := Fct;
       f := Cos(f);
       End
     Else If Copy(Formula, p, 6) = 'ARCTAN' Then
       Begin
       p := p + 5;
       NextP;
       F := Fct;
       f := ArcTan(f);
       End
     Else If Copy(Formula, p, 2) = 'LN' Then
       Begin
       p := p + 1;
       NextP;
       F := Fct;
       f := Ln(f);
       End
     Else If Copy(Formula, p, 3) = 'EXP' Then
       Begin
       p := p + 2;
       NextP;
       F := Fct;
       f := Exp(f);
       End
     Else If Copy(Formula, p, 4) = 'FACT' Then
       Begin
       p := p + 3;
       NextP;
       F := Fct;
       f := fact(Trunc(f));
       End
     Else
       Begin
       BreakPoint := p;
       End;
     End;
   End;

   (****************************************)
```

```
Begin (* process_as_standard_Function *)
If (Ch In Numbers) Then
  process_as_number
Else If (Ch = '(') Then
  process_as_new_Expr
Else
  process_as_standard_Function;
Fct := F;
End; (* process_as_standard_Function *)

(********************)

Begin
If Ch = '-' Then
  Begin
  NextP;
  S_Fact := -Fct;
  End
Else
  S_Fact := Fct;
End;

(********************)

Begin
T := S_Fact;
While Ch = '^' Do
  Begin
  NextP;
  t := Exp(Ln(t)*S_Fact)
  End;
Term := t;
End;

(********************)

Begin
s := term;
While Ch In ['*', '/'] Do
  Begin
  Operator := Ch;
  NextP;
    Case Operator Of
    '*' : s := s*term;
    '/' : s := s/term;
    End;
  End;
SmplExpr := s;
End;

(********************)

Begin
E := SmplExpr;
While Ch In ['+', '-'] Do
  Begin
  Operator := Ch;
```

```
  NextP;
    Case Operator Of
    '+' : e := e+SmplExpr;
    '-' : e := e-SmplExpr;
    End;
  End;
Expr := E;
End;

(********************)

Begin
For i := 1 To Length(Formula) Do
  Formula[i] := Upcase(Formula[i]);
If Formula[1] = '.' Then Formula := '0'+Formula;
If Formula[1] = '+' Then Delete(Formula, 1, 1);
p := 0;
NextP;
Value := Expr;

If Ch = #13 Then
  Error := False
Else
  Error := True;
BreakPoint := p;
End;

(********************)

Begin
Eval(Strg, r, p);
Compute_Formula := r;
End;

(********************)

Begin
ClrScr;
  Repeat
  Write('Enter Formula: ');
  Read(Formula);
  If Formula <> '' Then
    Begin
    Result := Compute_Formula(p,Formula,Error);
    If Error Then
      Begin
      WriteLn;
      WriteLn('Error!');
      WriteLn(Formula);
      For i := 1 To p-1 Do Write(' ');
      WriteLn('^');
      End
    Else
      WriteLn(' = ',Result:0:2);
    End;
  ReadLn;
  Until Formula = '';
End.
```

When you run this program, you will be asked to enter an equation, which the program stores in a string and passes to the function **Compute_Formula**. This function evaluates the equation through a series of recursive calls. If successful, the result is passed back to the program; if not, the Boolean parameter **Error** is set to TRUE, and the **Integer** parameter **p** indicates the point in the string at which the error was detected.

Coding this same procedure in a nonrecursive manner is possible, but given the nature of the algorithm, which lends itself to the recursive approach, it is undesirable.

DOS Devices

In Turbo Pascal, all input and output are performed using devices such as a keyboard, a monitor, or a disk file. To make things easier, Turbo Pascal lets you treat all devices as files. This allows you to treat all input and output uniformly, making your programming much easier.

All input and output in a program normally are performed using DOS devices. A DOS device is an input or output device that DOS is designed to handle. This includes keyboards, disk drives, and video monitors. Some devices, such as optical disks, tape backup units, mice, and other specialized equipment, are not supported by DOS and require their own *device drivers* to make them work with DOS. Writing device drivers is an advanced topic outside the range of this book, but every programmer should know how to use DOS devices.

The Standard Input and Output Devices

While all input and output in Turbo Pascal are performed through devices, you are not always aware of it. For example, the statement **ReadLn(s)** tells Turbo Pascal to accept input from the *standard input device*. Likewise, the statement **WriteLn(s)** indicates output using the *standard output device*.

The name of the standard output device is CON, as in console, and refers to the video display. The standard input device is also CON, but refers not to the screen, but to the keyboard. The following program demonstrates how the CON device can be used for input and output much like a disk file.

```
Program DeviceTest;
Uses CRT;
Var
  f : Text;
  s : String;
Begin
ClrScr;
Assign(f,'CON');
Rewrite(f);
WriteLn(f,'Output to CON');
WriteLn;

WriteLn('Enter string using ReadLn(s)');
Write('Type a string. Press ENTER when done: ');
ReadLn(s);
WriteLn('>',s);

Assign(f,'CON');
Reset(f);
WriteLn('Enter string from CON using ReadLn(f,s)');
Write('Type a string. Press ENTER when done: ');
ReadLn(f,s);
WriteLn('>',s);

WriteLn;
Write('Press ENTER...');
ReadLn;
End.
```

Notice that the CON device can be used with the **Reset** or **Rewrite** procedures, just like a disk file. In fact, the standard input and output devices use the same file handles used by disk files.

Printer Devices

DOS supports various printer devices: PRN, LPT1, LPT2, and LPT3. (LPT1 and PRN refer to the same device.) Most people use only one printer, and so use only LPT1 and PRN devices. Naturally, printers are used for output only. If you try to use **Reset** on a printer device, Turbo Pascal will generate an immediate end of file (the **Eof** function will return TRUE).

Turbo Pascal also offers another way to route output to the printer: the **PRINTER** unit. This unit declares a text-file variable name **Lst**, which directs output to the printer. This brief program demonstrates how the LST device is used:

```
Program TestPrt;
Uses Printer;
Begin
WriteLn(Lst,'ABC');
End.
```

Serial Devices

Most computers have serial ports, which they use for printers, modems, local area networks, and other communications purposes. Turbo Pascal supports two DOS serial devices: COM1 and COM2. In addition, Turbo Pascal supports an AUX (for auxiliary) device, which is the same as COM1.

While these devices make it easy to send and receive data through serial ports, they are far too limited for most purposes. Communications programs, for example, usually need to bypass DOS devices and go directly to the serial port.

The NUL Device

Turbo Pascal recognizes one more device; the NUL device. This device is special because it ignores everything you send to it. You might wonder what use such a device could possibly have. Generally, you will use the NUL device when you are programming an output function, but don't actually want to send out any data.

Merging, Sorting, and Searching

Merging
Sorting Methods
Searching Methods

Some programming tasks are so common that over the years standardized, highly efficient algorithms have been developed to take care of them. Searching, sorting, and merging are three of the most common, turning up in nearly every book on computer programming. While entire books have been devoted to these subjects, this chapter touches on only the most practical algorithms and how they are used in Turbo Pascal.

Merging

Merging files refers to the process by which two ordered files are combined to form one large ordered file. For example, a master file of historical transactions might be updated by merging a file of daily transactions into it. Both files must be ordered in the same way (for example, by date or account number); the updated file then becomes the master file that will be updated the next day.

Of course, you could add the daily file to the end of the historical file and sort the whole thing at one time, but sorting takes far longer than merging.

The merge process is straightforward. It starts by reading the first record from each file, after which the program enters a loop. Inside the loop, the program compares the two records and writes the one with the lower value to the newly created file. Another record is then read from the input file.

This process continues until all records in one or both files have been processed. Usually, one of the input files runs out of records before the other. When this occurs, the procedure continues to read records from the remaining file and write them to the newly created file.

This process is illustrated in Figure 11-1, where two input files of integers are merged. File 1 contains three integer records—1, 4, and 6—and File 2 contains four integer records— 2, 3, 7, and 9. The procedure reads and compares the first records from File 1 and from File 2. The record from File 1 is then written to the merged file because it is lower in value than the record from File 2.

The procedure then reads a new record from File 1 and compares it to the record already in Record 2. Record 1 has a greater value than the value already in Record 2. Therefore, Record 2 is written to the merged file and another record is read from File 2.

	File 1	**File 2**
	1	2
	4	3
	6	7
		9

Step 1:	record 1 = 1	record 2 = 2 → Write record 1
Step 2:	Read a new record 1	
Step 3:	record 1 = 4	record 2 = 2 → Write record 2
Step 4:	Read a new record 2	
Step 5:	record 1 = 4	record 2 = 3 → Write record 2
Step 6:	Read a new record 2	
Step 7:	record 1 = 4	record 2 = 7 → Write record 1
Step 8:	Read a new record 1	
Step 9:	record 1 = 6	record 2 = 7 → Write record 1
Step 10:	Read a new record 1—end of file	
Step 11:	record 1 = EOF	record 2 = 7 → Write record 2
Step 12:	Read a new record 2	
Step 13:	record 1 = EOF	record 2 = 9 → Write record 2
Step 14:	Read a new record 2—end of file	
Step 15:	Both input files are EOF: Procedure ends	

Figure 11-1.   Merging two sorted files

This process continues until the procedure reaches the end of File 1, at which point the procedure reads all the records remaining in File 2 and writes them to the merge file. The procedure ends when it reaches the end of File 2.

While the merge procedure is simple in concept, it is not so simple to express in Turbo Pascal. The major complexity is in determining when a new record is needed from an input file and when an input file is empty. In the following program, input is controlled through two Boolean functions, **GetItem1** and **GetItem2**:

```
Program MergeTest;
Uses CRT;
Type
  Str80 = String[80];

Var
  File1,
  File2,
  File3 : Str80;

(*************************************)

Procedure Merge(Fname1,Fname2,Fname3 : Str80);
Var
  ok1,ok2 : Boolean;
  f1,f2,f3 : Text;
  i1,i2 : Integer;

(*************************************)

Function GetItem1(Var i : Integer) : Boolean;
Begin
If Not Eof(f1) Then
  Begin
  ReadLn(f1,i);
  GetItem1 := True;
  End
Else
  GetItem1 := False;
End;

(*************************************)

Function GetItem2(Var i : Integer) : Boolean;
Begin
If Not Eof(f2) Then
  Begin
  ReadLn(f2,i);
  GetItem2 := True;
  End
Else
```

```
      GetItem2 := False;
End;

(*************************************)

Begin
Assign(f1,Fname1);
Reset(f1);
Assign(f2,Fname2);
Reset(f2);
Assign(f3,Fname3);
Rewrite(f3);

ok1 := GetItem1(i1);
ok2 := GetItem2(i2);

While ok1 Or ok2 Do
  Begin
  (* If ok1 is true, then a record from File 1 is present. *)
  (* If ok2 is true, then a record from File 2 is present. *)

  If ok1 And ok2 Then      (* records are present *)
    Begin                  (* from both files.    *)
    If i1 < i2 Then
      Begin
      WriteLn(f3,i1);
      ok1 := GetItem1(i1);
      End
    Else
      Begin
      WriteLn(f3,i2);
      ok2 := GetItem2(i2);
      End;
    End
  Else If ok1 Then      (* a record is present from *)
    Begin               (* the first file only.     *)
    WriteLn(f3,i1);
    ok1 := GetItem1(i1);
    End
  Else If ok2 Then      (* a record is present from *)
    Begin               (* the second file only.    *)
    WriteLn(f3,i2);
    ok2 := GetItem2(i2);
    End;
  End;

Close(f1);
Close(f2);
Close(f3);
End;

(*************************************)

Begin
ClrScr;
Write('Enter name of first file: ');
```

```
ReadLn(File1);
Write('Enter name of second file: ');
ReadLn(File2);
Write('Enter name of merged file: ');
ReadLn(File3);
Merge(file1,file2,file3);
End.
```

GetItem1 and **GetItem2** read the next record from their respective files. If successful, they return the value TRUE along with the record read; if unsuccessful (that is, if it reaches the end of the file), they return FALSE. By isolating the input process in these two functions, the structure of the merge procedure is simplified.

When the procedure **Merge** begins, the Boolean variables **ok1** and **ok2** are set with **GetItem1** and **GetItem2**. The loop controlled by the statement

While ok1 Or ok2 Do

executes as long as records are present from either file and terminates when the end is reached for both files.

Three program branches are contained in the **While-Do** loop. The first is executed when input from both files is present. In this case, the procedure compares the two records, the record with the lower value is written to the merge file, and another record is read in.

The two other branches execute when one of the input files reaches its end. When this occurs, the loop continues to read records from the remaining file and write them to the merged file. When the procedure reaches the end of the remaining file, the input files and the merged file are closed and the procedure ends.

Sorting Methods

Although many sorting algorithms have been developed over the years, three are the most frequently used: the bubble sort, the shell sort, and the quick sort.

The *bubble sort* is easy to write but terribly slow. The *shell sort* is moderately fast, but excels in its use of memory resources. The *quick sort*, the fastest of the three, requires extensive stack space for recursive calls. Knowing all three algorithms, and understanding why one is better than another, is important and illustrates the subtleties of good programming.

General Sorting Principles

The sorting algorithms presented in this section compare one element in an array to another, and, if the two elements are out of order, the algorithms switch their order in the array. This process is illustrated in this code segment:

```
If a[i] > a[i+1] Then
  Begin
  temp := a[i];
  a[i] := a[i+1];
  a[i+1] := temp;
  End;
```

The first line of code tests if two elements of the array are out of order. Generally, arrays are in order when the current element is smaller than the next element. If the elements are not properly ordered, that is, when the current element is greater than the next element, their order is switched. The switch requires a temporary storage variable of the same type as that of the elements in the array being sorted.

The main difference between the three sorting algorithms is the method by which array elements are selected for comparison. The comparison method has a tremendous impact on the efficiency of the sort. For example, the bubble sort, which compares only adjacent array elements, may require half a million comparisons to sort an array, while the quick sort requires only three or four thousand.

Bubble Sort

To computer programmers, there are good methods, there are bad methods, and there are kludges. A kludge is a method that works, but slowly and inefficiently. The bubble sort is a good example of a kludge: given enough time, it will sort your data, but you might have to wait a day or two.

The bubble-sort alogorithm is simple: it starts at the end of the array to be sorted and works toward the beginning of the array. The procedure compares each element to the one preceding it. If the elements are out of order, they are switched. The procedure continues until it reaches the beginning of the array.

Because the sort works backward through the array, comparing each adjacent pair of elements, the lowest element will always "float" to the top after the first pass. After the second pass, the second lowest element will "float" to the second position in the array, and so on, until the algorithm has passed through the array once for every element in the array.

This code shows this process in Turbo Pascal:

```
For i := 2 To n Do
For j := n DownTo i Do
  If a[j-1] > a[j] Then
    Switch(a[j],a[j-1]);
```

As you can see, the bubble-sort algorithm is compact; in fact, it is a single Turbo Pascal statement. The bubble sort receives two inputs: **a**, the array to be sorted, and **n**, the number of elements in the array. The inside loop, controlled by the statement

For j := n DownTo i Do

performs all the comparisons in each pass through the array. The outside loop, controlled by the statement

For i := 2 To n Do

determines the number of passes to execute. Notice that **j** executes from the end of the array (**n**) to **i** and that **i** decreases after every pass. Thus, each pass through the array becomes shorter as the bubble sort executes.

An example of how the bubble sort works is shown in Figure 11-2. An array of 10 integers is sorted in order of increasing value. The elements of the array are listed at the end of each pass. A pass consists of one complete execution of the inside **For-Do** loop.

The order of the original array is shown in the row labeled "Start." The values range from 0 to 92, and they are distributed randomly

Pass	Position in Array									
	1	2	3	4	5	6	7	8	9	10
Start:	91	6	59	0	75	0	48	92	30	83
1	0	91	6	59	0	75	30	48	92	83
2	0	0	91	6	59	30	75	48	83	92
3	0	0	6	91	30	59	48	75	83	92
4	0	0	6	30	91	48	59	75	83	92
5	0	0	6	30	48	91	59	75	83	92
6	0	0	6	30	48	59	91	75	83	92
7	0	0	6	30	48	59	75	91	83	92
8	0	0	6	30	48	59	75	83	91	92
9	0	0	6	30	48	59	75	83	91	92

Figure 11-2.   Sorting an array of integers with the bubble-sort algorithm

throughout the array. The first pass through the array places the lowest value (0) in the first position in the array, and the number 91 is shifted from the first position into the second position. The other elements are still more or less randomly scattered.

With each step of the bubble sort, the next lowest number takes its proper place in the array, and the higher numbers get shifted to the right. By the end of the eighth pass, the array is completely sorted, yet the sort continues to make one more pass over the array.

The following program contains the bubble-sort algorithm, which takes an **Integer** array and the number of elements in the array as parameters:

```
Program BubbleTest;
Type
  Int_Arr = Array [1..10] Of Integer;
Var
  i : Integer;
  a : Int_Arr;

(*****************************************)

Procedure Bubble(Var a : Int_Arr;
                 n : Integer);
Var
  i,j : Integer;

(*****************************************)

Procedure Switch(Var a,b : Integer);
Var
  c : Integer;
Begin
c := a;
a := b;
b := c;
End;

(*****************************************)

Begin
For i := 2 To n Do
For j := n DownTo i Do
  If a[j-1] > a[j] Then
    Switch(a[j],a[j-1]);
End;

(*****************************************)

Begin
a[1]  := 91;
a[2]  := 06;
a[3]  := 59;
a[4]  := 0;
a[5]  := 75;
a[6]  := 0;
a[7]  := 48;
a[8]  := 92;
a[9]  := 30;
a[10] := 83;
```

```
For i := 1 To 10 Do
  Write(a[i]:4);
WriteLn;
Bubble(a,10);

For i := 1 To 10 Do
  Write(a[i]:4);

WriteLn;
Write('Press ENTER...');
ReadLn;
End.
```

The program begins by assigning random values to array **a,** and displays the values on your terminal. The procedure **Bubble** sorts the array. When the sort is finished, the array is displayed again.

The weakness of the bubble sort is that it compares only adjacent array elements. If the sorting algorithm first compared elements separated by a wide interval, and then focused on progressively smaller intervals, the process would be more efficient. This train of thought led to the development of the shell-sort and quick-sort algorithms.

Shell Sort

The shell sort is far more efficient than the bubble sort. It first puts elements approximately where they will be in the final order and determines their exact placement later. The strength of the algorithm lies in the method it uses to estimate an element's approximate final position.

The key concept in the shell sort is the *gap,* which is the distance between the elements compared. If the gap is 5, the first element is compared with the sixth element, the second with the seventh, and so on. In a single pass through the array, all elements within the gap are put in order. For example, the elements in this array are in order given a gap of 2:

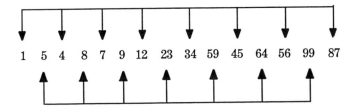

As you can see, the array is nearly completely sorted before the algorithm tests adjacent elements. In the next pass over this array, the gap is reduced to 1, which results in a completely sorted array. The initial value of the gap is arbitrary, although it is common to set it to one half the number of elements in the array (that is, **n div 2**).

The many versions of the shell sort vary in complexity and efficiency. The version presented in this chapter is extremely efficient, requiring few passes to complete the sort.

Unfortunately, there is no simple way to describe how this particular shell algorithm works. Efficient algorithms tend to be more complex than inefficient ones and are therefore harder to express in words. This is why poor algorithms are used so often. Figure 11-3 contains the essential code for the shell-sort algorithm. Review this code as you read the explanation.

The first line in the procedure sets the gap to **n div 2**. The outside loop in the shell sort, controlled by the statement

While (gap > 0) Do

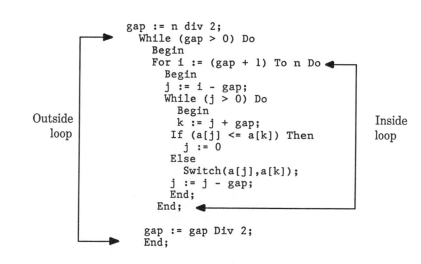

```
gap := n div 2;
   While (gap > 0) Do
      Begin
      For i := (gap + 1) To n Do
         Begin
         j := i - gap;
         While (j > 0) Do
            Begin
            k := j + gap;
            If (a[j] <= a[k]) Then
               j := 0
            Else
               Switch(a[j],a[k]);
            j := j - gap;
            End;
         End;

   gap := gap Div 2;
   End;
```

Outside loop

Inside loop

Figure 11-3.   The main loops in the shell-sort algorithm

determines the number of passes made through the array. After each pass through the array, the gap is reduced by half for each pass until the gap reaches 0. For example, if there were ten elements in the array, the first gap would be 5, followed by 2, 1, and 0. Because **Integer** division is used, **1 div 2** results in 0.

In each pass, three variables determine which elements to compare: **i**, **j**, and **k**. The variable **i** points to the far element, and **j** points to the near element. For example, if the **gap** is 5, **i** will equal 6 and **j** will equal 1. Before the comparison, **k** is set equal to **j + gap**, which, for the first comparison, equals **i**.

The comparison uses **k** instead of **i** because it may be necessary to backtrack through the array. To backtrack, **j** is reduced by **gap** and **k** is also changed so that a new pair of elements is compared. Because **i** controls the inside loop, it should not be changed in this backtracking process.

Consider the example in Figure 11-4 where a ten-element array is being sorted. At step 1, **gap** is 2, **j** is equal to 6, and **k** is equal to 8.

	Position in Array									
	1	2	3	4	5	6	7	8	9	10
Step 1:	19	9	32	63	86	85	87	49	35	86
						↑ j		↑ k		
Step 2:	19	9	32	63	86	49	87	85	35	86
				↑ j		↑ k				
Step 3:	19	9	32	49	86	63	87	85	35	86
		↑ j		↑ k						
Step 4:	19	9	32	49	86	63	87	85	35	86
							↑ j		↑ k	

Figure 11-4.   Sorting an array of integers with the shell-sort algorithm

Thus, the sixth and eighth elements in the array will be compared. Since element 6 is 85 and element 8 is 49, the two must be switched, as is shown in step 2.

Next, the algorithm sets **j** equal to **j − gap**, in this case 4. Since **j** is greater than zero, the inside loop executes again. Because **j** has been reduced by 2, the fourth and sixth elements are compared. Again, the elements are out of order and need to be switched. As before, **j** is set to **j − gap**, or 2, leading to step 3.

Elements 2 and 4 of the array are in the correct order, so rather than switching the elements, the program sets **j** to zero. Now, the result of **j − gap** is negative 2. Since this is less than zero, the inner loop is terminated and **i** is incremented. Working downward, **j** is set to **i − gap**, or 7, and **k** is set equal to **j + gap**, or 9.

In short, **i** keeps track of the overall flow of the algorithm, while **k** backtracks when necessary. This tricky bit of logic increases the efficiency by about 300% over the most simple shell sort.

The following sample program includes the procedure **Shell**, which contains the shell-sort algorithm.

```
Program ShellTest;
Uses CRT;
Type
  Int_Arr = Array [1..10] of Integer;
Var
  i : Integer;
  a : Int_Arr;

(*****************************)

Procedure Shell(Var a : Int_arr;
                    n : Integer);
Var
  gap,i,j,k,x : Integer;

(*****************************)

Procedure Switch(var a,b : Integer);
Var
  c : Integer;
Begin
c := a;
a := b;
b := c;
End;

(*****************************)
```

```
Begin
gap := n div 2;
While (gap > 0) Do
  Begin
  For i := (gap + 1) To n Do
    Begin
    j := i - gap;
    While (j > 0) Do
      Begin
      k := j + gap;
      If (a[j] <= a[k]) Then
        j := 0
      Else
        Begin
        Switch(a[j],a[k]);
        j := j - gap;
        End;
      End;
    End;

  gap := gap Div 2;
  End;
End;

(**********************)
Begin
ClrScr;
a[1] := 19;
a[2] := 9;
a[3] := 32;
a[4] := 63;
a[5] := 86;
a[6] := 85;
a[7] := 87;
a[8] := 49;
a[9] := 35;
a[10] := 86;

For i := 1 To 10 Do
  Write(a[i]:4);
WriteLn;

Shell(a,10);

For i := 1 To 10 Do
  Write(a[i]:4);
WriteLn;
Write('Press ENTER...');
ReadLn;
End.
```

Shell accepts the array to be sorted, including the number of elements in the array, and then returns the array in its sorted form. If you test this program against the bubble sort with an array of 1,000 elements, you will see an amazing difference in the time required to sort the array. Yet as efficient as the shell sort is, the quick sort is two or three times as efficient.

Quick Sort

The queen of all sorting algorithms is the quick sort: this algorithm is widely accepted as the fastest general-purpose sort available.

One of the pleasing aspects of the quick sort is that it sorts things in much the same way people do. It first creates large "piles," and then sorts those piles into smaller and smaller piles, eventually ending up with a completely sorted array.

The quick-sort algorithm begins by estimating a midrange value for the array. If the array consists of numbers 1 through 10, the midpoint could be 5 or 6. The midpoint's exact value is not crucial; the algorithm will work with a midpoint of any value. However, the closer the estimated midpoint is to the true midpoint of the array, the faster the sort.

The procedure calculates a midpoint by averaging the first and last elements in the portion of the array being sorted. Once the procedure selects a midpoint, it puts all the elements lower than the midpoint in the lower part of the array, and all the elements higher in the upper part. This is illustrated in Figure 11-5.

	Mid-Point	Position in Array									
		1	2	3	4	5	6	7	8	9	10
Step 1:	55	86	3	10	23	12	67	59	47	31	24
Step 2:	35	24	3	10	23	12	31	47	59	67	86
Step 3:	27	24	3	10	23	12	31	47	59	67	86
Step 4:	18	24	3	10	23	12	31	47	59	67	86
Step 5:	11	12	3	10	23	24	31	47	59	67	86
Step 6:	6	10	3	12	23	24	31	47	59	67	86
Step 7:	23	3	10	12	23	24	31	47	59	67	86
Step 8:	72	3	10	12	23	24	31	47	59	67	86
Step 9:	63	3	10	12	23	24	31	47	59	67	86
Final order:		3	10	12	23	24	31	47	59	67	86

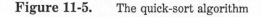

Figure 11-5.   The quick-sort algorithm

In step 1, the midpoint is 55, which is the average of 86 and 24. In step 2, the segment being sorted is 24 through 47, leading to a midpoint of 35. Notice that the elements in the segment rarely split evenly around the midpoint. This does not harm the algorithm, but does decrease its efficiency somewhat.

At each step in the process, the quick sort orders the elements of an array segment around the midpoint value. As the segments get smaller and smaller, the array approaches the completely sorted order.

In this program, the procedure **Quick** contains the quick-sort algorithm:

```
Program QuickTest;
Uses CRT;
Type
  Int_Arr = Array [1..10] Of Integer;
Var
  InFile : Text;
  i : Integer;
  a : Int_Arr;

(*****************************)

Procedure Quick(Var item : Int_Arr; count : integer);

(*****************************)

Procedure PartialSort(left, right : Integer;
                      Var a: Int_Arr);
Var
  ii,
  ll,rl,
  i,j,k : Integer;

(*****************************)

Procedure Switch(Var a,b : Integer);
Var
  c : Integer;
Begin
If a <> b Then
  Begin
  c := a;
  a := b;
  b := c;
  End;
End;

(*****************************)

Begin
k := (a[left] + a[right]) Div 2;
i := left;
```

```
  j := right;
   Repeat

   While a[i] < k Do
     Inc(i,1);

   While k < a[j] Do
     Dec(j,1);

   If i <= j Then
     Begin
     Switch(a[i],a[j]);
     Inc(i,1);
     Dec(j,1);
     End;
   Until i > j;

If left < j Then
  PartialSort(left,j,a);
If i < right Then
  PartialSort(i,right,a);
End;

(**********************)

Begin
PartialSort(1,count,item);
End;

(**********************)

Begin
ClrScr;
a[1] := 86;
a[2] := 3;
a[3] := 10;
a[4] := 23;
a[5] := 12;
a[6] := 67;
a[7] := 59;
a[8] := 47;
a[9] := 31;
a[10] := 24;

For i := 1 To 10 Do
  Write(a[i]:4);
WriteLn;

Quick(a,10);

For i := 1 To 10 Do
  Write(a[i]:4);
WriteLn;
Write('Press ENTER...');
ReadLn;
End.
```

The procedure begins by calling the subprocedure **PartialSort**, which takes three parameters: the lower bound of the array segment, the upper bound, and the array itself. When first called, the lower bound passed to **PartialSort** is 1, and the upper bound is the number of elements in the array.

PartialSort computes a midpoint and orders the elements in the array segment accordingly. It then calls itself by passing new lower and upper boundaries, thereby focusing on progressively smaller segments of the array. When it reaches the lowest level of the array, the recursion ends, and the procedure passes the sorted array back to the program.

Comparing Sorting Algorithms

The number of comparisons required to sort a list is the universal measure by which all sorting algorithms are judged. The number of comparisons is expressed as a multiple of the number of elements in the list. For example, if you are sorting an array of n elements with the bubble sort, the program will have to perform $1/2(n^2-n)$ comparisons. If n is 100, the number of comparisons is 4950.

This benchmark is fine for those with a theoretical bent, but most programmers find it easier to compare sorting methods by measuring the amount of time it takes for each method to sort the same array. Table 11-1 shows the results of tests performed using the bubble-sort, shell-sort, and quick-sort algorithms on arrays with 100, 500, and 1000 random numbers. As the table shows, the bubble sort is a poor algorithm compared to the shell and quick sorts, taking from 6 to 68 times as long to sort an array. Between the shell sort and quick sort, the difference in time is also significant. The shell sort takes twice as long as the quick sort and requires nearly four times as many comparisons.

	Bubble		Shell		Quick	
N	*Time*	*Comparisons*	*Time*	*Comparisons*	*Time*	*Comparisons*
100	0.66	4,950	0.11	849	0.06	232
500	15.88	124,750	0.77	5,682	0.44	1473
1000	63.66	499,500	1.87	13,437	0.93	3254

Table 11-1.   Relative Efficiency of Different Sorting Methods

The only drawback to the quick sort is the amount of space it requires on the stack. Because quick sort is a recursive procedure, space on the stack must be allocated every time the procedure calls itself. If you are concerned about stack space, you might want to use the shell sort: otherwise, use the quick sort.

Searching Methods

In programming, *searching* means finding a particular item within a group of items, for example, finding a particular **Integer** in an array of **Integer**s, finding a person's name in an array of strings, and so forth. The two methods of searching presented here, sequential and binary, accomplish the same end with different means.

Sequential Search

The *sequential search* is so simple it practically needs no explanation. The program simply starts at the beginning of the array to be searched and compares each element with the value you are seeking. The process of finding the number 10 in an array of **Integer**s is shown in Figure 11-6. The search compares **x**, which is equal to 10, to the first element, then the second, and so on. As soon as the value finds a match in the array, it exits from the search process and returns the index of the element found, which in this example is 4.

The following program includes the function **SeqSearch**, which takes three parameters: the value to search for, the array to search through, and the number of elements in the array.

```
Program SequentialSearch;
Type
  Int_Arr = Array [1..100] of Integer;

Var
  a : Int_Arr;
  i,j : Integer;

(*****************************)

Function SeqSearch(x : Integer;
                   a : Int_Arr;
                   n : Integer) : Integer;
Var
  i : Integer;
Begin
For i := 1 To n Do
```

```
If x = a[i] Then
  Begin
  SeqSearch := i;
  Exit;
  End;
SeqSearch := 0;
End;

(*****************************)

Begin
For i := 1 To 100 Do
  a[i] := Random(100);

  Repeat
  Write('Enter a number to search for (0 to exit): ');
  ReadLn(i);
  j := SeqSearch(i,a,100);
  If j = 0 Then
    WriteLn('Number not in list.')
  Else
    WriteLn(i,' is element number ',j);
  WriteLn;
  Until i = 0;
End.
```

Variable x equals 10:

Index	Array	Comparison	Result
1	3	x = 3?	False
2	21	x = 21?	False
3	4	x = 4?	False
4	10	x = 10?	True
5	55		
6	31		
7	9		
8	12		
9	15		Exit from search: Return index value 4

Figure 11-6. Locating a number with a sequential search

When **SeqSearch** finds a matching value, it assigns the value to the function and exits. Because a sequential search processes the array element by element, the order of the list is unimportant—the search works equally well with random lists as with sorted lists.

Binary Search

The *binary search* is one of the most efficient searching methods known and a big improvement over the sequential search. With an array of 100 elements, for example, a sequential search requires an average of 50 comparisons to find a match; the binary search requires at most seven comparisons and as few as four to accomplish the same goal. As the list gets longer, the relative efficiency of the binary search increases.

To perform a binary search, a list must be in sorted order. The search begins by testing the target element against the middle element in the array. If the target element is higher than the middle element, the search continues in the upper half of the list; if the target value is lower than the middle element, the target element is in the lower half.

The binary search process is shown in Figure 11-7. The array is searched for the target value 10. The fifth element, which is equal to 12, is tested first. Since 10 is less than 12, the target value must be in the

```
Variable x equals 10:
```

Index	Array	Comparison	Result
1	3	2	Higher
2	4	3	Higher
3	9	4	Equal
4	10	1	Lower
5	12		
6	15		
7	21		
8	31		
9	55		

Figure 11-7.   Searching a sorted array with the binary search algorithm

lower half of the array. The algorithm, therefore, selects element 2—midway between 1 and 4. The value of the second element is 4 (less than 10). The algorithm knows the target value must lie between elements 3 and 4. First, the algorithm tests element 3 and fails. This leaves element 4, which is equal to 10. The binary search now ends, returning a value of 4. Had element 4 been equal to 11, no match would have been found, and the function would have returned a zero.

Because the array in Figure 11-7 is so small, the benefit of the binary search is not fully illustrated. For example, a sequential search of a 1000-element array requires 500 comparisons on average, whereas a binary search requires between 5 and 10 comparisons.

The following program uses the function **Bsearch** to perform a binary search on an array of **Integer**s:

```
Program BinarySearch;
Type
  Int_Arr = Array [1..100] Of Integer;

Var
  a : Int_Arr;
  i,j : Integer;

(*****************************)
(*$i quick.inc*)
(*****************************)

Function Bsearch(x : Integer;
                 a : Int_Arr;
                 n : Integer) : Integer;
Var
  high, low, mid : integer;

Begin
low := 1;
high := n;
While high >= low Do
  Begin
  mid := Trunc((high+low) Div 2);
  If x > a[mid] Then
    low := mid + 1
  Else If x < a[mid] Then
    high := mid - 1
  Else
    high := -1;
  End;
If high = -1 Then
  Bsearch := mid
Else
  Bsearch := 0;
End;
```

```
(*****************************)
Begin
j := 2;
For i := 1 To 100 Do
  a[i] := Random(200);

Quick(a,100);

  Repeat
  Write('Enter a number to search for: (0 to exit): ');
  ReadLn(i);
  j := Bsearch(i,a,100);
  If j = 0 Then
    WriteLn('Number not in list.')
  Else
    WriteLn(i,' is element number ',j);
  WriteLn;
  Until i = 0;

End.
```

The program calls for an include file (with (**$i quick.inc***)), which holds the quick sort procedure described earlier in this chapter. The **Binary Search** program also illustrates the correct sequence. Notice that the **Quick** sort procedure is executed before the binary search function is executed.

The main code of the binary search algorithm, contained in the function **Bsearch**, is as follows:

```
low := 1;
high := n;
While high >= low Do
  Begin
  mid := Trunc((high+low) Div 2);
  If x > a[mid] Then
    low := mid + 1
  Else If x < a[mid] Then
    high := mid - 1
  Else
    high := -1;
  End;
If high = -1 Then
  Bsearch := mid
Else
  Bsearch := 0;
```

The variables **low** and **high** keep track of the portion of the array being searched. At the beginning, the program sets **low** equal to 1 and **high** equal to **n**, the number of elements in the array. Thus, the algorithm begins with the entire array.

The binary search loop is controlled by the statement

While high > = low Do

Each time the loop executes, either **high** is decremented or **low** is incremented by 1, bringing the two variables closer to each other. If **low** becomes greater than **high**, the element you are searching for does not exist in the sorted array and **Bsearch** returns zero.

If, at any point, **a[mid]** is equal to the value you are searching for, the program sets **high** equal to −1, causing the loop to terminate and the function to return the value of **mid**.

DOS and BIOS Functions

The 8088 Registers
The DOS Unit
The Register Set
Disk-Drive Services
Video Services
Time and Date Functions
Report Shift Status
The Turbo Pascal DOS Unit

Your PC consists of various physical devices: a keyboard, a monitor, disk drives, a printer, and so on. The *Disk Operating System* (DOS) and *Basic Input Output System* (BIOS) are comprised of software routines that control these devices, making sure data comes and goes to the right place without errors.

Your Turbo Pascal programs are constantly using DOS and BIOS services for such activities as writing to a disk file, displaying information on the monitor, getting the current time and date, and more. Because Turbo Pascal does all the work for you, you don't normally need to know anything about the DOS and BIOS services that are being called into play. Still, there are two reasons why you should know about these services and how to use them.

First, while Turbo Pascal gives you access to many services, it does not use them all. If you want complete control over your PC, you will have to learn to harness the power of DOS and BIOS services. Second, even if you never need to use these services, learning about them will greatly increase your understanding of personal computers and operating systems.

The 8088 Registers

The 8088 family of microprocessors (which includes the 8086 and 80286) contains a standard set of 14 *registers*, or internal memory locations, that computers use to execute commands. Each register is 16 bits long, which is why the 8088 is called a 16-bit microprocessor. (In Turbo Pascal, a 16-bit chunk of memory is known as a *word*.) The 8088's registers are shown in Figure 12-1.

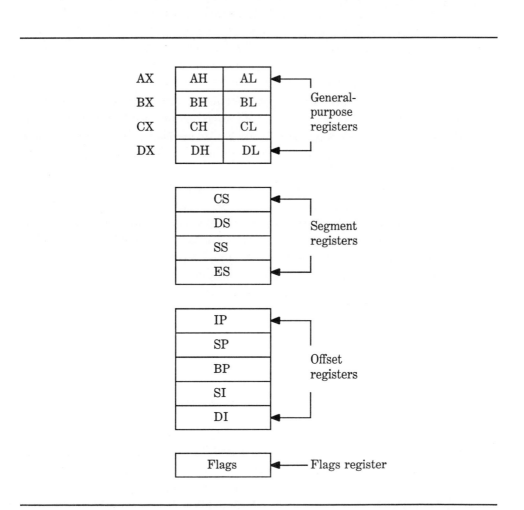

Figure 12-1.   The 8088 CPU registers

The first four registers—AX, BX, CX, and DX—are general-purpose areas that temporarily store data used in computations, comparisons, and other operations. Assembly-language programmers use these registers in the same way Pascal programmers use variables. Each of the general-purpose registers is divided into two one-byte registers; thus AX consists of AH and AL. These general registers are the ones most commonly used to call DOS and BIOS services.

The 8088 also has four segment registers: CS, DS, SS, and ES. CS stores the program's segment, DS contains the data segment, SS holds the stack segment, and ES holds temporary segments for special operations. The CS and SS registers hold critical data that is changed only at great risk to the program's integrity. Therefore, Turbo Pascal does not allow you to access these registers for DOS or BIOS calls, but DS and ES are used occasionally to pass segment addresses.

A memory address consists of a segment and an offset, and the 8088 contains five offset registers: IP, SP, BP, SI, and DI. These are used in conjunction with the segment registers to address specific locations in memory. Turbo Pascal allows access only to SI, DI, and BP; IP and SP are never used in DOS or BIOS calls.

Finally, the Flags register contains information about the status of the instruction last executed. Individual bits in the flag byte indicate specific conditions that result from CPU operations, although not all bits are used. The Flags register is used primarily to identify error conditions. While it can be used in Turbo Pascal, the Flags register is generally not necessary for DOS and BIOS calls, as they usually return error codes in one of the general registers.

The DOS Unit

Turbo Pascal 6 provides a standard unit, named DOS, which contains routines that call specific DOS and BIOS services as well as the data structures and procedures you need to call services on your own. With these routines you can get information on files, get a directory listing, set time and date for the system and individual files, and more. This section describes these new procedures and how you use them.

Some of the procedures in the DOS unit require special data types that you use to define variables. The DOS unit also contains two procedures, **MsDos** and **Intr**, that you can use to call specific DOS and BIOS services. Both procedures take a parameter of type **Registers**. With **MsDos, Intr,** and the **Registers** data structure, you can take advantage of all the services provided by DOS and BIOS. Fortunately, Borland has already packed the DOS unit full of easy-to-call procedures for the most commonly used services.

The Register Set

The **Registers** variable is the key to unlocking the power of DOS and BIOS services. This variable, passed to both **MsDos** and **Intr**, includes fields that match most of the 8088's registers:

```
Type
  Registers = Record
    Case Integer Of
    0: (AX,BX,CX,DX,BP,SI,DI,DS,ES,Flags : Word);
    1: (AL,AH,BL,BH,CL,CH,DL,DH : Byte);
    End;
```

The **Registers** data type contains only those CPU registers that are used in BIOS and DOS services. The record has two variant parts: one part consists of **Word** variables representing whole registers; the other part consists of bytes that define the high and low portions of the general registers. For example, the two **Byte** variables **AL** and **AH** refer to the same memory location that contains **AX**. The low-order byte (**AL**) precedes the high-order byte (**AH**) because the 8088 microprocessor stores bytes within words in reverse order. Therefore, if the integer 1 is stored in **AX**, it appears in memory as follows:

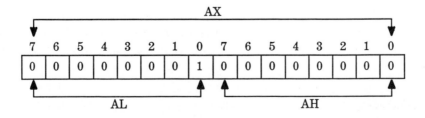

Before you can call **MsDos** or **Intr,** you must set the register-set variable to specific values that tell the computer which service you want and how you want to execute it. For example, to select a DOS service, place the code for the service in the AH register. DOS service **2Bh,** which sets the system date, is shown here:

```
Program SetTime;
Uses DOS, CRT;
Var
  Regs : Registers;

Begin
ClrScr;
FillChar(Regs,SizeOf(Regs),0);
With Regs Do
  Begin
  AH := $2B;
  DH := 12;      (* Month *)
  DL := 31;      (* Date  *)
  CX := 1991;    (* Year  *)
  End;

MsDos(Regs);    (* Call the DOS service *)

If Regs.AL <> 0 Then
  WriteLn('Error!')
Else
  WriteLn('Date has been set.');

WriteLn;
Write('Press ENTER...');
ReadLn;
End.
```

The procedure first initializes the register set to zero with the statement

FillChar(Regs,SizeOf(Regs),0);

and then puts **2Bh,** the code for setting the system date, in AH. Next, registers DH, DL, and CX are filled with date information.

MsDos accepts the register-set variable as a parameter and calls the DOS procedure that updates the system date to December 31, 1991. If the DOS service detects an error, it returns the register set with the error code in AL. The statement

```
If Regs.AL <> 0 Then
  WriteLn('Error!');
```

checks this code; if it is not equal to zero, an error occurs.

While the **MsDos** procedure is used for DOS services, the **Intr** procedure is used for BIOS services. **Intr** accepts two variables: the interrupt number and the register-set variable. For example, the BIOS call that prints the contents of a screen is invoked by setting register AH to 5 and calling interrupt 5, as follows:

```
FillChar(Regs,SizeOf(Regs),0);
Regs.AH := 5;
Intr(5,Regs);
```

The first parameter is the interrupt number. The example above calls interrupt 5, which can be used to do many things. Setting **Regs.AH** to 5, however, specifies the print-screen service (the same service invoked by pressing the SHIFT and PRTSC keys at the same time). In this service, no error indicator is returned in the register set.

The use of DOS and BIOS services greatly increases what you can do with Turbo Pascal, but learning to use them properly takes some time. The remainder of this chapter deals with procedures that incorporate the most useful of the DOS and BIOS services and serve as examples of how to use them.

Disk-Drive Services

The main purpose of the Disk Operating System is to manage your computer's disk drives and files. Fortunately, Turbo Pascal's standard procedures take care of the most difficult disk-related tasks, such as reading and writing files. This section presents several DOS functions not supported by Turbo Pascal that can improve your programs.

Report Free Disk Space

DOS service **36h** indicates how much space is available on a disk. The DL register selects the disk to check; 0 indicates the default drive, 1 indicates drive A, 2 indicates drive B, and so on. After **MsDos** is called, the general-purpose registers contain the following information:

AX	Sectors per allocation cluster
BX	Number of unused clusters
CX	Bytes per sector
DX	Total number of clusters

Using these values, you can easily calculate the total amount of free disk space with the equation

$$LongInt(AX) * BX * CX$$

(The **LongInt** typecast in the equation is necessary to avoid integer overflow.) If an invalid drive is specified, Turbo Pascal returns $FFFF in AX.

The function **FreeDiskSpace**, shown here, reports the number of free bytes for a drive:

```
Program DiskSpace;
Uses CRT, DOS;
Var
  Drive : Char;

(********************************************************)

Function FreeDiskSpace(Drive : Char) : LongInt;
Var
  Regs : Registers;
Begin
FillChar(Regs,SizeOf(Regs),0);
With Regs Do
  Begin
  AH := $36;
  DL := Ord(UpCase(Drive)) - 64;
  End;

MsDos(Regs);

With Regs Do
If AX = $FFFF Then
  FreeDiskSpace := -1
Else
  FreeDiskSpace := LongInt(AX)*BX*CX;
End;

(********************************************************)

Begin
ClrScr;
Write('Which Drive? (A/B/C/D): ');
```

```
ReadLn(Drive);
Drive := UpCase(Drive);
WriteLn(FreeDiskSpace(Drive):0,' bytes free.');
WriteLn;
Write('Press ENTER...');
ReadLn;
End.
```

The parameter in the preceding procedure is a character that indicates which drive to check. To assign the drive number to DL, the procedure changes the parameter **Drive** to uppercase, converts it into its ASCII value, and subtracts 64. If **drive** is equal to **a**, it is changed to **A**, which has an ASCII value of 65. Subtracting 64 from 65 gives 1, which is the correct drive number for DL.

After **MsDos** is called, the procedure checks the AX register. If AX contains $FFFF, an error occurred during the procedure and the function returns the value −1. If no error is indicated, the function computes the amount of free disk space.

Get and Set File Attributes

Disk files can have any of six attributes provided by DOS: *read-only, hidden, system, volume label, subdirectory,* and *archive.* File attributes are contained in a single byte, with individual attributes controlled by bits.

Bit 1 in the attribute byte represents a file's read-only status. Read-only files cannot be changed in any way. DOS blocks any attempt to write over or erase read-only files, just as a write-protect tab protects a floppy disk.

Bit 2 tells you if a file is hidden or not. Hidden files, which often contain sensitive information, are ignored by DOS: they are not listed by the **Dir** command, they cannot be erased or displayed, and so forth. As a result, hidden files are invisible unless the user has a program that can find them. While DOS does not acknowledge hidden files, Turbo Pascal allows them to be used for input or output.

Bit 3 controls the system attribute. System files, like hidden files, are not acknowledged by DOS commands. The system attribute, however, has no real role and is merely a carryover from CP/M.

Bit 4 in the attribute byte toggles the volume label, which is a statement that identifies a floppy disk or hard disk. This is an option set by the user when a disk is formatted.

Bit 5 in the attribute byte indicates that the file is a subdirectory. DOS uses subdirectory files, which contain no data, to keep track of directories and subdirectories.

Bit 6, the archive attribute bit, is turned on when a file is first created. The bit is turned off when the file is copied with the DOS **Backup** command, and it remains off until the file's contents are changed. The archive bit allows you to back up only those files that have changed since the previous backup. Bits 7 and 8 of the attribute byte are not used.

To find what attributes a file has, or to set the attributes you want, use DOS service **43h**. The value in register AL controls which action to execute: 0 to report a file's attributes; 1 to set a file's attributes.

When you report a file's attributes, service **43h** returns the attribute byte in register CL. By testing the individual bits, you can determine the status of each attribute. When setting a file's attributes, you must create an attribute byte and place it in CL prior to calling **MsDos**.

Whether setting or reporting a file's attribute byte, you must load the register set DS:DX with the segment and offset of an *ASCIIZ string* that contains the filename. An ASCIIZ string is an array of letters terminated by a binary zero. You can use a Turbo Pascal string as an ASCIIZ string by adding #0 to it. Turbo Pascal strings, however, have a length byte, while ASCIIZ strings do not. Therefore, you must use the address of the first character in the string to use it as an ASCIIZ string.

In the following procedure, DOS service **43h** sets six Boolean parameters, one for each possible file attribute:

```
Program FileAttributes;
Uses CRT, DOS;
Var
  Fname : String;
  RO, Hidden,
  Sys, Vol,
  SubDir, Arch, Error : Boolean;

(********************************************************)

Procedure GetFileAttributes( FileName : String;
                             Var RO,
                                 Hidden,
                                 Sys,
                                 Vol,
                                 SubDir,
                                 Arch,
                                 Error : Boolean);
```

```
Var
  Regs : Registers;

Begin
FillChar(Regs,SizeOf(Regs),0);
FileName := FileName + #0;

With Regs Do
  Begin
  AH := $43;
  DS := Seg(FileName);
  DX := Ofs(FileName) + 1;
  End;

MsDos(Regs);

Error  := (Regs.AL in [2,3,5]);
RO     := (Regs.CL And $01) > 0;
Hidden := (Regs.CL And $02) > 0;
Sys    := (Regs.CL And $04) > 0;
Vol    := (Regs.CL And $08) > 0;
SubDir := (Regs.CL And $10) > 0;
Arch   := (Regs.CL And $20) > 0;
End;

(*****************************************************)

Begin
ClrScr;
Write('Which file?: ');
ReadLn(Fname);

GetFileAttributes(Fname,
                  RO,
                  Hidden,
                  Sys,
                  Vol,
                  SubDir,
                  Arch,
                  Error);

If Error Then
  WriteLn('Error!')
Else
  Begin
  WriteLn(Fname,' has these attributes: ');
  WriteLn('Read only:    ',RO);
  WriteLn('Hidden:       ',Hidden);
  WriteLn('System file:  ',Sys);
  WriteLn('Volume label: ',Vol);
  WriteLn('Subdirectory: ',SubDir);
  WriteLn('Archive:      ',Arch);
  End;

WriteLn;
Write('Press ENTER...');
ReadLn;
End.
```

DOS service **43h** reports error conditions when the file is not found (AL register is 2), the path is not found (AL is 3), or access to the file is denied (AL is 5).

The following procedure sets a file's attribute byte. The procedure accepts four Boolean parameters for four file attributes. It does not include the volume-label and subdirectory attributes, since they cannot be set by this DOS service.

```
Program FileAttributes;
Uses CRT, DOS;
Var
  ch : Char;
  Fname : String;
  RO, Hidden,
  Sys, Arch : Boolean;

(******************************************************)

Procedure SetFileAttributes( FileName : String;
                             Var RO,
                                 Hidden,
                                 Sys,
                                 Arch : Boolean);
Var
  Regs : Registers;

Begin
FillChar(Regs,SizeOf(Regs),0);
FileName := FileName + #0;

With Regs Do
  Begin
  AH := $43;
  AL := 1;
  DS := Seg(FileName);
  DX := Ofs(FileName) + 1;

  If RO Then
    CL := (CL Or $01);
  If Hidden Then
    CL := (CL Or $02);
  If Sys Then
    CL := (CL Or $04);
  If Arch Then
    CL := (CL Or $20);
  End;

MsDos(Regs);

End;

(******************************************************)

Begin
ClrScr;
```

```
Write('Which file?: ');
ReadLn(Fname);

Write('Set to read only? (Y/N) ');
ReadLn(ch);
RO := UpCase(ch) = 'Y';

Write('Set to hidden (Y/N) ');
ReadLn(ch);
Hidden := UpCase(ch) = 'Y';

Write('Set to archive (Y/N) ');
ReadLn(ch);
Arch := UpCase(ch) = 'Y';

Write('Set to system file (Y/N) ');
ReadLn(ch);
Sys := UpCase(ch) = 'Y';

SetFileAttributes(Fname,
                  RO,
                  Hidden,
                  Sys,
                  Arch);

WriteLn(Fname,' has been set to these attributes: ');
WriteLn('Read only:      ',RO);
WriteLn('Hidden:         ',Hidden);
WriteLn('System file:   ',Sys);
WriteLn('Archive:        ',Arch);
WriteLn;
Write('Press ENTER...');
ReadLn;
End.
```

It is useful to change a file's attributes to hide files that you want to keep secret or to reveal files that are already hidden or are set to read-only status.

Directory Listing

Displaying a disk directory requires three different DOS services and an understanding of the program segment prefix (PSP) and the disk-transfer area (DTA), which is a part of the PSP.

When a program starts, DOS sets aside the first 256 bytes of memory for its PSP. Because it contains highly technical information, the PSP is normally never touched by the programmer, except for the DTA portion. The DTA is a 128-byte default buffer used for certain DOS operations, such as reading a disk directory, in which case the DTA contains the information shown in Table 12-1.

The filename and its extension constitute the last field in the DTA. The file attribute, time, date, and file size can be read and translated for a more complete directory listing.

Before obtaining information from the DTA, you must know its address, which is reported by DOS service **2Fh**. When executed, service **2Fh** places the DTA segment in ES and the DTA offset in BX, as shown here:

```
Regs.AH := $2F;
MsDos(Regs);
DTAseg := Regs.ES;
DTAofs := Regs.BX;
```

The preceding program segment stores the DTA segment in the variable **DTAseg** and the offset in **DTAofs**. These variables are used with the Turbo Pascal standard array **Mem** to extract information from the DTA. For example,

Mem[DTAseg:DTAofs + 21]

points to the location of the file-attribute byte in the DTA.

The DOS function **4Eh** searches for the first matching file in the directory and fills the DTA with the file's information. Before **4Eh** is

Description	Offset	Length
Data used by DOS	0	21
File attribute	21	1
Time stamp of file	22	2
Date stamp of file	24	2
File size in bytes	26	4
Filename and extension	30	13

Table 12-1.   Contents of DTA for a Directory Listing

called, however, the registers DS and DX must contain the segment and offset of an ASCIIZ string with the path and filename. This is shown in the following code segment:

```
Mask_In := Mask_In + #0;
With Regs Do
  Begin
  AH := $4E;
  DS := Seg(Mask_In);
  DX := Ofs(Mask_In) + 1;
  CL := $00;
  End;
MsDos(Regs);

If Regs.AL <> 0 Then Exit;
```

The CL register tells DOS what type of file it should include in its search. If the register is set to zero, DOS locates only standard files. To include hidden or system files in the directory listing, set CL to a value according to the guidelines in Table 12-2.

If CL is set to 16h (the sum of 2h, 4h, and 10h), hidden files, system files, and subdirectories will be included in the directory listing. If the AL register returns with a nonzero value, no file entries matching the file spec were found in the directory.

Attribute to Include	Value of CL
Hidden	$02
System	$04
Volume label	$08
Subdirectory	$10

Table 12-2.   Setting DOS File Attributes with the CL Register

The program **Directory** uses the procedure **DirList** to create an array of filenames for a file spec entered by the user:

```
Program Directory;
Uses CRT, DOS;
Type
  Dir_Files = Array [1..200] Of String[13];
Var
  FileSpec : String;
  i,
  fc : Integer;
  df : Dir_Files;

(*********************************************)

Procedure DirList( Mask_In : String;
                   Var Name_List : Dir_Files;
                   Var File_Counter : Integer);
Var
  i : Byte;
  Regs : Registers;

  DTAseg,
  DTAofs : Word;
  FileName : String[20];

Begin
FillChar(Regs,SizeOf(Regs),0);
File_Counter := 0;

Regs.AH := $2F;
MsDos(Regs);
With Regs Do
  Begin
  DTAseg := ES;
  DTAofs := BX;
  End;

FillChar(Regs,SizeOf(Regs),0);
Mask_In := Mask_In + #0;
With Regs Do
  Begin
  AH := $4E;
  DS := Seg(Mask_In);
  DX := Ofs(Mask_In) + 1;
  CL := $00;
  End;
MsDos(Regs);

If Regs.AL <> 0 Then Exit;
```

```
i := 1;
  Repeat
  FileName[i] := Chr(Mem[DTAseg:DTAofs+29+i]);
  i := i + 1;
  Until (FileName[i-1] < #32) Or (i > 12);

FileName[0] := Chr(i-1);
File_Counter := 1;
Name_List[File_Counter] := FileName;

  Repeat
  FillChar(Regs,SizeOf(Regs),0);
  With Regs Do
    Begin
    AH := $4F;
    CL := $00;
    End;
  MsDos(Regs);

  If Regs.AL = 0 Then
    Begin
    i := 1;
      Repeat
      FileName[i] := Chr(Mem[DTAseg:DTAofs+29+i]);
      i := i + 1;
      Until (FileName[i-1] < #32) Or (i > 12);

    Inc(File_Counter,1);
    FileName[0] := Chr(i-1);
    Name_List[File_Counter] := FileName;
    End;

  Until Regs.AL <> 0;

End;

(*********************************************)

Begin
ClrScr;
  Repeat
  Write('Enter file spec: ');
  ReadLn(FileSpec);
  If FileSpec <> '' Then
    Begin
    DirList(FileSpec,df,fc);
    For i := 1 To fc Do
      WriteLn(df[i]);
    WriteLn;
    End;
  Until FileSpec = '';
End.
```

The procedure **DirList** accepts the following three parameters: **mask_in**, **name_list**, and **file_counter**. The string parameter **mask_in** contains the file spec to match (for example, test.pas, *.pas, or

???.pas). Filenames that match the file spec are stored in **name _ list**, an array of strings. The **Integer file _ counter** returns the number of matching filenames **DirList** finds.

Note that DOS service **4Eh** locates only the first file; **4Fh** finds all subsequent files and continues to locate them until register AL contains a nonzero value, which indicates that there are no more matching files in the directory.

Video Services

Most users judge a program almost entirely by its use of video, largely because well-designed and attractive displays make programs easier to use. Unfortunately, Turbo Pascal provides only limited screen-control capabilities. The procedures presented in this section extend your control over the monitor and make possible more sophisticated video displays.

Report Current Video Mode

One fundamental aspect of screen control is determining what type of video adapter the computer has. The major categories are monochrome and color graphics adapter followed by the PCjr and enhanced graphics adapters.

BIOS interrupt **10h** reports the type of video adapter being used and is demonstrated in the function **CurrentVidMode**, shown here:

```
Program VideoMode;
Uses CRT, DOS;

(*********************************************)

Function CurrentVidMode : Char;
Var
  Regs : Registers;
Begin
FillChar(Regs,SizeOf(Regs),0);
Regs.AH := $0F;
Intr($10,Regs);

  Case Regs.AL of
  1..6   : CurrentVidMode := 'C'; (* CGA *)
```

```
   7     : CurrentVidMode := 'M'; (* Monochrome *)
   8..10 : CurrentVidMode := 'P'; (* PCjr *)
   13..16 : CurrentVidMode := 'E'; (* EGA *)
   End;

End;

(*******************************************)

Begin
ClrScr;
WriteLn('Current video mode is: ',CurrentVidMode);
WriteLn;
Write('Press ENTER...');
ReadLn;
End.
```

Before the interrupt is called, the function sets the AH register to 0Fh. The interrupt stores the screen width (as the number of characters per line) in AH, the video mode in AL, and the video page number in BH. The procedure determines the video mode by examining AL. If this register is equal to 7, the screen is monochrome and the function returns the letter M. A value from 1 to 6 indicates a color graphics monitor (C), 8 to 10 means PCjr (P), and 13 to 16 is for enhanced graphics (E).

Knowing the type of display is essential when you begin writing information directly to video memory, a topic covered in Chapter 14.

Set the Cursor Size

At times in a program, it is best not to show the cursor. At other times, a large cursor makes more sense than a small one. Typically, a cursor consists of two scan lines. A color graphics adapter, however, can display a cursor with as many as 8 scan lines, and a monochrome adapter can go up to 14. The more scan lines used, the larger the cursor; if no scan lines are used, the cursor disappears.

To set the cursor size, use BIOS interrupt **10h** with register AH set equal to 1. Put the number of the starting scan line in register CH and the ending scan line in CL. The color graphics adapter uses 8 scan lines (0 to 7); the monochrome adapter uses 14 lines (0 to 13). The lower scan lines appear toward the top of the screen. For example, a small cursor on a color graphics monitor consists of scan lines 6 and 7, the bottom two scan lines.

```
Program Cursor;
Uses DOS, CRT;

(****************************************************)

Procedure CursorSize(Stype, Size : Char);
Var
  Regs : Registers;
  i : Integer;
Begin
Size := UpCase(Size);
If UpCase(Stype) = 'M' Then
  i := 6
Else
  i := 0;

Regs.AH := $01;

  Case Size Of
  'O' :
    Begin
    Regs.CH := $20;
    Regs.CL := $20;
    End;
  'B' :
    Begin
    Regs.CH := $0;
    Regs.CL := $7+i;
    End;
  'S' :
    Begin
    Regs.CH := $6+i;
    Regs.CL := $7+i;
    End;
  End;

Intr($10,Regs);
End;

(****************************************************)

Begin
ClrScr;
WriteLn('Big cursor');
CursorSize('C','B');
WriteLn;
Write('Press ENTER...');
ReadLn;

WriteLn;
WriteLn;
WriteLn('No cursor');
CursorSize('C','O');
WriteLn;
Write('Press ENTER...');
ReadLn;
```

```
WriteLn;
WriteLn;
WriteLn('Small cursor');
CursorSize('C','S');
WriteLn;
Write('Press ENTER...');
ReadLn;

End.
```

This procedure sets the cursor size according to the parameters you pass to it. The parameter **stype** can be equal to M for monochrome or C for color graphics. The parameter **size** can take three values: B for big, S for small, or O for off.

If the computer uses a monochrome adapter, the variable **i** is set equal to 6; otherwise it is set to 0. The cursor is turned off by simply setting both CH and CL to 20h, while a large cursor is created by setting CH to 0, and CL to 7 for color-graphics adapters or 13 for monochrome adapters. For a small cursor, CH and CL are set to 6 and 7 for color graphics adapters or 12 and 13 for monochrome adapters.

Read a Character from the Screen

You can read characters from the video screen with BIOS interrupt **10h.** The function **ScreenChar,** as follows, demonstrates how to read characters from the screen with interrupt **10h.**

```
Program ScreenTest;
Uses DOS, CRT;
Var
  s : String;
  i : Integer;

(**************************************************)

Function ScreenChar : Char;
Var
  Regs : Registers;
Begin
FillChar(Regs,SizeOf(Regs),0);
Regs.AH := 8;
Regs.BH := 0; (* video page *)
Intr($10,Regs);
ScreenChar := Chr(Regs.AL);
End;

(**************************************************)
```

```
Begin
ClrScr;

WriteLn('ABCDE');

s := '';
For i := 1 To 5 Do
  Begin
  GotoXY(i,1);
  s := s + ScreenChar;
  End;
WriteLn;
WriteLn(s);

WriteLn;
Write('Press ENTER...');
ReadLn;
End.
```

Because **ScreenChar** reads the character at the current cursor position, you must position the cursor correctly before calling the interrupt. Put 8 in register AH and 0 in register BH. The number in register BH selects the video page to be used, but you will most likely use video page 0.

After the interrupt is called, the ASCII code for the character at the cursor position is returned in register AL. **ScreenChar** converts the ASCII code into a character and returns it as the function result.

Time and Date Functions

DOS maintains an internal clock that keeps track of the time and date. When a file is created or changed, DOS uses the clock to stamp the time and date on it. The DOS services shown in Table 12-3 give you control over the system date and time.

DOS Service	Function
2Ah	Report the system date
2Bh	Set the system date
2Ch	Report the system time
2Dh	Set the system time

Table 12-3.   DOS System Time and Date Services

Register	Information
AL	Day of week (0 = Sunday)
CX	Year
DH	Month
DL	Day

Table 12-4.   Contents of Registers After DOS Service 2Ah

Before calling one of these services, specify the appropriate DOS service code in the AH register.

Get the System Date

DOS service **2Ah**, which reports the current system date, puts date information in the registers displayed in Table 12-4.

This is demonstrated in the procedure **GetSystemDate** (as follows), which uses DOS service **2Ah** to report the system date and then formats that date into a string. The date is then passed back to the program.

```
Program Date;
Uses CRT, DOS;
Var
  s : String;

(****************************************************)

Procedure GetSystemDate(Var date : String);
Var
  Regs : Registers;
  st1, st2, st3, st4 : String[10];

Begin
FillChar(Regs,SizeOf(Regs),0);
Regs.AH := $2A;
MsDos(Regs);
With Regs Do
  Begin
    Case AL Of
    0 : st1 := 'Sunday';
    1 : st1 := 'Monday';
    2 : st1 := 'Tuesday';
    3 : st1 := 'Wednesday';
    4 : st1 := 'Thursday';
```

```
   5 : st1 := 'Friday';
   6 : st1 := 'Saturday';
   End;
  Str(CX, st2); (* Year *)
  Str(DH, st3); (* Month *)
  Str(DL, st4); (* Date *)
  End;
If Length(st3) = 1 Then
  st3 := '0' + st3;
If Length(st4) = 1 Then
  st4 := '0' + st4;
date := st1+' '+st3+'-'+st4+'-'+st2;
End;

(****************************************************)

Begin
ClrScr;

GetSystemDate(s);
WriteLn('The date is ',s);

WriteLn;
Write('Press ENTER...');
ReadLn;

End.
```

GetSystemDate uses a **Case** statement to determine the appropriate day of the week. The year, month, and day are converted into strings. (If the day or month consists of a single numeral, the strings are padded with a leading zero.)

Set the System Date

DOS service **2Bh** sets the system date. Before making a call to **MsDos**, you must insert the month in register DH, the day in DL, and the year in CX. The following procedure shows how Turbo Pascal uses this service:

```
Program Date;
Uses CRT, DOS;
Var
  Error : Boolean;

(****************************************************)
```

```
Procedure SetSystemDate( Month, Day, Year : Integer;
                         Var Error : Boolean);
Var
  Regs : Registers;
Begin
FillChar(Regs,SizeOf(Regs),0);
With Regs Do
  Begin
  AH := $2B;
  DH := Month;
  DL := Day;
  CX := Year;
  End;
MsDos(Regs);
Error := Regs.AL <> 0;
End;

(*****************************************************)

Begin
ClrScr;

SetSystemDate(1,1,1990, Error);

If Error Then
  WriteLn('Error!')
Else
  WriteLn('Date has been set.');

WriteLn;
Write('Press ENTER...');
ReadLn;

End.
```

If you enter an illegal date, an error will occur, in which case register AL returns an error code. If a nonzero value is found in AL, the Boolean parameter **Error** is set to TRUE.

Get and Set the System Time

DOS service **2Ch** reports the system time, and service **2Dh** sets the system time. Reporting and setting the system time are much like the same operations for the system date. The two following procedures demonstrate how the system time can be reported and set:

```
Program SysTime;
Uses DOS, CRT;
Var
  Hour,
  Minute,
  Second : Byte;
  Error : Boolean;
  s : String;

(*********************************************)

Procedure GetSystemTime(Var Time : String);
Var
  Regs : Registers;
  h, m, s : Word;
  st1, st2, st3, st4 : String[10];

Begin
FillChar(Regs,SizeOf(Regs),0);
Regs.AH := $2C;
MsDos(Regs);
With Regs Do
  Begin
  Str(CH, st1);
  Str(CL, st2);
  Str(DH, st3);
  Str(DL, st4);
  End;

If Length(st1) = 1 Then
  st1 := '0' + st1;

If Length(st2) = 1 Then
  st2 := '0' + st2;

If Length(st3) = 1 Then
  st3 := '0' + st3;

If Length(st4) = 1 Then
  st4 := '0' + st4;

Time := st1+':'+st2+':'+st3+':'+st4;
End;

(*********************************************)

Procedure SetSystemTime( Hour, Minute, Second : Byte;
                         Var Error : Boolean);
Var
  Regs : Registers;
Begin
FillChar(Regs,SizeOf(Regs),0);
```

```
With Regs Do
  Begin
  AH := $2D;
  CH := Hour;
  CL := Minute;
  DH := Second;
  End;
MsDos(Regs);
Error := Regs.AL <> 0;
End;

(*********************************************)

Begin
ClrScr;
Write('Hour  : ');
ReadLn(Hour);
Write('Minute: ');
ReadLn(Minute);
Write('Second: ');
ReadLn(Second);

SetSystemTime(Hour, Minute, Second, Error);

GetSystemTime(s);
WriteLn('Time now: ',s);

WriteLn;
Write('Press ENTER...');
ReadLn;

End.
```

If errors occur when setting the system time, register AL returns the error code. Any nonzero value returned in AL indicates an error condition.

Get and Set Time and Date for a File

DOS service **3Dh** can report or set a file's time and date stamp. Time and date functions for disk files are complicated by the fact that a *file handle* must be used, and the date and time are coded as a single numeric value. A file handle is a DOS convention used to process disk input and output.

To obtain a file handle, use DOS service **3Dh**, which opens a file and returns the file handle in register AX. The function **GetFileHandle**, used in the following program, accepts a filename and returns a file handle:

```
Function GetFileHandle( FileName : String;
                         Var Error : Boolean) : Integer;
Var
  Regs : Registers;
  i : Integer;
Begin
FileName := FileName + #0;
FillChar(Regs,SizeOf(Regs),0);
With Regs Do
  Begin
  AH := $3D;
  AL := $00;
  DS := Seg(FileName);
  DX := Ofs(FileName)+1;
  End;

MsDos(Regs);

i := Regs.AX;

If (Lo(regs.Flags) And $01) > 0 Then
  Begin
  Error := True;
  GetFileHandle := 0;
  Exit;
  End;
GetFileHandle := i;
End;
```

If an error occurs, **GetFileHandle** returns a zero and sets the error parameter to TRUE. If no error occurs, the file is opened, and you can proceed to report or set the file time and date. Before you finish, however, you must be sure to close the file that was opened to provide a file handle by using DOS service **3Eh**, as shown in this procedure:

```
Procedure CloseFileHandle(i : Integer);
Var
  Regs : Registers;
Begin
With Regs Do
  Begin
  AH := $3E;
  BX := i;
  End;
MsDos(Regs);
End;
```

In short, the reporting or setting of a file's time and date is a three-step procedure:

1. Open a file and store the file handle.

2. Use the file handle to report or set the file's time and date.

3. Close the file.

The two procedures that follow—**GetFileTimeAndDate** and **Set-FileTimeAndDate**—show how to use DOS service **57h**. If the AL register is set to 0, Turbo Pascal reports the time and date; if it is set to 1, Turbo Pascal sets the time and date. In either case, register BX stores the file handle.

```
Program FileStamp;
Uses DOS, CRT;
Var
  Fname,
  Time_st,
  Day_st : String;
  Month, Day,
  Year, Hour,
  Minute, Second : Word;
  Error : Boolean;

(*****************************************************)

Function GetFileHandle( FileName : String;
                        Var Error : Boolean) : Integer;
Var
  Regs : Registers;
  i : Integer;
Begin
FileName := FileName + #0;
FillChar(Regs,SizeOf(Regs),0);
With Regs Do
  Begin
  AH := $3D;
  AL := $00;
  DS := Seg(FileName);
  DX := Ofs(FileName)+1;
  End;

MsDos(Regs);

i := Regs.AX;

If (Lo(regs.Flags) And $01) > 0 Then
  Begin
  Error := True;
  GetFileHandle := 0;
  Exit;
  End;
GetFileHandle := i;
End;

(*****************************************************)
```

```
Procedure CloseFileHandle(i : Integer);
Var
  Regs : Registers;
Begin
With Regs Do
  Begin
  AH := $3E;
  BX := i;
  End;
MsDos(Regs);
End;

(*******************************************************)

Procedure GetFileTimeAndDate( File_Name : String;
                              Var Time_st,
                                  Day_st : String;
                              Var Error : Boolean);
Var
  Regs : Registers;
  i : Integer;
  st1,st2,st3 : String[4];
  y,m,d,r,h,s,Time,Day : Word;

Begin
Error := False;
Time_st := '';
Day_st := '';

i := GetFileHandle(File_Name,Error);
If Error Then Exit;

With Regs Do
  Begin
  AH := $57;
  AL := $00;
  BX := i;
  End;

MsDos(Regs);
CloseFileHandle(i);

(* Convert Time *)
r := Regs.CX;
h := r Div 2048;
r := r - (h*2048);
m := r Div 32;
r := r - (m*32);
s := r * 2;

Str(h:0,st1);
Str(m:0,st2);
Str(s:0,st3);
If Length(st1) = 1 Then st1 := '0'+st1;
If Length(st2) = 1 Then st2 := '0'+st2;
If Length(st3) = 1 Then st3 := '0'+st3;
Time_st := st1+':'+st2+':'+st3;
```

```
(* Convert Day *)
r := Regs.DX;
y := (r Div 512) + 1980;
r := r - ((y-1980)*512);
m := r Div 32;
r := r - (m * 32);
d := r;
Str(y:0,st1);
Str(m:0,st2);
Str(d:0,st3);
If Length(st1) = 1 Then st1 := '0'+st1;
If Length(st2) = 1 Then st2 := '0'+st2;
If Length(st3) = 1 Then st3 := '0'+st3;
Day_st := st2+'-'+st3+'-'+st1;
End;


(*********************************************)

Procedure SetFileTimeAndDate( File_Name : String;
                              Month, Day,
                              Year, Hour,
                              Minute, Second : Word;
                              Var Error : Boolean);

Var
  Regs : Registers;
  i,j,k : Word;
  t,d : Word;

Begin
Error := False;
i := GetFileHandle(File_Name,Error);
If Error Then Exit;

t := (Hour*2048)+(Minute*32)+(Second Div 2);
d := ((Year-1980)*512)+(Month*32)+Day;

With Regs Do
  Begin
  AH := $57;
  AL := $01;
  BX := i;
  CX := t;
  DX := d;
  End;

MsDos(Regs);
CloseFileHandle(i);
End;


(*****************************************************)
```

```
Begin
ClrScr;

Write('File: ');
ReadLn(Fname);
Write('Month: ');
ReadLn(Month);
Write('Day: ');
ReadLn(Day);
Write('Year: ');
ReadLn(Year);
Write('Hour: ');
ReadLn(Hour);
Write('Minute: ');
ReadLn(Minute);
Write('Second: ');
ReadLn(Second);

SetFileTimeAndDate( Fname,
                    Month, Day, Year,
                    Hour, Minute, Second,
                    Error);

GetFileTimeAndDate(Fname,Time_st, Day_st, Error);
If Error Then
  WriteLn('Error!')
Else
  WriteLn(Time_st,' ',Day_st);

WriteLn;
Write('Press ENTER...');
ReadLn;
End.
```

When it calls **MsDos, GetFileTimeAndDate** reports the time in register CX and the date in DX, which are then stored in **Word** variables. The variables are then broken down arithmetically into their components: hours, minutes, and seconds and day, month, and year. These components are combined into one string and passed back in the parameters **Time _ st** and **Day _ st**.

To set the time and date of a file, you must first compute the numerical value that represents the time and date. In **Set-FileTimeAndDate**, the input values (hour, minute, second, day, month, and year) are passed as parameters. The procedure converts them into two numbers, which are loaded into register CX (for time) and DX (for date). The call to **MsDos** then sets the time and date for that file.

Report Shift Status

Turbo Pascal is unable to directly read some of the most powerful keys on the PC: NUMLOCK, SCROLL LOCK, CTRL, ALT, the two shift keys, CAPSLOCK, and INS. BIOS interrupt **16h,** which reports the status of these keys, increases your control over the keyboard.

To check the status of these special keys, use interrupt **16h** with register AH set to 2. After interrupt **16h** is done, it returns a status byte in register AL. Each bit in this byte indicates the status for one of the eight special keys.

In the following procedure, interrupt **16h** checks on the status of the eight special keys:

```
Program Shift;
Uses CRT, DOS;
Var
  Ins,
  CapsLock,
  NumLock,
  ScrollLock,
  Alt,
  Ctrl,
  LeftShift,
  RightShift : Boolean;

(*****************************************************)

Procedure ShiftStatus(Var Ins,
                          CapsLock,
                          NumLock,
                          ScrollLock,
                          Alt,
                          Ctrl,
                          LeftShift,
                          RightShift : Boolean);
Var
  Regs : Registers;

Begin
Regs.AH := 2;
Intr($16,Regs);

RightShift      := (Regs.AL And $01) > 0;
LeftShift       := (Regs.AL And $02) > 0;
Ctrl            := (Regs.AL And $04) > 0;
Alt             := (Regs.AL And $08) > 0;
ScrollLock      := (Regs.AL And $10) > 0;
```

```
NumLock          := (Regs.AL And $20) > 0;
CapsLock         := (Regs.AL And $40) > 0;
Ins              := (Regs.AL And $80) > 0;

End;

(*****************************************************)

Begin
ClrScr;
WriteLn('Press Ins and then Ctrl to stop...');

  Repeat
  ShiftStatus(Ins,CapsLock,NumLock,ScrollLock,
           Alt,Ctrl,LeftShift,RightShift);

  GotoXY(1,4);
  WriteLn('Ins.........',Ins,' ');
  WriteLn('CapsLock....',CapsLock,' ');
  WriteLn('NumLock.....',NumLock,' ');
  WriteLn('ScrollLock..',ScrollLock,' ');
  WriteLn('Alt.........',Alt,' ');
  WriteLn('Ctrl........',Ctrl,' ');
  WriteLn('LeftShift...',LeftShift,' ');
  WriteLn('RightShift..',RightShift,' ');
  Until (Ins And Ctrl);

WriteLn;
Write('Press ENTER...');
ReadLn;
End.
```

The procedure **ShiftStatus,** which accepts a Boolean parameter for each of the eight special keys, checks each bit in the byte returned in register AL. Thus, the eight parameters are set according to the individual bits in the status byte.

The Turbo Pascal DOS Unit

DOS and BIOS are full of powerful services that can be called from within Turbo Pascal with the **MsDos** and **Intr** procedures. Borland has made things even easier by providing special routines that access the most popular DOS and BIOS services. The routines, and the data structures you need to use them, are contained in the DOS unit.

DOS Unit Constants

The DOS unit contains many constants that will help simplify your programming. These constants can be categorized under three broad headings: flags constants (used to interpret the CPU's Flags register), file mode constants (used by Turbo Pascal's file-handling procedures), and file attribute constants (used to interpret a file's attribute byte). The declarations of these constants are shown here:

```
{ Flags Constants }

Const
  FCarry    = $0000; (* Carry Flag     *)
  FParity   = $0004; (* Parity Flag    *)
  FAuxiliary = $0010; (* Auxiliary Flag *)
  FZero     = $0000; (* Zero Flag      *)
  FSign     = $0080; (* Sign Flag      *)
  FOverflow = $0800; (* Overflow Flag  *)

{ File Mode Constants }

Const
  fmClosed = $D7B0; (* File Closed *)
  fmInput  = $D7B1; (* File Open for Input *)
  fmOutput = $D7B2; (* File Open for Output *)
  fmInOut  = $D7B3; (* File Open for Input and Output *)

{ File Attribute Constants }

  Const
    ReadOnly   = $01;
    Hidden     = $02;
    SysFile    = $04;
    VolumeID   = $08;
    Directory  = $10;
    Archive    = $20;
    AnyFile    = $3F;
    End;
```

DOS Unit Data Types

The DOS unit contains declarations for several data types, which are used with routines found in the DOS unit. The **FileRec** data type is used for typed and untyped file variables, while the **TextRec** data type is used for text-file variables.

```
Type
  { Typed and untyped }
  FileRec = Record
```

```
    Handle  : Word;
    Mode    : Word;
    RecSize : Word;
    Private : Array [1..26] Of Byte;
    End;

  { Textfile Record }
  TextBuf = Array [0..127] Of Char;
  TextRec = Record
    Handle    : Word;
    Mode      : Word;
    Bufsize   : Word;
    Private   : Word;
    BufPos    : Word;
    BufEnd    : Word;
    BufPtr    : ^TextBuf;
    OpenFunc  : Pointer;
    InOutFunc : Pointer;
    FlushFunc : Pointer;
    CloseFunc : Pointer;
    UserData  : Array [1..16] Of Byte;
    Name      : Array [0..79] Of Char;
    Buffer    : TextBuf;
    End;
```

Both **FileRec** and **TextRec** contain a Mode field, which can be interpreted by using the file mode constants described previously.

The **Registers** data type is used with the **Intr** and **MsDos** routines to invoke DOS and BIOS functions:

```
Type
  Registers = Record
   Case Integer Of
    0 : (AX,BX,CX,DX,BP,SI,DI,DS,ES,Flags : Word);
    1 : (AL,AH,BL,BH,CL,CH,DL,DH : Word);
    End;
```

Each field in the **Registers** data type refers to a CPU register. By setting the values in this record, you can call system-level services just as you would in assembler.

The DOS unit also includes data types used for time and date functions (**DateTime**) and directory operations (**SearchRec**). The **Date-Time** data type is used with the **GetTime** and **SetTime** procedures, which read and set the time and date of the system clock.

The DateTime Type

```
Type
  DateTime = Record
```

```
Year, Month, Day, Hour, Min, Sec : Integer;
End;
```

The SearchRec Type

```
Type
  SearchRec = Record
    Fill : Array[1..21] Of Byte;
    Attr : Byte;
    Time : LongInt;
    Size : LongInt;
    Name : String[12];
    End;
```

The **SearchRec** record type is used with two procedures, **FindFirst** and **FindNext**, which read the file entries in a directory. The fields in the **SearchRec** record include the file attribute (Attr), the time stamp (Time), the size of the file (Size), and the filename (Name).

The DOS unit also declares three **String** data types: **DirStr**, **NameStr**, and **ExtStr**. The **DirStr** type is used to hold the directory path portion of a filename (for example, C:\TP\TEMP); **NameStr** is used for the filename; **ExtStr** is for the file extension.

```
Type
  DirStr   = String[67];
  NameStr  = String[8];
  ExtStr   = String[3];
```

These types are used with the **Fsplit** procedure, which takes a complete file spec and returns separately the path, filename, and extension.

The DosError Variable

In the event of an error, many of the routines in the DOS unit set the value of **DosError** to indicate which error occurred. **DosError** is an **Integer** variable that can take any of the values in Table 12-5.

DOS Unit Procedures and Functions

While you can access any DOS or BIOS function using the **Intr** and **MsDos** procedures, the DOS unit contains many routines that make it easy to access these functions. These routines are described briefly in the following sections. Detailed descriptions of these routines can be found in Appendix E.

Interrupt Support Routines

The interrupt support routines give you the tools to call any DOS or BIOS service or install your own interrupt service routines. **GetIntVec** returns the current address for the routine executed by a particular interrupt; **SetIntVec** replaces the existing interrupt routine with one of your own. The **Intr** procedure executes any interrupt service, while **MsDos** executes only DOS services.

Date and Time Routines

The system clock keeps track of the current date and time. You can get the date and time from the system clock with the **GetTime** and **GetDate** procedures. Likewise, you can set the time and date of the system clock with **SetTime** and **SetDate**.

Files have their own date stamp, a single long integer that contains both the time and date the file was created or last updated. You can get the time stamp for any file with **GetFTime**. Before you can interpret the file's time stamp, you must pass it through **UnPackTime**, which

0	No error
2	File not found
3	Path not found
5	Access denied
6	Invalid handle
8	Not enough memory
10	Invalid environment
11	Invalid format
18	No more files

Table 12-5.   Possible Values of DosError

produces a date and time. You can reverse this process with **PackTime**, which takes a time and date and returns a long integer that you can use in **SetFTime** to set a file's time and date.

Disk and File Routines

The DOS unit contains two disk-status routines: **DiskFree** and **Disk-Size**. **DiskFree** returns the number of free bytes on a disk, and **Disk-Size** returns the total number of used and unused bytes on a disk.

Some of the most useful routines in the DOS unit are those that operate on disk files. Two routines, **FindFirst** and **FindNext** let you read the files in any directory. **FindFirst**, as the name implies, reads information on the first file in the directory while **FindNext** gets information on each subsequent file. You can use the DOS wildcard characters in your search and even specify the type of file to search for (for example, archive, system, hidden).

If you want to know the attributes for a specific file, you can use **GetFAttr**, which returns the file attribute byte for the named file. **SetFAttr**, on the other hand, allows you to set the value of a file's attribute byte. The **FExpand** function takes a filename as a parameter and returns the complete file spec, including the disk drive, path, and filename. **FSplit** does just the opposite, taking a complete file spec and returning its components: path, name, and extension. **FSearch** looks for a file within a list of directories. If the file is found, **FSearch** returns the complete file spec; if not, it returns a blank string.

Process Routines

Exec and **Keep** are two of the more advanced routines in the DOS unit. **Exec** allows you to execute programs or a DOS shell from within a program, while **Keep** terminates a program, but keeps it resident in memory. The **SwapVectors** routine, when used with **Exec**, provides some margin of safety. When you use **Exec** to run a child program from within your Turbo Pascal program, you run the risk that the child program will permanently alter the interrupt vector table. By calling **SwapVectors** before and after the call to **Exec**, you can make sure that the interrupt vectors will be restored to their original state. One final process-control routine is **DosExitCode**, which provides a DOS error result upon program termination. This code can be used by other programs or by a batch file.

DOS maintains an area in memory that contains information about the computer's *environment* (for example, the number of file handles, the location of COMMAND.COM, and so on). This information is contained in a number of *environment strings*. The function **EnvCount** returns the number of environment strings in memory, and the function **EnvStr** returns a specified environment string. A third routine, **GetEnv**, returns the environment string for a specific environment element (for example, FILES, COMSPEC, PATH).

Finally, the DOS unit contains a number of miscellaneous routines that provide information and control over the computer. The **DosVersion** routine returns an **Integer** whose high and low bytes contain the version of DOS in use. The personal computer also has two features— control-break checking and disk-write verification—that can be turned on or off. The CTRL-BREAK key combination is used to terminate programs. When control-break checking is disabled, DOS checks for CTRL-BREAK only during console, printer, or communications I/O; when it is enabled, DOS checks for CTRL-BREAK at every system call. The **GetCBreak** routine returns a Boolean value that indicates if control-break checking is on or off. **SetCBreak** accepts a Boolean value that turns control-break checking on or off. Similarly, the **GetVerify** routine returns a Boolean value that indicates if disk-write verification is on or off, while **SetVerify** accepts a Boolean value that turns disk-write verification on or off. When disk-write verification is enabled, DOS verifies every disk write; when it is disabled, DOS performs no verification.

The use of each of these DOS unit routines is detailed in Appendix E. The following program, however, demonstrates each routine (except **Keep**) and should provide you with a good idea of how you can use them in your programs.

```
{$F+}
{$M 10000, 0, 0}
Program Test;
Uses DOS,CRT;
Var
  OldTimerVec : Pointer;
  Regs : Registers;
  ClockFlag  : Word;
  x,y : Byte;
  i : Integer;
  S : String;

(**************************************************)
```

```
Procedure CallOldInt(sub : Pointer);
Begin
{ This procedure calls an interrupt service by address }
Inline($9C/$FF/$5E/$06);
End;

(**************************************************)

Procedure XYChar(x,y : Byte;
                 c : Char;
                 fg,bg : Byte);

{
This routine writes a character to the screen using
a BIOS routine.
}
Begin
GotoXY(x,y);
FillChar(Regs,SizeOf(Regs),0);
With Regs Do
  Begin
  AH := $09;                   (* Call BIOS Service 9          *)
  AL := Ord(C);                (* Character in AL              *)
  BH := 0;                     (* Video page in BH             *)
  BL := (bg shl 4) + fg;       (* Attribute in BL              *)
  CX := 1;                     (* Number of repetitions in CX *)
  End;
Intr($10,Regs);               (* Call BIOS Interrupt 10h      *)
End;

(**************************************************)

Procedure Clock; Interrupt;
{
This procedure replaces the original clock interrupt.
}
Begin
CallOldInt(OldTimerVec);        (* Call the original routine *)
Inc(ClockFlag,1);               (* Increment the counter      *)
Str(ClockFlag,S);               (* Convert to string          *)
For i := 1 To Length(S) Do      (* Write string with XYChar  *)
  XYChar(i,10,s[i],Yellow,Black);
End;

(**************************************************)

Function PadRight(S : String; L : Word) : String;
{
This function adds blank characters to
a String until it reaches length L. If
the String is longer than L to begin with,
this function truncates the String.
}
Begin
If Length(S) > L Then
  S[0] := Chr(L);
While Length(S) < L Do
  S := S + ' ';
```

```
PadRight := S;
End;

(*************************************************)

Procedure InterruptSupportDemo;
Var
  I : Word;
  FileName : String;
  Regs : Registers;
Begin
ClrScr;

(* Use BIOS interrupt to determine video adapter *)

FillChar(Regs,SizeOf(Regs),0);
Regs.AH := $0F;
Intr($10,Regs);
  Case Regs.AL of
  1..6   : WriteLn('CGA');
  7      : WriteLn('Monochrome');
  8..10  : WriteLn('PCjr');
  13..16 : WriteLn('EGA');
  End;

(* Use DOS service to determine if file is read-only *)

WriteLn;
Write('Enter file name: ');
ReadLn(FileName);
FillChar(Regs,SizeOf(Regs),0);

(* Add null character to String *)
(* so String can be used as      *)
(* ASCIIZ String.                *)

FileName := FileName + #0;

With Regs Do
  Begin
  AH := $43;
  DS := Seg(FileName);
  DX := Ofs(FileName) + 1;  (* Skip length byte *)
  End;

MsDos(Regs);

If ((Regs.CL And $01) > 0) Then
  WriteLn('File is Read-Only')
Else
  WriteLn('File is not Read-Only');
WriteLn;
Write('Press ENTER...');
ReadLn;

ClockFlag := 0;
GetIntVec(8,OldTimerVec); (* Save interrupt address *)
SetIntVec(8,@Clock); (* Point timer interrupt to Clock *)
```

```
WriteLn;
Write('Press ENTER...');
ReadLn;
SetIntVec(8,OldTimerVec); (* Restore interrupt address *)
End;


(*************************************************)

Procedure DateAndTimeProcedures;
Const
  DayName: Array [0..6] of String[10] = ('Sunday',
                               'Monday',
                               'Tuesday',
                               'Wednesday',
                               'Thursday',
                               'Friday',
                               'Saturday');
Var
  Year, Month, Day, DayOfWeek,
  Hour, Minute, Second, Sec100 : Word;
  fname : String;
  f : File;
  T : LongInt;
  DT : DateTime;

Begin
ClrScr;

(* Display current date and time *)
WriteLn('Current date and time.');
GetDate(Year, Month, Day, DayOfWeek);
WriteLn('System Date = ',DayName[DayOfWeek],' ',Month,'/',Day,
        '/',Year);
GetTime(Hour, Minute, Second, Sec100);
WriteLn('System time = ',Hour,':',Minute,':',Second,':',Sec100);
WriteLn;

WriteLn('Set current date and time.');
(* Set new date and time *)
Write('Enter year (1980 Or later): ');
ReadLn(Year);
Write('Enter month: ');
ReadLn(Month);
Write('Enter day: ');
ReadLn(Day);
Write('Enter hour: ');
ReadLn(Hour);
Write('Enter minute: ');
ReadLn(Minute);
Second := 0;
Sec100 := 0;
SetDate(Year, Month, Day);
SetTime(Hour, Minute, Second, Sec100);

(* Display new date and time *)
WriteLn('New date and time.');
```

```
GetDate(Year, Month, Day, DayOfWeek);
WriteLn('System Date = ',DayName[DayOfWeek],' ',Month,'/',Day,'/
        ',Year);
GetTime(Hour, Minute, Second, Sec100);
WriteLn('System time = ',Hour,':',Minute,':',Second,':',Sec100);
WriteLn;
Write('Press ENTER...');
ReadLn;

(* Get time and date for a file *)
ClrScr;
WriteLn('Get date and time for a file.');
Write('Enter file name: ');
ReadLn(fname);
Assign(f,fname);
Reset(f);
GetFTime(f,T);
UnPackTime(T,DT);
With DT Do
  Begin
  WriteLn('File name: ',fname);
  WriteLn('Date:       ',Month,'/',Day,'/',Year);
  WriteLn('Time:       ',Hour,':',Min,':',Sec);
  End;

(* Set new time and date for file *)
WriteLn('Set file''s date and time.');
With DT Do
  Begin
  Write('Year: ');
  ReadLn(Year);
  Write('Month: ');
  ReadLn(Month);
  Write('Day: ');
  ReadLn(Day);
  Write('Hour: ');
  ReadLn(Hour);
  Write('Minute: ');
  ReadLn(Minute);

  Second := 0;
  End;
PackTime(DT,T);
SetFTime(f,T);

(* Get new time and date for file *)
WriteLn('Get new time and date for file.');
GetFTime(f,T);
UnPackTime(T,DT);
With DT Do
  Begin
  WriteLn('File name: ',fname);
  WriteLn('Date:       ',Month,'/',Day,'/',Year);
  WriteLn('Time:       ',Hour,':',Min,':',Sec);
  End;

Close(f);
WriteLn;
```

```pascal
Write('Press ENTER...');
ReadLn;
End;

(************************************************)

Procedure DiskStatusFunctions;
Var
  S : LongInt;
Begin
ClrScr;
WriteLn('Disk status.');
S := DiskFree(0);
WriteLn('Free space on disk = ',s,' bytes/ ',s Div 1024,
        ' Kbytes');
S := DiskSize(0);
WriteLn('Total space on disk = ',s,' bytes/ ',s Div 1024,
        ' Kbytes');
WriteLn;
Write('Press ENTER...');
ReadLn;
End;

(************************************************)

Procedure FileHandling;
Var
  Attr : Word;
  f : File;
  S : String;
  DT : DateTime;
  Srec : SearchRec;
  PS : PathStr;
  DS : DirStr;
  FN : NameStr;
  EN : ExtStr;

Begin
ClrScr;
WriteLn('Press ENTER for a directory listing.');
ReadLn;
FindFirst('*.*',AnyFile,Srec);
While DosError = 0 Do
  Begin
  With Srec Do
    Begin
    UnPackTime(Time,DT);
    With DT Do
      Begin
      S := FExpand(Name);
      Fsplit(S, DS, FN, EN);
      WriteLn(PadRight(DS,10),' ',
              PadRight(FN,9),' ',
              PadRight(EN,5),' ',
              Size:7,'  ',Year);
      End;
    End;
  FindNext(Srec);
  End;
```

```
WriteLn;
Write('Press ENTER...');
ReadLn;

WriteLn('Search for a file by name.');
ClrScr;
  Repeat
  Write('Enter file name: ');
  ReadLn(S);
  Write('Enter directory: ');
  ReadLn(DS);
  S := Fsearch(S,DS);
  If S = '' Then WriteLn('File not found...');
  Until S > '';

Assign(f,S);
GetFAttr(f,Attr);

If ((Attr And ReadOnly) > 0) Then
  WriteLn('File is read only')
Else
  WriteLn('File is not read only');

If ((Attr And Hidden) > 0) Then
  WriteLn('File is hidden')
Else
  WriteLn('File is not hidden');

If ((Attr And SysFile) > 0) Then
  WriteLn('File is system file')
Else
  WriteLn('File is not system file');

If ((Attr And VolumeID) > 0) Then
  WriteLn('File is Volume ID')
Else
  WriteLn('File is not Volume ID');

If ((Attr And Directory) > 0) Then
  WriteLn('File is Directory')
Else
  WriteLn('File is not Directory');

If ((Attr And Archive) > 0) Then
  WriteLn('File is Archive')
Else
  WriteLn('File is not Archive');

WriteLn;
Write('Press ENTER...');
ReadLn;
End;

(*************************************************)

Procedure ProcessHandling;
Begin
ClrScr;
```

```
WriteLn(''DOS SHELL: Type EXIT to return to program...');
SwapVectors;
Exec(GetEnv('COMSPEC'),'');
WriteLn('DosExitCode = ',DosExitCode);
SwapVectors;
WriteLn;
Write('Press ENTER...');
ReadLn;
End;

(************************************************)

Procedure EnvironmentHandling;
Var
  i : Integer;
Begin
ClrScr;
WriteLn('Environment info: ');
WriteLn('Number of Environment Strings = ',EnvCount);
For i := 1 To EnvCount Do
  WriteLn(i:2,': ',EnvStr(i));
WriteLn;
WriteLn('COMSPEC = ',GetEnv('COMSPEC'));
WriteLn('PATH = ',GetEnv('PATH'));
WriteLn;
Write('Press ENTER...');
ReadLn;
End;

(************************************************)

Procedure MiscProcs;
Var
  YN : Char;
  DosVer : Word;
  Verify,
  CBreak : Boolean;
Begin
ClrScr;
WriteLn('Other information.');
DosVer := DosVersion;
WriteLn('DOS Version: ',Lo(DosVer),'.',Hi(DosVer));
WriteLn;

GetCBreak(CBreak);
If CBreak Then
  Begin
  WriteLn('Ctrl-Break checking is ON.');
  Write('Turn Ctrl-Break checking OFF? Y/N: ');
  ReadLn(YN);
  If UpCase(YN) = 'Y' Then
    SetCBreak(FALSE);
  End
Else
  Begin
  WriteLn('Ctrl-Break checking is OFF.');
```

```
    Write('Turn Ctrl-Break checking ON? Y/N: ');
    ReadLn(YN);
    If UpCase(YN) = 'Y' Then
      SetCBreak(TRUE);
    End;

 GetVerify(Verify);
 If Verify Then
   Begin
   WriteLn('Disk write verification is ON.');
   Write('Turn disk write verification OFF? Y/N: ');
   ReadLn(YN);
   If UpCase(YN) = 'Y' Then
     SetVerify(FALSE);
   End
 Else
   Begin
   WriteLn('Disk write verify is OFF.');
   Write('Turn disk write verification ON? Y/N: ');
   ReadLn(YN);
   If UpCase(YN) = 'Y' Then
     SetVerify(TRUE);
   End;

 WriteLn;
 GetCBreak(CBreak);
 If CBreak Then
   WriteLn('Ctrl-Break checking is ON.')
 Else
   WriteLn('Ctrl-Break checking is OFF.');

 GetVerify(Verify);
 If Verify Then
   WriteLn('Disk write verification is ON.')
 Else
   WriteLn('Disk write verify is OFF.');

 WriteLn;
 Write('Press ENTER...');
 ReadLn;
 End;


 (***************************************************)

 Begin
 DateAndTimeProcedures;
 DiskStatusFunctions;
 FileHandling;
 EnvironmentHandling;
 MiscProcs;
 InterruptSupportDemo;
 ProcessHandling;
 End.
```

External Procedures and Inline Code

Extending Turbo Pascal
Inline Directives
External Procedures
Comparing Inline Code and External Procedures
Using Turbo Debugger

When the first computers were developed, no programming languages existed. Every program had to be entered directly into the computer in the form of *machine language*, which consists of numeric codes that represent instructions. Writing and maintaining programs in machine language was extremely difficult; assembler language was developed in response to this need.

Assembler uses mnemonic labels rather than numeric codes, which makes it easier both to write and maintain programs. Even so, assembler programming is still tedious and error prone. Many lines of code are needed to execute even simple tasks. In the early days, each type of computer had its own assembler language, which made it impossible to transfer a program from one computer to another.

High-level languages, such as COBOL and FORTRAN, are the next step up from assembler. Because one high-level statement does the job of many assembler statements, programs can be written faster. Another advantage is that programs written in high-level languages can be moved from one computer to another with only small modifications. So as time went on, assembler was relegated to special-purpose programs, while general applications, with few exceptions, were written in high-level languages.

Extending Turbo Pascal

As a high-level language, Turbo Pascal provides a great deal of power and exceptional speed. Yet procedures written in assembler run much faster and give you control over every aspect of your computer. Fortunately, you can extend the power of Turbo Pascal by incorporating assembler routines into your programs, thereby combining the logic and structure of Turbo Pascal with the speed of assembler.

There are two ways to incorporate assembly language into Turbo Pascal programs: *external procedures* and *inline code*. External procedures are assembly-language routines that you assemble to .OBJ files and link to your Turbo Pascal program when you compile it. Inline code consists of machine-language instructions that you insert directly into your Turbo Pascal program. Turbo Pascal will not catch errors in external procedures or inline code, so you must take great care to see that your inline and external procedures are fully debugged.

Inline Code

Using inline code is much like regressing to the earliest days of computers because you are dealing with the numeric codes that represent machine-language instructions. Writing inline code is no easy task—it requires a solid knowledge of both assembler and Turbo Pascal.

To use inline code, you must begin with the InLine compiler directive, which tells Turbo Pascal to interpret what follows as machine-language instructions. The instructions themselves are hexadecimal numbers preceded by a dollar sign and followed by a slash, as shown here:

```
Inline($8B/$46/<i/    (* MOV AX,I      *)
       $03/$46/<j/    (* ADD AX,J      *)
       $89/$46/$FE);  (* MOV [BP-2],AX *)
```

In this example, the comments show the assembler mnemonics that correspond to the inline code. This inline code moves variable **I** into the AX register, adds **J** to the value in AX, and then moves the contents of AX to a position on the stack. While it is not obvious from the code, both **I** and **J** are value parameters that are located on the stack. If these were global variables, different inline code would be required.

Notice the use of the size operators < and >. For lack of a better name, let's refer to < as the byte-size operator and > as the word-size operator. These operators are used to reference variables. In the preceding example, the variables are value parameters of type **Word**. The byte-size operator is used because the variables are located using single-byte offsets to the BP register. Using the correct size operator is vitally important. The only way to be absolutely sure you have done so is to use a debugger, like Turbo Debugger, to view your inline code in unassembled form.

In the example just given, all inline code is included in a single statement that spans three lines. Another approach is to declare each line as a separate inline statement, as shown here:

```
Inline($8B/$46/<i);      (* MOV AX,I      *)
Inline($03/$46/<j);      (* ADD AX,J      *)
Inline($89/$46/$FE);     (* MOV [BP-2],AX *)
```

While this approach is more cumbersome, it is also easier to debug with Turbo Debugger. If you were to code all three lines as a single statement, Turbo Debugger would only show the first line as part of the unassembled listing. But if you have made each line a statement, Turbo Debugger will show each line with its unassembled code, making debugging much easier.

The following listing demonstrates a simple inline function that adds two integers:

```
Program TestInline;
Uses CRT;

(***********************************************)

Function Sum(i,j : Integer) : Integer;
Begin
Inline($8B/$46/<i);      (* MOV AX,I      *)
Inline($03/$46/<j);      (* ADD AX,J      *)
Inline($89/$46/$FE);     (* MOV [BP-2],AX *)
End;

(***********************************************)

Begin
ClrScr;
Write('1 + 2 = ');
WriteLn(Sum(1,2));
WriteLn;
Write('Press ENTER...');
ReadLn;
End.
```

Notice that the function heading is the same as it would be for a Turbo Pascal function. The function block starts with **Begin** followed by the **Inline** statement and open parenthesis, which tells Turbo Pascal that machine code follows. Each byte of machine code is entered in hexadecimal format and separated by a slash. The **Inline** statement ends with a close parenthesis. The assembler mnemonics, added as comments, have no effect on the program, but help explain what the code is doing.

Now that you have coded the inline procedure, you might be interested to see what the machine-level instructions look like. Here is the unassembled code for the function **Sum**:

```
PUSH    BP
MOV     BP,SP
SUB     SP,+02

MOV     AX,[BP+08]
ADD     AX,[BP+06]
MOV     [BP-02],AX

MOV     AX,[BP-02]
MOV     SP,BP
POP     BP
RETF    0004
```

The three lines in the middle of the listing are the inline statements. To these, Turbo Pascal has added seven instructions. The first three lines set up the stack on entry to the procedure. Of these, the first two lines are standard to any procedure or function call. The third line, **SUB   SP,+02**, is used for functions that return one-byte or two-byte results. In other words, Turbo Pascal reserves two bytes on the stack as a temporary holding place for the function result.

The last four lines in the listing move the function result from the stack into the AX register, restore the SP and BP registers to their original values, and make a far return while popping the parameters off the stack.

Returning function results in inline procedures can be tricky. Turbo Pascal expects to find the function result at a specific location on the stack. You must make sure the function result gets placed on the stack before the procedure ends.

Notice that a far return is used to terminate the function because the {F+} compiler directive was enabled when the program was compiled. As you can see, writing inline procedures and functions is not easy. Not only do you need to work in machine language, but you also need to know how Turbo Pascal works at the assembler level.

All in all, it is far easier and more productive to use external assembler procedures assembled to .OBJ files and linked to Turbo Pascal with the **External** directive. There is one place, however, where inline code is indispensable—inline directives.

Inline Directives

An inline directive is like an inline procedure or function, except that Turbo Pascal adds no code to set up or clear the stack. An inline directive is declared much like an inline procedure or function, except that the **Begin** and **End** reserved words are omitted. The following listing demonstrates the difference between an inline function and an inline directive:

```
(* Inline Function *)
Function Sum(i,j : Integer) : Integer;
Begin
Inline($8B/$46/<i);       (* MOV AX,I      *)
Inline($03/$46/<j);       (* ADD AX,J      *)
Inline($89/$46/$FE);      (* MOV [BP-2],AX *)
End;

(************************************************)

(* Inline Directive *)
Function SumD(i,j : Integer) : Integer;
Inline($58/       (* POP AX - moves j into AX *)
       $5B/       (* POP BX - moves i into BX *)
       $03/$C3);  (* ADD AX,BX - sums values *)
```

When you compile this code, function **SumD** produces the following instructions:

```
POP AX
POP BX
ADD AX,BX
```

As you can see, Turbo Pascal has not added a single instruction. With inline directives, what you see is what you get. Notice, however, that the inline directive cannot access variables by name. And because Turbo

Pascal did not set up the stack, you can't refer to the parameters as offsets of BP (unless, of course, you set up the stack yourself). The inline directive accesses the parameters by popping them off the stack directly into registers.

As the example just given illustrates, procedures and functions written as inline directives are not easy to program. Generally speaking, inline directives are best used for short segments of code that perform a special function. For example, this inline directive stores the value of SP in **WordVar**, a variable of type **Word**.

```
Inline($89/$26/WordVar);    (* MOV WordVar,SP *)
```

Naturally, you aren't going to need to obtain the value of the SP register very often, but when you do, the most efficient way of doing this is through an inline directive. As your programming tasks become more advanced, you will find many uses for this special programming technique.

External Procedures

External procedures are routines that you write in assembler, assemble to an .OBJ file, and then link to your Turbo Pascal program when you compile it. Compared with inline code, assembler routines have many advantages. Assembler code is far easier to write, interpret, and maintain than is the machine language used in inline procedures. In fact, when programmers write an inline procedure, they usually code it as an external procedure and then convert it to inline code. Since inline procedures have no major advantages over external procedures, there is little reason to go that extra step.

More important, external routines give you direct access to Turbo Pascal global variables, local variables, parameters, procedures, and functions. In other words, you can access Turbo Pascal data and functions just as easily in assembler as in Turbo Pascal. These powerful features make writing external assembler routines an attractive alternative to Turbo Pascal when extra speed is required.

An External Function

Earlier you saw inline code for a function that adds two integers. The following assembler listing, written as an external routine, performs the same function:

```
CODE      SEGMENT BYTE PUBLIC
          ASSUME CS:CODE

PUBLIC SUM

SUM            PROC FAR

               PUSH    BP
               MOV     BP,SP

               MOV     AX,[BP+08]
               ADD     AX,[BP+06]

               POP     BP
               RET     4

SUM            ENDP
CODE           ENDS
               END
```

While it is small, this example routine demonstrates the essential aspects of assembler routines. It begins by defining the CODE segment and declaring the procedure **Sum** as a public procedure. (While assembler lets you use any code segment name, Turbo Pascal recognizes only two: CODE and CSEG.) The PUBLIC designation is important since it tells the assembler that this routine must be made available to other program modules. If you do not declare a routine PUBLIC, you will not be able to access it from Turbo Pascal.

The remainder of the assembler code defines the **Sum** routine. The procedure begins, as all external procedures should, by saving the base pointer (BP) and setting the stack pointer. The next two statements take the integer parameters from the stack, add them, and leave the result in the AX register. For functions that return scalars (for example, bytes, integers, words, and so on), Turbo Pascal will expect to find the result in the AX register. Notice that the procedure ends with the **RET 4** instruction. The value 4 refers to the four bytes (two integers) that Turbo Pascal pushed onto the stack when the routine was called. You must make sure that all parameters are removed from the stack when your procedure returns.

To use the external routine just given in a program, first assemble it to an .OBJ file. For the sake of example, assume the assembler code is in ADD.ASM and the object file is ADD.OBJ. Inside your Turbo Pascal program, you declare the external routine as follows:

```
{$F+}
{$L ADD}
Function Sum(i,j : Integer): Integer; External;
```

The first statement is a compiler directive that forces far calls. Since our external routine is declared a FAR PROC and terminates with a **RETF** command, we must ensure that Turbo Pascal treats it as a far call. The next line is a compiler directive that tells Turbo Pascal to look in the ADD.OBJ file to resolve any external references. Since the procedure **Sum** is contained in ADD.OBJ, the external reference will be resolved by the linker.

The final statement is the function declaration, which concludes with the **External** declaration, which tells Turbo Pascal that the code for this procedure will be found in an object file. The complete program, using the external routine, is shown here:

```
Program TestExternal;
Uses CRT;

(************************************************)

{$F+}
{$L ADD}
Function Sum(i,j : Integer) : Integer; External;

(************************************************)

Begin
ClrScr;
Write('1 + 2 = ');
WriteLn(Sum(1,2));
WriteLn;
Write('Press ENTER...');
ReadLn;
End.
```

Using Global Data and Procedures

One of the most valuable features of Turbo Pascal's assembler interface is the ability to use global procedures, variables, and typed constants in your assembler routines. This feature makes your code much easier to maintain because you can intersperse Pascal and assembler code with much greater flexibility.

As an example of how an assembler routine might use global data and procedures, consider a routine designed to change a string from lowercase to uppercase. The procedure takes a string as a variable parameter and returns it with all uppercase letters. In our example, however, a limitation states that passing a string of more than a certain number of characters is illegal and should cause the program to stop executing. Your assembler routine needs to know what the maximum number of characters is, and how to transfer control when an error is detected.

The following assembler code meets these criteria. The Turbo Pascal global variable **MaxStrLen** holds the number that signals an error. Of course, you could hard-code a number into the procedure, or pass a number as a parameter, but these solutions make the program more clumsy and difficult to maintain.

```
DATA      SEGMENT BYTE PUBLIC

          EXTRN MaxStrLen : BYTE;

DATA      ENDS

CODE      SEGMENT BYTE PUBLIC
          ASSUME CS:CODE, DS:DATA

          EXTRN       StrLenError : FAR

          PUBLIC      UPCASESTR

UPCASESTR     PROC FAR

          PUSH        BP
          MOV         BP,SP

          LDS         SI,[BP+6]          ; Move string length byte
          MOV         AL,BYTE PTR [SI]   ; into AL.

          XOR         CX,CX              ; Move string length
          MOV         CL,AL              ; into CL.
          CMP         CL,MaxStrLen  ; If the string is less than
          JL          LOOP1         ; the maximum length, go on.
          CALL        StrLenError   ; If not, call StrLenError.

LOOP1:    INC         SI                 ; Point to character.
          MOV         AL,BYTE PTR [SI]   ; Load char into AL.
          CMP         AL,97              ; Compare to 'a'.
```

```
        JB          NOTLOW              ; If lower, jump.
        CMP         AL,122              ; Compare to 'z'.
        JA          NOTLOW              ; If higher, jump.
        SUB         AL,32               ; Uppercase char.
        MOV         BYTE PTR [SI],AL    ; Move char to string.

NOTLOW: LOOP        LOOP1

        POP         BP
        RET         2

UPCASESTR       ENDP

CODE    ENDS
        END
```

Part of the CODE segment refers to an external procedure named
StrLenError, a global Turbo Pascal routine that is called when an
illegally long string is passed to the assembler routine. When the procedure starts, it looks at the length byte of the string parameter. If the
length is greater than or equal to the test value (**MaxStrLen**), control is
passed to Turbo Pascal procedure **StrLenError**, which prints a message
and halts execution. The program listed here shows how this routine can
be tested:

```
{$F+}
Program TestAsm;
Uses CRT;
Const
  MaxStrLen : Byte = 100;
  Var
  s : string;

{$L UPCASE}
Procedure UpCaseStr(Var s : String); External;

(************************************************)

Procedure StrLenError;
Begin
WriteLn('String length error encountered.');
WriteLn;
Write('Press ENTER...');
ReadLn;
Halt;
End;

(************************************************)

Begin
ClrScr;
s := 'abcdef';
```

```
WriteLn('Lower case = ',s);
UpCaseStr(s);
WriteLn('Upper case = ',s);
WriteLn(s);
WriteLn;
WriteLn('Force a string-length error condition.');
WriteLn;
Write('Press ENTER...');
ReadLn;
s[0] := Chr(101);
UpCaseStr(s);
End.
```

Make sure the **F** compiler directive is enabled when you compile this program because the external routine was defined as a far call. If you do not enable the **F** compiler directive, your program will crash when it attempts to return from the external procedure.

Using the Turbo Assembler

In the previous examples of external routines, all references to parameters were made using an offset to the base pointer (for example, **[BP+6]**). Using offsets is time consuming and is error prone. Fortunately, Borland has introduced a solution in Turbo Assembler.

Turbo Assembler is a full-fledged, high-performance assembler, with additional capabilities that make linking to Turbo Pascal easy. Consider the following example assembler routine—a procedure called **Switch** that swaps the values of two variables. The procedure requires three parameters—two pointers (one to each of the variables to be swapped), and a **Word** parameter that indicates the size of the parameters to be swapped (for example, integers would have a size of two). Normally, your assembler routine would need to define data and code segments and include entry and exit code to set up the stack and pop the correct number of parameters. With Turbo Assembler, much of the work is done for you.

```
.MODEL TPASCAL
.DATA

BUFFER DB 256 DUP(?)     ; Buffer to hold value during switch

.CODE
PUBLIC SWITCH

Switch  PROC FAR A : DWORD, B : DWORD, Dsize : WORD
```

```
; MOVE A INTO BUFFER

        LDS     SI,A        ; Load address of A into DS:SI
        LEA     DI,BUFFER ; Load address of Buffer in ES:DI
        MOV     CX,Dsize  ; Move Dsize into CX

        ; Move contents of A into Buffer
        REP     MOVS BYTE PTR ES:[DI],DS:[SI]

; MOVE B INTO A

        LDS     SI,B        ; Load address of B into DS:SI
        LES     DI,A        ; Load address of A in ES:DI
        MOV     CX,Dsize  ; Mov  Dsize into CX

        ; Move contents of B into A
        REP     MOVS BYTE PTR ES:[DI],DS:[SI]

; MOVE BUFFER INTO B

        LEA     SI,BUFFER ; Load address of Buffer into DS:SI
        LES     DI,B        ; Load address of B in ES:DI
        MOV     CX,Dsize  ; Move Dsize into CX

        ; Move contents of Buffer into B
        REP     MOVS BYTE PTR ES:[DI],DS:[SI]

        RET

SWITCH  ENDP
        END
```

The first line of the assembler routine, **.MODEL TPASCAL**, tells Turbo Assembler to generate code for linking to a Turbo Pascal program. The **.DATA** and **.CODE** directives replace the more cumbersome pseudo operation codes required by other assemblers. The procedure prototype

```
Switch  PROC FAR a : DWORD, b : DWORD, Dsize : WORD
```

tells Turbo Assembler the name of the procedure (**Switch**), that it is a far call, and that the procedure will take three variables—two addresses (**a** and **b**) and one numeric value parameter (**Dsize**).

Note that the procedure in the assembler listing given earlier does not include any entry or exit code. In fact, the RET instruction, at the end, does not even specify the number of bytes to pop off the stack— Turbo Assembler fills in the correct number for you. Moreover, Turbo Assembler lets you refer to parameters and global variables by their

Turbo Pascal names. As you can see, writing external routines in Turbo Assembler is far easier than using standard assemblers.

The program listed here shows how to use the assembler routine just given. The **L** compiler directive names the object file to link with. The program contains two switching procedures—**Switch**, the external routine, and **Switch1**, a routine written in Turbo Pascal. The Pascal procedure is offered as a comparison and, surprisingly, runs nearly as fast as the assembler routine—a testimony to the efficiency of Turbo Pascal.

```
{$F+}
Program SwitchTest;
Uses CRT;
Var
  a,b : Integer;
  c,d : Real;
  e,f : String;

{$L SWITCH}
Procedure Switch(Var a,b;
                 c : Integer); External;

Procedure Switch1(Var a,b;
                  c : Integer);
Var
  Buf : String;

Begin
Move(a,Buf,c);
Move(b,a,c);
Move(Buf,b,c);
End;

Begin
ClrScr;

a := 1;
b := 2;
c := 12.34;
d := 45.67;
e := 'ABCDEFG';
f := 'HIJKLMN';

WriteLn('Using assembler');
WriteLn;
WriteLn(a,' > ',b);
Switch(a,b,SizeOf(a));
WriteLn(a,' < ',b);
WriteLn;

WriteLn(c:0:2,' > ',d:0:2);
```

```
Switch(c,d,SizeOf(c));
WriteLn(c:0:2,' < ',d:0:2);
WriteLn;

WriteLn(e,' > ',f);
Switch(e,f,SizeOf(e));
WriteLn(e,' < ',f);
WriteLn;
WriteLn;

a := 1;
b := 2;
c := 12.34;
d := 45.67;
e := 'ABCDEFG';
f := 'HIJKLMN';

WriteLn('Using Pascal');
WriteLn;
WriteLn(a,' > ',b);
Switch(a,b,SizeOf(a));
WriteLn(a,' < ',b);
WriteLn;

WriteLn(c:0:2,' > ',d:0:2);
Switch(c,d,SizeOf(c));
WriteLn(c:0:2,' < ',d:0:2);
WriteLn;

WriteLn(e,' > ',f);
Switch(e,f,SizeOf(e));
WriteLn(e,' < ',f);
WriteLn;
WriteLn;

ReadLn;
End.
```

The example just given merely touches on the power of Turbo Assembler. If you are serious about writing external routines for Turbo Pascal, you should consider the advantages Turbo Assembler can offer.

Comparing Inline Code and External Procedures

Whether you write your procedures as external procedures or as inline code is largely a matter of personal taste. Inline procedures tend to be faster and compile along with your program, but they are harder to write and maintain. External routines are a bit simpler to write since you do not need to translate the assembler code into machine language; they are also easier to document and manage.

Generally speaking, inline code is best kept to a minimum; but there are times when inline code is not only desirable but necessary. For example, when you want to inject code into a program without creating a separate procedure or function, you must use inline code.

Using Turbo Debugger

You can't program in assembler without a debugger. Whether you use the venerable DEBUG.COM or a more advanced program, there is no substitute for tracing through your code one step at a time. Borland's Turbo Debugger is an invaluable tool for programmers who write assembler routines. With Turbo Debugger you can execute your program one machine instruction at a time, seeing exactly what happens to every register and location in memory. You will also learn a lot about the internal workings of Turbo Pascal—how parameters are passed to the stack, how arithmetic is performed, what registers are saved at certain points, and much more.

To see how Turbo Debugger works, let's use a program, given earlier in this chapter, that contains inline code:

```
{$D+,L+}
Program TestInline;
Uses CRT;

(*************************************************)

Function Sum(i,j : Integer) : Integer;
Begin
Inline($8B/$46/<i);      (* MOV AX,I        *)
Inline($03/$46/<j);      (* ADD AX,J        *)
Inline($89/$46/$FE);     (* MOV [BP-2],AX   *)
End;

(*************************************************)

Begin
ClrScr;
Write('1 + 2 = ');
WriteLn(Sum(1,2));
WriteLn;
Write('Press ENTER...');
ReadLn;
End.
```

When you compile this program, you must be sure that **Standalone debugging** is **On** and that the **D** and **L** compiler directives are enabled. Doing this gives Turbo Debugger the information it needs to match your program's source code to its executable code.

When you have compiled this program to disk, start Turbo Debugger by typing **TD** followed by the name of the program you want to examine. Assuming the program file is named TEST.PAS, the command would be

```
C > TD TEST
```

Turbo Debugger loads the TEST.EXE file and reads the TEST.PAS and TEST.MAP files. Using debugging information appended to the .EXE file, Turbo Debugger can display a line of source code along with the underlying machine-language instructions. Figure 13-1 shows how the TEST.PAS program looks in Turbo Debugger. Notice that an arrow is

```
 File   View   Run   Breakpoints   Data   Window   Options          READY
╔Module: TESTINLINE  File: TEST.PAS 24══════════════════════════════════1╗
║                                                                         ║
║  Function Sum(i,j : Integer) : Integer;                                 ║
║  Begin                                                                  ║
║  Inline($8B/$46/<i);        (* MOV AX,I      *)                         ║
║  Inline($03/$46/<j);        (* ADD AX,J      *)                         ║
║  Inline($89/$46/$FE);       (* MOV [BP-2],AX *)                         ║
║  End;                                                                   ║
║                                                                         ║
║  (***************************************************)                  ║
║                                                                         ║
║► Begin                                                                  ║
║  ClrScr;                                                                ║
║  Write('1 + 2 = ');                                                     ║
║  WriteLn(Sum(1,2));                                                     ║
║  WriteLn;                                                               ║
║  Write('Press ENTER...');                                              ║
║  ReadLn;                                                                ║
║  End.                                                                   ║
╚═════════════════════════════════════════════════════════════════════════╝
┌Watches──────────────────────────────────────────────────────────────2┐
│                                                                        │
└────────────────────────────────────────────────────────────────────────┘
Alt: F2-Bkpt at F3-Mod F4-Anim F5-User F6-Undo F7-Instr F8-Rtn F9-To F10-Local
```

Figure 13-1.   Pascal program in Turbo Debugger

pointing to the first **Begin** statement in the program. As you trace through your program, this arrow will always point to the next statement to be executed.

You can trace through your program by using the F7 and F8 keys. Either key executes one line at a time, but the F8 key skips over function calls, while F7 traces into function calls. Using the cursor keys on the numeric pad, you can scroll the program up and down to see different parts of your program. If you scroll down a few statements and press F4, Turbo Debugger will execute all previous statements leading to the current position.

To get the most from Turbo Debugger, you have to get down to the machine-level instructions. This is easy to do—simply press F10 to activate the main menu, select the **View** option, and then press C for **CPU** (see Figure 13-2). This will open the CPU window, which consists of four "panes." The upper-left pane shows your unassembled code (see Figure 13-3); to the right is the register frame, which displays the contents of the CPU's registers. The bottom-right pane keeps track of the stack,

```
  File  View  Run  Breakpoints  Data  Window  Options          MENU
 Module:           ┌───────────────────┐ S 20─────────────────────────1┐
                   │ Breakpoints       │
     Functi        │ Stack             │ nteger;
     Begin         │ Log               │
     Inline        │ Watches           │ AX,I        *)
     Inline        │ Variables         │ AX,J        *)
     Inline        │ Module...  Alt-F3 │ [BP-2],AX   *)
     End;          │ File...           │
                   │ CPU               │
     (*****        │ Dump              │ *******************)
                   │ Registers         │
     Begin         │ Numeric processor │
     ClrScr        │ User screen Alt-F5│
     Write(        ├───────────────────┤
    ►WriteL        │ Another           │
     WriteL        └───────────────────┘
     Write('Press ENTER...');
     ReadLn;
     End.
 ┌Watches─ 4BA9:0010 5D 28 2F 02 8C 2D 9F 13 ]{/♂î-ƒ!!│ ss:752E 0000 ├─2┐
           4BA9:0018 01 01 01 00 02 FF FF FF ☺☺☺ ◙ │ ss:752C►0000
 └Watches─
 F1-Help Esc-Abort
```

Figure 13-2.   Selecting the CPU screen from the View menu

```
   File    View    Run    Breakpoints    Data    Window    Options              READY
 ┌CPU 80286─────────────────────────────────────────────────┬──────────┬──3──┐
 │TESTINLINE.20: WriteLn(Sum(1,2));                          │ ax 0000  │ c=0 │
 │ ░cs:0059▶BF5001          mov     di,0150                  │ bx 0700  │ z=1 │
 │  cs:005C 1E              push    ds                       │ cx 0000  │ s=0 │
 │  cs:005D 57              push    di                       │ dx 03D5  │ o=0 │
 │  cs:005E B80100          mov     ax,0001                  │ si 01D8  │ p=1 │
 │  cs:0061 50              push    ax                       │ di 01D8  │ a=0 │
 │  cs:0062 B80200          mov     ax,0002                  │ bp 752C  │ i=1 │
 │  cs:0065 50              push    ax                       │ sp 752C  │ d=0 │
 │  cs:0066 E897FF          call    TESTINLINE.SUM           │ ds 4CA3  │     │
 │  cs:0069 99              cwd                               │ es 4CA3  │     │
 │  cs:006A 52              push    dx                       │ ss 4CCD  │     │
 │  cs:006B 50              push    ax                       │ cs 4BB9  │     │
 │  cs:006C 31C0            xor     ax,ax                    │ ip 0059  │     │
 │  cs:006E 50              push    ax                       ├──────────┤     │
 │  cs:006F 9A7807264C      call    4C26:0778                │ ss:7532 0000     │
 ├────────────────────────────────────────────────────────  │ ss:7530 0000     │
 │ ds:0000 00 00 00 00 00 00 00 00                          │ ss:752E 0000     │
 │ ds:0008 20 54 20 54 20 54 00 00    T T T                 │ ss:752C▶0000     │
 │ ds:0010 00 00 00 00 00 00 20 54           T              │ ss:752A 0246     │
 │ ds:0018 00 00 20 54 00 00 34 81    T  4ü                 │ ss:7528 4BB9     │
 │ ds:0020 00 00 00 00 00 00 00 00                          │ ss:7526 005A     │
 └──────────────────────────────────────────────────────────┴──────────────────┘
 F2-Bkpt F3-Close F4-Here F5-Zoom F6-Next F7-Trace F8-Step F9-Run F10-Menu
```

Figure 13-3.   Turbo Debugger's CPU screen

and the bottom-left pane displays a portion of RAM. You will be primarily concerned with the code and register frames. Notice that the code pane contains a Pascal statement:

TESTINLINE.20: WriteLn(Sum(1,2));

This is line 20 in your source file, which writes out a function result. Below this line, Turbo Debugger lists the machine instructions that carry it out:

```
cs:0059 BF5001          mov     di,0150
cs:005C 1E              push    ds
cs:005D 57              push    di
cs:005E B80100          mov     ax,0001
cs:0061 50              push    ax
cs:0062 B80200          mov     ax,0002
cs:0065 50              push    ax
cs:0066 E897FF          call    TESTINLINE.SUM
cs:0069 99              cwd
cs:006A 52              push    dx
cs:006B 50              push    ax
```

```
cs:006C 31C0            xor     ax,ax
cs:006E 50              push    ax
cs:006F 9A7807264C      call    4C26:0778
```

Each line consists of three parts—the location of the instruction in the code segment (for example, **cs:0059**), the machine-language instructions in hexadecimal (for example, **BF5001**), and the assembler code (for example, **mov   di,0150**). As you can see, the single line of source code produced 14 machine-language instructions, 2 of which are calls to other routines. In the middle of the code is the call to the procedure **Sum**, which contains inline code. Keep pressing F7 until Turbo Debugger traces into **Sum**. The screen will look like the one in Figure 13-4. Notice that the procedure begins with

```
cs:0000 55              push    bp
cs:0001 89E5            mov     bp,sp
cs:0003 83EC02          sub     sp,0002
```

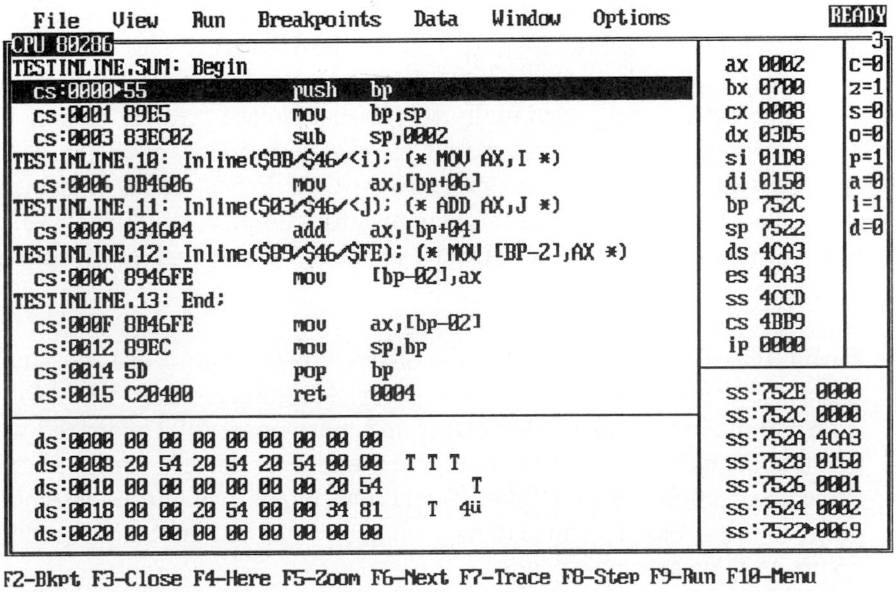

Figure 13-4.   Inline code in Turbo Debugger

Turbo Pascal added this code to the inline function to set up the stack before your procedure executes. The next three lines consist of inline code:

```
TESTINLINE.10: Inline($8B/$46/<i); (* MOV AX,I *)
   cs:0006 8B4606        mov    ax,[bp+06]
TESTINLINE.11: Inline($03/$46/<j); (* ADD AX,J *)
   cs:0009 034604        add    ax,[bp+04]
TESTINLINE.12: Inline($89/$46/$FE); (* MOV [BP-2],AX *)
   cs:000C 8946FE        mov    [bp-02],ax
```

Notice how the inline code compares with the machine instructions in the unassembled lines. By using Turbo Debugger, you can check your inline code to make sure it is doing what you expected.

The procedure ends with code that moves the function result into the AX register, cleans up the stack, and returns to the originating point in the program:

```
cs:000F 8B46FE        mov    ax,[bp-02]
cs:0012 89EC          mov    sp,bp
cs:0014 5D            pop    bp
cs:0015 C20400        ret    0004
```

Inline code is particularly difficult to debug because it consists of nothing but numeric machine instructions. Turbo Debugger lets you see the assembler instructions that your inline statements represent, and executes each statement individually so you can isolate problem areas. But Turbo Debugger is not restricted to use with inline code—it works equally well for external routines and straight Pascal code. It is also a great way to learn about assembler programming. With Turbo Debugger, you can inspect the handiwork of some of the best programmers around.

Turbo Pascal produces extremely efficient code, but there are times when you want or need to do even better. Assembler routines and inline code can make your programs faster and more powerful. Compared with inline code, external routines tend to be easier to develop and maintain. Whichever approach you take, Turbo Assembler will make assembler programming easier, and Turbo Debugger will aid in tracking down errors in your assembler code.

Text Display

Personal Computer Text Display
Using Display Memory
Locating Video Memory
Turbo Pascal Windows

People often judge programs primarily by the quality of their video display. Screen presentation is so important that often programs are successful simply because they "look like" other popular programs. Your computer is capable of producing screen displays that are both attractive and helpful. This chapter discusses these capabilities and how you can control them with Turbo Pascal.

Personal Computer Text Display

Personal computers have two video modes: Text and Graphics (the Graphics mode is covered in Chapter 15). When it is in Text mode, a personal computer can display any of the 256 standard ASCII characters it supports. These characters are locked permanently in the computer's memory, so your PC always knows how to draw them.

To display characters, your computer uses a *video adapter*, which is a circuit board that connects the computer to a monitor. Most computers have either a monochrome adapter or a color graphics adapter (CGA), though enhanced graphics adapters (EGA) and VGA are becoming more common. This chapter focuses on monochrome and color graphics adapters, but the concepts discussed can also apply to the enhanced graphics adapter.

The Video Adapter and Display Memory

Your monitor can display up to 80 characters horizontally and 25 vertically, or a total of 2000 characters in an entire screen. Each character has its own *foreground* and *background color.* The foreground color is the color of the character itself; the background color is the color of the space around the character.

Your computer stores characters and color information in a special part of memory known as the *display memory.* This is what tells your computer which characters and colors to display. Although it is located on the video adapter card, the display memory is considered to be part of RAM. The first byte of the display memory contains the first character on your monitor, which appears in the upper left corner.

Thus, if the first byte in the display memory contains the value 41h (the hexadecimal ASCII value for the letter "A"), the monitor displays the letter "A" in the upper left corner of the monitor. The second byte in display memory, the attribute byte for the first character, contains color and other display information.

This pattern—character, attribute, character, attribute—is repeated for all 2000 characters that appear on the monitor. Thus, the contents of a single screen require 4000 bytes of video memory.

The Attribute Byte

A computer with a color graphics adapter is capable of displaying 16 different colors, each of which consists of up to four elements: blue, red, green, and brightness. The color your computer displays depends on the particular combination of these elements. For example, the color black uses no elements, while light cyan uses the blue, green, and brightness elements. Video adapters also support a blinking element that makes the character flash on and off and has no effect on color.

An attribute byte stores the foreground and background color for the preceding character byte. Figure 14-1 shows how each bit in the attribute byte contributes to the color of the character and its background.

The first three bits (0, 1, and 2) in the attribute byte control a character's foreground color, while the fourth bit (bit 3) adds brightness to the color. You can combine these four elements to create 16 different foreground colors. Bits 4, 5, and 6 determine a character's background color, and bit 7, when on, makes the character blink. Because the background has no brightness element, only eight colors are available for it.

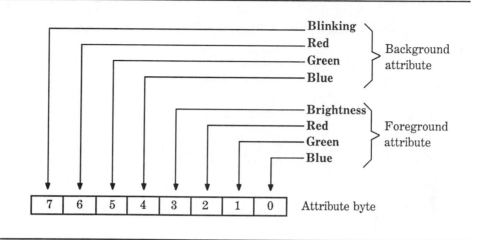

Figure 14-1.   Mapping the attribute byte

On the monochrome monitor, the attribute byte can create only five display formats: hidden, normal, bright, underlined, and reverse. As with the color graphics adapter, brightness is controlled by bit 3 and blinking is controlled by bit 7.

Characters are hidden when both the foreground and background colors are set to the same color. The brightness and blinking bits have no effect with hidden characters.

To display characters in *reverse video* (dark characters on a light background), set the background color to light gray (white without brightness) and the foreground color to black. Characters in reverse video cannot be made bright, but they can be made to blink.

Underlining, a specialty of the monochrome adapter, can only be displayed when the foreground is blue. An underlined character can be shown bright and be made to blink, but it cannot be shown in reverse video.

Personal Computer Text Modes

Personal computers support 16 different display modes, and five of these display text. These modes, listed in Table 14-1, control both the size of the characters and the colors in a display. Mode 0, for example, displays large characters (40 per line) in shades of gray.

Mode	Size	Colors	Adapter
0	40 × 25	Shades of gray	CGA,EGA
1	40 × 25	Colors	CGA,EGA
2	80 × 25	Shades of gray	CGA,EGA
3	80 × 25	Colors	CGA,EGA
7	80 × 25	Black and white	Monochrome

Table 14-1.   Personal Computer Text Modes

The first four display modes, 0 through 3, work only with color graphics adapters and enhanced graphics adapters, most of which can switch between the four modes. Mode 7, on the other hand, is used only by the monochrome adapter.

You can change your computer's Text mode with the Turbo Pascal command **TextMode** (see Figure 14-2). This command, which works only with the color graphics adapter (it has no effect on monochrome adapters), can be used with or without parameters. Without parameters, **TextMode** sets the video display to the previous setting. With parameters, it can set the video display to any of the first four modes. Turbo

Parameters	Settings
TextMode	Set to previous text mode
TextMode(BW40)	Black and white/40 characters per line
TextMode(BW80)	Black and white/80 characters per line
TextMode(CO40)	Color/40 characters per line
TextMode(CO80)	Color/80 characters per line

**Value of Turbo Pascal
Standard Constants**

BW40 = 0
BW80 = 1
CO40 = 2
CO80 = 3

Figure 14-2.   Turbo Pascal TextMode command

Pascal supplies four standard integer constants for the **TextMode** command; **BW40, BW80, CO40,** and **CO80.** Note that **TextMode** always clears the screen before changing the mode.

Controlling Color with Turbo Pascal

Turbo Pascal allows you to select the foreground and background colors for your text with the commands **TextColor** and **TextBackground.** The color graphics adapter provides 16 colors to choose from, as shown in Table 14-2. **TextColor,** which sets the foreground color (the color of the character), can use all 16 colors. **TextBackground,** which sets the background color, can use only the dark colors.

Turbo Pascal provides a standard constant called **Blink,** which when added to the foreground color causes the character to blink. Here are some examples of how to use Turbo Pascal's color commands:

```
TextBackground(Blue);

TextColor(Cyan);

TextColor(Cyan+Blink);
```

Once invoked, the new colors take effect with the next characters you display; the characters already on the screen retain their colors.

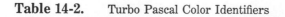

Dark Colors	Light Colors
0: Black	8: DarkGray
1: Blue	9: LightBlue
2: Green	10: LightGreen
3: Cyan	11: LightCyan
4: Red	12: LightRed
5: Magenta	13: LightMagenta
6: Brown	14: Yellow
7: LightGray	15: White

Table 14-2.   Turbo Pascal Color Identifiers

Using Screen Coordinates

Like a map, your computer monitor has locations that are defined by coordinates. Screen coordinates are commonly referred to as x and y, where x is the column position and y is the row position. (Coordinates are displayed in x:y format.) Thus, the upper left corner of the monitor has coordinate position 1:1, while the lower right corner is at coordinate 80:25.

You can move the cursor to any coordinate location on your monitor with the Turbo Pascal command **GotoXY**. For example, the command **GotoXY(1,10)** positions the cursor at column 1 of row 10. If you want to know the coordinates for the cursor's current position, use the Turbo Pascal functions **WhereX** and **WhereY**. **WhereX** returns an integer that represents the cursor column; **WhereY** does the same for the cursor row.

Turbo Pascal's standard screen commands give you the control you need to create attractive and informative screen displays. The following program demonstrates how to create a simple data-entry routine with all of the commands described thus far: **TextMode, TextColor, Text-Background, GotoXY, WhereX,** and **WhereY**.

```
Program Box;
Uses CRT;
Var
  i, code,
  x, y : Integer;
  s : String[20];

(*********************************************)

Procedure DrawBox(x1,y1,x2,y2,fg,bg : Integer);
Var
  i : Byte;
Begin
TextColor(fg);
TextBackground(bg);
For i := (x1+1) To (x2-1) Do
  Begin
  GotoXY(i,y1);
  Write(#205);
  GotoXY(i,y2);
  Write(#205);
  End;

For i := (y1+1) To (y2-1) Do
  Begin
  GotoXY(x1,i);
```

```
    Write(#186);
    GotoXY(x2,i);
    Write(#186);
    End;

GotoXY(x1,y1);
Write(#201);
GotoXY(x2,y1);
Write(#187);
GotoXY(x1,y2);
Write(#200);
GotoXY(x2,y2);
Write(#188);
End;

(**********************************************)

Procedure GetNumber;
Begin
DrawBox(5,14,35,16,White,Black);
GotoXY(7,15);
Write('Enter a number (1-10): ');
x := WhereX;
y := WhereY;
  Repeat
  GotoXY(x,y);
  s := '      ';
  Write(s);
  GotoXY(x,y);
  ReadLn(s);
  Val(s,i,code);
  Until ((i > 0) And (i < 11)) And (code = 0);

End;

(**********************************************)

Begin
ClrScr;
TextMode(c40);
GetNumber;

ClrScr;
TextMode(c80);
GetNumber;
GotoXY(1,20);
WriteLn;
Write('Press ENTER...');
ReadLn;
End.
```

The procedure **DrawBox** uses standard ASCII graphics characters to draw a rectangle anywhere on the screen. The procedure defines a data-entry portion on the screen.

Using Display Memory

The standard Turbo Pascal command **Write** uses a BIOS interrupt to send characters to the monitor. You can bypass BIOS, however, and write characters directly to display memory. This approach is far faster, but is complicated by vertical retrace, which creates a "snow" effect on CGA adapters. If you want your program to write directly to video memory, you must take special steps to eliminate snow. Fortunately, Turbo Pascal offers an easy solution in the form of the CRT unit. When you use the CRT unit in a program, Turbo Pascal automatically writes directly to video memory without generating snow.

While extremely useful, the video capabilities of the Turbo Pascal CRT unit do have limitations. For example, the CRT unit, even when writing directly to video memory, is still slower than the maximum speed you can get. This chapter provides several assembler routines that give your programs that extra burst of speed. In addition, the **Write** command always moves the cursor to the next position on the screen. So, if you write a character to the lower right corner of the screen, the display scrolls up one line. This makes it impossible to write out entire screens using Turbo Pascal statements. The remainder of this chapter will go into the technical details of your computer's video display and show how you can harness its power for your programs.

Locating Video Memory

Before you can use your computer's display memory, you must know where it is. On a monochrome adapter, the display memory starts at segment B000h, while on the color graphics adapter, it starts at B800h. Because each adapter uses different locations for video memory, you must determine which adapter is in use. One way to determine the adapter in use is through a BIOS interrupt. This technique is demonstrated in Chapter 12, with the **CurrentVidMode** procedure. Another way of obtaining the same information is shown here:

```
Function VidSeg : Word;
Begin
If Mem[$0000:$0449] = 7 Then
```

```
  VidSeg := $B000
Else
  VidSeg := $B800;
End;
```

The **VidSeg** function checks the memory location at segment 0000h and offset 0449h, where DOS stores the video adapter code. If the byte at this location is equal to 7, the adapter is monochrome; if not, it is safe to assume the adapter is color graphics.

While this method is more direct than using a BIOS interrupt, it is highly sensitive to IBM-PC compatibility: if your computer stores this information at a different memory address, this approach will not work. Fortunately, most PC manufacturers are careful to maintain the location of the video display type in the same place as the IBM PC does.

Once you know the type of video adapter in use, it is easy to bypass BIOS and write characters directly to the display memory. The program shown here determines the type of adapter used, and then fills the display memory with the letter "A" in white letters on a black background:

```
{$R-,S-}
Program FillScreen;
Uses CRT;
Var
  CharAtt,
  i,j,
  VS  : Word;

(**************************************************)

Function VidSeg : Word;
Begin
If Mem[$0000:$0449] = 7 Then
  VidSeg := $B000
Else
  VidSeg := $B800;
End;

(**************************************************)

Begin
ClrScr;
VS := VidSeg;

j := 0;

(* $41 is the character 'A' *)
(* $70 is White on Black *)
```

```
CharAtt := ($70 Shl 4) + $41;

For i := 1 To 2000 Do
  Begin
  MemW[VS:j] := CharAtt;  (* Write character and attribute *)
  Inc(j,2);               (* Point to next video character *)
  End;
GotoXY(1,1);
Write('Press ENTER...');
ReadLn;
End.
```

The program uses the function **VidSeg** to store the video display memory segment in the **Integer** variable **VS**. The **For-Do** loop uses the standard array **MemW** to move the character and attribute byte to video memory. Because **MemW** operates on a full word (16 bytes), both the attribute byte and character byte must be combined into a single word. The character is set to 41h, the ASCII code for the letter "A," and the attribute byte is set to 70h, which produces a white letter on a black background. The variable **j** holds the offset in display memory and is incremented by 2 after each character and attribute are written.

With the following procedure, **FastWrite**, you can write strings directly to display memory at specific x and y coordinates, as well as set the color attributes.

```
Procedure FastWrite(x,y : Byte;
                    Var s : String;
                    fg,bg : Byte);

Var
  w : Word;
  i,ColAtr : Byte;

Begin
ColAtr := (bg Shl 4) + fg;    (* create attribute byte *);
w := ((y-1)*80 + (x-1))*2;    (* calculate offset *)

For i := 1 To Length(s) Do
  Begin
  MemW[VS:w] := (ColAtr Shl 8) + Ord(s[i]);
  Inc(w,2);
  End;
End;
```

The procedure first creates the attribute byte (**ColAtr**) by shifting the background color left four bits and adding the foreground color. Next, the procedure computes the starting offset in display memory with the following formula:

x: = ((y-1)*80 + (x-1)) *2;

In each iteration of the loop, the Turbo Pascal array **MemW** sets the character byte and the attribute byte at the same time. The procedure combines them by shifting the color byte to the left eight bits and adding the character byte. Notice that this puts the attribute byte in the high-order portion of the word, yet the attribute byte should be placed after the character byte in display memory. Once again, Intel's backward storage method forces you to think in reverse when operating with words.

Avoiding Vertical Retrace

If you use a CGA video adapter, you will soon find out why avoiding vertical retrace is so important. Try running the following program, which uses the Turbo Pascal **FastWrite** procedure to display a large "V" on your monitor.

```
{$R-}
Program FastWriteDemo;
Uses CRT;
Var
  VS  : Word;
  i,j : Byte;
  s : String;

(***************************************************)

Function VidSeg : Word;
Begin
If Mem[$0000:$0449] = 7 Then
  VidSeg := $B000
Else
  VidSeg := $B800;
End;

(***************************************************)

Procedure FastWrite(x,y : Byte;
                    Var s : String;
                    fg,bg : Byte);

Var
  w : Word;
  i,ColAtr : Byte;

Begin
ColAtr := (bg Shl 4) + fg;    (* create attribute byte *);
w := ((y-1)*80 + (x-1))*2;    (* calculate offset *)
```

```
For i := 1 To Length(s) Do
  Begin
  MemW[VS:w] := (ColAtr Shl 8) + Ord(s[i]);
  Inc(w,2);
  End;
End;

(**************************************************)

Begin
ClrScr;
VS := VidSeg;
s := 'XXXXXXX';
j := 5;

For i := 1 To 25 Do
  Begin
  FastWrite(j,i,s,Yellow,Black);
  Inc(j,1);
  End;

For i := 25 DownTo 1 Do
  Begin
  FastWrite(j,i,s,Yellow,Black);
  Inc(j,1);
  End;
GotoXY(1,24);
Write('Press ENTER...');
ReadLn;
End.
```

When you run this program with a CGA adapter, you will notice some "snow" on your screen. This is caused by the *vertical retrace,* a process that updates your screen from display memory many times per second (each vertical retrace takes approximately 1.25 milliseconds). If you move bytes directly to display memory while a vertical retrace is in progress, you will get snow.

The only way to avoid snow is to write to display memory between vertical retraces; in other words, the program must wait until the retrace has ended and then write the characters to display memory before the next retrace begins. Turbo Pascal is simply not fast enough to do this; you must use an external assembler procedure or inline code.

The following listing is an assembler procedure that writes out a string to video memory without generating snow. The assembler listing uses the special features of the Turbo Assembler, so you must use TASM.EXE to assemble it.

```
.MODEL TPASCAL

.DATA
```

```
VIDTYPE DB ?

.CODE

FastWrite PROC FAR x:BYTE, y:BYTE, s:DWORD, fg:BYTE, bg:BYTE

               PUBLIC    FASTWRITE

FASTSTR:

;-------------------------------------------------------------
; Compute offset into display memory--((y-1)*80 + (x-1)) * 2
;-------------------------------------------------------------
               PUSH    DS
               XOR     BX,BX
               XOR     AX,AX
               MOV     BL,x        ; Get x from stack;
               MOV     AL,y        ; Get y from stack;
               DEC     BX          ; Decrement x and y to get
               DEC     AX          ;   correct offset.
               MOV     CX,0080     ; Multiply y (in AX) by
               MUL     CX          ;   80 (in CX).
               ADD     AX,BX       ; Add x to y;
               MOV     CX,0002     ; Multiply the
               MUL     CX          ;   sum by 2.
               MOV     DI,AX       ; Store starting offset in DI.

;-------------------------------------------------------------
; Create the attribute byte
;-------------------------------------------------------------
               MOV     BL,bg       ; Get the background color.
               MOV     AL,fg       ; Get the foreground color.
               MOV     CL,4        ; Shift the foreground color
               SHL     BX,CL       ;   into the high nybble.
               ADD     BX,AX       ; Add in the foreground.
               XCHG    BL,BH       ; Move into the upper byte.
               MOV     DX,3DAH     ; Load CRT port address in DX.

;-------------------------------------------------------------
; Get the monitor type
;-------------------------------------------------------------
               XOR     AX,AX       ; Assign 0000h to ES.
               MOV     ES,AX

               MOV     AX,0449h    ; Assign offset of
               MOV     SI,AX       ; video type location.

               MOV     AX,ES:[SI]  ; If video type is 7
               CMP     AL,7        ; then monitor is
               JZ      MONO        ; monochrome.

               MOV     AX,0B800H   ; Load the color
               MOV     ES,AX       ;   segment into ES.
               MOV     VIDTYPE,1
               JMP     CHKSTR      ; Continue.
```

```
MONO:
                MOV     AX,0B000H  ; Load the monochrome
                MOV     ES,AX      ;   segment into ES.
                MOV     VIDTYPE,0


;------------------------------------------------------------
; Load the string and check for zero length
;------------------------------------------------------------

CHKSTR:         LDS     SI,s     ; Load string address into DS:SI.
                MOV     CL,[SI]    ; Move string length into CL.
                CMP     CL,0       ; If string length is zero,
                JZ      ENDSTR     ;   exit procedure.
                CLD                ; Clear direction flag.

NEXTCHAR:       INC     SI         ; Point to next character.
                MOV     BL,[SI]    ; Move it into BL.
                CMP     VIDTYPE,0  ; If monochrome, don't check
                JE      MOVECHAR   ; for retrace.

WLOW:           IN      AL,DX      ; Get CRT status.
                TEST    AL,1       ; Is retrace off?
                JNZ     WLOW      ; If off, wait for it to start.
                CLI                ; No interrupts, please.

WHIGH:          IN      AL,DX      ; Get CRT status.
                TEST    AL,1       ; Is retrace on?
                JZ      WHIGH      ; If on, wait for it to stop.

MOVECHAR:       MOV     AX,BX  ; Move color and character to AX.
                STOSW         ; Move color & character to screen.
                STI                ; Interrupts are now allowed.

LOOP            NEXTCHAR           ; Done yet?

ENDSTR:         POP     DS
                RET

FASTWRITE       ENDP
CODE            ENDS
                END
```

The **FastWrite** procedure checks the adapter I/O port number 3DAh for a status bit known as the *vertical sync signal.* When this status bit is on, a vertical retrace is in progress. The procedure first checks to see if the monitor is between retraces (the status bit equals 0). If so, the loop repeats until a retrace begins. The procedure then waits for the retrace to end.

As soon as the retrace ends, the procedure moves characters to the display memory. Because the procedure waited until the very end of a retrace, there should be ample time to move the characters before the next retrace begins.

Use TASM, the Turbo Assembler, to assemble this code to an object file (FASTWRIT.OBJ) and declare the external routine as shown in the program listed here:

```
{$R-,F+}
Program FastWriteDemo;
Uses CRT;
Var
  VS  : Word;
  i,j : Byte;
  s : String;

{$L FASTWRIT}
Procedure FastWrite(x,y : Byte;
                    Var s : String;
                    fg,bg : Byte); External;

Begin
ClrScr;
s := 'XXXXXXX';
j := 5;

For i := 1 To 25 Do
  Begin
  FastWrite(j,i,s,Yellow,Black);
  Inc(j,1);
  End;

For i := 25 DownTo 1 Do
  Begin
  FastWrite(j,i,s,Yellow,Black);
  Inc(j,1);
  End;
GotoXY(1,24);
Write('Press ENTER...');
ReadLn;
End.
```

The technique used in **FastWrite** works on most IBM-compatible personal computers and greatly improves the speed of video displays.

Turbo Pascal Windows

Normally, your programs will take advantage of the PC's entire 80×25 video display. There are times, however, when it is desirable to restrict output to just a portion of your monitor, using the Turbo Pascal command **Window**. For example, the command

Window(10,10,20,15)

restricts your program's display to a 10 by 5 rectangle starting at column 10 and row 10; the remainder of the display is off limits to the **Write** command. (Note that the **FastWrite** procedure pays no attention to Turbo Pascal and can write outside the active window.) When you want to return to the full screen, the command

Window(1,1,80,25)

returns the monitor to normal operation.

The **Window** command's most useful feature is its ability to realign the screen coordinates so that they fit the active window; that is, screen coordinates refer only to the active window, not to the entire screen. Thus, the command

GotoXY(1,1)

positions the cursor at the upper left corner of the active window, not the entire screen. In fact, Turbo Pascal treats the window as if it were the entire screen: when text runs off the bottom of the window, the screen scrolls up one line.

Pop-Up Windows

While useful in its own right, the Turbo Pascal **Window** command is simply not powerful enough to create professional-looking pop-up windows. The problem is that a Turbo Pascal window wipes out the portion of the screen it uses. Most people expect windows to act the way they do in the popular program SideKick; that is, when a window disappears, the text that was on the screen "beneath" the window reappears.

To create true pop-up windows, save the contents of the screen before you open the window and then restore the screen when you close the pop-up window.

To save a screen, define a variable that can store all the information contained in the screen: 2000 characters, 2000 color attributes, and the x and y coordinates of the cursor. The following data structure, **Screen-Type**, provides all you need.

```
Type
  ScreenType = Record
    Pos : Array [1..80, 1..25] Of Record
```

```
    Ch : Char;
    At : Byte;
    End;
CursX,
CursY : Byte;
End;
```

ScreenType, a nested **Record** data type, stores characters and attributes in the array named **Pos**, which has dimensions that match the coordinates of your monitor. Thus, to refer to the character in column 10 and row 20, you would use the following statement:

    Screen.Pos[10,20].Ch

The **Integer** variables **CursX** and **CursY** are used to store the cursor position.

The **ScreenType** variable is quite powerful. You can use it not only to store a screen's contents, but also to change the contents of the variable in memory, and then move it directly to video display, updating an entire video display in one shot.

There are several ways you can use a **ScreenType** variable to save and restore video images. One way to do this is to declare the variable **Absolute** at the display memory location. If you have a color graphics adapter, you would use this declaration:

    Var
        Screen : ScreenType Absolute $B800;

Unfortunately, this approach requires you to choose the offset in advance, which means you can service only one type of video adapter (unless you define separate screens for monochrome and color). A better approach is to define the screen as a **pointer** variable. The program then sets the pointer to the correct offset in display memory, depending on the adapter in use. The following program demonstrates this technique:

```
Program WindowPointer;
Uses CRT;

Const
  MaxWin = 5;
Type
```

```
  ScreenPtr = ^ScreenType;
  ScreenType = Record
    Pos : Array [1..80, 1..25] Of Record
      Ch : Char;
      At : Byte;
      End;
    CursX, CursY : Integer;
    End;

Var
  Screen : ScreenPtr;

(***************************************************)

Function VidSeg : Word;
Begin
If Mem[$0000:$0449] = 7 Then
  VidSeg := $B000
Else
  VidSeg := $B800;
End;

(***************************************************)

Begin
ClrScr;

Screen := Ptr(VidSeg,$0000);
Screen.Pos[1,1].Ch := 'A';

ReadLn;
End.
```

The program begins by clearing the screen and then uses the **Ptr** command to point the **Screen** variable to the correct location in the display memory. Because of this repositioning, any changes made to the variable **Screen** will show up on your monitor.

When you use this method, do not use the **Dispose** command on the **Screen** variable, or Turbo Pascal will try to deallocate memory from the display adapter, most likely crashing your program.

Multiple Logical Screens and Pop-Up Windows

Your program can have as many screen variables as its memory will hold. Screens that are held in memory, and not displayed, are often called *logical* screens to distinguish them from the *physical screen* (the computer monitor). A program can write to a logical screen without disturbing the display on the physical screen. Then, when you want to display the logical screen, simply move its contents into the physical screen.

The use of logical screens is best explained by an example. This program uses one physical screen variable (**Screen**) and three logical screen variables (**Screen1**, **Screen2**, and **Screen3**). By typing **1**, **2**, or **3** on the keyboard, you can display any of the three logical screens.

```pascal
Program FastScreenDemo;
Uses CRT;

Const
  MaxWin = 5;

Type
  ScreenPtr = ^ScreenType;
  ScreenType = Record
    Pos : Array [1..80,1..25] Of Record
      Ch : Char;
      At : Byte;
      End;
    CursX,
    CursY : Byte;
    End;

Var
  Screen,
  Screen1,
  Screen2,
  Screen3 : ScreenPtr;
  Ch : Char;
  i,j : Byte;

(*********************************************)

Function VidSeg : Word;
Begin
If Mem[$0000:$0449] = 7 Then
  VidSeg := $B000
Else
  VidSeg := $B800;
End;

(*********************************************)

Begin
New(Screen1);
New(Screen2);
New(Screen3);
```

```
For i := 1 To 80 Do
For j := 1 To 25 Do
  Begin
  Screen1^.Pos[i,j].Ch := '1';
  Screen2^.Pos[i,j].Ch := '2';
  Screen3^.Pos[i,j].Ch := '3';
  Screen1^.Pos[i,j].At := $07;
  Screen2^.Pos[i,j].At := $07;
  Screen3^.Pos[i,j].At := $07;
  End;

ClrScr;
Screen := Ptr(VidSeg,$0000);

  Repeat
  GotoXY(1,1);
  Write('Press 1,2,3 to change screens or 0 to exit.');

  Ch := ReadKey;
    Case Ch Of
    '1' : Screen^ := Screen1^;
    '2' : Screen^ := Screen2^;
    '3' : Screen^ := Screen3^;
    End;
  Until Ch = '0';

End.
```

Screen, which is superimposed on the display memory, acts as the physical device. The program changes the display memory by setting the physical device variable **Screen** equal to one of the logical screens. The transfer is fast, and the entire screen is updated in one statement. A program can also move the contents of the physical screen to a logical screen with a statement like this:

```
PhysicalScreen^ := LogicalScreen^;
```

Manipulating logical screens is the technique you need to create pop-up windows. Before you open a pop-up window, save a copy of the physical screen in a logical screen variable. Then, when you close the window, restore the screen to its original appearance. Thus, your windows seem to pop up from nowhere and, when no longer needed, disappear without a trace.

The following program uses an array of logical screens to create up to five pop-up windows. When you run the program, you will see how windows can overlap without causing problems.

```
(*$R-*)
Program WindowDemo;
Uses CRT;
Const
  MaxWin = 5;
Type
  ScreenType = Record
    Pos : Array [1..80,1..25] Of Record
      Ch : Char;
      At : Byte;
      End;
    CursX,
    CursY : Byte;
    End;

  WindowPtr = ^WindowType;
  WindowType = Record
    Scr : ScreenType;
    WinX1,
    WinY1,
    WinX2,
    WinY2 : Byte;
    End;

Var
  Ch : Char;
  i : Integer;
  ActiveWin : WindowPtr;
  Windo : Array [0..MaxWin] Of WindowPtr;
  CurrentWindow : Integer;

(*********************************************)

Function VidSeg : Word;
Begin
If Mem[$0000:$0449] = 7 Then
  VidSeg := $B000
Else
  VidSeg := $B800;
End;

(*********************************************)

{$L FASTWRIT}
Procedure FastWrite(x, y : Byte;
                    S : String;
                    bc, fc : Byte); External;

(*********************************************)

Procedure FastBox(x1,y1,x2,y2,fg,bg : Byte);
Var
  i : Byte;
  s : String[1];
```

```
Begin
TextColor(fg);
TextBackground(bg);

s := #205;
For i := (x1+1) To (x2-1) Do
  Begin
  FastWrite(i,y1,s,fg,bg);
  FastWrite(i,y2,s,fg,bg);
  End;

s := #186;
For i := (y1+1) To (y2-1) Do
  Begin
  FastWrite(x1,i,s,fg,bg);
  FastWrite(x2,i,s,fg,bg);
  End;

s := #201;
FastWrite(x1,y1,s,fg,bg);
s := #187;
FastWrite(x2,y1,s,fg,bg);
s := #200;
FastWrite(x1,y2,s,fg,bg);
s := #188;
FastWrite(x2,y2,s,fg,bg);
End;

(**************************************)

Procedure SetUpWindows;
Var
  i : Integer;
Begin
New(ActiveWin);
For i := 0 To MaxWin Do
  New(Windo[i]);

With ActiveWin^ Do
  Begin
  WinX1 := 1;
  WinY1 := 1;
  WinX2 := 80;
  WinY2 := 25;
  With Scr Do
    Begin
    CursX := WhereX;
    CursY := WhereY;
    End;
  End;

ActiveWin := Ptr(VidSeg,$0000);
CurrentWindow := 0;
With Windo[CurrentWindow]^ Do
  Begin
```

```
    WinX1 := 1;
    WinY1 := 1;
    WinX2 := 80;
    WinY2 := 25;
    With Scr Do
      Begin
      CursX := 1;
      CursY := 1;
      End;
    End;
End;

(****************************************)

Procedure OpenWindow;
Begin
If CurrentWindow < MaxWin Then
  Begin
  Windo[CurrentWindow]^.Scr := ActiveWin^.Scr;
  Windo[CurrentWindow]^.Scr.CursX := WhereX;
  Windo[CurrentWindow]^.Scr.CursY := WhereY;

  CurrentWindow := CurrentWindow + 1;
  With Windo[CurrentWindow]^ Do
    Begin
    WinX1 := CurrentWindow * 10;
    WinY1 := CurrentWindow * 2;
    WinX2 := WinX1 + 20;
    WinY2 := WinY1 + 5;
    With Scr Do
      Begin
      CursX := 1;
      CursY := 1;
      End;
    Window(WinX1,WinY1,WinX2,WinY2);
    FastBox(WinX1-1,WinY1-1,WinX2+1,WinY2+1,Yellow,Black);
    TextColor(Yellow);
    TextBackGround(Black);
    ClrScr;
    End;
  End;
End;

(****************************************)

Procedure CloseWindow;
Begin
If CurrentWindow > 0  Then
  Begin
  Windo[CurrentWindow]^.Scr.CursX := WhereX;
  Windo[CurrentWindow]^.Scr.CursY := WhereY;

  CurrentWindow := CurrentWindow - 1;
  ActiveWin^.Scr := Windo[CurrentWindow]^.Scr;
```

```
  With Windo[CurrentWindow]^ Do
    Begin
    Window(WinX1,WinY1,WinX2,WinY2);
    GotoXY(Scr.CursX,Scr.CursY);
    End;
  End;
End;

(**************************************)

Procedure FillWindow;
Var
  Ch : Char;
Begin
Ch := ReadKey;
  Repeat
  Write(Chr(Random(80)+30));
  Delay(20);
  Until KeyPressed;
End;

(**************************************)

Begin
ClrScr;
SetUpWindows;

TextColor(Yellow+Blink);
GotoXY(1,25);
Write('Press any key to open windows...');
GotoXY(1,1);
TextColor(Yellow);

FillWindow;
For i := 1 To MaxWin Do
  Begin
  OpenWindow;
  FillWindow;
  End;

For i := 1 To MaxWin Do
  Begin
  CloseWindow;
  FillWindow;
  End;
End.
```

When you run **WindowDemo**, CGA users will notice snow on the screen. There is just no way to avoid it with code written in Turbo Pascal. An external procedure written in assembler, however, can eliminate the snow while making the screen update even faster. Listed here are two assembler procedures you can use as external procedures. The first moves a logical screen to video memory. The second moves the screen currently in video memory to a logical screen. In both cases, snow is eliminated. Be sure to use the Turbo Assembler to assemble this listing.

```
.MODEL TPASCAL

.DATA

VIDTYPE DB ?

.CODE

PUBLIC READSCR
PUBLIC WRITESCR

WRITESCR PROC FAR s:DWORD

;-----------------------------------------------------------
; Save registers.
;-----------------------------------------------------------

            PUSH      DS


;-----------------------------------------------------------
; Get the monitor type.
;-----------------------------------------------------------

            XOR       AX,AX       ; Assign 0000h to ES.
            MOV       ES,AX

            MOV       AX,0449h    ; Assign offset of
            MOV       SI,AX       ; video type location.

            MOV       AX,ES:[SI]  ; If video type is 7
            CMP       AL,7        ; then monitor is
            JZ        MONO1       ; monochrome.

            MOV       AX,0B800H   ; Load the color
            MOV       ES,AX       ;    segment into ES.
            MOV       VIDTYPE,1
            JMP       CONT1       ; Continue.

MONO1:
            MOV       AX,0B000H   ; Load the monochrome
            MOV       ES,AX       ;    segment into ES.
            MOV       VIDTYPE,0

;-----------------------------------------------------------
; Load buffer to screen.
;-----------------------------------------------------------

CONT1:      LDS       SI,s        ; Load buffer address in DS:SI.
            MOV       DI,0        ; Point to start of memory.
            MOV       CX,2000     ; Move 2000 characters.
            CLD                   ; Clear direction flag.
```

```
                MOV     DX,3DAh     ; Load CRT port address.

NEXTCHAR1:      CMP     VIDTYPE,0   ; If monochrome, don't check
                JE      MOVECHAR1   ; for retrace.

WLOW1:          IN      AL,DX       ; Get CRT status.
                TEST    AL,1        ; Is retrace off?
                JNZ     WLOW1       ; If off, wait for it to start.
                CLI                 ; No interrupts, please.

WHIGH1:         IN      AL,DX       ; Get CRT status.
                TEST    AL,1        ; Is retrace on?
                JZ      WHIGH1      ; If on, wait for it to end.

MOVECHAR1:      LODSW               ; Get word from buffer to AX.
                STOSW               ; Move word from AX to screen.
                STI                 ; Interrupts are allowed.
                LOOP    NEXTCHAR1   ; Done yet?

ENDSTR1:

;-------------------------------------------------------------
; Restore registers.
;-------------------------------------------------------------

                POP     DS
                RET

WRITESCR        ENDP

READSCR  PROC FAR s:DWORD

;-------------------------------------------------------------
; Save registers.
;-------------------------------------------------------------

                PUSH    DS

;-------------------------------------------------------------
; Get the monitor type
;-------------------------------------------------------------

                XOR     AX,AX       ; Assign 0000h to ES.
                MOV     ES,AX

                MOV     AX,0449h    ; Assign offset of
                MOV     SI,AX       ; video type location.

                MOV     AX,ES:[SI]  ; If video type is 7
                CMP     AL,7        ; then monitor is
                JZ      MONO2       ; monochrome.
```

```
                MOV       VIDTYPE,1
                MOV       AX,0B800H  ; Load the color
                MOV       DS,AX      ;   segment into DS.
                JMP       CONT2      ; Continue.

MONO2:
                MOV       VIDTYPE,0
                MOV       AX,0B000H  ; Load the monochrome
                MOV       DS,AX      ;   segment into DS.

CONT2:
                LES       DI,s       ; Load buffer address in ES:DI.
                MOV       SI,0       ; Point to start of memory.
                MOV       CX,2000    ; Characters in screen.
                CLD                  ; Clear direction flag.

;------------------------------------------------------------
; Transfer display memory to buffer.
;------------------------------------------------------------

                MOV       DX,3DAh ; Load CRT port address into DX.

NEXTCHAR2:      CMP       ES:VIDTYPE,0 ; If monochrome, don't check
                JE        MOVECHAR2    ; for retrace.

WLOW2:          IN        AL,DX      ; Get CRT status.
                TEST      AL,1       ; Is retrace off?
                JNZ       WLOW2      ; If off, wait for it to start.
                CLI                  ; No interrupts please.

WHIGH2:         IN        AL,DX      ; Get CRT status.
                TEST      AL,1       ; Is retrace on?
                JZ        WHIGH2     ; If on, wait for it to end.

MOVECHAR2:      LODSW                ; Move word from screen to AX.
                STOSW                ; Move AX to buffer.
                LOOP      NEXTCHAR2  ; Done yet?
                STI                  ; Interrupts are allowed.

ENDSTR2:

;------------------------------------------------------------
; Restore registers.
;------------------------------------------------------------

                POP       DS

                RET

READSCR         ENDP

CODE            ENDS

                END
```

The assembler listing just given contains two procedures, **WriteScr** and **ReadScr.** You can use these two procedures in the program **WindowDemo** as shown here:

```
(*$R-,F+*)
Program WindowDemo;
Uses CRT;
Const
  MaxWin = 5;
Type
  ScreenType = Record
    Pos : Array [1..80,1..25] Of Record
      Ch : Char;
      At : Byte;
      End;
    CursX,
    CursY : Byte;
    End;

  WindowPtr = ^WindowType;
  WindowType = Record
    Scr : ScreenType;
    WinX1,
    WinY1,
    WinX2,
    WinY2 : Byte;
    End;

Var
  Ch : Char;
  i : Integer;
  Windo : Array [0..MaxWin] Of WindowPtr;
  CurrentWindow : Integer;

(*********************************************)

Function VidSeg : Word;
Begin
If Mem[$0000:$0449] = 7 Then
  VidSeg := $B000
Else
  VidSeg := $B800;
End;

(*********************************************)

{$L FASTWRIT}
Procedure FastWrite(x, y : Byte;
                    s : String;
                    bc, fc : Byte); External;

{$L FASTSCR}
Procedure WriteScr(Var s : ScreenType); External;
Procedure ReadScr(Var s : ScreenType);  External;
```

```
(****************************************)

Procedure FastBox(x1,y1,x2,y2,fg,bg : Byte);
Var
  i : Byte;
  s : String[1];
Begin
TextColor(fg);
TextBackground(bg);

s := #205;
For i := (x1+1) To (x2-1) Do
  Begin
  FastWrite(i,y1,s,fg,bg);
  FastWrite(i,y2,s,fg,bg);
  End;

s := #186;
For i := (y1+1) To (y2-1) Do
  Begin
  FastWrite(x1,i,s,fg,bg);
  FastWrite(x2,i,s,fg,bg);
  End;
s := #201;
FastWrite(x1,y1,s,fg,bg);
s := #187;
FastWrite(x2,y1,s,fg,bg);
s := #200;
FastWrite(x1,y2,s,fg,bg);
s := #188;
FastWrite(x2,y2,s,fg,bg);
End;

(****************************************)

Procedure SetUpWindows;
Var
  i : Integer;
Begin
For i := 0 To MaxWin Do
  Begin
  New(Windo[i]);
  FillChar(Windo[i]^,SizeOf(Windo[i]^),0);
  End;

CurrentWindow := 0;
With Windo[CurrentWindow]^ Do
  Begin
  WinX1 := 1;
  WinY1 := 1;
  WinX2 := 80;
  WinY2 := 25;
  With Scr Do
    Begin
    CursX := 1;
    CursY := 1;
    End;
```

```
  End;
End;

(****************************************)

Procedure OpenWindow;
Begin
If CurrentWindow < MaxWin Then
  Begin
  ReadScr(Windo[CurrentWindow]^.Scr);
  Windo[CurrentWindow]^.Scr.CursX := WhereX;
  Windo[CurrentWindow]^.Scr.CursY := WhereY;

  CurrentWindow := CurrentWindow + 1;
  With Windo[CurrentWindow]^ Do
    Begin
    WinX1 := CurrentWindow * 10;
    WinY1 := CurrentWindow * 2;
    WinX2 := WinX1 + 20;
    WinY2 := WinY1 + 5;
    With Scr Do
      Begin
      CursX := 1;
      CursY := 1;
      End;
    Window(WinX1,WinY1,WinX2,WinY2);
    FastBox(WinX1-1,WinY1-1,WinX2+1,WinY2+1,Yellow,Black);
    TextColor(Yellow);
    TextBackGround(Black);
    ClrScr;
    End;
  End;
End;

(****************************************)

Procedure CloseWindow;
Begin
If CurrentWindow > 0   Then
  Begin
  Windo[CurrentWindow]^.Scr.CursX := WhereX;
  Windo[CurrentWindow]^.Scr.CursY := WhereY;

  CurrentWindow := CurrentWindow - 1;
  WriteScr(Windo[CurrentWindow]^.Scr);
  With Windo[CurrentWindow]^ Do
    Begin
    Window(WinX1,WinY1,WinX2,WinY2);
    GotoXY(Scr.CursX,Scr.CursY);
    End;
  End;
End;

(****************************************)
```

```
Procedure FillWindow;
Var
  Ch : Char;
Begin
Ch := ReadKey;
  Repeat
  Write(Chr(Random(80)+30));
  Delay(20);
  Until KeyPressed;
End;

(***************************************)

Begin
ClrScr;
SetUpWindows;

TextColor(Yellow+Blink);
GotoXY(1,25);
Write('Press any key to open windows...');
GotoXY(1,1);

TextColor(Yellow);
FillWindow;
For i := 1 To MaxWin Do
  Begin
  OpenWindow;
  FillWindow;
  End;

For i := 1 To MaxWin Do
  Begin
  CloseWindow;
  FillWindow;
  End;
End.
```

Within the program, delete all references to the variable **activewin** and replace the line

ActiveWin^.Scr := Windo[CurrentWindow]^.Scr;

with the line

WriteScr(Windo[CurrentWindow]^.Scr);

and replace

Windo[CurrentWindow]^.Scr := ActiveWin^.Scr;

with the line

ReadScr(Windo[CurrentWindow]^.Scr);

These fast, clean screen procedures make your windows look professional. Now you can spend your time on filling the windows with
useful information and tools (calendars, calculators, note pads, and so
on) and not on getting the windows started in the first place.

Graphics

**F
I
F
T
E
E
N**

Your computer's graphics capability is one of its strongest features. Using graphics you can create drawings, charts, multi-font text, or anything that can be drawn. But using graphics requires far more work than using the PC's Text mode. You must develop methods for drawing lines and characters and be able to scale them in the proper perspective. What's more, there are now more than ten commonly available graphics adapters comprising more than two dozen different graphics modes. Fortunately, Turbo Pascal provides an exceptionally rich set of graphics routines that can make graphics programming much easier. This chapter covers some of the basics of programming graphics using Turbo.

Graphics Versus Text

Compared with the Graphics mode, the PC's Text mode is easy to use. Displaying information on the screen is as simple as placing ASCII characters in specific memory locations. The text screen is neatly divided into 80 columns and 25 rows, and your computer already knows how to draw the ASCII characters, sparing you most of the headaches.

The Graphics mode requires a completely different orientation. Instead of characters and attribute bytes, you have *pixels*, the smallest picture element on your computer's display. A single character on your computer's screen is made up of many pixels arranged in a pattern that forms a character. In the Graphics mode, you can light pixels anywhere on your display. The program listed here, which demonstrates some fundamental graphics programming techniques, lights pixels at random locations on your screen.

```
Program DemoPixel;
Uses CRT, GRAPH;
Var
  x,y,
  ErrorCode,
  GraphMode,
  GraphDriver : Integer;

Begin
(* Initiate the CGA high resolution mode. *)
GraphDriver := CGA;
GraphMode := CGAhi;
InitGraph(GraphDriver,GraphMode,'D:\TP5');
ErrorCode := GraphResult;
If ErrorCode <> grOK Then
  Begin
  WriteLn('Graphics error: ',GraphErrorMsg(ErrorCode));
  Halt;
  End;

  Repeat
  x := Random(640); (* CGA high resolution coordinates *)
  y := Random(200); (* 640 x 200 *)
  PutPixel(x,y,White);
  Delay(100);
  Until KeyPressed;

CloseGraph;
End.
```

The preceding program not only demonstrates the concept of the pixel, but also highlights some of the difficulties involved in writing graphics programs. The program begins by initializing the Turbo Pascal CGA graphics driver. It does this by first specifying the type of adapter and the Graphics mode and then calling **InitGraph**. You must also tell **InitGraph** where to look for the .BGI file that corresponds to the adapter. A .BGI file contains information on a specified graphics adapter. This information is needed to draw a graph properly. In the example, this file is found in the D:\TP5 directory.

```
GraphDriver := CGA;
GraphMode := CGAhi;
InitGraph(GraphDriver,GraphMode,'D:\TP5');
```

After calling **InitGraph**, the program calls **GraphResult**, a function that returns a status code. If the code is not equal to **grOK**, you know that an error occurred. (**grOK** is a constant defined in the GRAPH unit and has a value of zero.) If an error is detected, the program passes the error code to the **GraphErrorMsg** function, which then returns a string that describes the error condition.

```
ErrorCode := GraphResult;
If ErrorCode <> grOK Then
  Begin
  WriteLn('Graphics error: ',GraphErrorMsg(ErrorCode));
  Halt;
  End;
```

While checking for graphics errors is not required, it is a good idea. Nearly every graphics procedure and function can produce serious errors when used improperly. Always remember, though, to store the value of **GraphResult** in a variable because once the function is called, it will thereafter return the value 0 until another error occurs.

Specifying the display adapter in your program is fine if you know in advance what adapter will be used. If you're wrong, however, the program won't run. Notice also that the screen coordinate limits (640 and 200) are hard-coded into the program. If your computer uses a graphics adapter that has a different coordinate system, the program will not work properly. To make a graphics program truly useful, it must be able to run on any graphics adapter and, ideally, would use that adapter's advanced features as much as possible.

Graphics Adapters and Coordinate Systems

Your graphics screen consists of pixels ordered in horizontal and vertical lines. This is true of all computer graphics modes; the major difference is the size of the pixel. In CGA's Low-resolution mode, the pixels are quite large, so only 320 fit horizontally and 200 fit vertically. The VGA adapter, a relatively new video display controller, has a High-resolution mode with pixels so small that 640 fit horizontally and 480 fit vertically. The smaller the pixel, the more pixels per image, and the higher the quality of the graphic display.

(0,0)   (319,0)

(0,199)   (319,199)

Figure 15-1.   CGA high-resolution coordinates

Each adapter has one or more graphics modes, and each mode has an associated coordinate system. The coordinate system for high-resolution CGA graphics is 320 × 200, as shown in Figure 15-1. Graphics coordinates begin at position (0,0), which is located at the upper left corner of the screen. The right-most pixel is number 319 and the bottom-most is number 199. By referring to pixels by coordinates, you can light the pixels you want for your graphic image.

Now you can see why it is so important to know what graphics adapter is installed and which mode is active. Screen coordinate systems vary from adapter to adapter and from mode to mode. For example, the CGA adapter supports High- and Low-resolution modes, each having different coordinate systems. If you want to light a pixel at the lower right corner of the screen, you must know what the screen coordinates are. Fortunately, Turbo Pascal provides the answer with two GRAPH unit functions, **GetMaxX** and **GetMaxY**, which return the maximum x and y coordinates for the active graphics display adapter and mode. Here is the program given earlier, but updated to be used on any graphics adapter:

```
Program DemoPixel2;
Uses CRT, GRAPH;
Var
  MaxX,
```

```
    MaxY,
    x,y,
    ErrorCode,
    GraphMode,
    GraphDriver : Integer;

Begin
GraphDriver := Detect;
InitGraph(GraphDriver,GraphMode,'D:\TP5');
ErrorCode := GraphResult;
If ErrorCode <> grOK Then
  Begin
  WriteLn('Graphics error: ',GraphErrorMsg(ErrorCode));
  Halt;
  End;

MaxX := GetMaxX;
MaxY := GetMaxY;

  Repeat
  x := Random(MaxX)+1;
  y := Random(MaxY)+1;
  PutPixel(x,y,White);
  Delay(100);
  Until KeyPressed;

CloseGraph;
End.
```

This program, while simple in function, demonstrates how complicated even simple graphics programs can be. Given the rich set of tools that the Turbo Pascal graphics unit provides, the possibilities could fill a book on their own. The remainder of this chapter will touch on the important aspects of graphics programming and how to use the basics of the GRAPH unit.

The GRAPH Unit

The GRAPH unit is by far the most complex of all the units supplied by Borland. It contains more than 50 procedures, over 20 functions, and scores of constants, variables, and data types. What's more, Borland includes drivers for all the major graphics adapters and fonts for drawing a wide range of character styles. If you are serious about graphics programming, the GRAPH unit alone is worth the price of the Turbo Pascal compiler.

Drawing Lines

A fundamental task in graphics is drawing a line between two points. The GRAPH unit provides a **Line** procedure that does this. Still, you may find it useful to understand how such a routine works because, as you do more complicated graphics programming, you will probably decide to write your own specialized graphics routines.

Drawing horizontal or vertical lines is easy—you simply hold one coordinate value fixed and plot pixels along the other coordinate. Once you begin to slant the line, however, the process becomes much more complicated. Somehow, you must determine which pixels to light. This is done with an algorithm that computes one coordinate given a value of the other coordinate.

Graphics systems based on algorithms (as opposed to fixed bit maps) are the basis of nearly all graphics and provide a great deal of flexibility because an algorithm need not be tied to a particular scaling factor. This means that you can use the same algorithm to draw a small box or a large box, a circle or an ellipse, a thick line or a thin line. The algorithm for drawing a straight line is fairly straightforward, though somewhat complicated.

The straight-line algorithm is based on the algebraic equation for a straight line:

$$Y = a + bX$$

where **Y** is the vertical coordinate, **X** is the horizontal coordinate, **a** is a constant factor, and **b** is the slope of the line. Once you have determined the value of **a** and **b**, drawing the line is easy.

To compute **a** and **b**, you need two coordinate pairs. In the code extract shown here, x1:y1 and x2:y2 are pairs of coordinates representing points on the graphics screen.

```
dx := (x2 - x1);
dy := (y2 - y1);
If dx <> 0 Then
  b := dy / dx
Else
  b := 0;
a := y1 - x1*b;
```

The **b** variable is defined as the difference between the x coordinates divided by the difference between the y coordinates. If **x1** equals **x2**, then **b** is defined as zero. Once **b** is calculated, **a** is easily calculated using one of the two coordinate pairs.

With **a** and **b** both defined, the algorithm is complete. To draw the line, you need only trace along the x axis, compute the corresponding y coordinate, and plot the pixel. One problem with this approach, however, is that lines will become very sparse when the range between the x coordinates is small compared to the range of the y coordinates. To compensate for this, the line-drawing procedure must compare the distances between the vertical coordinates and between the horizontal coordinates. If the gap between the y coordinates is greater than the gap between the x coordinates, tracing should move along the vertical axis. The complete line-drawing process is contained in the procedure **PlotLine**, in the following program:

```
Program LineDemo;
Uses CRT, GRAPH;
Var
  MaxX,
  MaxY,
  ErrorCode,
  GraphMode,
  GraphDriver : Integer;

(****************************************************)

Procedure PlotLine(x1, y1, x2, y2, color : Integer);
Var
  a,b   : Real;
  dx,dy,
  x,y,i : Integer;

(****************************************************)

Procedure Switch(var x,y : Integer);
Var
  t : Word;
Begin
t := x;
x := y;
y := t;
End;

(****************************************************)

Begin
```

```pascal
If Abs(x1-x2) > Abs(y1-y2) Then
  Begin
  (* Gap between x's is greater than y's.
     Trace horizontally*)
  If x1 > x2 Then
    Begin
    Switch(x1,x2);
    Switch(y1,y2);
    End;

  dx := (x2 - x1);
  dy := (y2 - y1);
  If dx <> 0 Then
    b := dy / dx
  Else
   b := 0;
  a := y1 - x1*b;
  For x := x1 to x2 do
    Begin
    y := Round(a+x*b);
    PutPixel(x,y,color);
    End;
  End
Else
  Begin
  (* Gap between y's is greater than x's.
     Trace vertically. *)
  If y1 > y2 Then
    Begin
    Switch(y1,y2);
    Switch(x1,x2);
    End;

  dx := (x2 - x1);
  dy := (y2 - y1);

  If dx <> 0 Then
    b := dy / dx
  Else
   b := 0;
  a := y1 - x1*b;

  For y := y1 to y2 do
    Begin
    If b <> 0 Then
      x := Round((y-a)/b)
    Else
      x := 0;
    PutPixel(x,y,color);
    End;
  End;
End;

(****************************************************)

Begin
GraphDriver := Detect;
```

```
InitGraph(GraphDriver,GraphMode,'D:\TP5');
ErrorCode := GraphResult;
If ErrorCode <> grOK Then
  Begin
  WriteLn('Graphics error: ',GraphErrorMsg(ErrorCode));
  Halt;
  End;

MaxX := GetMaxX;
MaxY := GetMaxY;

  Repeat
  PlotLine(Random(MaxX),
           Random(MaxY),
           Random(MaxX),
           Random(MaxY),
           White);
  Until KeyPressed;

CloseGraph;
End.
```

This program draws lines between random points on the computer screen (see Figure 15-2). To stop the program, simply press any key.

Figure 15-2.   Drawing lines in Graphics mode

If drawing a straight line is difficult, as the program just given demonstrates, imagine the difficulty in writing complete graphics routines for drawing polygons, ellipses, pie charts, and, perhaps most difficult, text characters. The GRAPH unit is a tremendous asset to all graphics programmers.

Circles, Lines, and Patterns

With the GRAPH unit's procedures you can create extremely complex graphics with relative ease, controlling color, shape, and size. **Line** and **Circle** are two important procedures: most common graphics, such as bar charts, pie charts, histograms, and polygons, are combinations of lines and circles.

The procedure **Line** takes four parameters in the form of coordinate pairs. The statement

```
Line(MaxX Div 2, 0, MaxX Div 2, MaxY);
```

draws a line that runs down the center of the screen, from top to bottom. Using **MaxX Div 2** to determine the center of the horizontal axis makes the statement independent of the coordinate system in use.

The procedure **Circle** takes three parameters. The first two form a coordinate pair that determines the center of the circle, while the third parameter is the radius of the circle in horizontal pixels—**Circle** computes the appropriate number of vertical pixels to maintain the proper proportions. The ratio of vertical to horizontal pixels is known as the *aspect ratio*. Each graphics driver has an aspect ratio that determines the scaling of graphic images. While Turbo Pascal allows you to alter the aspect ratio, you will probably never need to do so.

Returning to the example, the statement

```
Circle(MaxX Div 2, MaxY Div 2, 10);
```

draws a circle at the center of the screen with a radius of ten horizontal pixels. You can increase the size of the radius to a point where parts of the circle run off the edge of the screen. When this occurs, the image is *clipped*, or truncated, to protect you from writing into memory outside that allocated for graphic images.

The example program listed here demonstrates the use of the **Line** and **Circle** procedures as well as some other important graphics techniques. The program begins by drawing lines that intersect at the center

of the screen and then draws concentric circles from the edge of the
screen toward the center (see Figure 15-3). Next, the program saves a
rectangular area around the center of the screen and flashes it in reverse
and normal colors. Finally, the program fills the sectors of the circle
with a random selection of colors and patterns (see Figure 15-4).

```
Program CircleDemo;
Uses CRT, GRAPH;
Var
  Palette : PaletteType;
  MaxX,
  MaxY,
  i,
  ErrorCode,
  GraphMode,
  GraphDriver : Integer;
  Size : Word;
  P : Pointer;

Begin
GraphDriver := Detect;
InitGraph(GraphDriver,GraphMode,'D:\TP5');
ErrorCode := GraphResult;
If ErrorCode <> grOK Then
  Begin
  WriteLn('Graphics error: ',GraphErrorMsg(ErrorCode));
  Halt;
  End;

MaxX := GetMaxX;
MaxY := GetMaxY;

(* Draw lines on screen *)
Line(MaxX Div 2, 0, MaxX Div 2, MaxY);
Line(0, MaxY Div 2, MaxX, MaxY Div 2);
Line(0, 0, MaxX, MaxY);
Line(MaxX, 0, 0, MaxY);

(* Draw concentric circles *)
i := MaxY;
While i > 20 Do
  Begin
  Circle(MaxX Div 2, MaxY Div 2, i);
  i := i - 10;
  End;

(* Save a portion of the screen *)
Size := ImageSize(Round(MaxX * 0.25),
                  Round(MaxY * 0.25),
                  Round(MaxY * 0.75));
GetMem(P, Size);
GetImage(Round(MaxX * 0.25),
         Round(MaxY * 0.25),
         Round(MaxX * 0.75),
         Round(MaxY * 0.75),P^);
```

```
(* Flash a portion of the screen *)
For i := 1 To 6 Do
  Begin
  PutImage(Round(MaxX * 0.25),
           Round(MaxY * 0.25),
           P^,NotPut);

  GetImage(Round(MaxX * 0.25),
           Round(MaxY * 0.25),
           Round(MaxX * 0.75),
           Round(MaxY * 0.75),P^);
  End;

GetPalette(Palette);

(* Fill in portions of the graphic image *)
  Repeat
  SetFillStyle(Random(9),Random(Palette.Size)+1);
  FloodFill(Random(MaxX),Random(MaxY),White);
  Until KeyPressed;

ReadLn;
CloseGraph;
End.
```

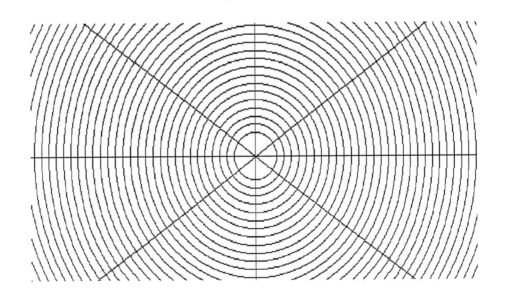

Figure 15-3.   Drawing lines and circles

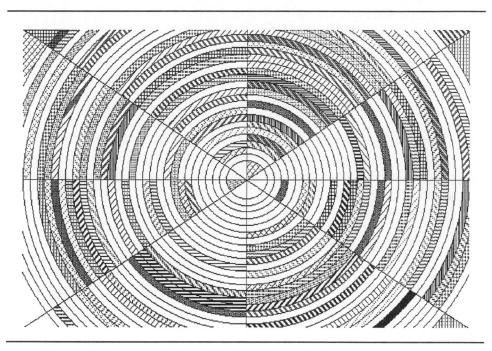

Figure 15-4.   Filling with colors and patterns

Saving and Changing the Image

The example program just given demonstrates how you can save a portion of a graphic screen and redisplay it in an altered form. The process of saving a graphic image requires three steps:

1. Determine how much memory you will need to store the graphic image.

2. Allocate a buffer of that size.

3. Save the image in the buffer.

This is accomplished with the following code:

```
Size := ImageSize(Round(MaxX * 0.25),
                  Round(MaxY * 0.25),
                  Round(MaxX * 0.75),
                  Round(MaxY * 0.75));
```

```
GetMem(P, Size);
GetImage(Round(MaxX * 0.25),
         Round(MaxY * 0.25),
         Round(MaxX * 0.75),
         Round(MaxY * 0.75),P^);
```

The first statement uses the function **ImageSize** to calculate the amount of memory required to store a rectangular image defined by two coordinate pairs defining upper left and lower right points on the screen. The amount of memory will vary dramatically with the display adapter and graphics mode in use, but cannot exceed 64K. The **GetMem** procedure then allocates memory from the heap to **pointer** variable P. Finally, the procedure **GetImage** moves the image defined by the coordinate pairs to the buffer that **P** points to.

Once you have saved a graphic image, you can retrieve it any time. In the example program, this is done with the procedure **PutImage**:

```
PutImage(Round(MaxX * 0.25),
         Round(MaxY * 0.25),
         P^,NotPut);
```

PutImage takes four parameters. The first two are a coordinate pair that indicate where the upper left corner of the saved image should appear on the screen. The third parameter is the pointer to the buffer where the image is stored. The fourth parameter is the most interesting because it determines how the image will appear. The example above uses the constant **NotPut**, which uses a bit-wise negation process (in which the value of individiual bits is reversed) to reverse the colors of the image, producing a reverse video effect.

The last part of the program fills the graphic with different colors and patterns. This process begins with the **GetPalette** procedure, which returns information about the color capabilities of the current graphics driver and mode.

```
GetPalette(Palette);

(* Fill in portions of the graphic image *)
  Repeat
  SetFillStyle(Random(9),Random(Palette.Size)+1);
  FloodFill(Random(MaxX),Random(MaxY),White);
  Until KeyPressed;
```

GetPalette takes a single parameter of type **PaletteType**, which is defined as follows:

```
Type
  PaletteType = Record
    Size : Byte;
    Colors : Array[0..MaxColors] of ShortInt;
```

The **Size** field contains the number of colors currently available, and **Colors** contains the numeric codes that correspond to the colors. With a single call to **GetPalette** you know exactly what you have to work with in terms of graphic colors.

The procedures that do the hard work—drawing different patterns in varying colors—are **SetFillStyle** and **FloodFill**. The GRAPH unit defines 12 different patterns to use as filler in graphics. The procedure **SetFillStyle** lets you choose the pattern you want to use and the color you want to display it in. **FloodFill** "paints" the inside of a polygon or circle using the pattern and color you defined using **SetFillStyle**. To do its job, **FloodFill** needs two pieces of information: (1) the location of a pixel inside the area to fill and (2) the color of the boundary of the area. The boundary color is the only way **FloodFill** can determine where to stop filling.

Dragging an Image

The **PutImage** procedure was used in an earlier example to produce a reverse video effect. It can also be used to "drag" an image across the screen. The important quality of dragging an image is that when the image moves, it does not disturb the pixels "underneath" the image. Anyone who has worked with desktop publishing or other "paint" programs is familiar with the dragging concept.

To drag an image, you must do two things. First, the image to be dragged must be stored in a buffer separate from the underlying image. Second, you must use the procedure **PutImage** with **XORPut** as the third parameter. The following sample program demonstrates how this is done. It saves the image of a circle, draws lines on the screen, and then drags the circle around the screen (see Figure 15-5).

```pascal
Program CircleDemo2;
Uses CRT, GRAPH;
Var
  Direction : (up,down,right,left);
  XX,YY,
  MaxX,
  MaxY,
  ErrorCode,
  GraphMode,
  GraphDriver : Integer;
  Size : Word;
  P : Pointer;

Begin
GraphDriver := Detect;
InitGraph(GraphDriver,GraphMode,'D:\TP5');
ErrorCode := GraphResult;
If ErrorCode <> grOK Then
  Begin
  WriteLn('Graphics error: ',GraphErrorMsg(ErrorCode));
  Halt;
  End;

MaxX := GetMaxX;
MaxY := GetMaxY;


(* Draw a circle, save it, and clear the screen. *)

Circle(MaxX Div 2, MaxY Div 2, 20);

XX := Round(MaxX * 0.45);
YY := Round(MaxY * 0.45);
Size := ImageSize(XX, YY,
                   Round(MaxX * 0.55),
                   Round(MaxY * 0.55));
GetMem(P, Size);
GetImage(XX,YY,
         Round(MaxX * 0.55),
         Round(MaxY * 0.55),P^);

ClearViewPort;

(* Draw lines on screen *)
Line(MaxX Div 2, 0, MaxX Div 2, MaxY);
Line(0, MaxY Div 2, MaxX, MaxY Div 2);
Line(0, 0, MaxX, MaxY);
Line(MaxX, 0, 0, MaxY);

(* Start dragging the circle. *)
```

```
Direction := down;
PutImage(XX, YY, P^,XORPut);

  Repeat
  PutImage(XX, YY, P^,XORPut);

    Case Direction Of

    Down :
      Begin
      YY := YY + 5;
      If YY > (MaxY * 0.75) Then
        Direction := Left;
      End;

    Left :
      Begin
      XX := XX - 5;
      If XX < (MaxX * 0.25)  Then
        Direction := Up;
      End;

    Up :
      Begin
      YY := YY - 5;
      If YY < (MaxY * 0.25)  Then
        Direction := Right;
      End;

    Right :
      Begin
      XX := XX + 5;
      If XX > (MaxX * 0.75)  Then
        Direction := Down;
      End;
    End;

  PutImage(XX, YY, P^,XORPut);

  Until KeyPressed;

CloseGraph;
End.
```

The dragging is accomplished with the statement

```
PutImage(XX, YY, P^,XORPut);
```

This statement is used twice for each step in the movement. The first time it is used, **PutImage** erases the circle; the second time, it redraws it at the new location. As the circle moves around the screen, the lines are left undisturbed. An important point in using this technique is to define the smallest possible buffer to store the dragged image—the larger the buffer, the longer it takes to update the image, and the slower the dragging will seem.

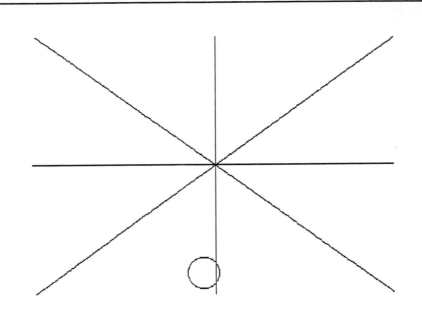

Figure 15-5.   Dragging a circle in Graphics mode

Graphic Text

Graphics wouldn't be much use without text. The ability to combine text and graphics is the foundation of the desktop publishing industry. The GRAPH unit contains five fonts: one bit-mapped font and four "stroked" fonts. A bit-mapped font is one that is created from a static number of elements. When it is enlarged, the bit-mapped characters become "blocky" because their definition is not changed to match their larger size (see Figure 15-6).

Stroked fonts, on the other hand, create characters by means of an algorithm. Because the algorithms are insensitive to scale, stroked fonts actually become more precise as they are enlarged (see Figure 15-7). The program listed here demonstrates the difference between bit-mapped and stroked fonts. It displays each of the five GRAPH fonts, starting with the default bit-mapped font, in increasing size.

```
Program TextDemo;
Uses CRT, GRAPH;
Const
  CharType : Array [0..4] of String[20] =
             ('Default','Triplex','Small','Sans Serif','Gothic');
Var
  S : String;
  MaxX,
  MaxY,
  i,j,k,
  ErrorCode,
  GraphMode,
  GraphDriver : Integer;

Begin
GraphDriver := Detect;
InitGraph(GraphDriver,GraphMode,'D:\TP5');
GraphMode := GetMaxMode;
InitGraph(GraphDriver,GraphMode,'D:\TP5');
ErrorCode := GraphResult;
If ErrorCode <> grOK Then
  Begin
  WriteLn('Graphics error: ',GraphErrorMsg(ErrorCode));
  Halt;
  End;

MaxX := GetMaxX;
MaxY := GetMaxY;

For i := 0 To 4 Do
  Begin
  k := 0;
  For j := 1 To 10 Do
    Begin
    SetTextStyle(i,HorizDir,j);
    OutTextXY(j*20,k,CharType[i]);
    k := k + TextHeight(CharType[i]) + 10;
    End;

  SetTextStyle(0,HorizDir,2);
  S := 'Press ENTER...';
  OutTextXY(MaxX - TextWidth(S),MaxY - TextHeight(S),S);
  ReadLn;
  ClearDevice;
  End;

CloseGraph;
End.
```

To select a font, use the procedure **SetTextStyle**, which takes three parameters. The first parameter is the font, and can range from 0 (default) to 4 (Gothic). The second parameter is the direction in which the text is to be written. You have two choices here: 0 (horizontal) or 1

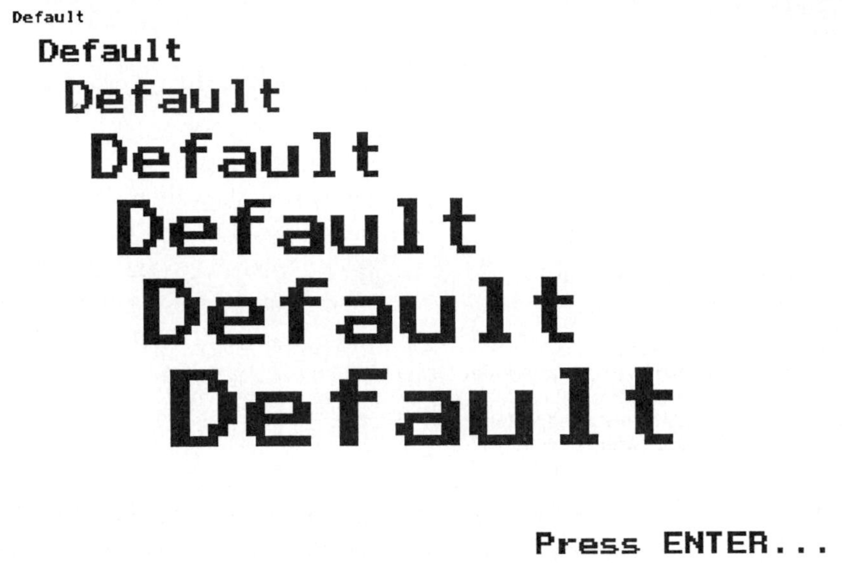

Default

Default

Default

Default

Default

Default

Default

Press ENTER...

Figure 15-6.   A bit-mapped font

Triplex

Triplex

Triplex

Triplex

Triplex

Triplex

Triplex

TriplexPress ENTER...

Figure 15-7.   A stroked font

(vertical). The third parameter controls the size of the characters. The normal font size is 1 for the default font and 4 for the stroked fonts, but these can be increased to ten times the normal size.

Once you have selected a font, you can display text with the **OutTextXY** procedure, which displays a string starting at coordinates you supply as parameters. Notice that in the example program, **OutText-XY** is used in conjunction with the function **TextHeight** to determine where the next line of text should be placed. **TextHeight** is necessary because each font has a different scale. If you wish to place one line of text below another, you must determine the height of the current text and use that number to calculate the distance you have to move down in order to write the next line. In the program, the statement

```
k := k + TextHeight(CharType[i]) + 10;
```

moves the next line of text down by the size of the current line plus ten pixels. As you can see, using text in the Graphics mode is not easy, even when the fonts are defined for you.

More on Colors

To round out the discussion on Turbo Pascal graphics, let's consider the use of color with a procedure named **FillPoly**. The **FillPoly** procedure creates a polygon with any number of sides and fills it with a color and pattern you define with the **SetFillStyle** procedure.

To use the **FillPoly** procedure you must first define a variable array of **PointType**, a record type defined in the GRAPH unit that contains an x and y coordinate. The following example program shows how this is done.

```
Program ColorDemo;
Uses CRT, GRAPH;

Type
  TriType = Array [1..3] of PointType;

Var
  Tri : TriType;
  S : String;
```

```
      MaxX,
      MaxY,
      x1,y1,
      i,j,k,
      ErrorCode,
      GraphMode,
      GraphDriver : Integer;

      Palette : PaletteType;

Begin
GraphDriver := Detect;
InitGraph(GraphDriver,GraphMode,'D:\TP5');
GraphMode := GetMaxMode;
InitGraph(GraphDriver,GraphMode,'D:\TP5');
ErrorCode := GraphResult;
If ErrorCode <> grOK Then
  Begin
  WriteLn('Graphics error: ',GraphErrorMsg(ErrorCode));
  Halt;
  End;

MaxX := GetMaxX;
MaxY := GetMaxY;

GetPalette(Palette);
SetFillStyle(3,3);

While Not Keypressed Do
  Begin
  SetFillStyle(Random(13),Random(Palette.Size)+1);

  Tri[1].X := Random(MaxX);
  Tri[1].Y := Random(MaxY);
  Tri[2].X := Random(MaxX);
  Tri[2].Y := Random(MaxY);
  Tri[3].X := Random(MaxX);
  Tri[3].Y := Random(MaxY);

  FillPoly(3,Tri);
  Delay(100);

  x1 := x1 + (MaxX Div 12);
  y1 := y1 + (MaxY Div 12);
  End;

ReadLn;
CloseGraph;
End.
```

The example program uses the **FillPoly** procedure to draw triangles. Since a triangle is completely defined by three points, the following definition is sufficient:

```
Type
  TriType = Array [1..3] of PointType;
```

A variable named **Tri** is declared as **TriType**. To create a triangle, the program first defines the three coordinate pairs in **Tri**. The call to **FillPoly** passes the number of points in the polygon (three in this case) and the variable **Tri**, which contains the coordinates. As the following listing shows, the triangle's coordinates are determined randomly.

```
Tri[1].X := Random(MaxX);
Tri[1].Y := Random(MaxY);
Tri[2].X := Random(MaxX);
Tri[2].Y := Random(MaxY);
Tri[3].X := Random(MaxX);
Tri[3].Y := Random(MaxY);

FillPoly(3,Tri);
```

For each triangle drawn, colors and patterns are also selected randomly using **SetFillStyle**, as shown here:

```
Set FillStyle(Random(13),Random(Palette.Size)+1);
```

This statement randomly selects one of the 12 fill patterns defined in the GRAPH unit and also randomly selects a color from the Video mode

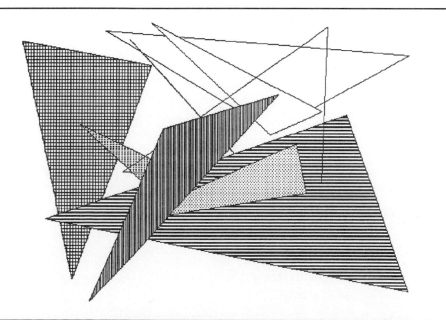

Figure 15-8.   Filling triangles with color and patterns

palette (see Figure 15-8). Thus, when you run this program, you will see randomly generated triangles with randomly selected patterns and colors.

The graphics potential of the PC is great, but tapping into it is a challenge for even the most experienced programmer. For the beginner, Turbo Pascal's GRAPH unit provides an easy way to learn about graphics programming. For the professional programmer, the GRAPH unit's rich set of routines and data structures provides the building blocks for sophisticated applications.

Interrupts, Telecommunications, and Memory-Resident Programs

Using Interrupts
Writing the Interrupt Handler
Memory-Resident Programs

Life is full of interruptions—and so is computing. In computer programming, interruptions are called *interrupts*. If you own a telephone, you will understand the concept of an interrupt. When your telephone rings, you stop what you are doing, answer the phone, and resume working when your conversation is over. In a way, computers have little telephones ringing inside the microprocessor that make it stop and do something else for a moment.

This chapter introduces the concept of interrupts and how they are used in Turbo Pascal. Interrupts are fundamental to the operation of your computer; and if you want to tap the full power of the personal computer, you must understand them. Because telecommunications commonly use interrupt programming, the concepts will be illustrated with examples from a Turbo Pascal communications program that is listed at the end of this chapter.

Using Interrupts

Do you occasionally find it inconvenient when your telephone rings? Imagine how inconvenient it would be to have a telephone that does not ring. You would have to pick up the receiver from time to time to see if anyone were calling. Not only would this waste time, but you would run the risk of missing a call if someone called and hung up before you picked up the receiver.

Of course, our phones do ring, and so we can do other things and answer the telephone only when we know someone is calling. In similar fashion, interrupts allow your computer to work until something happens that requires your computer's attention.

One interrupt controls your computer's internal clock. About 18 times each second, this interrupt stops your microprocessor and asks it to increment the DOS time and date. You do not notice this because it happens so quickly. Other interrupts occur when you press a key on your keyboard or data comes into a serial port. In fact, interrupts occur all the time, but you do not notice them because they generally require the microprocessor to do very little work.

Hardware and Software Interrupts

Interrupts are of two types: hardware and software. *Hardware interrupts,* generated by such actions as pressing a key, a tick of the system clock, or data entering a serial port, originate in the computer's circuitry and are controlled by a special chip, the 8259 interrupt controller. When a hardware interrupt occurs, this chip acts as a traffic cop, making sure the interrupt goes in the correct direction. The 8259 receives an interrupt request, evaluates its priority, and routes the request to the procedure it needs.

Software interrupts are generated by programs that request special BIOS and DOS services. In Turbo Pascal, the commands **Intr** and **MsDos** create software interrupts (see Chapter 12). Whether hardware or software, however, all interrupts use the *interrupt vector table.*

The Interrupt Vector Table

The interrupt vector table is an array of memory addresses located at the lowest part of the PC's memory. The array is 1024 bytes long and contains the addresses of all the routines that are triggered by interrupts. Because an address requires 4 bytes, the 1024-byte interrupt vector table can hold a maximum of 256 interrupt addresses.

An interrupt, when initiated, fetches an address from the interrupt vector table, jumps to that memory location, and executes the routine located there. Each address in the interrupt vector table is used exclusively by a single interrupt. For example, Interrupt 8, the clock timer, always fetches the address at offset 0020h. Table 16-1 contains the PC's

| Interrupt | | | |
Dec	Hex	Offset	Purpose
8	8	0020h	System clock tick
9	9	0024h	Keyboard interrupt
10	A	0028h	Not used
11	B	002Ch	Second serial port (COM2)
12	C	0030h	First serial port (COM1)
13	D	0034h	Hard-disk interrupt
14	E	0038h	Floppy-disk interrupt
15	F	003Ch	Printer interrupt

Table 16-1.   Location of Hardware Interrupts in the Interrupt Vector Table

eight hardware interrupts, numbers 8 through 15, and their offsets in the interrupt vector table.

Of the hardware interrupts, the most useful to program are the clock tick (number 8), the keyboard interrupt (number 9), and the COM1 serial port (number 12). Interrupt 12 is used for serial communications with other computers. Interrupts 8 and 9 are used for many purposes, including pop-up terminate-stay-resident (TSR) programs.

Replacing Interrupts

Each time you start your computer, DOS fills the interrupt vector table with addresses to standard interrupt routines. As soon as the computer is running, however, you can change addresses in the interrupt vector table to point to interrupt handling procedures that you have written; the interrupt will then execute your procedure instead of the default procedure. In short, by changing addresses in the interrupt vector table, you can usurp DOS and BIOS and take charge of your computer's basic functions.

Although programmers are not usually interested in altering the addresses of software interrupts, they are interested in changing hardware interrupt addresses. By changing the keyboard interrupt address, for example, a memory-resident program can intercept a keystroke and interpret it before it ever gets to the main program. This is how memory-resident programs such as SuperKey and SideKick work.

An interrupt address can be changed in two ways: by changing the interrupt vector table directly or by using a DOS service to do it for you. To change memory directly, you must overlay an array of addresses on the interrupt vector table, as follows:

```
Var
  AsyncVector : Pointer;

  InterruptVector : Array [0..$FF] of Pointer
                    Absolute $0000:$0000;
```

The example code just given uses the **pointer** data type. **Pointers** are 4-byte data types that hold a segment and offset that together constitute a memory address. The variable **InterruptVector**, an array of 256 (0oh through FFh) addresses, is declared absolute at the very beginning of RAM, where the interrupt vector table resides. Since **InterruptVector** and the table share the same space, when you change a value in one, you also change it in the other. To change an address in the interrupt vector table, use the following statements:

```
AsyncVector := InterruptVector[$0C];
InterruptVector[$0C] := @AsyncInt;
```

The first statement stores the vector for Interrupt 12 (0C in hexadecimal) in the variable **AsyncVector**. Saving the original address is important since you will need to restore it eventually. The second statement replaces the original vector with the address of a Turbo Pascal procedure named **AsyncInt**.

The Turbo Pascal operator @ returns a four-byte address (segment and offset) of the procedure **AsyncInt**. The address is then loaded into the interrupt vector table. Now, when Interrupt 0Ch is triggered by data arriving at the serial port, **AsyncInt** will execute instead of the normal procedure.

When you are done using the interrupt vector, you must restore the original address that you saved in the **pointer** variable **AsyncVector**. If you do not restore the address, you may crash your computer and have to reboot. This single line of code is all you need to restore the original interrupt vector address:

```
InterruptVector[$0C] := AsyncVector;
```

With the interrupt vector now restored to its original value, your computer will operate normally.

It is simple to change interrupt addresses directly, but it is safer to use DOS services, which apply to a wider range of computers. DOS service **35h** reports a vector's contents, and service **25h** changes an address in the interrupt vector table. Fortunately, the Turbo Pascal DOS unit provides two routines— **GetIntVec** and **SetIntVec**—that do exactly what is needed. Both procedures take two parameters: the interrupt number (for example, **0Ch**) and a **pointer** variable. The process of saving an interrupt vector and replacing it with a new vector is shown here:

```
GetIntVec($0C,AsyncVector);
SetIntVec($0C,@AsyncInt);
```

When you are done using the interrupt, you can restore the old interrupt address, as shown here:

```
SetIntVec($0C,AsyncVector);
```

Using the procedures from the DOS unit is safer than directly altering the interrupt vector table. But, now that you know how to change a vector to point to your own procedure, what does that procedure look like?

Writing the Interrupt Handler

Interrupt handler is a term that refers to the code that executes as the result of an interrupt. In the previous examples, the handler was a Turbo Pascal procedure named **AsyncInt**, which was attached to Interrupt **0Ch**. Interrupt handlers are different from other types of procedures because you do not always control when they will execute. For example, Interrupt **0Ch** is triggered when a byte is ready in COM1. You have no way of knowing when that will occur, so your interrupt handler must be extra cautious so as not to disturb the normal processing of the computer. In other words, a well-written interrupt handler is like a cat burglar: it enters when you least expect it, steals some computing time, and leaves without a trace.

The trick to writing interrupt handlers is leaving without a trace. To do this, the handler must save all the CPU's registers before executing and restore them when done. (The handler need not save the CS, IP, or Flags registers because DOS saves these for you prior to calling the interrupt.) But saving the CPU registers alone is not enough—you must also conquer the problem presented by the data segment.

Restoring the Data Segment

When an interrupt handler is invoked, only the code segment (CS) and instruction pointer (IP) registers are correctly set to the values your handler needs. The data segment (DS) register, on the other hand, contains the value used by the procedure being interrupted and may not contain the correct value for the interrupt handler. Without the correct data segment, your handler cannot refer to its own global variables. Your interrupt handler must, therefore, store its DS value someplace in the code segment, so that the correct DS can be set.

Turbo Pascal Interrupt Support

While all of this may seem a bit intimidating, Borland comes to the rescue. Turbo Pascal lets you write interrupt handler procedures that automatically save all registers, set up the DS register, and restore all registers when done. To declare a procedure as an interrupt handler, you need only append the **Interrupt** directive to the end of the procedure declaration, as shown here:

```
Procedure IntHandler; Interrupt;
```

The **Interrupt** directive instructs Turbo Pascal to insert the appropriate code to save registers, set up the DS register, restore registers, and issue an **IRET** command to terminate the procedure. You may optionally declare in your handler a list of pseudo-variables that represent the CPU registers:

```
Procedure IntHandler(Flags,CS,IP,AX,BX,CX,DX,SI,DI,DS,ES,BP);
         Interrupt;

Procedure IntHandler(SI,DI,DS,ES,BP); Interrupt;
```

As you can see in the preceding listing, the parameter list can include all the CPU registers (Flags through BP) or a subset of the registers (for example, SI through BP). There are, however, two restrictions. First, you cannot change the order of the parameters. Second, if you delete parameters, you may only do so from the left. For example, if you want only the SI and DS registers, you must include SI, DI, DS, ES, and BP in your parameter list, in that order.

When your interrupt handler executes, you will have access to all the pseudo-parameters that you listed in the procedure heading. The values in the parameters will represent the contents of the CPU registers *prior to the interrupt.*

Note that the SP and SS registers are not included as pseudo-parameters. This means that your interrupt handler will be using the stack of the program it interrupted. This is a bit risky since you have no idea how large the stack of the interrupted program is. The safest approach is to avoid as much as possible using the stack in your interrupt handler. The next section of this chapter demonstrates how an interrupt handler can be used to create a telecommunications program.

PC Telecommunications

Telecommunications, the transmission of data from one computer to another via telephone lines, is simple in concept, but complicated in practice. In concept, the computer sends a byte to a serial port, which sends it on to the modem. The modem translates the bits into tones and sends the tones to another modem, which translates them back into bits. The translated bits are sent to the receiving serial port where they wait to be picked up by the software.

In practice, writing a program to do all these things is not so simple. The complexity is partly due to the number of hardware elements you must control: the RS-232 serial port, the INS8250 universal asynchronous receiver transmitter (UART), the 8259 interrupt controller, and the modem itself. In addition, there are many variations of modem speed, parity, stop bits, data bits, which serial port to use, and so on.

The Telecommunications Program

The following program, called **AsyncCommunications**, provides simple telecommunications capability using Interrupt 12. The program assumes you have a Hayes-compatible modem connected to your first serial port. Before you run the program, set the values in the **SelectModemSet** procedure to those of the remote computer you want to call.

```pascal
Program CommX;
{$S-,R-,I-,V-,F+}
Uses CRT, DOS;
Type
  ModemSetType = Record
    ComPort,
    BPS,
    DataBits,
    StopBits        : Integer;
    Parity          : Char;
    PhoneNumber     : String;
    End;

Const
  MainDseg : Integer = 0;
  MaxBufLen = 1024;
  CR        = #13;

  (******************************)
  (* ISN8250 UART Registers.    *)
  (******************************)
  DataPort = $03F8;
  (* Contains 8 bits to transmit or receive.      *)
  IER      = $03F9;
  (* Enables the serial port when set equal to 1. *)
  LCR      = $03FB;
  (* Sets communications parameters.              *)
  MCR      = $03FC;
  (* Bits 1, 2 and 4 are turned on to ready modem.*)
  LSR      = $03FD;
  (* When bit 6 is on, it is safe to send a byte. *)
  MDMMSR   = $03FE;
  (* Initialized to 80h when starting.            *)

  ENBLRDY = $01;    (* Initial value for Port[IER].     *)
  MDMMOD  = $0B;    (* Initial value for Port[MCR].     *)
  MDMCD   = $80;    (* Initial value for Port[MDMMSR].  *)

  INTCTLR = $21;    (* Port for 8259 Interrupt Controller. *)
Var
  ModemSet        : ModemSetType;
  AsyncVector     : Pointer;
  Regs            : Registers;
  Buffer          : Array [1..MaxBufLen] Of Char;
  I,
```

```
            CharsInBuf,
            CircOut,
            CircIn        : Word;
            Orig          : Char;

(*********************************************************)

Procedure ClearBuffer;
Begin
CircIn := 1;
CircOut := 1;
CharsInBuf := 0;
FillChar(Buffer,SizeOf(Buffer),0);
End;

(*********************************************************)

Procedure SelectModemSet;
Begin
With ModemSet Do
  Begin
  ComPort     := 1;           (* Must be 1 in this program. *)

    Repeat
    Write('BPS (300,1200): ');
    ReadLn(BPS);
    Until (BPS = 300) Or (BPS =1200);

    Repeat
    Write('Data bits (7,8): ');
    ReadLn(DataBits);
    Until DataBits in [7,8];

    Repeat
    Write('Stop bits (0,1): ');
    ReadLn(StopBits);
    Until StopBits in [0,1];

    Repeat
    Write('Parity (N,E,O): ');
    ReadLn(Parity);
    Parity := UpCase(Parity);
    Until Parity in ['N','E','O'];

  Write('Phone number: ');
  ReadLn(PhoneNumber);
  End;
End;

(*********************************************************)

Procedure AsyncInt; Interrupt;
Begin
Inline($FB);        (* STI *)

If (CharsInBuf < MaxBufLen) Then
  Begin
```

```pascal
    Buffer[CircIn] := Char(Port[DataPort]);
    If (CircIn < MaxBufLen) Then
      Inc(CircIn,1)
    Else
      CircIn := 1;
    Inc(CharsInBuf,1);
    End;

Inline($FA);        (* CLI *)

Port[$20] := $20;
End;

(******************************************************)

Procedure SetSerialPort(ComPort,
                        BPS,
                        StopBits,
                        DataBits: Integer;
                        Parity : Char);
Var
  Regs : Registers;
  Parameter : Byte;
Begin
  Case BPS Of
  300  : BPS := 2;
  1200 : BPS := 4;
  End;

If StopBits = 2 Then
  StopBits := 1
Else
  StopBits := 0;

If DataBits = 7 Then
  DataBits := 2
Else
  DataBits := 3;

Parameter := (BPS Shl 5) + (StopBits Shl 2) + DataBits;

  Case Parity Of
  'E' : Parameter := Parameter + 8;
  'O' : Parameter := Parameter + 24;
  End;

With Regs Do
  Begin
  DX := ComPort - 1;
  AH := 0;
  AL := Parameter;
  Flags := 0;
  Intr($14,Regs);
  End;
End;

(******************************************************)
```

```
Procedure EnablePorts;
Var
  B : Byte;
Begin
MainDseg := Dseg;
ClearBuffer;
GetIntVec($0C,AsyncVector);
SetIntVec($0C,@AsyncInt);

B := Port[INTCTLR];
B := B And $0EF;
Port[INTCTLR] := B;
B := Port[LCR];
B := B And $7F;

Port[LCR] := B;
Port[IER] := ENBLRDY;
Port[MCR] := $08 Or MDMMOD;
Port[MDMMSR] := MDMCD;
Port[$20] := $20;
End;

(********************************************************)

Function GetCharInBuf : Char;
Begin
If CharsInBuf > 0 Then
  Begin
  GetCharInBuf := Buffer[CircOut];
  If CircOut < MaxBufLen Then
    Inc(CircOut,1)
  Else
    CircOut := 1;
  Dec(CharsInBuf,1);
  End;
End;

(********************************************************)

Function CarrierDetected : Boolean;
Var
  Ch : Char;
  Timer  : Integer;
Begin
CarrierDetected := False;
Timer:=40;
While (Port[MDMMSR] And $80) <> $80 Do
  Begin
  If KeyPressed Then
    Begin
    Ch := ReadKey;
    If Ch = #27 Then
      Exit;
    End;
  If (CharsInBuf > 0) Then
    Begin
```

```
      Ch := GetCharInBuf;
      Write(Ch);
      If Ch = CR Then
        WriteLn;
      End;
    If Timer = 0 Then
      Exit
    Else
      Begin
      Dec(Timer,1);
      Delay(1000);
      End;
    End
CarrierDetected := True;
End;

(*******************************************************)
Procedure SendChar(B: Byte);
Begin
While ((Port[LSR] And $20) <> $20) Do
  Begin
  End;
Port[Dataport] := B;
End;

(*******************************************************)
Procedure StringToPort(S : String);
Var
  I : Integer;
Begin
For I := 1 To Length(S) Do
  SendChar(Ord(S[I]));
SendChar(Ord(CR));
End;

(*******************************************************)
Procedure DisablePorts;
Var
  B : Byte;
Begin
(* Turn off carrier signal. *)
StringToPort('ATC0');

(* Turn off the communication interrupt for COM 1. *)
B := Port[INTCTLR];
B := B Or $10;
Port[INTCTLR] := B;

(* Disable 8250 Data Ready Interrupt. *)
B := Port[LCR];
B := B And $7F;
Port[LCR] := B;
Port[IER] := $0;

(* Disable OUT2 on 8250. *)
Port[MCR] := $0;
```

```pascal
Port[$20] := $20;

SetIntVec($0C,AsyncVector);

MsDos(Regs);
End;

(*********************************************************)

Function SuccessfulConnect(PhoneNumber : String) : Boolean;
Var
  S : String;
Begin
(* ATDT assumes touch-tone dial. *)
S := 'ATDT'+PhoneNumber;
StringToPort(S);
Delay(300);
If CarrierDetected Then
  SuccessfulConnect:=True
Else
  Begin
  Write('Error: Unable To Connect.');
  StringToPort('ATC0'); (* Turn off carrier signal. *)
  SuccessfulConnect:=False;
  End;
End;

(*********************************************************)

Procedure SetHayesModem;
Begin
StringToPort('ATC0');      (* Turn off carrier signal.      *)
Delay(1000);               (* Wait a second.                *)
StringToPort('ATZ');       (* Reset modem to cold-start.    *)
Delay(1000);               (* Wait a second.                *)
StringToPort('ATF1');      (* Full Duplex.                  *)
Delay(1000);               (* Wait a second.                *)
StringToPort('ATE0');      (* Do not echo in command state. *)
Delay(1000);               (* Wait a second.                *)
StringToPort('ATV1');      (* Verbal result codes.          *)
Delay(1000);               (* Wait a second.                *)
StringToPort('ATQ0');      (* Send result codes.            *)
Delay(1000);               (* Wait a second.                *)
End;

(*********************************************************)

Procedure StartCommunicating;
Var
  OutChar,
  InChar : Char;
Begin
ClearBuffer;

  Repeat
  If (CharsInBuf > 0) Then
    Begin
    InChar := GetCharInBuf;
```

```
      If InChar in [#32..#126] Then
        Write(InChar)
      Else If (InChar = CR) Then
        WriteLn;
      End;
    If KeyPressed Then
      Begin
      OutChar := ReadKey;
      If (OutChar <> #27) Then
        Begin
        SendChar(Ord(OutChar));
        If OutChar = CR Then
          WriteLn
        Else
          Write(OutChar);
        End;
      End;
    Until OutChar = #27;
End;

(******************************************************)

Begin
ClrScr;

SelectModemSet;

With ModemSet Do
  SetSerialPort(ComPort,BPS,StopBits,DataBits,Parity);

EnablePorts;

SetHayesModem;

If SuccessfulConnect(ModemSet.PhoneNumber) Then
  StartCommunicating;

WriteLn;
Write('Logging off...');
StringToPort('ATZ');          (* Reset modem to cold-start.   *)
Delay(1000);                  (* Wait a second.               *)
DisablePorts;
End.
```

The main block of this program calls several procedures and functions, and outlines the steps necessary to establish asynchronous communications. The first procedure called is **SelectModemSet**, which allows the user to specify the communications port to use, the bits per second, the number of stop and data bits, the parity, and the telephone number. (Note that this program is designed to use communications port number 1 (COM1) only.) These data items are stored in a record of type **ModemSetType**, which is defined in the following listing.

```
Type
  ModemSetType = Record
    ComPort,
    BPS,
    DataBits,
    StopBits      : Integer;
    Parity        : Char;
    PhoneNumber   : String;
    End;
```

After this record is initialized, its contents are passed to the procedure **SetSerialPort**, which uses BIOS Interrupt **14h** to set the serial port to your parameters. To use this interrupt, you must set AH to 0, which tells BIOS to initialize a serial port, set AL to a parameter byte whose bits contain the communications settings, and set DX to 0 for COM1 or 1 for COM2.

7	6	5	4	3	2	1	0

Parameter	Bits Used	Bit Pattern	Meaning
Data Bits	Bits 0-1	00	5 data bits
		01	6 data bits
		10	7 data bits
		11	8 data bits
Stop Bits	Bit 2	0	1 stop bit
		1	2 stop bits
Parity	Bits 3-4	00	No parity
		01	Odd parity
		10	No parity
		11	Even parity
Speed (BPS)	Bits 5-7	000	100 BPS
		001	150 BPS
		010	300 BPS
		011	600 BPS
		100	1200 BPS
		101	2400 BPS
		110	4800 BPS
		111	9600 BPS

Table 16-2.   Contents of AL Register for BIOS Interrupt 14h

The most difficult part of using Interrupt 14 is setting the bits in the parameter byte. Table 16-2 lists definitions of each bit in this byte.

Once the modem has been set, the interrupt is installed by procedure **EnablePorts**. This procedure saves the old interrupt vector address, installs the address of procedure **AsyncInt**, and prepares the INS8250 UART chip for communications.

The final step in preparation is to initialize the modem to the proper settings with the **SetHayesModem** procedure. While there are many modems available, the Hayes Smartmodem is the commonly accepted standard for personal computers. The modem commands used here should work on any modem compatible with the Hayes Smartmodem. Table 16-3 lists the commands available for the Hayes Smartmodem. For a full explanation of the internal operation of the Hayes Smartmodem, see the *Smartmodem 1200 Hardware Reference Manual* by Hayes Microcomputer Products, Inc. If you use an incompatible modem, change this procedure to match your modem.

Now that the serial port is set, the interrupt is installed, and the modem is initialized, it is time to begin communications. The Boolean function **SuccessfulConnect(ModemSet.PhoneNumber)** dials the phone number passed to it and waits for a carrier-detect signal from the modem, indicating that the connection has been established, in which case the function returns TRUE, and communications begin. If no carrier-detect signal is obtained, the function returns FALSE and the program ends.

After the carrier-detect signal is received, control is passed to the procedure **StartCommunicating**, which transmits the characters you type and displays the characters received from the remote computer. This procedure continues until you press ESC, which produces an ASCII code 27.

The **DisablePorts** procedure, the final step, installs the original interrupt in the interrupt vector table and resets the UART chip.

The Circular Input Buffer

The *circular input buffer* is one of the central elements of an interrupt-driven communications program. Because data can arrive at the serial port at any time, the interrupt handler must be able to capture and process that data while the computer is busy doing something else. If the interrupt does not store the character in a buffer, the character will be lost before the program has time to capture it.

Command	Parameters	Description
A	None	Modem answers a telephone call without waiting for a ring. This is used to change from Voice mode, where you speak to someone, to Data mode, where two computers communicate
A/	None	Repeats the last command
Cn	0,1	Transmitter off. When $n = 1$, the modem calls, answers, or connects to another modem. All other times, $n = 0$
,(Comma)	None	Causes a two-second delay when dialing a telephone number
Ds	Number	Puts the modem in the Originate mode and dials the telephone number represented by s
En	0,1	When $n = 0$, the modem in the command state does not echo back characters. When $n = 1$, characters are echoed
Fn	0,1	When $n = 0$, the modem operates in half-duplex; when $n = 1$, the modem operates in full-duplex
Hn	0,1,2	This command controls your telephone's dial tone. When $n = 0$, the modem is "on-hook" and no dial tone is present. When $n = 1$, the modem is "off-hook" and the dial tone is present. The parameter 2 is used for special applications using amateur radio equipment
In	0,1	This command requests the Smartmodem's three-digit product code. The first two digits indicate the product (for example, 12 indicates a Smartmodem 1200) and the third digit represents the revision number
Mn	0,1,2	The **M** command controls the speaker. When $n = 0$, the speaker is always off. When $n = 1$, the speaker is on until a carrier is detected. When $n = 2$, the speaker is always on
O	None	When the modem is on-line, the **O** command returns the modem to the Command state. In the Command state, any of the modem commands can be initiated
P	None	Tells the modem to dial the telephone using pulses rather than tones
Qn	0,1	The modem can send result codes that report the modem's status. The command **Q0** tells the modem to send status codes. **Q1** turns this feature off

Table 16-3.   Hayes Smartmodem Commands

Command	Parameters	Description
R	None	Put **R** at the end of a telephone number when calling an originate-only modem
Sr?	1..16	Reads the contents of one of the 16 modem registers, specified by **r**
Sr=n	r = 1..16	Sets modem register **r** to the value **n**
;	None	Places a semicolon at the end of the dial command to force the modem back to the Command state after the modem connects with the remote modem
T	None	Tells the modem to dial in Tone mode rather than Pulse mode
Vn	0,1	The modem can return codes in numbers or words. **V0** selects numeric codes; **V1** selects words
Xn	0,1	The modem can return a basic set of codes or an extended set. **X0** selects the basic set; **X1** selects the extended set
Z	None	Sets the modem to its cold-start configuration, which is like turning the modem off and on

Table 16-3.   Hayes Smartmodem Commands (*continued*)

A circular buffer, which is an array of characters, resolves this problem by storing characters temporarily until your computer can catch up with the stream of input characters. The circular buffer is controlled by three **Integer** variables: **CircIn**, **CircOut**, and **CharsInBuf**. **CircIn** points to the next character that the interrupt routine puts into the input buffer, and **CircOut** points to the next character to be taken out of the buffer. **CharsInBuf** is the number of characters waiting in the buffer.

When no characters are in the input buffer, **CircIn** and **CircOut** are equal and **CharsInBuf** is zero. When data comes into the serial port, the interrupt routine adds the incoming characters to the buffer and increments both **CircIn** and **CharsInBuf**. Note that when the end of the buffer is reached, **CircIn** is set to 1, the beginning of the buffer. This is why the buffer is called circular.

The procedure **GetCharInBuf** checks whether **CharsInBuf** is greater than zero, which indicates that characters are present in the buffer. If **CharsInBuf** is greater than zero, the character in the buffer is removed, **CharsInBuf** is decremented, and **CircOut** is incremented. Thus, **CircOut** is constantly chasing **CircIn** to make sure that there are no characters in the input buffer. Generally, your computer communicates at either 300 or 1200 bits per second. This is fairly slow compared to the speed at which the 8088 processes data. Therefore, the circular buffer should never be full. The **AsyncCommunications** program uses a 1K buffer, which should be more than enough for most communications purposes.

Memory-Resident Programs

When Borland's SideKick program burst onto the software market in 1984, it seemed like magic. Anytime, anywhere, a key stroke could call up a notepad, calculator, and other useful utilities. SideKick could do this because it is a memory-resident program, that is, one that locks itself in memory and is always there even when you run other programs.

Now, years later, memory-resident programs are fairly common. Even so, they remain a mystery to most programmers. This section explains how you can write limited-function memory-resident programs using Turbo Pascal.

The Reentrance Issue

Memory-resident programs are often referred to as TSRs because they terminate but stay resident in your computer's memory. Locking a program into memory is easy; getting it to do something useful once it is there can be terribly complicated. Most of the problems have to do with the fact that DOS is not reentrant. If you are not familiar with the term *reentrant*, don't be too concerned; it's a technical term with a simple explanation.

DOS provides a rich set of services to the programmer. These services are used for disk I/O, controlling the video display, keyboard input, and more. The problem is that a DOS service will not work if it is interrupted by another DOS service. Normally, this will never occur because DOS executes only one program at a time. With TSRs, however, the picture becomes more complicated. Consider this scenario: a program calls a DOS service to retrieve some data from a disk file. The DOS service begins executing, and at that moment, a TSR executes another DOS service. In short, the first DOS service is interrupted by the second. The result is disaster—the two DOS services collide and, most likely, your system crashes. That's what reentrance is all about.

There are two ways to deal with reentrance. The first approach is the easiest: make sure that your TSR never uses any DOS services. The second approach is more complicated: make sure that your TSR never executes a DOS service while another DOS service is active. With the second approach, your TSR has the full power of the PC at its disposal, but requires some very complex programming. This chapter will limit its scope to the easy way, avoiding the use of DOS services at all times.

Going Resident

Included in the Turbo Pascal DOS unit is a procedure named **Keep**, which terminates your program but keeps it resident. **Keep** takes a single **Word** parameter, which is passed to DOS as an exit code. With the **Keep** procedure, making your program resident is the easiest, and last, step of the TSR process. Much has to be done before you get to the **Keep** command. For one thing, you have to decide how to activate your TSR once it's resident. You also have to install the interrupt handlers that will do the work of the TSR. Once you understand some basic concepts, you will be surprised how straightforward a TSR can be.

Activating the TSR

For a TSR to do anything, it has to be triggered. If you use SideKick, you know that the trigger is pressing the hot keys. In that case, the keyboard is the trigger. The computer's clock timer is another good trigger—one that is pulled about 18 times a second. In fact, the keyboard and the timer are the triggers used most often to activate TSRs. The one you select will depend on the application. The timer interrupt is great if you need to constantly check for something, like a value of a flag. The keyboard is better suited to TSRs that need to respond at the user's request. The program example given here uses both the timer and the keyboard to create a TSR that blanks your computer's screen after a certain amount of time has passed without keyboard activity. Pressing a key instantly restores the screen. Screen-blanking programs protect your monitor from "burn in," a problem that occurs when computers are left on, but unused, for long periods.

```
{$M 2000,0,0}
{$R-,S-,I-,D+,F+,V-,B-,N-,L+ }
Program ScreenSaver;
Uses
  DOS, CRT;

Const
  TimerInt = $08;            (* Timer interrupt *)
  KbdInt   = $09;            (* Keyboard interrupt *)
  TimeLimit : Word = 5460; (* Wait 5 minutes before blanking *)

Var
  Regs       : Registers;

  Cnt        : Word; (* Counts timer ticks          *)
  PortNum    : Word; (* Port used to disable video *)
  PortOff    : Word; (* Value to disable video      *)
  PortOn     : Word; (* Value to enable video       *)

  OldKbdVec   : Pointer;
  OldTimerVec : Pointer;

  i    : Real;
  Code : Word;

(*********************************************************)

Procedure STI;
InLine($FB);

(*********************************************************)

Procedure CLI;
InLine($FA);

(*********************************************************)

Procedure CallOldInt(Sub:Pointer);
Begin
InLine($9C/           { PUSHF                    }
      $FF/$5E/$06);  { CALL DWORD PTR [BP+6] }
End;

(*********************************************************)

Procedure Keyboard(Flags,CS,IP,AX,BX,CX,DX,
                   SI,DI,DS,ES,BP : Word); Interrupt;
Begin
CallOldInt(OldKbdVec);       (* Call original interrupt *)

If (Cnt >= TimeLimit) Then  (* Restore screen, if disabled *)
  Port[PortNum] := PortOn;
Cnt := 0;                    (* Reset counter *)
STI;
End;
```

```
(********************************************************)
Procedure Clock(Flags,CS,IP,AX,BX,CX,DX,
                SI,DI,DS,ES,BP : Word); Interrupt;
Begin
CallOldInt(OldTimerVec);        (* Call original interrupt *)

If (Cnt > TimeLimit) Then       (* If timer limit is reached, *)
  Port[PortNum] := PortOff       (* disable video              *)
Else
  Inc(Cnt,1);                   (* Otherwise, increment counter *)
STI;
End;

(********************************************************)

Begin
(* If user entered a number parameter, *)
(* compute the delay factor.           *)

If ParamCount = 1 Then
  Begin
  Val(ParamStr(1),i,code);
  If (Code = 0) and (i > 0) and (i < 11) Then
    TimeLimit := Trunc(i*18.2*60);
  End;

Regs.AH := $0F;          (* Determine the type of video  *)
Intr($10,Regs);          (* adapter in use (Mono or CGA) *)

If Regs.AL = 7 Then      (* Mono adapter *)
  Begin
  PortNum  := $3B8;
  PortOff  := $21;
  PortOn   := $29;
  End
Else                     (* Color adapter *)
  Begin
  PortNum  := $3D8;
  PortOff  := $25;
  PortOn   := $2D;
  End;
(* Save original interrupts *)
GetIntVec(KbdInt, OldKbdVec);
GetIntVec(TimerInt, OldTimerVec);

(* Install new interrupts *)
SetIntVec(TimerInt, @Clock);
SetIntVec(KbdInt, @Keyboard);

Cnt := 0;  (* Initialize counter *)
Keep(0);   (* Terminate and stay resident *)
End.
```

Notice that the listing just given begins with the following compiler directive:

{$M 2000,0,0}

This directive limits the stack segment to 2000 bytes and allocates space for the heap. You must limit the amount of memory your TSR will use, especially the heap. If you do not limit the heap, your TSR will grab all available memory and leave none for any other programs.

Blanking the Screen

The TSR just given relies on a useful feature found on monochrome and CGA video adapters. This feature allows you to turn the video display off and on, without affecting the contents of the display. The function is accessed through a port: writing a specific value to the port turns the video off, another value turns it on. Unfortunately, the port address and the off/on values differ depending on the adapter in use (see Table 16-4). When the TSR starts, it must determine which adapter is in use and select the appropriate port address and off/on values.

How the TSR Works

Once installed, the TSR starts counting seconds. When the elapsed time passes a limit, the TSR blanks the screen. Time is counted from the last keystroke. Thus, if the limit is two minutes, the screen will go blank two

	Monochrome	CGA
Port Address	3B8h	3D8h
Turn Off	21h	25h
Turn On	29h	2Dh

Table 16-4. Video On/Off Control Values

minutes after the last keystroke. Once the screen is blank, pressing any key restores the screen, and the TSR begins counting time again.

This process depends on a counter that is continuously incremented. When a keystroke is detected, the counter is set back to zero and begins incrementing again. When the counter reaches a limit defined by the programmer, the TSR blanks the screen.

The Interrupt Handlers

The TSR relies on two interrupt handlers—**Keyboard** and **Clock**. The program attaches **Keyboard** to the keyboard interrupt ($09), so that anytime a key is pressed, **Keyboard** is activated. Likewise, **Clock**, the handler attached to the timer interrupt ($08), executes with every tick of the system clock. Notice that both handlers start out by calling the original interrupt (the one they replaced). This point is critical—your TSR must never interfere with the normal functioning of the keyboard and clock interrupts. The procedure **CallOldInt** is designed specifically for executing interrupts.

```
Procedure Keyboard(Flags,CS,IP,AX,BX,CX,DX,
                   SI,DI,DS,ES,BP : Word); Interrupt;
Begin
CallOldInt(OldKbdVec);         (* Call original interrupt *)

If (Cnt >= TimeLimit) Then     (* Restore screen, if disabled *)
  Port[PortNum] := PortOn;
Cnt := 0;                      (* Reset counter *)
STI;
End;


(**********************************************************)

Procedure Clock(Flags,CS,IP,AX,BX,CX,DX,
                SI,DI,DS,ES,BP : Word); Interrupt;
Begin
CallOldInt(OldTimerVec);       (* Call original interrupt *)

If (Cnt > TimeLimit) Then      (* If time limit is reached, *)
  Port[PortNum] := PortOff     (* disable video             *)
Else
  Inc(Cnt,1);                  (* Increment counter *)
STI;
End;
```

The **Clock** handler performs two tasks. First, it checks to see if the counter has passed the time limit. If so, the handler blanks the screen; if not, it increments the counter. The **Keyboard** handler does just the opposite. If the counter has passed the time limit, the handler restores the screen. In any case, the counter is reset to zero. As you can see, TSRs need not be complicated to be useful.

Installing the TSR requires four simple steps:

1. Save the original interrupts for the keyboard and timer.

2. Install your interrupt handlers.

3. Initialize the counter to zero.

4. Call **Keep** to terminate and stay resident.

```
(* Save original interrupts *)
GetIntVec(KbdInt, OldKbdVec);
GetIntVec(TimerInt, OldTimerVec);

(* Install new interrupts *)
SetIntVec(TimerInt, @Clock);
SetIntVec(KbdInt, @Keyboard);

Cnt := 0;   (* Initialize counter *)
Keep(0);    (* Terminate and stay resident *)
```

The example TSR sets the default time limit at 5460, about five minutes. When loading the TSR, the user can override the default by adding a number to the command line. The number indicates the number of minutes to wait before blanking the screen. For example, the command

```
SCRSAVE 1.5
```

sets the time interval to 90 seconds (1.5 minutes). You can specify any time limit up to ten minutes.

Interrupt processing is one of the most useful and challenging aspects of PC programming. With Turbo Pascal, you can easily write interrupt handlers for use in telecommunications and memory-resident programs. Though the concept of interrupts may be new to you, it is an area well worth exploring, for mastery of the use of interrupts is a sign of a well-versed programmer.

Turbo Pascal Procedure and Function Library

Fundamental Routines
Buffered String Input
Large String Procedures
Arithmetic Functions
File Encryption

Good programmers are pack rats; they store every function and procedure they come across because they know that sooner or later they will use them. Putting together a good library of procedures and functions takes years of coding, testing, and swapping information with other programmers. You can get a head start on your library with the procedures and functions in this chapter.

Fundamental Routines

Certain routines are so generally useful that you include them in almost all programs. Some of the most valuable ones write directly to screen memory, control the PC's sound generator, and center a string on the screen.

FastWrite

The fastest way to display text is to write directly to video memory. When you do so, you must use either an external assembler procedure or inline code; otherwise your procedure will create snow on the screen. This inline procedure writes a string to coordinates x and y in the colors you specify. The parameter **stype** must contain either "M" for monochrome displays or "C" for color displays.

```
Procedure FastWrite( x, y : Integer;
                     Var S : String;
                     fg, bg : Integer;
                     stype : Char);
Var
  i, b : Byte;
Begin
If UpCase(Stype) = 'M' Then
  Begin
  b := (bg Shl 4) + fg;
  x := ((x-1)*2) + ((y-1)*160);
  For i := 1 To Length(S) Do
    Begin
    Mem[$B000:X] := Byte(s[i]);
    Mem[$B000:X+1] := b;
    Inc(x,2);
    End;
  End
Else
Inline($50/              (* PUSH     AX                   *)
       $53/              (* PUSH     BX                   *)
       $51/              (* PUSH     CX                   *)
       $52/              (* PUSH     DX                   *)
       $1E/              (* PUSH     DS                   *)
       $06/              (* PUSH     ES                   *)
       $57/              (* PUSH     DI                   *)
       $56/              (* PUSH     SI                   *)
       $8B/$5E/<x/       (* MOV      BX,x                 *)
       $8B/$46/<y/       (* MOV      AX,y                 *)
       $4B/              (* DEC      BX                   *)
       $48/              (* DEC      AX                   *)
       $B9/$50/$00/      (* MOV      CX,0050              *)
       $F7/$E1/          (* MUL      CX                   *)
       $03/$C3/          (* ADD      AX,BX                *)
       $B9/$02/$00/      (* MOV      CX,0002              *)
       $F7/$E1/          (* MUL      CX                   *)
       $8B/$F8/          (* MOV      DI,AX                *)
       $8B/$5E/<bg/      (* MOV      BX,bg                *)
       $8B/$46/<fg/      (* MOV      AX,fg                *)
       $B9/$04/$00/      (* MOV      CX,0004              *)
       $D3/$E3/          (* SHL      BX,CL                *)
       $03/$D8/          (* ADD      BX,AX                *)
       $86/$DF/          (* XCHG     BL,BH                *)
       $BA/$DA/$03/      (* MOV      DX,03DA              *)
       $B8/$00/$B8/      (* MOV      AX,B800              *)
       $8E/$C0/          (* MOV      ES,AX                *)
       $C5/$76/<s/       (* LDS      SI,s                 *)
       $8A/$0C/          (* MOV      CL,[SI]              *)
       $80/$F9/$00/      (* CMP      CL,00                *)
       $74/$15/          (* JZ       2E06                 *)
       $FC/              (* CLD                           *)
       $46/              (* INC      SI                   *)
       $8A/$1C/          (* MOV      BL,[SI]              *)
       $EC/              (* IN       AL,DX                *)
       $A8/$01/          (* TEST     AL,01                *)
       $75/$FB/          (* JNZ      2DF5                 *)
```

```
$FA/              (* CLI                        *)
$EC/              (* IN      AL,DX               *)
$A8/$01/          (* TEST    AL,01               *)
$74/$FB/          (* JZ      2DFB                *)
$8B/$C3/          (* MOV     AX,BX               *)
$AB/              (* STOSW                       *)
$FB/              (* STI                         *)
$E2/$EC/          (* LOOP    2DF2                *)
$5E/              (* POP     SI                  *)
$5F/              (* POP     DI                  *)
$07/              (* POP     ES                  *)
$1F/              (* POP     DS                  *)
$5A/              (* POP     DX                  *)
$59/              (* POP     CX                  *)
$5B/              (* POP     BX                  *)
$58/              (* POP     AX                  *)
$E9/$00/$00/      (* JMP     2E11                *)
$8B/$E5/          (* MOV     SP,BP               *)
$5D/              (* POP     BP                  *)
$C2/$0E/$00);     (* RET     000E                *)
End;
```

GetScreenType

To use **FastWrite** and many other routines in this chapter, you must know what type of display adapter the computer uses. This information is reported by the procedure **GetScreenType**, which is shown here. **GetScreenType** uses BIOS interrupt **10h** with register AH set to **0Fh**, which returns the current video mode. If the returned mode is 7, the screen is monochrome.

```
Procedure GetScreenType(Var stype : Char);
Var
  Regs : Registers;
Begin
Regs.AH := $0F;
Intr($10,Regs);
If Regs.AL = 7 Then
  stype := 'M'
Else
  stype := 'C';
End;
```

Controlling the Cursor

The following three procedures control the size of the cursor, making it small or large, and also turn it off. The parameter **stype** contains the type of adapter in use ("M" or "C"). The color screen uses up to 8 lines for the cursor, while the monochrome screen uses as many as 14.

```
Procedure Cursor_Off(Stype : Char);
Var
  Regs : Registers;

Begin
With Regs Do
  Begin
  AH :=$01;
  CH :=$20;
  CL :=$20;
  END
Intro($10, Regs);
End;

(******************************************)

Procedure Cursor_Small(Stype : Char);
Var
  Regs : Registers;

Begin
  Case Stype Of
  'M' :
    Begin
    With Regs Do
      Begin
      AH := $01;
      CH := 12;
      CL := 13;
      End;
    End;

  'C' :
    Begin
    With Regs Do
      Begin
      AH := $01;
      CH := 6;
      CL := 7;
      End;
    End;
  End;
  Intr($10, Regs);
End;

(******************************************)

Procedure Cursor_Big(Stype : Char);
Var
  Regs : Registers;
```

```
Begin
  Case Stype Of
  'M' :
    Begin
    With Regs Do
      Begin
      AH := $01;
      CH := 0;
      CL := 13;
      End;
    End;

  'C' :
    Begin
    With Regs Do
      Begin
      AH := $01;
      CH := 0;
      CL := 7;
      End;
    End;
  End;
Intr($10, Regs);
End;
```

Centering Text

Center displays a string in the middle of a screen line you specify. The syntax of the command is just like that of the **FastWrite** command, except that no x coordinate is specified. Instead, the procedure calculates which x coordinate will properly center the string.

```
Procedure Center(y : Integer;
                 s : String;
                 fg,
                 bg : Integer;
                 stype : Char);
Var
    x : Integer;

Begin
x := 40 - (Length(s) Div 2);
FastWrite(x, y, s, fg, bg, Stype);
End;
```

Generating Sound

The Turbo Pascal commands **Sound** and **NoSound** control the PC's sound generator. **Sound** takes an **Integer** parameter that specifies the pitch of the tone. The tone continues until you issue the **NoSound** command. By using the **Delay** command, you can produce a tone that lasts a specified amount of time. The procedure **Beep**, presented here, uses these three commands to create a tone of a certain pitch and duration. The parameter **Freq** determines the pitch, and **Time** specifies the duration in milliseconds.

```
Procedure Beep(Freq, Time : Integer);
Begin
Sound(Freq);
Delay(Time);
NoSound;
End;
```

Buffered String Input

Turbo Pascal's input procedures **Read** and **ReadLn** are quite limited. When entering data, you can only delete backward with the BACKSPACE key. There is no direct way to know if a function key has been pressed. The two procedures in this section, **InKey** and **InputStringShift**, extend your ability to control the keyboard.

InKey

Each time you press a function key, the PC generates a scan code along with a character. For example, function key F1 generates a scan code (#0) followed by ASCII character 59, the semicolon. The procedure **InKey** checks for the scan code when a key is pressed. If the code is present, **InKey** sets the parameter **FunctionKey** to TRUE.

    InKey also allows you to control the cursor in two ways. The parameter **BeginCursor** determines the way the cursor looks when the procedure is waiting for a key to be pressed: "B" creates a big cursor, "S" a small cursor, and "O" no cursor. The parameter **EndCursor** tells **InKey** how it should leave the cursor after the key has been read.

    Since keeping track of function-key codes is difficult, **InKey** sets a global scalar variable that refers to the function keys by name. This scalar is defined as shown here:

```
Type
  Keys = (NullKey, F1, F2, F3, F4, F5, F6, F7, F8, F9, F10,
          CarriageReturn, Tab, ShiftTab, Bksp, UpArrow,
          DownArrow, RightArrow, LeftArrow, DeleteKey,
          InsertKey, HomeKey, Esc, EndKey, TextKey,
          NumberKey, Space, PgUp, PgDn);

Var
  Key : Keys;
```

You can use this definition to easily program control loops by testing for a specific key, as shown here:

```
Repeat
InKey(Fk, Ch, 'O','O');
Until Key = F1;
```

In this example, the program keeps accepting keyboard input until you press the F1 key. The complete **InKey** procedure is shown here:

```
Procedure InKey(Var FunctionKey : Boolean;
                Var ch : Char;
                BeginCursor,
                EndCursor : Char);
Begin

  Case BeginCursor Of
  'B' : Cursor_Big(Stype);
  'S' : Cursor_Small(Stype);
  'O' : Cursor_Off(Stype);
  End;

FunctionKey := False;
ch := ReadKey;
If (ch = #0) Then
  Begin
  FunctionKey := True;
  ch := ReadKey;
  End;

If FunctionKey Then
  Case Ord(ch) Of
  15: (* shift Tab *)     key := ShiftTab;
  72: (* up arrow *)      key := UpArrow;
  80: (* down arrow *)    key := DownArrow;
  82: (* insert key *)    key := InsertKey;
  75: (* left arrow *)    key := LeftArrow;
  77: (* right arrow *)   key := RightArrow;
  73: (* pge up *)        key := PgUp;
  81: (* pge down *)      key := PgDn;
  71: (* home *)          key := HomeKey;
```

```
 79: (* End *)            key := EndKey;
 83: (* delete *)         key := DeleteKey;
 82: (* insert *)         key := InsertKey;
 59: (* Fl *)             key := F1;
 60: (* F2 *)             key := F2;
 61: (* F3 *)             key := F3;
 62: (* F4 *)             key := F4;
 63: (* F5 *)             key := F5;
 64: (* F6 *)             key := F6;
 65: (* F7 *)             key := F7;
 66: (* F8 *)             key := F8;
 67: (* F9 *)             key := F9;
 68: (* F10 *)            key := F10;
 End
Else
  Case Ord(ch) Of
    8: (* back Space *)     key := Bksp;
    9: (* Tab key *)        key := Tab;
   13: (* return *)         key := CarriageReturn;
   27: (* escape *)         key := Esc;
   32: (* Space bar *)      key := Space;

   33..44, 47, 58..254:
     (* TextKey *)          key := TextKey;

   45..46, 48..57:
     (* number key *)       key := NumberKey;
  End;

  Case EndCursor Of
  'B' : Cursor_Big(Stype);
  'S' : Cursor_Small(Stype);
  'O' : Cursor_Off(Stype);
  End;

End;
```

InputStringShift

A good input procedure allows you to use all the keys on the PC keyboard to delete characters with both the BACKSPACE and DEL keys, move back and forth with RIGHT and LEFT ARROW keys, and switch between Insert and Overwrite modes by pressing the INS key.

InputStringShift, provides your program with all these features. This procedure also lets you enter a string that is longer than the space on the screen you provided for input. For example, even if you set aside only 10 spaces on the screen for input, you still can accept strings as long as 255 characters. **InputStringShift** shifts the string back and forth in the input window as you type or use the arrow and DEL keys.

InputStringShift takes seven parameters, which are shown here:

```pascal
Procedure InputStringShift(Var S : String;
                           WindowLength,
                           MaxLength,
                           X,Y : Integer;
                           FT : Char;
                           BackgroundChar : Integer);
```

S, a string variable, accepts the input; **WindowLength** specifies the size of the data-entry field (from 1 to 255); **MaxLength** is the maximum length of the string (from 1 to 255), and x and y are the screen coordinates of the first character of the input field. **FT** specifies the field type and can be either "T" for text or "N" for numeric. When the field is empty, blank spaces are filled with a character specified by the parameter **BackgroundChar**. Character 176 is a good choice because it creates a lightly shaded background.

```pascal
Procedure InputStringShift(Var S : String;
                           WindowLength,
                           MaxLength,
                           X,Y : Integer;
                           FT : Char;
                           BackgroundChar : Integer);
Var
  xx, i, j, p : Integer;
  ch : Char;
  InsertOn,
  SpecialKey : Boolean;
  offset : Integer;
  TempStr : String;

Procedure XY(x, y : Integer);
Var
  Xsmall : Integer;
Begin
  Repeat
  Xsmall := x-80;
  If Xsmall > 0 Then
    Begin
    y := y+1;
    x := Xsmall;
    End;
  Until Xsmall <= 0;
GotoXY(x, y);
End;

(***********************************)

Procedure SetString;
Var
  i : Integer;
Begin
```

```
i := Length(s);
While s[i] = Char(BackgroundChar) Do
  i := i-1;
s[0] := Char(i);
cursor_small(stype);
End;


(**********************************)


Begin
j := Length(s)+1;
For i := j To MaxLength Do
  s[i] := Char(BackgroundChar);
s[0] := Char(MaxLength);

TempStr := Copy(s, 1, WindowLength);
FastWrite(x,y,TempStr,Yellow,Black,stype);
p := 1;
offset := 1;
InsertOn := True;

  Repeat
  xx := X+(p-offset);
  If (p-offset) = WindowLength Then
    xx := xx-1;

  XY(XX, Y);

  If InsertOn Then
    InKey(SpecialKey, ch, 'S', 'O')
  Else
    InKey(SpecialKey, ch, 'B', 'O');

  If (FT = 'N') Then
    Begin
    If (key = TextKey) Then
      Begin
      beep(100,250);
      key := NullKey;
      End
    Else If (ch = '-') And ((p > 1) Or (s[1] = '-')) Then
      Begin
      beep(100,250);
      key := NullKey;
      End
    Else If (ch = '.') Then
      Begin
      If Not((Pos('.', s) = 0) Or (Pos('.', s) = p)) Then
        Begin
        beep(100,250);
        key := NullKey;
        End
      Else If (Pos('.', s) = p) Then
        Delete(s, p, 1);
      End;
    End;
```

```
Case key Of

  NumberKey,
  TextKey,
  Space :
    Begin
    If (Length(s) = MaxLength) Then
      Begin
      If p = MaxLength Then
        Begin
        Delete(s, MaxLength, 1);
        s := s+ch;
        If p = WindowLength+offset Then
          offset := offset+1;
        TempStr := Copy(s, offset, WindowLength);
        FastWrite(x,y,TempStr,Yellow,Black,stype);
        End
      Else
        Begin
        If InsertOn Then
          Begin
          Delete(s, MaxLength, 1);
          Insert(ch, s, p);
          If p = WindowLength+offset Then
            offset := offset+1;
          If p < MaxLength Then
            p := p+1;
          TempStr := Copy(s, offset, WindowLength);
          FastWrite(x,y,TempStr,Yellow,Black,stype);
          End
        Else      (* overwrite *)
          Begin
          Delete(s, p, 1);
          Insert(ch, s, p);
          If p = WindowLength+offset Then
            offset := offset+1;
          If p < MaxLength Then
            p := p+1;
          TempStr := Copy(s, offset, WindowLength);
          FastWrite(x,y,TempStr,Yellow,Black,stype);
          End;
        End;
      End
    Else
      Begin
      If InsertOn Then
        Begin
        Insert(ch, s, p);
        End
      Else
        Begin
        Delete(s, p, 1);
        Insert(ch, s, p);
        End;
      If p = WindowLength+offset Then
        offset := offset+1;
      If p < MaxLength Then
        p := p+1;
```

```
        TempStr := Copy(s, offset, WindowLength);
        FastWrite(x,y,TempStr,Yellow,Black,stype);
        End;
     End;

  Bksp :
    Begin
    If p > 1 Then
      Begin
      p := p-1;
      Delete(s, p, 1);
      s := s+Char(BackgroundChar);
      If offset > 1 Then
        offset := offset-1;
      TempStr := Copy(s, offset, WindowLength);
      FastWrite(x,y,TempStr,Yellow,Black,stype);
      ch := ' ';
      End
    Else
      Begin
      beep(100,250);
      ch := ' ';
      p := 1;
      End;
    End;

  LeftArrow :
    Begin
    If p > 1 Then
      Begin
      p := p-1;
      If p < offset Then
        Begin
        offset := offset-1;
        TempStr := Copy(s, offset, WindowLength);
        FastWrite(x,y,TempStr,Yellow,Black,stype);
        End;
      End
    Else
      Begin
      SetString;
      Exit;
      End;
    End;

  RightArrow :
    Begin
    If (s[p] <> Char(BackgroundChar)) And (p < MaxLength)
      Then Begin
      p := p+1;
      If p = (WindowLength+offset) Then
        Begin
        offset := offset+1;
        TempStr := Copy(s, offset, WindowLength);
```

```
            FastWrite(x,y,TempStr,Yellow,Black,stype);
          End;
        End
      Else
        Begin
        SetString;
        Exit;
        End;
    End;
  DeleteKey :
    Begin
    Delete(s, p, 1);
    s := s+Char(BackgroundChar);
    If ((Length(s)+1)-offset) >= WindowLength Then
      Begin
      TempStr := Copy(s, offset, WindowLength);
      FastWrite(x,y,TempStr,Yellow,Black,stype);
      End
    Else
      Begin
      TempStr := Copy(s, offset, WindowLength);
      FastWrite(x,y,TempStr,Yellow,Black,stype);
      End;
    End;

  InsertKey :
    Begin
    If InsertOn Then
      InsertOn := False
    Else
      InsertOn := True;
    End;

  Else If Not(key In [CarriageReturn, UpArrow, DownArrow,
                  PgDn, PgUp, NullKey, Esc, Tab,
                  F1, F2, F3, F4, F5, F6,
                  F7, F8, F9, F10]) Then beep(100,250);

  End;

  Until (key In [CarriageReturn, UpArrow, DownArrow, PgUp,
              PgDn, Esc, Tab, F1, F3, F4, F5, F6, F7, F8,
              F9, F10]);

SetString;
End;
```

Large String Procedures

Turbo Pascal limits strings to a maximum of 255 characters. While this is long enough for most strings, there are times when you will need longer strings. The procedures in this section allow you to define strings up to 32,767 characters long. The procedures assume a record type that includes an **Integer** field, which keeps track of the string length, and an array of characters. An example of this record type, **BigString**, follows:

```
Const
  MaxBigStrLen = 1000;
Type
  BigString = record
                length : Integer;
                ch : array [1..MaxBigStrLen] of Char;
                End;
```

BigString can hold up to 1000 characters, and it can be easily extended by changing the value of **MaxBigStrLen**.

The procedures and functions in this section mimic the standard Turbo Pascal string commands; they use the same syntax and names, but begin with the word "Big." For example, the equivalent of Turbo Pascal's **Insert** command is the **BigInsert** command.

SetBigString

SetBigString initializes a big string, **st1**, to a value specified in parameter **s**.

```
Procedure SetBigString(Var st1 : BigString;s : String);
Var
  i : Integer;
Begin
For i := 1 To Length(s) Do
  st1.ch[i] := s[i];
st1.length := Length(s);
End;
```

BigConcat

Big strings cannot use the Turbo Pascal concatenation operator **+**. You can, however, simulate the **Concat** command, as shown in the procedure **BigConcat**, which concatenates **st2** to **st1**.

```
Procedure BigConcat(Var st1 : BigString;
                        st2 : BigString);
  Var
```

```
    i : Integer;
Begin
Move(st2.ch[1],st1.ch[st1.length+1],st2.length);
st1.length := st1.length + st2.length;
End;
```

BigInsert

BigInsert inserts one **BigString** inside a target **BigString** starting at character **p**.

```
Procedure BigInsert(Var st1,st2 : BigString; p : Integer);
Var
  st3 : BigString;
  i,j : Integer;
Begin
Move(st2.ch[1],st3.ch[1],p-1);

Move(st1.ch[1],st3.ch[p],st1.length);

Move(st2.ch[p],st3.ch[p+st1.length],(st2.length-p)+1);

st3.length := st1.length + st2.length;
If st3.length > MaxBigStrLen Then
  st3.length := MaxBigStrLen;

Move(st3.length,st2.length,st3.length+2);
End;
```

BigDelete

BigDelete removes characters from a **BigString** starting at character **p**. It deletes as many characters as specified in the parameter **len**.

```
Procedure BigDelete(Var st1 : BigString; p,len : Integer);
Var
  st2 : BigString;

Begin
Move(st1.ch[1],st2.ch[1],p-1);
Move(st1.ch[(p+len)],st2.ch[p],(st1.length-(p+len))+1);
st2.length := (st1.length - len);
Move(st2.length,st1.length,st2.length+2);
End;
```

BigPos

The function **BigPos** returns the position of one **BigString** inside another **BigString**. To indicate the position, **BigPos** returns a positive number; if no match is found, it returns 0.

```
Function BigPos(Var st1,st2 : BigString) : Integer;
Var
   found : Boolean;
   i,j,StopFlag : Integer;
Begin
StopFlag := (st2.length - st1.length) + 1;
For i := 1 To StopFlag Do
   Begin
   found := True;
   j := 1;

     Repeat
     If st2.ch[i+j-1] <> st1.ch[j] Then
        found := False;
     j := j + 1;
     Until (Not found) Or (j = st1.length);

   If found Then
     Begin
     BigPos := i;
     Exit;
     End;
   End;
BigPos := 0;
End;
```

BigLength

The **BigLength** procedure returns an **Integer** with the length of a **BigString**.

```
Function BigLength(Var St1 : BigString) : Integer;
Begin
BigLength := st1.length;
End;
```

BigCopy

Because the Turbo Pascal string function **Copy** cannot be directly duplicated for large strings (Turbo Pascal cannot define a function using a **Record** data type) you must use **BigCopy**, which provides a result in the form of a procedure. **BigCopy** takes **len** characters from **st1**, starting from character **p**, and assigns them to **st2**.

```
Procedure BigCopy(Var st1,st2 : BigString; p,len : Integer);
Begin
Move(st1.ch[p],st2.ch[1],len);
st2.length := len;
End;
```

Arithmetic Functions

Most of the numerical procedures and functions your programs need are available in Turbo Pascal. One thing these procedures cannot do, however, is convert a fraction that is stored in a string to a decimal equivalent or convert a decimal value into a fraction. The two functions listed here, **Real _ To _ Frac** and **Frac _ To _ Real**, do just that.

Real _ To _ Frac

Real _ To _ Frac accepts two parameters: **r,** the value to convert to decimal, and **d,** the denominator of the fraction. The function returns a string that contains the integer portion of the fraction, as well as the fractional portion. The two are separated by a space.

```
Function Real_To_Frac(r : Real; d : Integer) : String;
Var
  is, ns, ds, s1, s2 : String[20];
  r1, r2, i, f : Real;
  code, p, n : Integer;

Begin
If r = 0 Then
  Begin
  Real_To_Frac := '0';
  Exit;
  End;

is := '0';
ds := '0';
ns := '0';

Str(r:0:8, s2);
p := Pos('.', s2);
If p > 0 Then
  s1 := Copy(s2, 1, p-1);

Delete(s2, 1, p-1);
Val(s1, i, code);
Str(i:0:0, is);

Val(s2, f, code);
If f > 0.0 Then
  Begin
  n := 0;
    Repeat
    n := n+1;
    r1 := n/d;
```

```
    Until rl >= f;
  If (rl-f) > (1.0/(d*2.0)) Then
    n := n-1;

  While (Not Odd(n)) And (n > 0) Do
    Begin
    n := n DIV 2;
    d := d DIV 2;
    End;
  Str(n:0, ns);
  Str(d:0, ds);
  End;

If (ns = '1') And (ds = '1') Then
  Begin
  ns := '0';
  Val(is,rl,code);
  rl := rl + 1;
  Str(rl:0:0,is);
  End;

If (is = '0') And (ns = '0') Then
  Real_To_Frac := '0'
Else If ns = '0' Then
  Real_To_Frac := is
Else If is = '0' Then
  Begin
  If (ns = '1') And (ds = '1') Then
    Real_To_Frac := '1'
  Else
    Real_To_Frac := ns+'/'+ds;
  End
Else
  Real_To_Frac := is+' '+ns+'/'+ds
End;
```

Frac _ To _ Real

Frac _ To _ Real, a function of type **Real**, converts a string that contains a fraction into a real number. The procedure takes two parameters: **Frac**, the string that contains the fraction, and **code**, an integer that indicates an error in conversion. If **code** is equal to zero, no error occurred; if it is not equal to zero, an error did occur. The fraction is formed by an integer, a space, the numerator, a slash, and a denominator. The following are all legal fractions:

```
14 1/2
3/16
29
```

As you can see, both the whole number and the fractional portion
are optional.

```pascal
Function Frac_To_Real(Frac : String;
                      Var code : Integer) : Real;
Var
  n, d, i : Real;
  ns, ds, is : String[8];
  l,p,
  p_slash,
  p_space,
  j : Integer;

Begin
While (frac[1] = ' ') and (Length(frac) > 0) Do
  Delete(frac,1,1);
If frac = '' Then
  Begin
  Frac_To_Real := 0;
  Exit;
  End;

p_slash := Pos('/',frac);
p_space := Pos(' ',frac);

is := '';
ns := '';
ds := '';

If (p_slash > 0) Then
  Begin
  If (p_space > 0) Then
    Begin (* slash and space *)
    For j := 1 To (p_space-1) Do
      is := is + frac[j];
    For j := (p_space+1) To (p_slash-1) Do
      ns := ns + frac[j];
    For j := (p_slash+1) To Length(frac) Do
      ds := ds + frac[j];

    Val(is,i,code);
    Val(ns,n,code);
    Val(ds,d,code);

    Frac_To_Real := i + n / d;
    End
  Else
    Begin (* slash and no space *)
    For j := (p_space+1) To (p_slash-1) Do
      ns := ns + frac[j];
    For j := (p_slash+1) To Length(frac) Do
      ds := ds + frac[j];

    Val(ns,n,code);
    Val(ds,d,code);
```

```
      Frac_To_Real := n / d;
      End
   End
Else
   Begin
   If (p_space > 0) Then
      Begin (* no slash and space *)
      For j := 1 To (p_space-1) Do
         is := is + frac[j];

      Val(is,i,code);
      Frac_To_Real := i;
      End
   Else
      Begin (* no slash and no space *)
      is := is + frac;
      Val(is,i,code);
      Frac_To_Real := i;
      End
   End;
End;
```

File Encryption

Protecting letters, data, and programs is a common task. The only sure protection is to encode the file itself. The programs presented here do this, and offer some extra features as well.

Encode

The **Encode** program encrypts a file based on a password you provide. To encrypt a file, type

ENCODE FILENAME PASSWORD

If you enter the name of a file that does not exist, the program will abort with the message **File not found.** The program also checks to see whether the file was already encrypted. Files encrypted with **Encode** contain the word "LOCKED" in the first 6 bytes. When **Encode** finds these letters, it aborts and displays the message **File already locked.** This protection is necessary to keep you from encrypting the same file twice.

Note also that this program overwrites the original file with binary zeros and then erases the file. This keeps out snoopers who might browse through your disk with a special program for this purpose.

The password can be up to six characters long. It generates two seed values, which control the encryption. **Encode** stores these two seed values in the encrypted file so that the file can never be decoded with an incorrect password.

```pascal
Program Encode;
Const
  MaxBuf = 30000;
Var
  password : String[6];
  seed1,
  seed2 : Byte;
  source,
  dest : File;
  buffer : Array [1..MaxBuf] Of Byte;
  BytesRead : Real;
  i : Integer;

(**********************************)

Procedure OpenFiles;
Const
  s : Array [1..6] Of Char = ('L','O','C','K','E','D');
Begin
Assign(source,ParamStr(1));
(*$I-*)
Reset(source,1);
(*$I+*)
If IOresult <> 0 Then
  Begin
  WriteLn('File not found.');
  Halt;
  End;

BlockRead(source,buffer,6);
If ((buffer[1] = ord('L')) And
    (buffer[2] = ord('O')) And
    (buffer[3] = ord('C')) And
    (buffer[4] = ord('K')) And
    (buffer[5] = ord('E')) And
    (buffer[6] = ord('D'))) Then
    Begin
    WriteLn('File already locked.');
    Halt;
    End;

Reset(source,1);
Assign(dest,'$$$$$.$$');
Rewrite(dest,1);
```

```
BlockWrite(dest,s,6);
BlockWrite(dest,seed1,1);
BlockWrite(dest,seed2,1);
End;

(**********************************)

Procedure Getseed;
Var
  i,j : Integer;
Begin
seed1 := 0;
seed2 := 0;
password := ParamStr(2);

j := Length(password);
For i := 1 To Length(password) Do
  Begin
  seed1 := seed1 + (Ord(password[i]) * i);
  seed2 := seed2 + (Ord(password[i]) * j);
  j := j - 1;
  End;
End;

(***********************************)

Procedure EncodeFile;
Var
  i1,i2 : Byte;
  rr : Integer;
Begin
i1 := seed1;
i2 := seed2;
BytesRead := 0;
BlockRead(source,buffer,MaxBuf,rr);
BytesRead := BytesRead + rr;
While rr > 0 Do
  Begin
  For i := 1 To rr Do
    Begin
    i1 := i1 - i;
    i2 := i2 + i;
    If odd(i) Then
      buffer[i] := buffer[i] - i1
    Else
      buffer[i] := buffer[i] + i2;
    End;
  BlockWrite(dest,buffer,rr);
  BlockRead(source,buffer,MaxBuf,rr);
  BytesRead := BytesRead + rr;
  End;
End;

(***********************************)
```

```
Procedure CloseFiles;
Var
  i : Integer;
Begin
Rewrite(source,1);
FillChar(buffer,MaxBuf,0);
While BytesRead > 0 Do
  Begin
  If BytesRead > MaxBuf Then
    BlockWrite(source,buffer,MaxBuf)
  Else
    Begin
    i := Trunc(BytesRead);
    BlockWrite(source,buffer,i)
    End;
  BytesRead := BytesRead - MaxBuf;
  End;
Close(source);
Close(dest);
Erase(source);
Rename(dest,ParamStr(1));
End;

(************************************)

Begin
If Paramcount <> 2 Then
  Begin
  WriteLn('Syntax: ENCODEIT Filename password');
  Halt;
  End;
Getseed;
OpenFiles;
EncodeFile;
CloseFiles;
End.
```

Decode

Decode restores files that have been encrypted with the **Encode** program. The syntax for **Decode** is

DECODE FILENAME PASSWORD

Decode first checks to see if the file is locked; locked files have the letters "LOCKED" in the first 6 bytes. Next it uses the password to generate two seed values and compares those to the seed values stored in the encrypted file. If the seed values match, the program continues; if not, it displays the message **Wrong password** and stops.

```
Program Decode;
Const
  MaxBuf = 30000;
Var
  password : String[6];
  source,
  dest     : File;
  buffer   : Array [1..MaxBuf] Of Byte;
  BytesRead : Real;
  seed1,
  seed1x,
  seed2,
  seed2x : Byte;
  i : Integer;

(***********************************)

Procedure OpenFiles;
Const
  s : Array [1..6] Of Char = ('L','O','C','K','E','D');
Begin
Assign(source,ParamStr(1));
(*$I-*)
Reset(source,1);
(*$I+*)
If IOresult <> 0 Then
  Begin
  WriteLn('File not found.');
  Halt;
  End;
BlockRead(source,buffer,6);
If Not ((buffer[1] = ord('L')) And
        (buffer[2] = ord('O')) And
        (buffer[3] = ord('C')) And
        (buffer[4] = ord('K')) And
        (buffer[5] = ord('E')) And
        (buffer[6] = ord('D'))) Then
         Begin
         WriteLn('File not locked.');
         Halt;
         End;

BlockRead(source,seed1x,1);
BlockRead(source,seed2x,1);

If ((seed1 <> seed1x) Or (seed2 <> seed2x)) Then
  Begin
  WriteLn('Wrong password.');
  Halt;
  End;

Assign(dest,'$$$$$.$$');
Rewrite(dest,1);
End;

(***********************************)
```

```
Procedure Getseed;
Var
  i,j : Integer;
Begin
seed1 := 0;
seed2 := 0;
password := ParamStr(2);

j := Length(password);
For i := 1 To Length(password) Do
  Begin
  seed1 := seed1 + (ord(password[i]) * i);
  seed2 := seed2 + (ord(password[i]) * j);
  j := j - 1;
  End;
End;

(***********************************)

Procedure DecodeFile;
Var
  i1,i2 : Byte;
  rr : Integer;
Begin
i1 := seed1;
i2 := seed2;
BytesRead := 0;
BlockRead(source,buffer,MaxBuf,rr);
BytesRead := BytesRead + rr;
While rr > 0 Do
  Begin
  For i := 1 To rr Do
    Begin
    i1 := i1 - i;
    i2 := i2 + i;
    If odd(i) Then
      buffer[i] := buffer[i] + i1
    Else
      buffer[i] := buffer[i] - i2;
    End;
  BlockWrite(dest,buffer,rr);
  BlockRead(source,buffer,MaxBuf,rr);
  BytesRead := BytesRead + rr;
  End;
End;

(***********************************)

Procedure CloseFiles;
Var
  i : Integer;
Begin
Rewrite(source,1);
FillChar(buffer,MaxBuf,0);
While BytesRead > 0 Do
  Begin
  If BytesRead > MaxBuf Then
```

```
      BlockWrite(source,buffer,MaxBuf)
    Else
      Begin
      i := Trunc(BytesRead);
      BlockWrite(source,buffer,i)
      End;
    BytesRead := BytesRead - MaxBuf;
    End;
Close(source);
Close(dest);
Erase(source);
Rename(dest,ParamStr(1));
End;

(***********************************)

Begin
If ParamCount <> 2 Then
  Begin
  WriteLn('Syntax: DECODEIT Filename password');
  Halt;
  End;
Getseed;
OpenFiles;
DecodeFile;
CloseFiles;
End.
```

Optimizing Turbo Pascal Programs

At the very least, a program should be free from bugs. Users expect programs to work as advertised, from start to finish, day in and day out. But the fact that a program functions properly is not always enough: users also want programs that work quickly. Optimization is the process of making sure your program runs as fast as it can without compromising the basic functions it performs. This chapter suggests methods you can use to optimize your programs, streamline your code, and eliminate unnecessary bottlenecks.

Optimization: Perfection Versus Excellence

The cost of excellence is reasonable; the cost of perfection is exorbitant. Some programmers spend hours optimizing even unimportant sections of code. Good programmers, however, learn to select the code that can benefit most from optimization, and avoid wasting time on trivial improvements.

There are two criteria to consider when selecting the parts of a program to optimize. First, can the code be improved enough to make a difference? It's quite possible, especially if you are an experienced programmer, that you wrote the section optimally the first time. In most cases, however, even well-written sections can benefit from closer inspection.

Second, the improvements you make must be noticeable to the user. If the user will not notice the difference in speed, your efforts at optimization are wasted. If, however, you feel a section of code can be improved and that the improvement will be noticed by the user, start optimizing.

Approaches to Optimization

Speed is just one goal of optimization; others include minimizing code size and reducing the data space required. With RAM in plentiful supply, however, speed is by far the highest concern. Therefore, the suggestions presented in this chapter are directed to making your programs faster.

The most obvious way to speed up a program is to write sections in assembler and include them in your code as external procedures or inline code. This approach, discussed in Chapter 13, requires time and an extensive knowledge of assembler. Before going to this extreme, you can gain a lot of speed simply by using Turbo Pascal more efficiently. A well-written Turbo Pascal procedure can run quite fast and is much easier to write, debug, and maintain than assembler code.

Timing Program Execution

You cannot optimize without having a way to measure just how much you gain or lose when you change a section of code. You may be surprised to find that a minor change can lead to a substantial increase in speed, while larger changes may do little to increase speed.

The guideline you need is contained in the procedures **ClockOn** and **ClockOff**, listed as follows in a unit named **TIMER**.

```
Unit TIMER;
(*****************************************************)
Interface
(*****************************************************)
Uses DOS;

Procedure ClockOn;
```

```
Procedure ClockOff;

(****************************************************)
Implementation
(****************************************************)

Var
  h,m,s,s100 : Word;
  StartClock,
  StopClock : Real;

(****************************************************)

Procedure ClockOn;
Begin
GetTime(h,m,s,s100);
StartClock := (h * 3600) + (m * 60) + s + (s100 / 100);
End;

(****************************************************)

Procedure ClockOff;
Begin
GetTime(h,m,s,s100);
StopClock := (h * 3600) + (m * 60) + s + (s100 / 100);
WriteLn('Elapsed time = ',(StopClock - StartClock):0:2);
End;

End.
```

The **TIMER** unit uses the procedure **GetTime** from the **DOS** unit to get the time from the system clock. The procedures **ClockOn** and **ClockOff** both call **GetTime**; both use the result to calculate the current time in seconds. **ClockOn** stores its result in the variable **StartClock**, while **ClockOff** computes the value of **StopClock**, subtracts **StartClock** from it, and reports the elapsed time in seconds. The program named **TestLoop** demonstrates how to use the procedures in the **TIMER** unit.

```
Program TestLoop;
Uses CRT, TIMER;
Var
  i,j : integer;

Begin
ClrScr;
j := 0;

ClockOn;  (* Initialize value of StartClock. *)

For i := 1 To MaxInt Do
  j := j + 1;
```

```
ClockOff; (* Display elapsed time. *)

WriteLn;
Write('Press ENTER...');
ReadLn;
End.
```

TestLoop times the execution of a simple **For-Do** loop by preceding it with a call to **ClockOn** and following it with a call to **ClockOff**. When you run this program, you will see the following message:

```
Elapsed time = 0.99

Press ENTER...
```

This message indicates that the **For-Do** loop took 0.99 seconds to execute. All timings reported in this chapter are based on a PC-compatible computer running at 4.77 MHz. Your timings may differ, depending on the computer you use. The specific time you get, however, is unimportant. The value of the timing procedures is to evaluate the relative speed of different procedures that produce the same result. The program listed here demonstrates how to compare the speed of two similar routines.

```
Program TestProcs;
Uses CRT, TIMER;
Const
  ArrLen = MaxInt;
Type
  ArrType = Array [1..ArrLen] Of Char;
Var
  a : ArrType;
  i : Integer;

(*******************************)

Procedure Init1(Var a : ArrType;
                    L : Integer);
Begin
FillChar(a,L,0);
End;

(*******************************)

Procedure Init2(Var a : ArrType;
                    L : Integer);
Var
  i : Integer;
```

```
Begin
For i := 1 To L Do
  a[i] := #0;
End;

(*******************************)

Begin
ClrScr;

ClockOn;
Init1(a,ArrLen);
ClockOff;

ClockOn;
Init2(a,ArrLen);
ClockOff;

WriteLn;
Write('Press ENTER...');
ReadLn;
End.
```

The program just given uses two procedures, **Init1** and **Init2**, both of which initialize an array of characters to all binary zeros. **Init1** uses the Turbo Pascal standard procedure **FillChar** to initialize the array, while **Init2** accomplishes the same goal with a **For-Do** loop.

The results of this program show that **Init1** takes 0.05 seconds to execute, while **Init2** requires 1.38 seconds. It is easy to see which is the better routine.

Optimizing Control Structures

When you optimize a program, control structures should be one of the first things you check. Because Turbo Pascal offers so many flexible control structures, it is easy to write control structures your first time through that are less than optimal.

Nested If-Then Statements

If-Then statements execute Boolean comparison statements, which can include numerous individual comparisons. When you optimize **If-Then**

statements, the goal is to minimize the number of comparisons the computer executes. The procedure listed here demonstrates a very poor use of **If-Then** statements:

```
Procedure BooleanTest1;
Begin
If (i = 1) Then   (* Comparison number 1 *)
  Begin
  a := '1';
  End;
If (i = 2) Then   (* Comparison number 2 *)
  Begin
  a := '2';
  End;
If (i = 3) Then   (* Comparison number 3 *)
  Begin
  a := '3';
  End;
If (i = 4) Then   (* Comparison number 4 *)
  Begin
  a := '4';
  End;
If (i <> 1) and
   (i <> 2) and
   (i <> 3) and
   (i <> 4) Then   (* Comparison number 5 *)
  Begin
  a := 'X';
  End;
End;
```

This routine executes one of five branches, depending on the value of variable **i**. Notice that all five comparisons are executed each time the code section is processed. This process can be made far more efficient with the following code:

```
Procedure BooleanTest2;
Begin
If (i = 1) Then          (* Comparison number 1 *)
  Begin
  a := '1';
  End
Else If (i = 2) Then     (* Comparison number 2 *)
  Begin
  a := '2';
  End
Else If (i = 3) Then     (* Comparison number 3 *)
  Begin
  a := '3';
  End
Else If (i = 4) Then     (* Comparison number 4 *)
```

```
      Begin
      a := '4';
      End
Else                        (* Comparison number 5 *)
      Begin
      a := 'X';
      End;
End;
```

Here, the **Else-If** statement reduces the number of comparisons required. For example, if **i** equals 1, only one comparison is executed. At the other extreme, when **i** is less than 1 or greater than 4, all four comparisons are required.

While the **If-Then-Else** structure is clearly efficient, the **Case** control structure is even more efficient. This code section shows how the **Case** command would replace the **If-Then-Else** statements:

```
Procedure BooleanTest3;
Begin

   Case i Of

   1 :
     Begin
     a := '1';
     End;

   2 :
     Begin
     a := '2';
     End;

   3 :
     Begin
     a := '3';
     End;

   4 :
     Begin
     a := '4';
     End;

   Else
     Begin
     a := 'X';
     End;

   End;

End;
```

While the **Case** statement does not eliminate the number of potential comparisons, under certain circumstances, it does perform them a bit more efficiently. These three procedures were compared in the following program, which repeated each procedure 30,000 times.

```pascal
Program BooleanTest;
Uses CRT, TIMER;
Var
  j,i : Word;
  a : Char;

(*****************************************************)

Procedure BooleanTest1;
Begin
If (i = 1) Then   (* Comparison number 1 *)
  Begin
  a := '1';
  End;
If (i = 2) Then   (* Comparison number 2 *)
  Begin
  a := '2';
  End;
If (i = 3) Then   (* Comparison number 3 *)
  Begin
  a := '3';
  End;
If (i = 4) Then   (* Comparison number 4 *)
  Begin
  a := '4';
  End;
If (i <> 1) and
   (i <> 2) and
   (i <> 3) and
   (i <> 4) Then  (* Comparison number 5 *)
  Begin
  a := 'X';
  End;
End;

(*****************************************************)

Procedure BooleanTest2;
Begin
If (i = 1) Then          (* Comparison number 1 *)
  Begin
  a := '1';
  End
Else If (i = 2) Then     (* Comparison number 2 *)
  Begin
  a := '2';
  End
Else If (i = 3) Then     (* Comparison number 3 *)
  Begin
  a := '3';
  End
Else If (i = 4) Then     (* Comparison number 4 *)
  Begin
```

```
    a := '4';
    End
Else                     (* Comparison number 5 *)
  Begin
  a := 'X';
  End;
End;

(***************************************************)

Procedure BooleanTest3;
Begin

  Case i Of

  1 :
    Begin
    a := '1';
    End;

  2 :
    Begin
    a := '2';
    End;

  3 :
    Begin
    a := '3';
    End;

  4 :
    Begin
    a := '4';
    End;

  Else
    Begin
    a := 'X';
    End;
  End;
End;

(***************************************************)

Begin
ClrScr;

WriteLn('Random values of i...');
WriteLn;
RandSeed := 0;
ClockOn;
For j := 1 To 30000 Do
  Begin
  i := Random(7);
  BooleanTest1;
  End;
ClockOff;
```

```
RandSeed := 0;
ClockOn;
For j := 1 To 30000 Do
  Begin
  i := Random(7);
  BooleanTest2;
  End;
ClockOff;

RandSeed := 0;
ClockOn;
For j := 1 To 30000 Do
  Begin
  i := Random(7);
  BooleanTest3;
  End;
ClockOff;

WriteLn;
WriteLn;
WriteLn('i = 1...');
WriteLn;

i := 1;
ClockOn;
For j := 1 To 30000 Do
  BooleanTest1;
ClockOff;

ClockOn;
For j := 1 To 30000 Do
  BooleanTest2;
ClockOff;

ClockOn;
For j := 1 To 30000 Do
  BooleanTest3;
ClockOff;

WriteLn;
WriteLn;
WriteLn('i = 5...');
WriteLn;

i := 5;
ClockOn;
For j := 1 To 30000 Do
  BooleanTest1;
ClockOff;

ClockOn;
For j := 1 To 30000 Do
  BooleanTest2;
ClockOff;

ClockOn;
For j := 1 To 30000 Do
```

```
  BooleanTest3;
ClockOff;

WriteLn;
Write('Press ENTER...');
ReadLn;

End.
```

This program produced the results shown in Table 18-1. Overall, the **If-Then-Else** statement is almost as efficient as the **Case** statement, but both are much more efficient than the **If-Then** statements.

Testing Values in Boolean Expressions

If-Then statements, Repeat-Until loops, and While-Do loops all require Boolean expressions, expressions that compare a variable to one or more test values. These tests can take several forms, from chained comparisons to set comparisons. Which one is most efficient?

Perhaps some will be surprised that set comparisons, while more compact to write, are far less efficient in operation. For example, the following **Set Inclusion** statement tests if a character variable **Ch** contains a letter in the set ['A','B','C']:

```
If Ch in ['A','B','C'] Then ...
```

The same comparison is performed far more efficiently with this chained comparison:

```
If (Ch = 'A') Or (Ch = 'B') Or (Ch = 'C') Then
```

	Random	Value of i 1	5
BooleanTest1	9.00	3.18	3.96
BooleanTest2	7.97	1.98	2.91
BooleanTest3	7.63	2.03	2.53

Table 18-1.   Results of Boolean Tests

If that surprises you, try tracing through both statements using the Turbo Debugger. You will find that the chained comparison requires far less code.

The program called **TestChar** demonstrates the difference in speed between a **Set Inclusion** statement and two similar forms of **If-Then** statements.

```
Program TestChar;
Uses CRT, TIMER;
Var
  i : Integer;
  Ch : Char;

Begin
ClrScr;
Ch := 'A';

(* Set Inclusion Statement. *)

ClockOn;
For i := 1 to MaxInt Do
  Begin
  If Ch in ['A','B','C'] Then
    Begin
    End;
  End;
ClockOff;

(* If-Then Statement *)

ClockOn;
For i := 1 To MaxInt Do
  Begin
  If (Ch = 'A') or (Ch = 'B') or (Ch = 'C') Then
    Begin
    End;
  End;
ClockOff;

(* Nested If-Then statement *)

ClockOn;
For i := 1 To MaxInt Do
  Begin
  If (Ch = 'A') Then
    Begin
    End
  Else If (Ch = 'B') Then
    Begin
    End
  Else If (Ch = 'C') Then
    Begin
    End;
  End;
ClockOff;
```

```
WriteLn;
WriteLn;
WriteLn;

Ch := 'C';

(* Set Inclusion Statement. *)

ClockOn;
For i := 1 To MaxInt Do
  Begin
  If Ch in ['A','B','C'] Then
    Begin
    End;
  End;
ClockOff;

(* If-Then Statement *)

ClockOn;
For i := 1 To MaxInt Do
  Begin
  If (Ch = 'A') or (Ch = 'B') or (Ch = 'C') Then
    Begin
    End;
  End;
ClockOff;

(* Nested If-Then statement *)

ClockOn;
For i := 1 To MaxInt Do
  Begin
  If (Ch = 'A') Then
    Begin
    End
  Else If (Ch = 'B') Then
    Begin
    End
  Else If (Ch = 'C') Then
    Begin
    End;
  End;
ClockOff;
WriteLn;
Write('Press ENTER...');
ReadLn;

End.
```

When the character in question is "A," the loop using the set-inclusion comparison requires 2.96 seconds to execute (Table 18-2), while the chained comparison and nested **If-Then-Else** statements require only 1.05 and 1.04 seconds, respectively. When the character is the last

	Value of Ch	
Comparison	**"A"**	**"C"**
Set inclusion	2.96	3.13 (Seconds)
Chained comparison	1.05	1.43
Nested If-Then-Else	1.04	1.54

Table 18-2.   Timings for Character Comparisons

one tested (in this case the letter "C"), the results are similar, though the performance of the set-inclusion comparison degrades less than the other two.

Optimizing Arithmetic

The speed of your calculations depends largely on the type of variables involved (**Integer** or **Real**) and the type of operation involved (addition, subtraction, multiplication, or division). **Integer** computations always require much less time than computations with **Real** variables. The following program, **MathComp**, compares the speed of integer and real computations for addition operations. You can change the program to test other operations.

```
Program MathComp;
Uses CRT,TIMER;
Var
  i,
  a, b, c : Integer;
  x, y, z : Real;

Begin
ClrScr;
a := 1;
b := 1;
ClockOn;
For i := 1 To 10000 Do
  Begin
  c := a + b;
  End;
ClockOff;

x := 1.0;
y := 1.0;
```

```
ClockOn;
For i := 1 To 10000 Do
  Begin
  z := x + y;
  End;
ClockOff;
WriteLn;
Write('Press ENTER...');
ReadLn;
End.
```

Table 18-3 shows the execution times for **Integer**s and **Real**s for the four arithmetic operators. As you can see, **Integer** computations are almost ten times faster than **Real** computations across the board.

Division involving **Real** variables is the slowest of all the computations, requiring over twice as much time as multiplication operations and four times as much as addition or subtraction.

In general, avoid using **Real**s when **Integer**s will do. If you must use **Real**s, avoid division when possible. For example, the equation

X / 4.0

can be changed to

X * 0.25

which is far faster.

Some programs that use a lot of calculations contain many complicated formulas. In such programs, optimization should be second to readability. If, in the process of optimization, you make a subtle change to a complicated formula, you may never find your error.

	Integer	Real
Addition	0.33	2.03
Subtraction	0.33	3.19
Multiplication	0.60	4.89
Division	0.66	13.02

Table 18-3.   Timings for Various Arithmetic Operations

Optimizing File Operations

Even when you use a hard disk, disk file input and output are slow operations. This is especially true for Turbo Pascal text files. You can speed up your text-file operations by specifying a text buffer for the file. The process is demonstrated in the program listed here:

```pascal
Program TestTextBuf;
Uses CRT, TIMER;
Var
  Buf1 : Array [1..256] of Char;
  Buf2 : Array [1..1023] of Char;
  Buf3 : Array [1..1024] of Char;
  Buf4 : Array [1..4096] of Char;
  T : Text;

(**************************************************)

Procedure WriteFile;
Var
  s : String;
  i : Integer;
Begin
FillChar(s,SizeOf(s),'A');
s[0] := Chr(255);
For i := 1 To 100 Do
  WriteLn(T,s);
End;

(**************************************************)

Begin
ClrScr;
Assign(T,'TEST.X');

Rewrite(T);
ClockOn;
WriteFile;
ClockOff;

Rewrite(T);
SetTextBuf(T,Buf1);
ClockOn;
WriteFile;
ClockOff;

Rewrite(T);
SetTextBuf(T,Buf2);
ClockOn;
WriteFile;
ClockOff;
```

```
Rewrite(T);
SetTextBuf(T,Buf3);
ClockOn;
WriteFile;
ClockOff;

Rewrite(T);
SetTextBuf(T,Buf4);
ClockOn;
WriteFile;
ClockOff;

Close(T);
Erase(T);

WriteLn;
Write('Press ENTER...');
ReadLn;
End.
```

This program declares a text file named **T** and four buffers of different sizes: 256 bytes, 1023 bytes, 1024 bytes, and 4096 bytes. If you do not specify a buffer to a text file, Turbo Pascal assigns a default buffer of 128 bytes.

Generally speaking, the larger the buffer, the faster your input and output operations will be. This is not strictly the case with Turbo Pascal text files, as Table 18-4 shows.

Output to the default 128-byte buffer is fairly slow (5.38 seconds) as is output to a 200-byte buffer (5.16 seconds). Surprisingly, a 1023-byte buffer is actually slower than the default buffer. Yet, increasing the buffer by one byte, to 1024 bytes, cuts the elapsed time to just 2.20 seconds. Increasing the buffer to 4096 bytes brings the elapsed time down to 1.43 seconds.

Buffer size	Time
128 bytes (Default)	5.38
256 bytes	5.16
1023 bytes	6.87
1024 bytes	2.20
4096 bytes	1.43

Table 18-4.   Impact of Text Buffers of Various Sizes

As for the difference in time between the 1023-byte buffer and the 1024-byte buffer, why does adding one byte cause a significant increase in speed? Disks are organized into 512-byte sectors that are organized into clusters of 1024 bytes for floppy disk and from 2048 to 8192 bytes for hard disks. When a buffer's size is set equal to the size of a cluster, the disk drive does less work with each read and write. In general, the best buffer sizes are multiples of 1024 bytes.

Optimizing String Operations

The **String** data type is an important part of Turbo Pascal, largely due to the standard procedures provided for string manipulation. However, string procedures, especially concatenation, can be quite slow.

The program called **TestProcs** uses two procedures, each of which creates a string that contains 100 characters, all of which are "A's."

```
Program TestProcs;
Uses CRT, TIMER;
Var
  i : Integer;

(*******************************)

Procedure Concat1;
Var
  i : Integer;
  s : String;
Begin
s := '';
For i := 1 To 100 Do
  s := s + 'A';
End;

(*******************************)

Procedure Concat2;
Var
  i : Integer;
  s : String;
Begin
For i := 1 To 100 Do
  s[i] := 'A';
s[0] := Chr(100); (* Set string length. *)
End;
```

```
(********************************)

Begin
ClrScr;

ClockOn;
For i := 1 To 100 Do Concat1;
ClockOff;

ClockOn;
For i := 1 To 100 Do Concat2;
ClockOff;

WriteLn;
Write('Press ENTER...');
ReadLn;
End.
```

Procedure **Concat1**, which uses the Turbo Pascal concatenation operator, requires 6.32 seconds, while procedure **Concat2**, which uses an index to the string's characters, needs only 0.27 second.

The **Copy** command can also be replaced to increase speed, as demonstrated by the **CopyString** program:

```
Program CopyString;
Uses CRT, TIMER;
Var
  p,i,j : Integer;
  s1,s2 : String;

Begin
ClrScr;

s1 := 'ABCDEFGHIJKLMNOP';

ClockOn;
For i := 1 To 10000 Do
  s2 := Copy(s1,3,5); (* Using the Copy command. *)
ClockOff;

ClockOn;
For i := 1 To 10000 Do
  Begin
  Move(s1[3],s2[1],5); (* Using the Move command. *)
  s2[0] := Chr(5);     (* Set the length byte. *)
  End;
ClockOff;

WriteLn;
Write('Press ENTER...');
```

```
ReadLn;
End.
```

In **CopyString**, the command

```
s2 := Copy(s1,3,5);
```

is replaced by the statements

```
Move(s1[3],s2[1],5);
s2[0] := Chr(5);
```

The **Move** command copies a portion of **s1** into **s2**, while the second statement correctly sets the length of **s2**. The **Copy** command requires 2.58 seconds for 10,000 iterations, compared with only 1.32 seconds for the optimized code.

Compiler Directives

Compiler directives control error checking features in Turbo Pascal. The three directives that have an impact on execution speed are the **R** directive, which checks the range of indexes; the **S** directive, which checks the stack errors; and the **B** directive, which enables short-circuit Boolean evaluation.

Range Checking

When enabled, the Range Checking (**R**) compiler directive adds code that checks for out-of-range conditions when assigning numeric values or accessing array elements. This additional code significantly increases overhead in your program, with noticeable results.

```
{$R+}
Program DirectiveTest;
Uses CRT, TIMER;
Var
  i,j : Integer;
  a : array [1..100] of Byte;
```

```
Begin
ClrScr;

Write('Range checking...');
ClockOn;
For i := 1 To 1000 Do
For j := 1 To 100 Do
  a[j] := 1;
ClockOff;

WriteLn;
Write('Press ENTER...');
ReadLn;
End.
```

When run with the **{$R +}** directive, this program takes 9.45 seconds; with **{$R −}**, it takes only 3.08 seconds. While range checking is essential during program development, you must disable this compiler directive to get the best performance for your program.

Stack Checking

The Stack Checking compiler directive (**{$S +}**) instructs the compiler to make sure that the stack has enough memory for local variables before calling a procedure. This is extremely important because stack errors are among the most difficult to trace. The program listed here demonstrates what effect stack checking can have on a program's performance.

```
Program DirectiveTest;
Uses CRT, TIMER;
Var
  i : Integer;
  s : String;

(****************************************************)

Procedure Proc;
Var
  x : array [1..5000] of Word;
Begin
End;

(****************************************************)

Begin
ClrScr;
s := 'AAAAAAAAAAAAAAAAAAAAAAAAAAAAAAAAAAAAAAAAAAAAAAAA';
```

```
Write('Stack checking...');
ClockOn;
For i := 1 To 10000 Do
Proc;
ClockOff;

WriteLn;
Write('Press ENTER...');
ReadLn;
End.
```

This program makes repeated calls to a procedure, **Proc**, that uses a large local array variable. When the stack checking directive is enabled ({$S+}), the program executes in 0.88 second; when disabled ({$S−}), it executes in just 0.49 second. As with range checking, stack checking is essential during program development and testing. Once completed, however, the directive should be turned off to maximize performance.

Boolean Evaluation

Turbo Pascal supports two types of Boolean evaluation: complete and short-circuit. Which one you choose can have a dramatic impact on the efficiency of your program. Consider the following Boolean evaluation:

```
If (a = 1) Or (a = 2) Or (a = 3) Then
```

If **a** is equal to 1, then there is no need to test any of the other conditions in the statement. Yet, under complete evaluation, that is exactly what happens. Short-circuit evaluation, as its name implies, jumps out of the Boolean expression as soon as a condition is met that assures a correct answer. The program listed here demonstrates the impact of Boolean evaluation on program performance.

```
{$B+}
Program DirectiveTest;
Uses CRT, TIMER;
Var
  a,i : Integer;

(*****************************************************)

Begin
ClrScr;
```

```
ClockOn;
a := 1;
For i := 1 To 10000 Do
  Begin
   If (a = 1) Or (a = 2) Or (a = 3) Then
     Begin
     End;
  End;
ClockOff;

WriteLn;
Write('Press ENTER...');
ReadLn;
End.
```

When short-circuit evaluation is enabled ({$B −}), the program executes in 0.27 second; under complete evaluation ({$B +}), execution takes 0.71 second. Unless you have good reason to insist on complete evaluation, you should always select short-circuit evaluation for your programs.

Procedures and Functions

Pascal allows the programmer to break a program down into procedures and functions, providing a more orderly framework for the program. Unfortunately, every time a procedure is called, Turbo Pascal must perform housekeeping tasks to keep track of memory. You can easily increase the speed of a program by putting a procedure's code directly into the main body of another procedure or into the main program. The impact of declaring a separate procedure is demonstrated by **TestProc3**:

```
Program TestProc3;
Uses CRT, TIMER;
Var
  i,j : Integer;

(*******************************)

Procedure DemoProc;
Begin
j := 0;
j := 0;
j := 0;
j := 0;
End;

(*******************************)
```

```
Begin
ClrScr;

ClockOn;
For i := 1 To 30000 Do
   DemoProc;                        (* Procedure call. *)
ClockOff;

ClockOn;
For i := 1 To 30000 Do
   Begin
   j := 0;                          (* No procedure call. *)
   j := 0;
   j := 0;
   j := 0;
   End;
ClockOff;

WriteLn;
Write('Press ENTER...');
ReadLn;
End.
```

Procedure **DemoProc** in **TestProc3** sets the **Integer** variable **j** equal to zero four times. The same process is also repeated in the main program block. When you run the program, the procedure requires 2.26 seconds for 30,000 iterations compared with only 1.48 seconds for the code in the program block.

Clearly, calling a procedure adds to a program's overhead. However, putting the code directly in the program has several disadvantages. First, if the procedure is called several times in the program, you must duplicate its code each time, adding to your program's code size. Second, when you want to change the procedure, you have to change it in each place it occurs. You must weigh these disadvantages against the speed you gain by removing the procedure call.

Reference Parameters Versus Value Parameters

When Turbo Pascal passes a reference parameter to a procedure, it passes the variable's address, not the value of the variable. Value parameters, on the other hand, pass the entire contents of the variable. If the value parameter is a 4000-byte array, 4000 bytes are passed to the procedure, compared with only 4 bytes when Turbo Pascal passes an address.

As the program **TestParams1** demonstrates, it takes longer to pass value parameters:

```
Program TestParams1;
Uses CRT, TIMER;
Type
  AType = Array [1..2000] Of Integer;

Var
  a : AType;
  i,j : Integer;

(*******************************)

Procedure a1(var a : AType);
Begin
End;

(*******************************)

Procedure a2(a : AType);
Begin
End;

(*******************************)

Begin
ClrScr;

ClockOn;
For i := 1 To 1000 Do
  a1(a);
ClockOff;

ClockOn;
For i := 1 To 1000 Do
  a2(a);
ClockOff;

WriteLn;
Write('Press ENTER...');
ReadLn;
End.
```

TestParams1 uses two procedures, **a1** and **a2**. Procedure **a1** accepts a reference parameter and **a2** accepts a value parameter. In both procedures, the parameter is an array of 2000 integers. When you run this program, you will find that procedure **a1** requires only 0.06 second for 1000 iterations, while **a2** requires 15.32 seconds to complete the same number of iterations. If you want to maximize the performance of your programs, try substituting reference parameters for value parameters. But, be careful—reference parameters retain any changes you make to them inside the procedure.

Performance is a concern for all programmers. Fortunately, Turbo Pascal produces some of the fastest, most efficient code of any compiler available. By using Turbo Pascal creatively, taking advantage of all its power, you can create programs that really fly. But remember that speed is just one consideration, and it can work to the detriment of maintainability. Optimized code often uses tricks and special logic that you might not remember a year later. If you must optimize, make sure that the benefits are worth the effort.

Debugging

As a general rule, programs do not run correctly the first time. Unfortunately, they often don't run correctly the tenth time, either. Tracking down and fixing program bugs can be time-consuming, painful, and unproductive. Fortunately, Turbo Pascal now includes an integrated debugger that can help you spot problems in seconds and can make your programming more rewarding.

NINETEEN

The Integrated Debugger

Debuggers have been around for a long time. One of the first, DEBUG-.COM, was included with the PC operating system. With DEBUG, a programmer could trace through a program one assembly-language instruction at a time, view segments of memory, and uncover bugs through a painstaking process. While useful in its own right, DEBUG suffered from several shortcomings. First, you could only see your program in assembler, a real limitation if you wrote the program in C, Pascal, or another high-level language. Second, variables were shown as addresses and offsets. Tracing a specific variable throughout a program was difficult, to say the least.

Programmers needed a better debugger—one that showed variables by name and could match source code to the underlying assembler instructions. Microsoft packaged a symbolic debugger—SYMDEB—with their assembler, and other software developers soon offered products of their own with additional desirable features. Recently, Borland introduced its own stand-alone debugger, Turbo Debugger, with a wide array of powerful features. Yet, as powerful as they are, all of these debuggers have one disadvantage—you have to get out of Turbo Pascal to use them.

While it lacks the advanced features you will find in Turbo Debugger, Turbo Pascal's integrated debugger does provide an easy-to-use way to track down all but the most subtle software bugs. Best of all, you don't need to leave the integrated development environment to use it. Even if you've never used a debugger before, you'll find the integrated debugger a pleasure. With it you can watch how variables change as you move through your program a line at a time, or you can set break points and jump from place to place in your program. The integrated debugger, combined with fast compilation, makes Turbo Pascal perhaps the most productive programming environment available.

Getting Ready to Debug

Before you debug a program, there are several things you must do. First, you must enable the **D** compiler directive either by adding the compiler directive **{$D+}** to your source code, or by enabling the **Debug Information** selection on the Options/Compiler menu. This tells Turbo Pascal to store program information that links a program's source code to its object code. If your program uses local variables, you should also enable the **L** compiler directive by either including the **{$L+}** compiler directive to your source code or by enabling the **Local Symbols** selection on the Options/Compiler menu. When this directive is enabled, Turbo Pascal stores information about local variables, allowing you to view them by name.

Finally, before you compile your program, you must be sure to enable the **Integrated Debugging** selection on the Options/Debugger menu. With this option enabled, the resulting executable code will contain debug information. If you do not intend to debug a program and you need extra RAM, disable this feature. With these details attended to, you can proceed to debug your program.

Debugger Features

Now that you know how to prepare to debug a program, what can you do next? The answer is nearly anything you want to. The integrated debugger gives you complete control over the execution of your program. You can set break points, trace from line to line, watch variables change, and more. The important point is that you'll never have to guess what your program is doing—you'll be able to watch every step.

The Execution Bar

When you are debugging a program, the *execution bar* highlights the program statement that will execute next. You can move the cursor around the source file, and even load other source files into the editor, but the integrated debugger will always keep track of the execution bar. The execution bar remains active until the program terminates or until you end the debugging session by selecting the **Program Reset** option on the Run menu.

Go to Cursor (F4)

The **Go to Cursor** feature lets you specify a temporary stopping point for your program. To use this feature, place the cursor on a line of code in your program and press F4. Turbo Pascal will execute your program until it reaches the program line containing the cursor, at which point control will be returned to you. This feature is especially handy if you want to go directly, rather than step by step, to a spot deep within your program.

To see how **Go to Cursor** works, consider the program shown in Figure 19-1. The execution bar is the first **Begin** statement in the program, and the cursor is four lines down. When you press F4, the program executes the first two statements, skips the blank line, and halts execution at the line where the cursor is (see Figure 19-2).

While **Go to Cursor** is like a break point, it is less restrictive. Break points have to be set and remain set until removed, while **Go to Cursor** relies only on the current position of the cursor. Note, however, that when you use this feature, the program will return control only if it

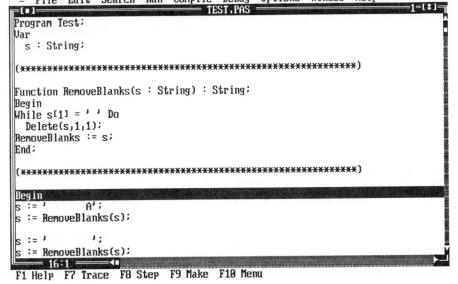

Figure 19-1.   Program at start of execution

Figure 19-2.   After using Go to Cursor

reaches the line you selected. If, on the other hand, your program never executes that line, you will not receive control.

Trace Into (F7)

A fundamental feature of any debugger is the ability to execute one statement at a time. The **Trace Into** feature, activated by the F7 key, executes the statement highlighted by the execution bar, moves the bar to the next statement, and returns control to you. If the execution bar is a function or procedure call, **Trace Into** will jump to that part of the program and continue executing from there. In Figure 19-3, the execution bar is located on the statement that calls the function **RemoveBlanks**. When F7 is pressed, the debugger traces into the **RemoveBlanks** function (see Figure 19-4).

If you are not interested in tracing into a procedure call, but wish to execute the procedure and move to the next line, use the **Step Over** feature.

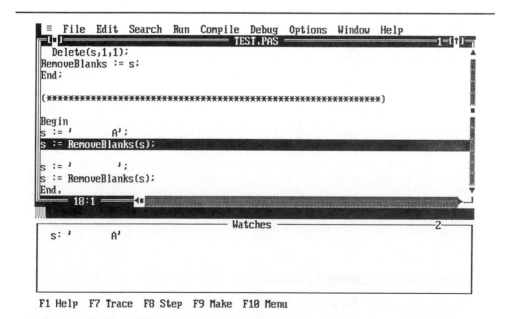

Figure 19-3.   Before executing a function

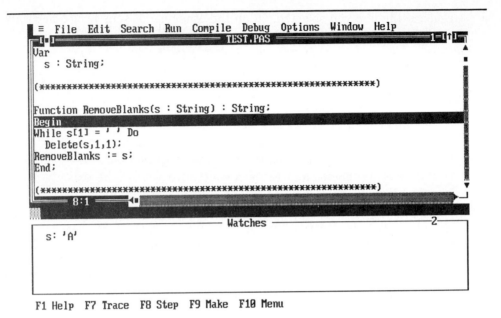

Figure 19-4. After tracing into a function

Step Over (F8)

Like **Trace Into,** the **Step Over** feature executes one line of code at a time. **Step Over,** however, will not trace into function or procedure calls. Instead, it executes the procedure or function as a single statement, moves the execution bar to the next statement, and returns control to you at that point. This feature is useful for avoiding procedures and functions that do not need to be debugged.

To see how this works, consider Figure 19-3, where the execution bar is positioned on the statement that calls the function **Remove-Blanks.** When you press F8, the debugger executes the entire statement, including the function call, at one time and moves the bar forward to the next statement (see Figure 19-5).

Evaluate and Modify (CTRL-F4)

Pressing CTRL-F4 pops up the Evaluate and Modify window, a special window that lets you evaluate a variable or expression or modify the

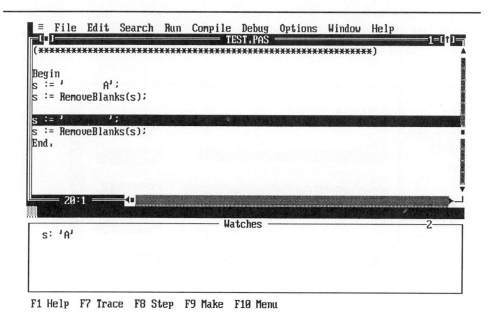

Figure 19-5.   After stepping over a function

value of a variable. This window contains three input fields — Expression, Result, and New value (see Figure 19-6). In the Expression field you type the name of a variable, an expression, or a numeric value. For example, if you enter a hexadecimal number in the Expression field and press ENTER, the decimal equivalent will appear in the Result field (see Figure 19-7). You can also use the Evaluate and Modify window to change the value of a variable. For example, in Figure 19-8, the string variable s is found to contain only space characters. Use the TAB key to move to the New value field and type the letters **ABC**. Now the value of s has been modified to include the character string 'ABC'. Modifying the value of a variable is an easy way to test how your program reacts to a variety of situations.

Call Stack (CTRL-F3)

In large programs, it is easy to lose track of the function and procedure calls that preceded a particular point in the program. The Call Stack

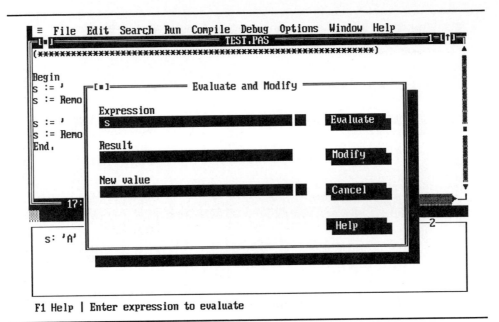

Figure 19-6. The Evaluate and Modify window

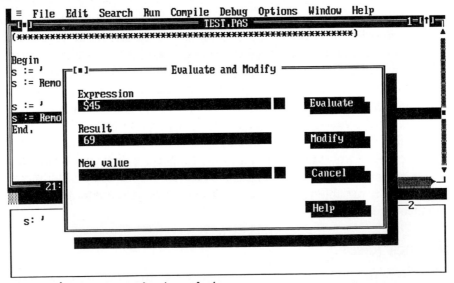

Figure 19-7. Converting a hexadecimal value

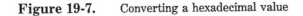

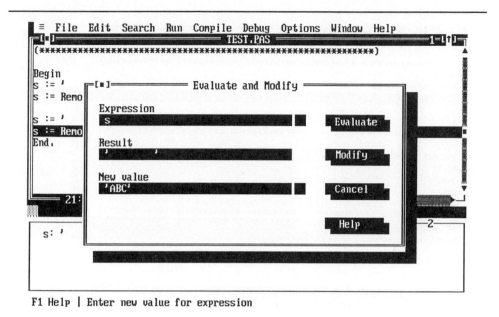

Figure 19-8. Modifying a variable

window provides an easy way to find out how you got to the current location in your program. When you press CTRL-F3 (or select **Call stack** from the Window menu), Turbo Pascal opens the Call Stack window, which lists all previous procedure and function calls. For example, in Figure 19-9, the Call Stack window shows four entries—PROC3, PROC2, PROC1, and TEST, which is the name of the program itself. If a procedure takes parameters, the Call Stack window will display the values of those parameters along with the name of the procedure.

Inside the Call Stack window, you can use the cursor keys to highlight any of the entries. If you press ENTER, Turbo Pascal will take you to the source code location of the highlighted routine. Now you can be certain of what events brought you to your current position in the program.

Add Watch (CTRL-F7)

The ability to watch variables is one of the most important features of the integrated debugger. A program bug is almost always related to or

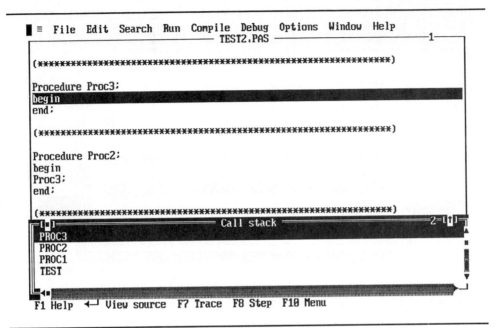

Figure 19-9. The Call Stack window

signaled by an unexpected value in a variable. You can open the Watch window by selecting **Watch** from the Window menu, or you can press CTRL-F7 to add a watch variable or expression, which will automatically open the Watch window.

When you press CTRL-F7, the Add Watch input window appears (Figure 19-10). If the cursor in your source file happened to be positioned on a symbol, that symbol will automatically appear in the Watch expression field. If this symbol is the correct one, simply press ENTER to add it to the watch list. Otherwise, enter the expression you want to watch. The symbol and its current value immediately appear in the Watch window (Figure 19-11). As you trace through your program, you can see how the variable changes. If the variable changes in a way that you don't expect, you may have found a bug.

Once you have created a Watch window, you can add new variables to it by activating the Watch window (by using the F6 key or the mouse) and pressing INS. The Add Watch window pops up, and in it you type the name of the variable you wish to add. Press ENTER to complete the process.

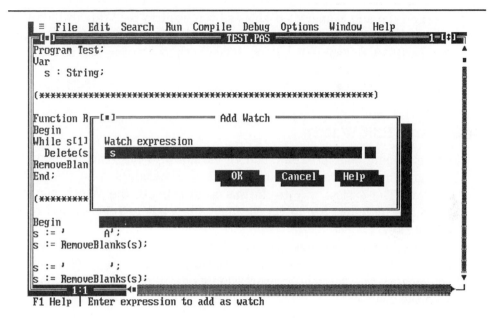

Figure 19-10.   Adding a variable to the Watch window

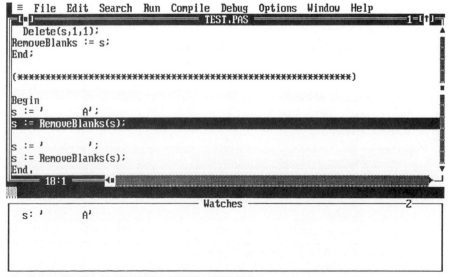

Figure 19-11.   A variable in the Watch window

You can add as many variables as you want to the Watch window or display a single variable in a number of different ways. For example, in Figure 19-12, the variable **s** is displayed both as a string and as the first character of the string.

Delete and Edit Watch

As you debug your program, adding variables to the Watch window as you go, you may want to remove unneeded variables from the Watch window. The easiest way to do this is to activate the Watch window, move the highlight bar to the variable you want to remove, and press the DEL key.

You can also change the way you view a variable in the Watch window by highlighting the desired variable and pressing ENTER. You can now change the variable or expression as desired. Press ENTER again to save the change.

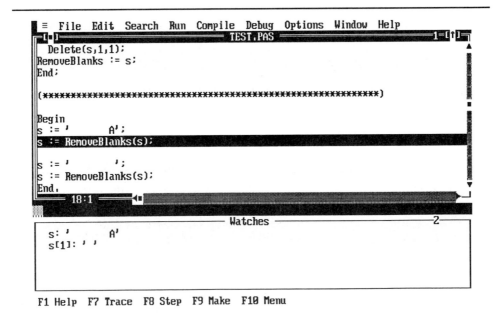

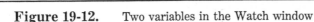

Figure 19-12.   Two variables in the Watch window

Remove All Watches

If you want to remove all variables from the Watch window, select **Remove all watches** from the Watch menu.

Toggle Breakpoint (CTRL-F8)

A break point is a flag attached to a line of source code that tells Turbo Pascal to stop execution when it reaches that line. Using break points can be more efficient than tracing when you have a good idea of the location of the bug. You can set up to 16 break points within a program by simply positioning the cursor on the line to break at and pressing CTRL-F8 or by selecting **Toggle breakpoint** from the Debug menu.

Always set break points on lines that contain an executable statement. Do not set break points on blank lines, comment lines, compiler directives, data declarations, or other non-executable parts of your program.

Once a break point has been set for a line, it can be removed by repeating the same sequence used to set it; place the cursor on the line with the break point and press CTRL-F8. Break points are also cleared when you end your debugging session, and they are not made part of the .EXE program file.

Clear All Breakpoints

To clear all the break points you have set in a program, choose **Clear all breakpoints** from the Breakpoints dialog box.

View Next Breakpoint

If you use a lot of break points in a program, it is easy to lose track of them. To locate break points, select **View next breakpoint** from the Breakpoints dialog box. Turbo Pascal will find the next break point, load the appropriate source file, and position the cursor on the line at which the break point has been set.

CTRL-BREAK

You can halt your program's execution at any point by pressing CTRL-BREAK, which halts the program and positions the execution bar at the next statement to be executed. When you break a program from the outside, you cannot always be sure where you will be placed in the program. Still, this technique is useful for jumping in and out of a program at random points and is especially good for terminating endless loops.

Debugging: An Example

As with most things, debugging is best learned by example. To see how the debugger can help uncover subtle errors in program code, consider the following program that consists of a unit (UNIT1.PAS) and a main program file (BUG.PAS). But, before you read on, take a look at the following listing and see if you can find the two bugs contained in it.

```
Unit Unit1;
{$D+,L+}
Interface

Procedure Proc1;

Implementation

Procedure Proc1;
Var
  i : Integer;
Begin
WriteLn('This is Proc1');
While i < 2 Do
  Begin
  WriteLn('i = ',i);
  Inc(i,1);
  End;
End;

End.

(***************************************************)

Program Bug;
{$D+,L+}
Uses CRT, Unit1;
Var
  w : Integer;
  r1,r2 : Real;

Begin
ClrScr;
```

```
Proc1;

r1 := 1.0E+38;
For w := 1 To 10 Do
  Begin
  r2 := r1 + 1.0;
  WriteLn(r1,' + 1.0 = ',r2);
  r1 := r2;
  End;

WriteLn;
Write('Press ENTER...');
ReadLn;
End.
```

If you couldn't find the bugs, don't be too concerned. That's why we have debuggers in the first place. In fact, after using a debugger for a while, you will become much more adept at avoiding bugs altogether.

Starting Up

Type in and compile the program and unit just given. (Before compiling, check the Debug menu to be sure that integrated debugging is on.) When you are ready, load the main program file into the editor, place the cursor on the call to **Proc1**, and press F4. Turbo Pascal will begin executing your program (performing a **Make** first, if needed) and stop with the execution bar highlighting the call to **Proc1** (see Figure 19-13). At this point, you can do several things. You can press F8 to step over the call to **Proc1**; you can press F7 to trace into **Proc1**; you can go to another point in the program and press F4 again; you can press CTRL-F2 to reset the program to the beginning; or you can press CTRL-F9 to let the program run. Let's press F7 to trace into **Proc1**.

Adding Watch Variables

When you trace into **Proc1**, the execution bar is placed on the first **Begin** (see Figure 19-14). Notice that the variable i has been added to the Watch window and that it has a value of 30468. By now you may have spotted the bug in this procedure. As the following listing shows, the procedure assumes that i will start out at a value less than two.

```
While i < 2 Do
  Begin
  WriteLn('i = ',i);
  Inc(i,1);
  End;
```

Notice that **i** is never initialized, so you cannot know in advance what value **i** will have when the procedure executes. In this case, **i** has a value far above 2, so the loop will not execute at all. Without the ability to watch the value of **i**, you might spend a lot of time tracking down this little bug.

More on the Watch Window

Continue pressing F7 until you are back at the main program file. Position the cursor on the **WriteLn** statement and press F4 (see Figure 19-15). At the bottom you can see that the Watch window now has three

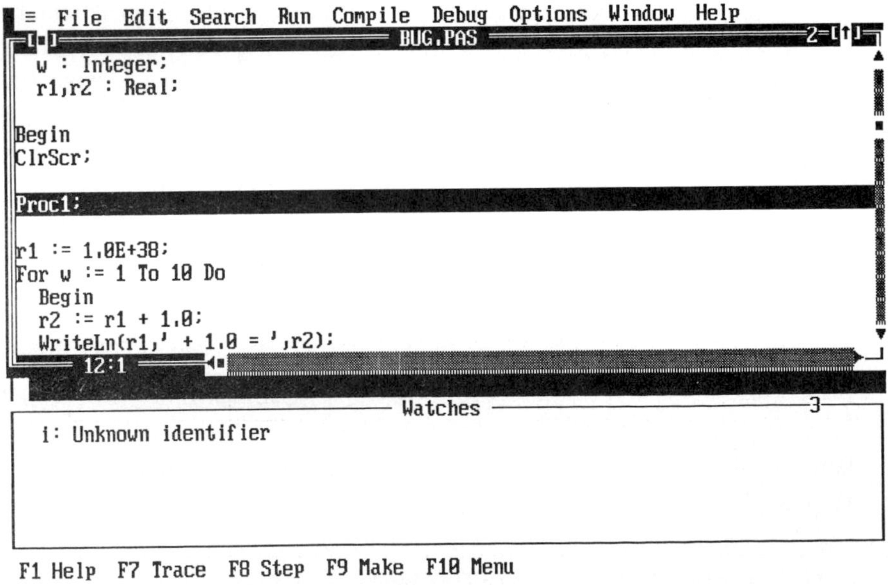

Figure 19-13. Starting a debugging session

```
 ≡  File  Edit  Search  Run  Compile  Debug  Options  Window  Help
[■]═══════════════════════UNIT1.PAS═══════════════════1═[↑]
Unit Unit1;
{$D+,L+}
Interface

Procedure Proc1;

Implementation

Procedure Proc1;
Var
  i : Integer;
Begin
WriteLn('This is Proc1');
═══ 12:1 ═══◄■
─────────────────────── Watches ───────────────────3──
   i: 30507
```

```
F1 Help  F7 Trace  F8 Step  F9 Make  F10 Menu
```

Figure 19-14.   Tracing into Proc1

```
 ≡  File  Edit  Search  Run  Compile  Debug  Options  Window  Help
[■]════════════════════════BUG.PAS═══════════════════2═[↑]
  w : Integer;
  r1,r2 : Real;

Begin
ClrScr;

Proc1;

r1 := 1.0E+38;
For w := 1 To 10 Do
  Begin
  r2 := r1 + 1.0;
  WriteLn(r1,' + 1.0 = ',r2);
═══ 18:1 ═══◄■
─────────────────────── Watches ───────────────────3──
   i: Unknown identifier
   r1: 1.0E38
   r2: 1.0E38
```

```
F1 Help  F7 Trace  F8 Step  F9 Make  F10 Menu
```

Figure 19-15.   Checking variables in the Watch window

variables — **i**, **r1**, and **r2**. Notice that **i** is now called an unknown identifier. Why? The variable **i** was local to procedure **Proc1**. We are now outside that procedure and beyond the scope of the variable, which is why the identifier is unknown.

If, on the other hand, a global variable **i** had been declared, the Watch window would reflect the value of the global variable. The Watch window can display the value of variables only within the variable's scope.

Looking at the Watch window, you might have been surprised to find that **r1** and **r2** have the same value, despite the fact that **r2** was assigned the value of **r1** plus 1.0. What happened? Floating-point variables retain only a fixed number of significant digits. When the number gets large, it will not reflect additions of small values. So, while you might expect **r1** to increase in value with each loop, the Watch window shows that this is not the case.

Display Format

You can use the Watch window to display the contents of any data type. If you do not specify otherwise, data is displayed in a default format (see Table 19-1). The Watch window, however, allows you to use format specifiers that alter the way the data is displayed. For example, you can view a value in hexadecimal format or as a raw memory dump. Table 19-2 lists the format specifiers and describes how they work.

Data Type	Default Display Format
Bytes, Integers, Words	Numeric scalars are displayed as their decimal value
Reals	Floating-point variables are displayed in decimal format without exponents, if possible
Characters	Characters from ASCII code 32 and up are displayed as themselves. Control characters, ASCII codes 0 to 31, are displayed as decimal values preceded by the # sign
Booleans	Displayed as either TRUE or FALSE

Table 19-1.   Default Display Formats

Data Type	Default Display Format
Pointers	Pointers are displayed as segments and offsets. If the segment portion matches the code segment or data segment, the CSEG or DSEG specifier will be displayed. Addresses are displayed in hexadecimal format
Strings	Strings are displayed as concatenated characters, enclosed in quotes. Control characters are displayed as decimal numbers preceded by the # sign
Arrays	Array contents are displayed within parentheses, separated by commas. If the array is multidimensional, nested parentheses are used
Records	The contents of records are displayed as lists surrounded by parentheses. Elements in the record are separated by commas. Nested records are shown as nested lists

Table 19-1. Default Display Formats (*continued*)

Format Specifier	Result
$, H, X	Displays scalars
C	Displays special characters as their ASCII graphic value instead of as decimal values
D	Displays scalars as decimal values
Fn	Displays a floating-point number with n significant digits. The value of n can range from 2 to 18; the default is 11
M	Displays a memory dump of a variable as hex bytes. Adding the **D** specifier causes the dump to be shown in decimal, and the **C** or **S** specifier displays the dump as a string of ASCII and special characters
P	Displays pointers in segment-and-offset format with both values in four-digit hex format
R	Displays the record's field names along with their values
S	Displays a string using ASCII and special characters. Normally, special characters are shown as decimal values

Table 19-2. Watch Window Format Specifiers

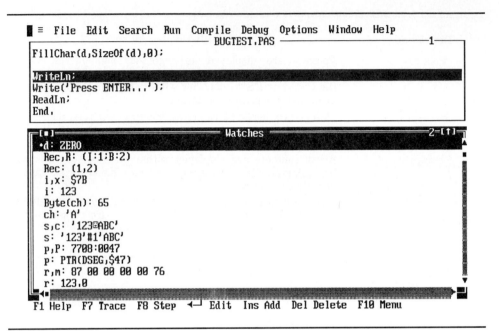

Figure 19-16. The Watch window

Using format specifiers is fairly simple. When you add a variable to the Watch window, simply add a comma and list the format specifiers you want to use. For example, if you want to view an integer **i** in hexadecimal format, you would enter **i, X**. The following example program declares a variety of data types. Figure 19-16 shows how these variables look when displayed using format specifiers. Notice in the figure that a typecast is used to display the **ch** variable as a decimal value. Using typecasts in the Watch window is a powerful method of viewing your data in a variety of ways.

```
Program BugTest;
Uses CRT;

Var
  Rec : Record
    i : Integer;
    b : Byte;
    End;

  ch : Char;
  i : Integer;
  r : Real;
```

```
  s : String;
  p : Pointer;
  d : (Zero, One, Two, Three);

Begin
ClrScr;

r := 123;
i := 123;
ch := 'A';
s := '123' + #1 + 'ABC';
p := @ch;
Rec.i := 1;
Rec.b := 2;
FillChar(d,SizeOf(d),1);

WriteLn;
Write('Press ENTER...');
ReadLn;
End.
```

Programming for Debugging

When writing your program, keep in mind that the integrated debugger can only debug one statement per line. For example, Turbo Pascal allows you to write the following line of code:

```
s := 1 * z; z := i Div Trunc(Sqrt(s)); s := z Div 0;
```

This single line contains three statements. If an error occurs in any of the three, the integrated debugger will not be able to tell you which statement caused the error. In this case, it would be better to code as follows:

```
s := 1 * z;
z := i Div Trunc(Sqrt(s));
s := z Div 0;
```

Now when an error occurs, you will know exactly which statement caused the error.

On the other hand, if you have sections of code that you are certain are correct, you might consider lumping them into one line to save time when tracing through the program. For example, the following code is efficient because you can trace past it in one step instead of four:

```
s := 1; x := 2; i := 3; j := 4;
```

Another important programming point is not to get sloppy just because you have the integrated debugger. It's always better to avoid problems by using proper programming techniques than to catch the problems afterward with the debugger. As much as is possible and practical, break up programs into modules, rely on parameters rather than on global variables, and test modules as much as possible before integrating them into your programs.

Memory Requirements

The integrated debugger requires memory and, with large programs, you might find that too little is left over to run a debugging session. You can maximize the use of memory through several techniques. First, if you have expanded memory installed in your computer, make sure that at least 64K is available; Turbo Pascal will use this memory to store the editor file.

If your program allocates more stack-and-heap memory than it uses, you can reduce the size of these data areas, freeing memory for the debugger. Removing RAM-resident programs, like SideKick, will also give the debugger more memory to work with.

When you compile your program, turn off error-checking compiler directives, such as the **S** and **R** directives. These directives increase the size of your programs. Where local symbols will not be watched, use the **{$L −}** compiler directive to reduce the size of the local symbol table. Likewise, where debugging is unnecessary, use the **{$D −}** compiler directive to conserve memory.

You can also save memory by organizing your program into overlays. This will slow down your program, but give you more memory for debugging. As much as possible, test procedures and functions separately from the main program. This will speed up your testing and provide memory for debugging.

Finally, you can gain memory by modifying the TURBO.TPL file. Use the TPUMOVER program to remove any unused units from TURBO.TPL. This method, however, is a bit drastic and should be used only as a last resort.

Debugger Limitations

While the integrated debugger is powerful, it does have some limitations. It will not, for example, trace into any of the standard Turbo Pascal units (**CRT, DOS, GRAPH, GRAPH3, PRINTER, SYSTEM,** and **TURBO3**). Of course, these units are supplied by Borland and do not require any debugging.

The integrated debugger will not trace into external procedures, interrupt procedures, procedures that are written entirely in inline code, any procedure not compiled with the **{$D+}** compiler directive, any procedure for which the source code is not available, or any procedure set up as an exit procedure. In short, the integrated debugger will help you in 99% of the situations most programmers run into. If, however, you absolutely need to trace through every part of your program, consider purchasing the Turbo Debugger, which is more powerful than the integrated debugger built into Turbo Pascal.

Bugs are a natural part of programming. No matter how carefully you code, you simply can't avoid errors in logic. Tracking down and correcting bugs used to be time-consuming and clumsy. With its built-in debugger, Turbo Pascal greatly increases your programming productivity and will help you produce better programs.

Objects

An Object Lesson
Inheritance
Encapsulation
Static and Virtual Methods
Object Type Compatibility
Dynamic Allocation of Objects
Polymorphism

By now, almost all programmers have heard the term *OOP*. Object oriented programming is the hottest method of software development today. In version 5.5, Borland introduced OOP to the Pascal world. Now with version 6, support for objects in Turbo Pascal is even better.

If you have never used OOP techniques, do not fear. Once you learn the new terms and map those to concepts that you already know, you will be well on your way to mastering OOP. Contrary to popular belief, you need not relearn programming to understand OOP.

You are not forced to program with objects now that they are supported by Turbo Pascal—you can use them as little or as much as you like. With the addition of Turbo Vision in Turbo Pascal 6, however, you might become a little more motivated to master OOP concepts. Turbo Vision is an extremely powerful toolset, but it is based almost entirely on objects. Chapter 21 covers Turbo Vision.

An Object Lesson

As its name implies, object oriented programming relies heavily on the concept of the object. In our daily lives, we are familiar with all kinds of objects—televisions, lamps, checkbooks, and so on. But when we turn on a television, we don't distinguish between its physical elements (the tuning dial, the picture tube, the antenna) and its behavior (providing an image and sound). We simply turn it on and select a channel.

Like the television, objects make programs more accurately conform to the way we deal with the real world. To gain this quality, objects depend on three main concepts: (1) combining code and data, (2) inheritance, and (3) encapsulation.

Code + Data = Object

As a Pascal programmer, you are used to defining data structures to hold information and defining procedures and functions to manipulate information. In OOP, data and procedures are combined into *objects*. An object contains both the characteristics of an entity (its data) and its behavior (its procedures). By melding these characteristics and behaviors, an object knows everything it needs to do its work.

To understand objects, it is useful to think in terms of metaphors. An airplane can be described in physical terms—the number of passengers it can hold, the amount of thrust it generates, its drag coefficient, and so on. Alternatively, an airplane can be described in functional terms—it takes off, ascends and descends, it turns and lands, and so on. Yet neither the physical description nor the functional description alone captures the essence of what the airplane is—you need both.

In traditional programming, you would define an airplane's physical characteristics as a data structure, such as this:

```
Type
  Airplane = Record
    AirSpeed : Word;
    Altitude : Word;
    Flaps    : (Up, Down);
    End;
```

You would separately define the airplane's behaviors as procedures and functions:

```
Procedure Accelerate;
Begin
{...}
End;

Procedure Decelerate;
Begin
```

```
{...}
End;

Procedure FlapsUp;
Begin
{...}
End;

Procedure FlapsDown;
Begin
{...}
End;
```

In OOP, characteristics (data) and behaviors (procedures) are combined into a single entity known as an object. An airplane defined as an object might look like this:

```
Type
  Airplane = Object
    AirSpeed : Word;
    Altitude : Word;
    Flaps    : (Up, Down);
    Procedure Init;
    Procedure Accelerate;
    Procedure Decelerate;
    Procedure Ascend;
    Procedure Descend;
    Procedure FlapsUp;
    Procedure FlapsDown;
    End;
```

The object just given contains declarations for both data and procedures. In the language of OOP, procedures and functions declared within an object are known as *methods*. Notice that the object defines only the methods header; the actual code for the methods is specified separately, like this:

```
Procedure Airplane.Init;
Begin
Flaps := Down;
AirSpeed := 0;
Altitude := 0;
End;

Procedure Airplane.FlapsUp;
Begin
Flaps := Up;
End;
```

Notice that the method is defined by both the object name (**Airplane**) and the procedure name (**FlapsUp**), just as you would refer to a field in a record. In fact, you can think of an object as a record that contains both data fields and method declarations.

Within these methods, the data field Flaps is referred to without specifying the object name. Specifying **Airplane.** in the procedure declaration acts like a **With** statement for the body of the procedure.

Once an object has been defined, you can declare variables using the object's name, as shown here:

```
Var
  A : Airplane;
```

In your program, you can now write statements like these:

```
With A Do
  Begin
  Init;
  FlapsUp;
  Accelerate;
  Ascend;
  End;
```

Now you can begin to see the advantages of OOP—all actions affecting an object can be made by reference to the object itself. There can be no confusion about which data structure procedure **FlapsUp** will use. Given the previous definition of the **Airplane** object, you are allowed to access the data fields directly. For example, it is perfectly legal to write

```
A.Flaps := Up;
```

As you become better acquainted with OOP, you will learn that accessing an object's fields directly is both unnecessary and undesirable. In fact, Turbo Pascal 6 enables you to prevent access to an object's fields, as you will see later in this chapter.

Inheritance

Although objects contain data and methods of their own, they can also inherit both from other objects. Inheritance in OOP has as its roots a concept that is familiar to Turbo Pascal programmers: nesting records. Consider the following record definitions:

```
Type
  Ages = 0..150;
  PersonInfo = Record
    LastName  : string[30];
    FirstName : string[20];
    Age       : Ages;
    End;

  Grades = 0..12;   (* 0 is K *)
  StudentInfo = Record
    Person  : PersonInfo;
    Grade   : Grades;
    Teacher : string[30];
    End;
```

The record **PersonInfo** contains fields used to describe any person. The second record, **StudentInfo**, declares **Person**, which contains the fields in the **PersonInfo** record. This type of nesting allows you to build increasingly complex record structures.

In OOP, you use this same concept to build increasingly complex objects. The following listing shows how to use objects to replace nested record declarations:

```
Type
  Ages = 0..150;
  Person = Object
    LastName  : string[30];
    FirstName : string[20];
    Age       : Ages;
    Procedure Init;
    Procedure SetName(NewFirst, NewLast : string);
    End;

  Grades = 0..12;   (* 0 is K *)
  Student = Object(Person)
    Grade   : Grades;
    Teacher : string[30];
    Procedure Init;
    End;
```

Notice that the declaration of **Student** includes a reference to the **Person** object:

```
Student = Object(Person)
```

By this declaration, **Student** inherits everything contained in **Person** — data and methods. You can refer to the data field Student.LastName just as if you had declared it explicitly. In OOP terminology, **Person** is an ancestor type and **Student** is a descendant type. An object can have more than one ancestor type. In the example just given, **Person** is the immediate ancestor of **Student** and **Student** is the immediate descendant of **Person**. The overall lineage of ancestors and descendants is known as the *object hierarchy*.

Not only do objects inherit data, they also inherit methods. In the previous example, the **Person** object included the method **SetName**, which presumably assigns a name to the person. Because the **Student** object is a descendant of **Person**, it inherits the **SetName** method. This is reasonable because you would assign a name to a student the same way you assign a name to a person. With inheritance, you avoid writing the same method to support two objects.

You might have noticed that both **Person** and **Student** contain a method called **Init**. You would use a duplicated name when you don't want to inherit the method of an ancestor. In this particular example, you probably need to do more initializing for **Student** objects than you would for **Person** objects. The two **Init** procedures might look something like this:

```
Procedure Person.Init;
Begin
LastName := ' ';
FirstName := ' ';
Age := 0;
End;

Procedure Student.Init;
Person.Init;
Teacher := ' ';
Grade := 0;
End;
```

Notice that the first step in initializing an object of type **Student** is to call the **Init** method of its immediate ancestor, **Person**. This helps to avoid duplication of code by saving **Student.Init** from initializing data fields defined by **Person**.

Although method names can (and probably will, as you will see with virtual methods) be duplicated for inherited objects, data field names cannot. Once an object's data field is named, no data field in any descendant object can share that field's name. You cannot override data fields like you can methods.

Since data fields and methods exist all the way down an object's hierarchy, it is often difficult to determine all of the fields and methods included with an object. You must trace carefully through the hierarchy, noting which methods are overridden and which are not. You will find this exercise very important when examining the Turbo Vision objects (covered in Chapter 21).

Inheritance is a complex subject with many ramifications, which will be covered in detail in the remainder of this chapter. Although at first these complexities make OOP appear difficult to use, with practice you will find that they are easily mastered.

Encapsulation

One of the overriding goals of OOP is *encapsulation,* the creation of objects that function as complete entities. One of the rules of encapsulation is that the programmer need never directly access the data fields within an object. Instead, methods should be defined within the object to handle all data manipulation. Consider the following object definition:

```
Person = Object
  LastName  : String[30];
  FirstName : String[20];
  Age       : Ages;
  Procedure Init;
  Procedure Display;
  Function GetLastName  : String;
  Function GetFirstName : String;
  Function GetAge       : Ages;
  Procedure SetLastName(NewLastName : String);
  Procedure SetFirstName(NewFirstName : String);
  Procedure SetAge(NewAge : Ages);
  End;
```

This expanded form of the **Person** object contains the same three data fields you saw in a previous example: LastName, FirstName, and Age. To provide access to these three fields, the object defines all the possible methods to either report or alter the value of a field.

Your first reaction to encapsulation is probably to notice its drawbacks: it's fairly code intensive and appears to be much more cumbersome than simple field access. The primary benefit of encapsulation is that by limiting access to just the methods, you are free to change the fields without any side effects. Suppose you discover that memory space is a problem with your application. You are forced to shorten the size of the name fields by several characters. If you have used encapsulation properly, you can make the change without affecting other code.

Using Units

One way to help provide encapsulation is to use units. Units have been part of Turbo Pascal since version 4.0. If you have been writing any large programs, you probably already use units to help break your code into manageable pieces.

Objects and OOP lend themselves very easily to units. You place the object declarations in the Interface section of the unit, and you place the bodies of the methods in the Implementation section. The number of objects you have in a unit is up to you. Many programmers define only one object per unit.

Take a look at the complete implementation of the **Person** object, in unit form:

```
Unit PERSONS;

Interface

Type
  Ages = 0..150;      (* in years *)
  Person = Object
    LastName  : String[30];
    FirstName : String[20];
    Age       : Ages;
    Procedure Init;
    Procedure Display;
    Function GetLastName  : String;
    Function GetFirstName : String;
    Function GetAge       : Ages;
    Procedure SetLastName(NewLastName : String);
    Procedure SetFirstName(NewFirstName : String);
    Procedure SetAge(NewAge : Ages);
    End;
```

```
Implementation

Procedure Person.Init;
Begin
LastName := ' ';
FirstName := ' ';
Age := 0;
End;

Procedure Person.Display;
Begin
Writeln('Person: ', FirstName, ' ', LastName);
Writeln('Age: ', Age);
End;

Function Person.GetLastName : String;
Begin
GetLastName := LastName;
End;

Function Person.GetFirstName : String;
Begin
GetFirstName :=  FirstName;
End;

Function Person.GetAge : Ages;
Begin
GetAge := Age;
End;

Procedure Person.SetLastName(NewLastName : String);
Begin
LastName := NewLastName;
End;

Procedure Person.SetFirstName(NewFirstName : String);
Begin
FirstName := NewFirstName;
End;

Procedure Person.SetAge(NewAge : Ages);
Begin
Age := NewAge;
End;

End.
```

You will see several examples throughout this chapter that build on this unit, so study it carefully. Notice how placing all of the code associated with the **Person** object into one unit reduces confusion and enforces encapsulation.

Private Areas

Version 6 of Turbo Pascal introduces a new reserved word: **Private.**
This word enables you to divide an object declaration into two sections:
the public area and the private area. The public area contains the data
and methods that you are making available to all other modules. The
private area contains fields and methods that are available only to
subprograms in the same module.

Consider this simple object definition:

```
Type
  Positions = (On, Off);
  LightSwitch = Object
    Position : Positions;
    Function GetPosition : Positions;
    Procedure TurnOn;
    Procedure TurnOff;
  End;
```

Since methods provide complete functionality for the **LightSwitch** object, the data field can be moved into the private area:

```
Type
  Positions = (On, Off);
  LightSwitch = Object
    Function GetPosition : Positions;
    Procedure TurnOn;
    Procedure TurnOff;
  Private
    Position : Positions;
  End;
```

Moving **Position** to the private area prevents other modules from accessing the field directly. Since the methods are defined in the same
module as the object declaration, they have complete access to the
private fields.

The addition of a private area to objects allows you to enforce the
concepts behind encapsulation. Study the following unit, the complete
definition of the **Student** object:

```
Unit STUDENTS;

Interface

Uses PERSONS;

Type
  Grades = 0..12;   (* 0 is K *)
  Student = Object(Person)
    Procedure Init;
    Procedure Display;
    Function GetGrade   : Grades;
    Function GetTeacher : String;
    Procedure SetGrade(NewGrade : Grades);
    Procedure SetTeacher(NewName : String);
  Private
    Grade      : Grades;
    Teacher    : String[30];
    End;

Implementation

Procedure Student.Init;
Begin
Person.Init;
Grade := 0;
Teacher := ";
End;

Procedure Student.Display;
Begin
Writeln('Student: ', GetLastName, ', ', GetFirstName,
    '; Age ', GetAge);
Writeln('Grade: ', Grade);
Writeln('Teacher: ', Teacher);
End;

Function Student.GetGrade : Grades;
Begin
GetGrade := Grade;
End;

Function Student.GetTeacher : String;
Begin
GetTeacher := Teacher;
End;

Procedure Student.SetGrade(NewGrade : Grades);
Begin
Grade := NewGrade;
End;

Procedure Student.SetTeacher(NewName : String);
Begin
Teacher := NewName;
End;

End.
```

As in the previous example, the methods provide complete access to the data fields, so the fields are placed in the private area. If you needed to change the fields in any way, you could do so without fear of unwanted side effects.

Look closely at the method **Student.Display**. This method was written assuming that the fields defined in the **Person** object were also moved to the private section. It had to call the **GetAge** method to output the age instead of using the Age field directly. Since the two objects were declared in different units, the descendant object loses access to the fields in its own ancestor.

There may also be cases where you want to place methods in the private area. For example, you may want to maintain a sorted list as part of an object. For that you would probably write a **Sort** method. But because the data is always sorted, and you don't want to allow other modules to call **Sort**, you place that method in the private area.

Static and Virtual Methods

Methods in OOP actually come in two flavors: static and virtual. The examples you have seen thus far in this chapter have all been *static methods*. These methods are simple to understand, and they execute almost exactly like normal procedures and functions. They are called static methods because when they call other methods, they always call the same ones. The calls are bound at compile time. This process is known as early binding.

Virtual methods, on the other hand, act much differently. When you call a virtual method, the actual call is bound at run time, when the call is made. This is called *late binding*. To make these terms clearer, and to understand the advantages of virtual methods, a comprehensive example is presented.

Where Static Methods Fall Short

If you are starting your reading in the middle of this chapter, you need to go back and study the object declarations for **Person** and **Student**. Given those two object declarations, suppose you want to add the following method to the **Person** object:

```
Procedure Person.HappyBirthday;
Begin
Age := Age + 1;
Writeln('The following record has been updated:');
Display;
End;
```

This method automatically updates the person's age and then calls the **Display** method to display the update.

Because the **Student** object is a descendant of **Person**, it inherits this new method. Now you write a short program to create a student, assign all the proper values, and then call the **HappyBirthday** method to update the student's age. Here is that sample program:

```
Program Static_vs_Virtual;

Uses PERSONS, STUDENTS, CRT;

Var
  AStudent : Student;

Begin
ClrScr;
With AStudent Do
  Begin
  Init;
  SetLastName('Judd');
  SetFirstName('Jessica');
  SetAge(5);
  SetGrade(1);
  SetTeacher('Mr. Spillman');
  Display;
  Writeln;
  HappyBirthday;
  End;
Readln;
End.
```

When you run this program, you get the output shown in Figure 20-1. Notice that when the age is updated, the program displays the record as though it were just a person, not a full-fledged student. How did this occur?

The problem was caused by the use of static methods. The method **HappyBirthday** resides in the **Person** object; therefore, a call to **AStudent.HappyBirthday** causes Turbo Pascal to trace up the hierarchy from the **Student** object to the **Person** object to locate the method.

```
Student: Judd, Jessica; Age 5
Grade: 1
Teacher: Mr. Spillman

The following record has been updated:
Person: Jessica Judd
Age: 6
```

Figure 20-1.   Output from Static _ vs _ Virtual using static methods

Once **HappyBirthday** executes, it encounters a call to a method named **Display**. With static methods, this call was automatically bound to the **Display** method that resides in the **Person** object (see Figure 20-2). So instead of displaying a student, it displays a person.

Overcoming the Shortfall with Virtual Methods

One way to overcome this problem is to redefine the **HappyBirthday** method within the **Student** object. But that solution runs counter to the philosophy of OOP, which strives to reduce redundant code. The OOP solution is to use virtual methods. As mentioned earlier, virtual methods use late binding, which determines the exact path of execution at run time.

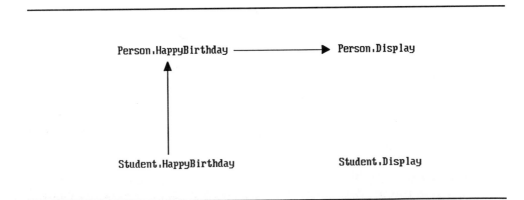

Figure 20-2.   Path of static method calls

There are two steps to turn a static method into a virtual one. The first step is to create a constructor method. The constructor tells Turbo Pascal that virtual methods will be used for that object. To create a constructor, you simply substitute the word **Constructor** for **Procedure** in both the object declaration and the method definition.

The second step is just as simple: you add the reserved word **Virtual** to the method heading in the object declaration. Here are the revised declarations of the **Person** and **Student** objects:

```
Type
  Ages = 0..150;    (* in years *)
  Person = Object
    Constructor Init;
    Procedure Display; Virtual;
    Function GetLastName  : String;
    Function GetFirstName : String;
    Function GetAge       : Ages;
    Procedure SetLastName(NewLastName : String);
    Procedure SetFirstName(NewFirstName : String);
    Procedure SetAge(NewAge : Ages);
    Procedure HappyBirthday;
  Private
    LastName  : String[30];
    FirstName : String[20];
    Age       : Ages;
    End;

  Grades = 0..12;  (* 0 is K *)
  Student = Object(Person)
    Constructor Init;
    Procedure Display; Virtual;
    Function GetGrade   : Grades;
    Function GetTeacher : String;
    Procedure SetGrade(NewGrade : Grades);
    Procedure SetTeacher(NewName : String);
  Private
    Grade     : Grades;
    Teacher   : String[30];
    End;
```

The method **Display** is now a virtual method for both objects, and the method **Init** is now a constructor for both objects. Once these changes are made, the call to **AStudent.HappyBirthday** traces up to **Person.HappyBirthday** as before. But when **Person.HappyBirthday** encounters a call to **Display**, it knows to execute the version in **Student**, not **Person** (see Figure 20-3). If you make these few changes, the output of the previous program will change from that shown in Figure 20-1 to the output pictured in Figure 20-4.

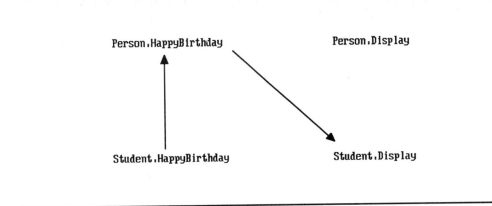

Figure 20-3. Path of virtual method calls

Three rules govern the declaration of virtual methods. First, you must call a constructor method for an object before calling any virtual methods. (The internal reasons for this will be discussed in the next section.) Second, once a method has been declared virtual in an object, the same method in any descendant object must also be declared virtual. And third, once a virtual method has been declared, its header cannot change in any descendants. This means that you cannot add, change, or delete parameters or change between a function and a procedure.

Inside Virtual Methods

The primary structure that supports virtual methods is the *VMT*, or *virtual method table*. As the name implies, a VMT is a table of addresses that point to virtual methods. Turbo Pascal sets up a VMT for

```
Student: Judd, Jessica; Age 5
Grade: 1
Teacher: Mr. Spillman

The following record has been updated:
Student: Judd, Jessica; Age 6
Grade: 1
Teacher: Mr. Spillman
```

Figure 20-4. Output from Static _ vs _ Virtual using virtual methods

every object type that contains or inherits a virtual method. By maintaining a table of addresses for each object type, Turbo Pascal can determine a path of execution that would be impossible to determine at compile time.

The structure of the VMT begins with two words. The first word contains the size of the object. The second word contains the negative value of the first word and is used to validate that the VMT has been properly initialized. The compiler directive **{$R+}** enables VMT validation. When it is enabled, Turbo Pascal tests to see if the sum of the first two words of the VMT is zero. If it is not, Turbo Pascal generates run-time error 210.

The role of the constructor method is to initialize the VMT. This is why you must call a constructor of an object before you can call any of its virtual methods. If you are using objects with virtual methods, be sure to initialize the object by calling its constructor at the beginning of your program.

The other fields in the VMT contain the addresses of the proper virtual methods for that object. All variables of the same object type point to the same VMT. Given the declarations of the **Person** and **Student** objects from the previous example, the VMT would contain only one other entry: the address of the proper **Display** method. The entire structure for the two objects is given in Figure 20-5.

When a virtual method is called, Turbo Pascal passes the address of the calling variable on the stack of the virtual method. Thus, when **AStudent.Display** is called, the address of the variable **AStudent** is passed on the stack. This address is known as the self parameter, and it is always the last item passed on the stack. Using this address, the method picks up the VMT address of the variable and executes the appropriate method by using the address found in the VMT. In other words, the variable passes a pointer to itself to the method, the method uses that pointer to locate the VMT, and the VMT tells the method which code to execute.

Object Type Compatibility

Object variables follow slightly different compatibility rules than do normal Turbo Pascal variables. The primary difference is that an ances-

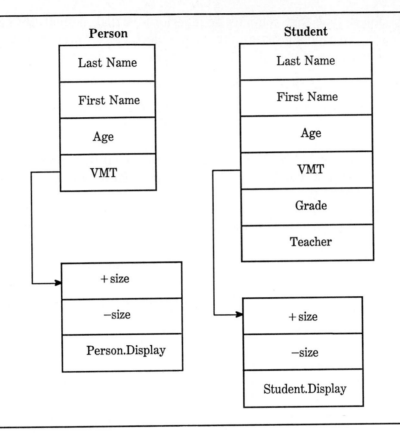

Figure 20-5. Internal structure of object variables

tor type is compatible with a descendant type, but the reverse is not true. For example, given the variables defined in a previous program, the statement

```
APerson := AStudent;
```

would be legal, but

```
AStudent := APerson
```

would generate a compiler error. The reasoning is that, through inheritance, **AStudent** contains everything in **APerson**, but **APerson** does not (or probably does not) contain everything in **AStudent**. The valid statement just listed assigns to **APerson** all values that it shares in common with **AStudent**. The other fields are ignored.

Similarly, a procedure that accepts a **Person** object variable as a **Var** parameter can also accept a variable of type **AStudent**. Thus, a procedure declared as

```
Procedure ChangeValue(Var AnyPerson : Person);
Begin
{...}
End;
```

could be called with

```
ChangeValue(AStudent);
```

The flexibility of object type compatibility may seem unimportant at first, but it is the simpler form of an extremely powerful OOP concept: polymorphism. *Polymorphism* is just a fancy way of saying that a procedure is willing to accept a wide range of object types, even if it is unaware of them at compile time. As long as the parameter variable is a descendant of the **Var** parameter type, the procedure will accept it. You could define 10 (or 100) different ancestors to **Person**, and the **Change-Value** procedure would not only accept them, it would also use them as you intended.

Polymorphism has another important implication. If the procedure that accepts the object gets its information about that variable at run time, you will be able to define compatible objects without recompiling the unit that contains the procedure. This adds the important quality of extensibility. You can compile a unit of routines that accept polymorphic variables, and distribute the compiled unit without the source code, and the users will be able to create their own objects to work with the compiled procedures. In other words, you don't have to think of everything in advance—the end users can add what they want.

Although the passing of objects as **Var** parameters gives you both polymorphism and extensibility, it still has its limitations. The code inside the **ChangeValue** procedure, for instance, knows only about **Person** objects and therefore cannot modify any fields other than the ones contained in **Person**. The real power of polymorphism comes when you add a few more concepts: virtual methods, which you already know, and dynamic objects, which are covered next.

Dynamic Allocation of Objects

When you talk about dynamic allocation of objects, you must understand that there are two kinds of dynamic objects. There are objects that contain pointers as data fields, and there are variables that are pointers to objects. You could also have a third kind, which is the combination of the first two. This section examines the first two in depth. The third kind needs no further elaboration once you've mastered the others.

Objects That Contain Pointers

When an object includes a pointer field, the constructor method gets a new function: it is responsible for allocating the memory for the dynamic field. Consider the following object definition:

```
Type
  BufferType = Array[1..1000] Of Byte;
  Buffer = Object
    Buff : ^BufferType;
    Constructor Init;
    Procedure SetB(NewBuff : BufferType);
    Procedure WriteToFile(var TheFile : File); virtual;
    Destructor Done;
    End;
```

The **Buffer** object contains a dynamic data field, so the constructor **Init** will allocate the memory:

```
Constructor Buffer.Init;
Begin
New(Buff);
End;
```

Since the **Buffer** object contains a virtual method, the constructor serves its second function of initializing the VMT.

When working with dynamic data fields, you also use a destructor method. The following is the simple code required to perform the deallocation:

```
Destructor Buffer.Done;
Begin
Dispose(Buff);
End;
```

Pointers to Objects

Turbo Pascal 6 also supports the creation of variables that are pointers to objects. The following is a simple example of using a dynamic variable that allocates a **Person** object:

```
Program Dynamic_Objects;

Uses PERSONS;

Var
  APersonPtr : ^Person;

Begin
New(APersonPtr, Init);
APersonPtr^.SetLastName('Lederman');
Writeln('The Last name is ', ApersonPtr^.GetLastName);
Dispose(APersonPtr);
Readln;
End.
```

Unlike the previous kind of dynamic objects, this kind requires no changes to the unit that defined the object.

You may have noticed a strange syntax in the call to **New** in the preceding listing. Turbo Pascal extends the traditional use of the **New** and **Dispose** standard procedures. Now both routines can take two parameters—a dynamic variable and a procedure name. The call

```
New(APersonPtr, Init);
```

performs the same task as these two calls:

```
New(APersonPtr);
APersonPtr^.Init;
```

By combining the syntax, you help to ensure that you remember both steps. You also guarantee that they're in the right order.

Dynamic deallocation is a mirror image of allocation. The **Dispose** command can also include a call to a destructor method. This would be the equivalent of calling the destructor and then doing a traditional **Dispose**.

Because the use of pointer variables is very common in OOP, you should include a pointer type for every object declaration. For the units discussed in this chapter, the type

```
PPerson = ^Person;
```

should be added to the PERSONS unit, and the type

```
PStudent = ^Student;
```

should be added to STUDENTS. The remainder of this chapter assumes that these additions were done.

Polymorphism

Earlier in the chapter you learned about how polymorphism is applied to **Var** parameters in subprograms that act on objects. In this last section, you will see how dynamic objects and virtual methods combine to give you an even more powerful form of polymorphism.

One of the rules of Turbo Pascal is that all pointer types are assignment compatible. This means that you can pass a pointer to any variable to a subprogram. If you pass a pointer to an object variable to a method, that method can in turn call a virtual method, which gives you extremely powerful polymorphism. Confused? Following is a detailed example.

Setting Yourself Up

Suppose you want to keep track of a list of people. You start with the PERSONS unit, which contains the declaration of the **Person** object.

You can then build a dynamic linked-list object that stores pointers to variables of type **Person**. Here is the interface section of the PERS-LIST unit:

```
Unit PERSLIST;

Interface

Uses PERSONS;

Type
  PPersonNode = ^PersonNode;
  PersonNode = Record
    PersonPtr : PPerson;
    Next : PPersonNode;
    End;

  PersonList = Object
    Constructor Init;
    Procedure AddPerson(ThisPerson : PPerson);
    Procedure DisplayList;
  Private
    First : PPersonNode;
    End;
```

If you never saw a linked-list data structure before, go back and study Chapter 8. If you have seen one, you should recognize that there is a record type to represent each node. The nodes contain only pointers to objects; this is critical.

The second structure is an object that is the linked list. To initialize that list, you need a constructor. The **Init** constructor is very simple and looks like this:

```
Constructor PersonList.Init;
Begin
First := nil;
End;
```

To add an object to the end of this list, you need code similar to the algorithm described in Chapter 8:

```
Procedure PersonList.AddPerson(ThisPerson : PPerson);
Var
  TempNode,
  NewNode : PPersonNode;
Begin
New(NewNode);
```

```
New(NewNode^.PersonPtr, Init);
NewNode^.PersonPtr := ThisPerson;
NewNode^.Next := Nil;
If First = Nil Then
  First := NewNode
Else
  Begin
  TempNode := First;
  While TempNode^.Next <> Nil Do
    TempNode := TempNode^.Next;
  TempNode^.Next := NewNode;
  End;
End;
```

Note that although the method accepts a pointer to a **Person** object, it allocates no space for the object (only for a new pointer to that object). Therefore, any module that calls this method must have already allocated memory for that object.

The final part of the implementation is the code to display the entire list:

```
Procedure PersonList.DisplayList;
Var
  Current : PPersonNode;
Begin
Current := First;
While Current <> Nil Do
  Begin
  Current^.PersonPtr^.Display;
  Writeln;
  Current := Current^.Next;
  End;
End;
```

This method accomplishes the display by calling **Person.Display**. Remember, **Display** is a virtual method (this will be important soon).

Next is a program that tests the linked-list program. This program generates some simple names just to validate the code:

```
Program TestList;

Uses PERSLIST, PERSONS, CRT;

Var
  APerson : PPerson;
  AList : PersonList;
  Count : Integer;
```

```
Begin
ClrScr;
AList.Init;
For Count := 1 To 4 Do
  Begin
  New(APerson, Init);
  With APerson^ Do
    Begin
    SetLastName('Last' + Chr(Count+48));
    SetFirstName('First' + Chr(Count+48));
    SetAge(Count);
    AList.AddPerson(APerson);
    End;
  End;

AList.DisplayList;
Readln;
End.
```

If you were to run this program, with all of its supporting units, you would see the output shown in Figure 20-6.

Where Polymorphism Comes In

At this point, assuming that you've understood the example, you're probably thinking of several simpler ways to accomplish the same task. The complexity is required for one critical reason: you can now use the same code for inherited objects, even *different* objects in the *same* list.

```
Person: First1 Last1
Age: 1

Person: First2 Last2
Age: 2

Person: First3 Last3
Age: 3

Person: First4 Last4
Age: 4
```

Figure 20-6.   Output from TestList program

This is polymorphism at its finest—using the same methods to support objects of "many forms" (the term "polymorphism" combines the Latin word for "many" with the Latin word for "form").

In case you find this hard to swallow, study the following example. It contains a slight change to the previous test program:

```
Program Polymorphism;

Uses PERSLIST, PERSONS, STUDENTS, CRT;

Var
  AStudent : PStudent;
  APerson : PPerson;
  AList : PersonList;
  Count : Integer;

Begin
ClrScr;
AList.Init;
For Count := 1 To 4 Do
  If Odd(Count) Then
    Begin
    New(APerson, Init);
    With APerson^ Do
      Begin
      SetLastName('Last' + Chr(Count+48));
      SetFirstName('First' + Chr(Count+48));
      SetAge(Count);
      End;
    AList.AddPerson(APerson);
    End
  Else
    Begin
    New(AStudent, Init);
    With AStudent^ Do
      Begin
      SetLastName('Last' + Chr(Count+48));
      SetFirstName('First' + Chr(Count+48));
      SetAge(Count);
      SetGrade(Count+5);
      SetTeacher('Teacher' + Chr(Count+48));
      End;
    AList.AddPerson(AStudent);
    End;

AList.DisplayList;
Readln;
End.
```

In this program, the object type alternates between **Person** objects and **Student** objects. Since the linked list is storing only pointers, it can handle objects of different types and different sizes. And because the

```
Person: First1 Last1
Age: 1

Student: Last2, First2; Age 2
Grade: 7
Teacher: Teacher2

Person: First3 Last3
Age: 3

Student: Last4, First4; Age 4
Grade: 9
Teacher: Teacher4
```

Figure 20-7.   Output from Polymorphism program

DisplayList method calls the virtual method **Display**, it can display objects of any type that is a descendant of **Person**. The output of this program appears in Figure 20-7.

If you are still confused, type the code from this chapter into your computer and experiment with it. You should be warned that almost all of the objects in Turbo Vision are polymorphic. This means that you must understand polymorphism to take full advantage of the structures that Turbo Vision provides. Once you have mastered the concepts in this chapter, you are ready for Chapter 21.

Turbo Vision

What Is Turbo Vision?
Creating and Using Flash Cards
Writing Applications with Turbo Vision

Occasionally, having the title *The Complete Reference* can be somewhat of a curse. A reference book that is too complete is often useless—readers spend most of their time wading through irrelevant information to find the needed data. Advanced readers, however, can get frustrated because the tiny detail they are looking for is not in the book.

Turbo Vision, the primary addition for Turbo Pascal 6, is a prime candidate for this dilemma. It contains hundreds of new types, objects, procedures, and methods. One could conceivably write a thousand pages, covering the underlying implementation of each construct. That tome would be useful to only a handful of readers. Alternatively, 95 to 98 percent of readers will require only enough detail to fill about 50 pages.

This chapter follows the second course. It attempts to break Turbo Vision into meaningful portions and then covers those portions enough so that you can write very complex programs. The chapter goes through the development of one complete example, so each section flows into the next. Shortly after an object type is introduced and explained, you will find a summary of methods and related subprograms and constants defined for that object. The methods are divided between primary methods, which you will use often, and other methods, which are either internal or seldom-required methods. With this organization, you can read the chapter from beginning to end once and then use the summary areas later as a reference.

What Is Turbo Vision?

Turbo Vision is the interface for the underlying mechanisms that Borland used to write the Integrated Development Environment (IDE) for Turbo Pascal 6. By giving you access to these mechanisms, Borland has allowed you to develop software that has the look and feel of the IDE.

The largest benefit of Turbo Vision is that it becomes a huge collection of reusable software. The next time you need to create a menu, for example, you'll simply define an object variable of type **TMenuBox** and insert the menu items into the object. If **TMenuBox** doesn't quite handle a specific capability, you can create a new object type that inherits all the functionality of **TMenuBox** but adds the new capability.

Turbo Vision is extremely flexible. A side effect of this flexibility is that it is also fairly complicated. You will find yourself calling Turbo Vision methods and procedures without any idea of why you're calling them—you're simply copying an example. This is fine; the details will make sense as you gain experience. Some details are never unveiled, but that is the wonder of OOP. By the way, Turbo Vision is entirely built around the concepts of inheritance and polymorphism. If you aren't familiar with these terms, reread Chapter 20.

Creating and Using Flash Cards

Throughout this chapter you will follow the development of a single application. Each example will therefore have some context, making it easier to understand. The application being developed is a program that allows you to create and use flash cards on the screen. As with all Turbo Vision programs, this application has the same look and feel as the Turbo Pascal environment.

As a user of this program, you would start by entering data for the flash cards. Each card has a question "side" and an answer "side." For simplicity, each side can contain only one 50-character line of text. The following illustration shows the screen used to enter a card:

```
┌─[■]═══════ Add Card ═══════
│ Card Number : 1
│
│ Question:
│ North Carolina
│
│ Answer:
│ Raleigh
│
│    ┌── OK ──┐   ┌─ Cancel ─┐
```

Notice that it looks exactly like the dialog boxes you use in the IDE.

Once the data for each card is entered, you can save those cards to a file on disk. Then you can run through the cards, either in random or sequential order. First, the question side of the card is displayed, as you can see here:

```
┌─[■]═════════════════ Question ═════════════════
│
│  North Carolina
│
│  ┌ Show Answer ┐          ┌ Cancel ┐    ┌ Card: 1 ┐
```

Once you read the question side, you can either look at the answer side or go directly to the next card. Figure 21-1 shows a screen in which both sides of a flash card are displayed. You can leave the program at any time by selecting a menu option or status-line command or by pressing a predefined hot key, in this case ALT-X. Many other commands are also bound to hot keys.

Writing Applications with Turbo Vision

Now that you understand what the **Flashcard_App** program does, you are ready to learn how it was made. The rest of this chapter takes you step by step through the development of this program. This will help you to create your own programs using Turbo Vision.

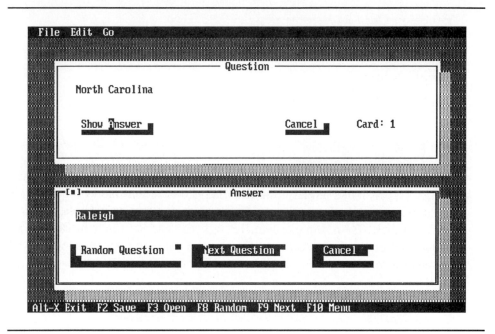

Figure 21-1.   Dialog box to display the answer side of a flash card

Creating an Application Object

When you first decide to tackle a large programming effort, you will probably find it difficult to determine a starting place. Often, if you start by prototyping your user interface, you can iron out the functionality of your application. Turbo Vision makes it easy for you to start this way. It allows you to achieve visual results of your efforts almost immediately.

The first step in creating a Turbo Vision application is to create a descendant of the **TApplication** object type. You can start by creating a simple descendant, with no new data fields and no overridden virtual methods. This gives you the following program:

```
Program Just_an_Application;

Uses App;

Type
  TFlashCardApp = Object(TApplication)
    End;
```

```
Var
  FlashCardApp : TFlashCardApp;

Begin
FlashCardApp.Init;
FlashCardApp.Run;
FlashCardApp.Done;
End.
```

After declaring the new object type, the preceding program creates a variable of that type and calls three inherited methods.

Figure 21-2 shows the screen displayed when you run this simple program. The top line, blank at the moment, will contain the menu bar. The entire middle of the screen is called the desktop. Finally, the status line takes up the bottom line, which contains hints and hot keys. The default status line includes a single entry, ALT-X, which enables you to exit the application. You should already be familiar with these terms from the Turbo Pascal IDE.

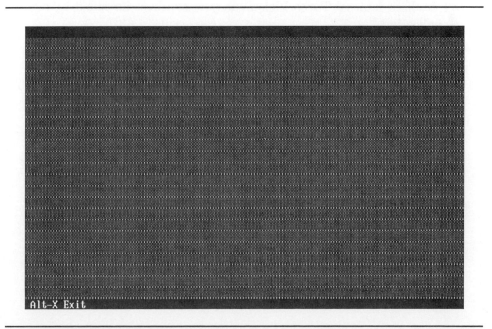

Figure 21-2.   Display of the default application desktop

To run any Turbo Vision application, you must call three methods: **Init, Run,** and **Done.** The **Init** method initializes all the internal structures required by Turbo Vision. You may choose to override this to include your own initializations. If you do, be sure to call the parent method, **TApplication.Init.** The **Run** method executes the application based on the way you set it up. Finally, **Done** cleans everything up.

TApplication Object Summary   APP.TPU

Heritage

TApplication → TProgram → TGroup → TView → TObject

Primary Methods

```
Constructor Init;
```

Initializes internal Turbo Vision subsystems; must be called by every application.

```
Destructor Done; Virtual;
```

Cleans up internal Turbo Vision subsystems; should be called by every application.

Primary Inherited Methods

Inherited from **TProgram** (see **TProgram** summary):

```
Procedure HandleEvent(Var Event: TEvent); Virtual;
Procedure InitMenuBar; Virtual;
Procedure InitStatusLine; Virtual;
Procedure Run; Virtual;
```

Inherited from **TView** (see **TView** summary):

```
Procedure GetExtent(Var Extent : TRect);
```

Creating Event Commands

Once you have the outline for your application, you need to determine the commands that will be available. By convention, these commands should be defined as constants and should start with the letters "cm". Turbo Vision reserves all constants from 0 to 99 and from 256 to 999. This leaves you with the values 100 to 255 and 1000 to 65535 for your own commands. The vast majority of the reserved commands are handled internally by Turbo Vision, so you need not be concerned about them. The few exceptions are covered in later discussions.

For the flash card application, the following commands are defined initially:

```
Const
(* valid event commands *)
  cmFileOpen   = 201;
  cmFileSave   = 202;
  cmEditAdd    = 211;
  cmEditChange = 212;
  cmEditDelete = 213;
  cmNextCard   = 221;
  cmRandomCard = 222;
```

The numbering scheme used for these commands reflects the menu structure that will support the commands. There is no requirement to use any specific values, other than using only nonreserved values.

Creating a Menu Bar

You can use Turbo Vision to create menus in two forms: horizontal and vertical. Their associated object types are **TMenuBar** and **TMenuBox**, respectively. Turbo Vision creates a global variable, **MenuBar**, for the menu bar associated with the main application. To assign menu items to this global variable, you must override the virtual method **TApplication** **.InitMenuBar**.

Here is the definition of the menu bar for the flash card application:

```
Procedure TFlashCardApp.InitMenuBar;

Var
  R : TRect;

Begin
GetExtent(R);
R.B.Y := 1;
MenuBar := New (PMenuBar, Init (R, NewMenu(
    NewSubMenu ('~F~ile', hcNoContext, NewMenu (
      NewItem ('~O~pen', 'F3', kbF3, cmFileOpen, hcNoContext,
      NewItem ('~S~ave', 'F2', kbF2, cmFileSave, hcNoContext,
      NewItem ('~Q~uit', 'Alt-X', kbAltX, cmQuit, hcNoContext,
      Nil)))),
    NewSubMenu ('~E~dit', hcNoContext, NewMenu (
      NewItem ('~A~dd', '', 0, cmEditAdd, hcNoContext,
      NewItem ('~C~hange', '', 0, cmEditChange, hcNoContext,
      NewItem ('~D~elete', '', 0, cmEditDelete, hcNoContext,
      Nil)))),
    NewSubMenu ('~G~o', hcNoContext, NewMenu(
      NewItem ('~R~andom', 'F8', kbF8, cmRandomCard, hcNoContext,
      NewItem ('~N~ext', 'F9', kbF9, cmNextCard, hcNoContext,
      Nil))),
    Nil))))));
End;
```

The first step in creating a menu is to define its dimensions. This is done by first calling method **GetExtent** for the application object. All dimension rectangles are given relative to the view, so they all include (0,0) as their first corner. Since the menu bar takes only one line, you should set the bottom line to 1. Note that a menu's dimensions are for the main part of the menu only, not for any of its submenus.

The global variable **MenuBar** is actually a pointer to a menu, so it must be assigned a value using the procedure **New**. Using the extended form of this procedure, the second parameter to **New** is a call to **TMenuBar.Init**. **Init** is a fairly complex constructor because it must handle menus of any size. It requires the dimension rectangle and the menu items as parameters.

When you define the menu items, you are actually inserting them into a linked list. The functions **NewMenu**, **NewSubMenu**, and **New-Item** are required to define the list. The last parameter in each of these functions is a pointer to the next menu item (or submenu item), which will be **Nil** for the last item.

Each menu entry contains five parts: the name of the entry, the name of a shortcut key for that entry (if applicable), the key code for the shortcut key, the command to be executed, and a help context key. The entry name can include a character enclosed by tilde ($\sim$) characters; this defines the letter that can be pressed to access that menu entry. For now, set all help context keys to the global constant **hcNoContext**, which defines no related help. The key codes are all defined as constants in the **Drivers** unit, and all start with the letters "kb".

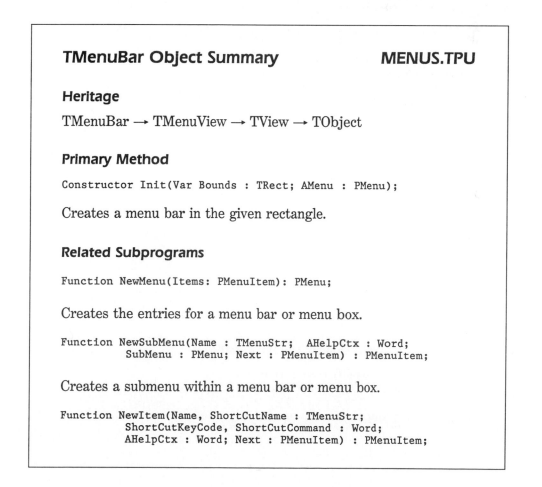

TMenuBar Object Summary   **MENUS.TPU**

Heritage

TMenuBar → TMenuView → TView → TObject

Primary Method

```
Constructor Init(Var Bounds : TRect; AMenu : PMenu);
```

Creates a menu bar in the given rectangle.

Related Subprograms

```
Function NewMenu(Items: PMenuItem): PMenu;
```

Creates the entries for a menu bar or menu box.

```
Function NewSubMenu(Name : TMenuStr;  AHelpCtx : Word;
        SubMenu : PMenu; Next : PMenuItem) : PMenuItem;
```

Creates a submenu within a menu bar or menu box.

```
Function NewItem(Name, ShortCutName : TMenuStr;
        ShortCutKeyCode, ShortCutCommand : Word;
        AHelpCtx : Word; Next : PMenuItem) : PMenuItem;
```

Defines an item within a menu or submenu.

```
Function NewLine(Next : PMenuItem) : PMenuItem;
```

Adds a horizontal line within a menu box.

Related Types

```
TMenu = Record
  Items : PMenuItem;
  Default : PMenuItem;
```

Defines a menu, including its entries and which entry is the default.

```
PMenuItem = ^TMenuItem;
TMenuItem = Record
  Next : PMenuItem;  Name : PString;  Command : Word;
  Disabled : Boolean;  KeyCode, HelpCtx : Word;
  Case Integer Of
    0 : (Param : PString);     (* PString = ^String *)
    1 : (SubMenu : PMenu);
    End;
  End;
```

Defines a menu entry.

```
TMenuStr = String[31];
```

The maximum length for a menu entry is 31 characters.

Other Methods

```
Procedure Draw; Virtual;
```

Called internally to display the menu bar.

```
Procedure GetItemRect(Item : PMenuItem;
        Var R : TRect); Virtual;
```

Called internally to determine if a mouse click occurred in the menu box.

TMenuBox Object Summary   MENUS.TPU

Heritage

TMenuBox → TMenuView → TView → TObject

Primary Methods

```
Constructor Init(Var Bounds : TRect; AMenu : PMenu;
        AParentMenu : PMenuView);
```

Creates a menu box, often as a submenu.

Related Subprograms

See list in **TMenuBar** summary.

Other Methods

See list in **TMenuBar** summary.

kbXXXX Constant Summary   DRIVERS.TPU

Primary Values

```
kbF1 .. kbF10, kbCtrlF1 .. kbCtrlF10, kbShiftF1 .. kbShiftF10,
        kbAltF1 .. kbAltF10
kbAlt1 ..  kbAlt0
kbAltA .. kbAltZ
kbEnter, kbEsc, kbTab, kbCtrlEnter
kbUp, kbDown, kbLeft, kbRight, kbHome, kbEnd, kbPgUp,
        kbPgDn, kbCtrlLeft, kbCtrlRight, kbCtrlHome, kbCtrlEnd,
        kbCtrlPgUp, kbCtrlPgDn
kbIns, kbDel, kbShiftIns, kbShiftDel, kbCtrlIns, kbCtrlDel
```

TRect Object Summary   OBJECTS.TPU

Heritage

None

Primary Method

```
Procedure Assign(XA, YA, XB, YB : Integer);
```

Assigns values to the corners of the rectangle.

Related Types

```
TPoint = Object
  X, Y : Integer;
  End;
```

Defines a point on the screen.

Other Methods

```
Function Contains(P : TPoint): Boolean;
```

Determines whether the point is inside the rectangle.

```
Procedure Copy(R : TRect);
```

Assigns the values in **R** to the values in the object.

```
Function Empty: Boolean;
```

Determines whether any characters can fit in the rectangle.

```
Function Equals(R : TRect) : Boolean;
```

Determines whether the two rectangles are equal.

```
Procedure Grow(ADX, ADY : Integer);
```

Changes the size of the rectangle using the deltas.

```
Procedure Intersect(R : TRect);
```

Reduces the size of the rectangle to become the intersection with the **R** rectangle.

```
Procedure Move(ADX, ADY : Integer);
```

Adds the deltas to both dimensions of the rectangle.

```
Procedure Union(R : TRect);
```

Increases the size of the rectangle to become the union with the **R** rectangle.

Creating a Status Line

Defining the status line is similar to defining menus. This is the code that defines the status line for the flash card application:

```
Procedure TFlashCardApp.InitStatusLine;

Var
  R : TRect;

Begin
GetExtent(R);
R.A.Y := R.B.Y - 1;
StatusLine := New (PStatusLine, Init (R,
    NewStatusDef (0, $FFFF,
      NewStatusKey ('~Alt-X~ Exit', kbAltX, cmQuit,
      NewStatusKey ('~F2~ Save', kbF2, cmFileSave,
      NewStatusKey ('~F3~ Open', kbF3, cmFileOpen,
      NewStatusKey ('~F8~ Random', kbF8, cmRandomCard,
      NewStatusKey ('~F9~ Next', kbF9, cmNextCard,
      NewStatusKey ('~F10~ Menu', kbF10, cmMenu,
      Nil)))))),
    Nil)));
End;
```

As with the menu bar, this method starts by assigning a rectangle to the dimensions of the status line (at the bottom of the screen, this time).

Then it initializes the pointer **StatusLine** with a call to **Init**, which requires a list of status key items.

Each status key has three parts: the string entry that normally includes the key name and the command name, the code for the hot key, and the command to be executed. The key name is normally enclosed in tilde characters, so it appears in a highlighted color.

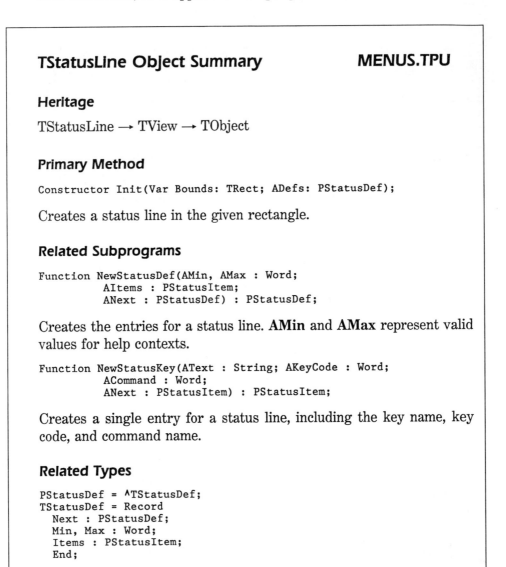

TStatusLine Object Summary   MENUS.TPU

Heritage

TStatusLine → TView → TObject

Primary Method

```
Constructor Init(Var Bounds: TRect; ADefs: PStatusDef);
```

Creates a status line in the given rectangle.

Related Subprograms

```
Function NewStatusDef(AMin, AMax : Word;
        AItems : PStatusItem;
        ANext : PStatusDef) : PStatusDef;
```

Creates the entries for a status line. **AMin** and **AMax** represent valid values for help contexts.

```
Function NewStatusKey(AText : String; AKeyCode : Word;
        ACommand : Word;
        ANext : PStatusItem) : PStatusItem;
```

Creates a single entry for a status line, including the key name, key code, and command name.

Related Types

```
PStatusDef = ^TStatusDef;
TStatusDef = Record
  Next : PStatusDef;
  Min, Max : Word;
  Items : PStatusItem;
  End;
```

Defines a status line, including the help context range.

```
PStatusItem = ^TStatusItem;
TStatusItem = Record
  Next : PStatusItem;  Text : PString;
  KeyCode : Word;  Command : Word;
  End;
```

Defines an item on the status line.

Other Methods

```
Destructor Done; Virtual;
```

Releases memory containing the status line; normally called internally.

```
Procedure Draw; Virtual;
```

Called internally to draw the status line on the screen.

```
Function GetPalette : PPalette; Virtual;
```

Can be overridden to change the color scheme.

```
Procedure HandleEvent(Var Event : TEvent); Virtual;
```

Called internally to handle status line events.

```
Procedure Hint(AHelpCtx : Word): String; Virtual;
```

Must be overridden to provide a one-line help message in the status line.

```
Constructor Load(Var S : TStream);
```

Called internally to load a status line from a stream.

```
Procedure Store(Var S : TStream);
```

Called internally to store the status line to a stream.

```
Procedure Update;
```

Redraws the status line based on the help context.

Creating the Event Handler

The final piece in the outer layer of each application object is the event handler. You can create an event handler by overriding the method **TProgram.HandleEvent**.

Any event handler must first call its ancestor's event handler. The rest of the structure is easier to copy as a template than to understand. For the flash card application, the event handler looks like this:

```
Procedure TFlashCardApp.HandleEvent(Var Event: TEvent);

Begin
TApplication.HandleEvent(Event);
If Event.What = evCommand Then
  Begin
  Case Event.Command Of
    cmFileOpen    : OpenFile;
    cmFileSave    : SaveFile;
    cmEditAdd     : AddCard;
    cmEditChange  : ChangeCard;
    cmEditDelete  : DeleteCard;
    cmNextCard    : NextCard;
    cmRandomCard  : RandomCard;
  Else
    Exit;
    End;
  ClearEvent(Event);
  End;
End;
```

All event handlers should have the same **Case** statement nested inside the **If** statement. The options for the case statement are the applications commands.

Notice that when a command is received, the event handler simply calls a procedure to process the command. For prototyping purposes, you might consider making null stubs for each command processor. Here are the stubs for the flash card commands:

```
Procedure AddCard;

Begin
End;


Procedure SaveFile;

Begin
End;
```

```
Procedure OpenFile;

Begin
End;


Procedure ChangeCard;

Begin
End;


Procedure DeleteCard;

Begin
End;


Procedure NextCard;

Begin
End;


Procedure RandomCard;

Begin
End;
```

Although nonfunctional now, these procedures will later be implemented and tested one at a time.

Given the three methods just defined, you can create the final definition of the **TFlashCardApp** object:

```
Type
  TFlashCardApp = Object(TApplication)
    Procedure InitMenuBar; Virtual;
    Procedure InitStatusLine; Virtual;
    Procedure HandleEvent(Var Event : TEvent); Virtual;
    End;
```

Almost every application you write will override these three methods. You may also choose to override **TApplication.Init** to include program initialization code, although it's usually better to keep them separate.

TProgram Object Summary   APP.TPU

Heritage

TProgram → TGroup → TView → TObject

Primary Methods

```
Procedure HandleEvent(Var Event : TEvent); Virtual;
```

Overridden to allow for event handling in each application. Any method that overrides this should call this method as its first statement. Without an override, it handles only internal events.

```
Procedure InitMenuBar; Virtual;
```

Overridden to create a menu bar at the top of the screen. Without an override, it creates an empty menu bar.

```
Procedure InitStatusLine; Virtual;
```

Overridden to create a status line at the bottom of the screen. Without an override, it creates a status line with the ALT-X **Quit** command only.

```
Procedure Run; Virtual;
```

Called internally to start the application's event handler.

Related Global Variables

```
Application : PApplication = Nil;
```

Stores a pointer to the main application object.

```
DeskTop : PDeskTop = Nil;
```

Stores a pointer to the desktop for the application.

```
MenuBar : PMenuView = Nil;
```

Stores a pointer to the main menu (bar or box) for the application.

```
StatusLine : PStatusLine = Nil;
```

Stores a pointer to the status line for the application.

Related Types

```
TEvent = Record
  What : Word;
  Case Word Of
    {...}
    evMessage: (Command : Word {...} );
    End;
```

Defines an event (internal information has been omitted).

Other Methods

```
Destructor Done;
```

Called internally to dispose of the desktop, main menu, and status line.

```
Procedure GetEvent(Var Event : TEvent); Virtual;
```

Called internally to see if an event has occurred.

```
Procedure GetPalette : PPalette; Virtual;
```

Can be overridden to change the color schemes for the entire application.

```
Procedure Idle; Virtual;
```

Can be overridden to accomplish tasks in background mode while no events have occurred.

```
Constructor Init;
```

Called internally to initialize internal variables.

```
Procedure InitScreen; Virtual;
```

Called internally to change the screen mode.

```
Procedure OutOfMemory; Virtual;
```

Can be overridden to handle the inability of the program to access enough memory. By default, it does nothing.

```
Procedure PutEvent(Var Event : TEvent); Virtual;
```

Called internally to store the current event in an internal buffer.

```
Procedure SetScreenMode(Mode : Word);
```

Sets the screen mode. Valid constants are **smCO80**, **smBW80**, and **smMono**. For extended line mode, **smFont8x8** can also be included.

```
Function ValidView(P : PView) : PView;
```

Called internally to check the validity of a view and make sure there was enough memory to create it.

TDeskTop Object Summary   APP.TPU

Heritage

TDeskTop → TGroup → TView → TObject

Primary Methods

```
Procedure Cascade(Var R: TRect);
```

Cascades all windows that are tileable (normally this excludes dialog boxes).

```
Procedure Tile(Var R : TRect);
```

Tiles all windows that are tileable (normally this excludes dialog boxes).

Primary Inherited Methods

Inherited from **TGroup** (see **TGroup** summary):

```
Procedure Delete(P : PView);
Function ExecView(P : PView): Word;
Procedure Insert(P : PView);
```

Other Methods

```
Procedure HandleEvent(Var Event : TEvent); Virtual;
```

Called internally to handle events in the desktop.

```
Constructor Init(Var Bounds : TRect);
```

Called internally to create the desktop.

```
Function NewBackground : PView; Virtual;
```

Can be overridden to change the default background.

```
Procedure TileError; Virtual;
```

Called internally when an error has occurred attempting to tile. By default, it does nothing.

TGroup Object Summary   VIEWS.TPU

Heritage

TGroup → TView → TObject

Primary Methods

```
Procedure Delete(P : PView);
```

Removes a view from the group.

```
Function ExecView(P : PView) : Word;
```

Executes a modal view. Control stays in that view until an appropriate command exits the view. The exit command is returned by the function.

```
Procedure Insert(P : PView);
```

Adds a view to the group. This normally causes the view to appear on the screen.

Other Methods

Group objects are almost never created explicitly, so their internal methods are of little value. See the methods for each descendant object type.

Creating a Simple Dialog Box

Although the previous stubs compile and execute, they do little to support program development. A much more effective way to show that a particular section of code has yet to be developed is to tell that to the user. This can be done in Turbo Vision by using a dialog box.

Being familiar with the Turbo Pascal environment, you already know how dialog boxes operate, and what types of I/O can be represented. Creating your own dialog box is a matter of initializing an empty box and then inserting the pieces you want.

To ease you into the methods of dialog box design, consider the creation of a very simple box. This box will have one button on it. When the box is displayed on the screen, a user must press that button in order to continue.

Study the code for the procedure that creates this simple dialog box:

```
Procedure SimpleBox(Name : String);

Var
  Dialog : PDialog;
  R : TRect;
  Control : Word;
```

```
Begin
R.Assign(20, 9, 55, 15);
Dialog := New(PDialog, Init(R, Name));
With Dialog^ Do
  Begin
  R.Assign(4, 2, 29, 4);
  Insert(New(PButton, Init(R, '(not implemented yet)',
      cmOK, bfDefault)));
  End;
Control := DeskTop^.ExecView(Dialog);
End;
```

The first step in creating a dialog box is to assign the area of the screen where the box will appear. For this you use **R.Assign**, just like you did for menus and status lines. Then you allocate memory to a dialog pointer, using **New**. This creates a blank dialog box with the title taken from a parameter.

The next step is to insert one or more standard objects. In this case a button was chosen. After you assign a rectangular area for the button, **Insert** is called with an initialization of the button. This initialization includes the text that will appear and the event that will be generated when the button is pressed.

When you've completely defined the dialog box, you make a call to **ExecView**. This function displays the dialog box and accepts no commands other than the ones defined by the box itself. This exclusiveness makes this dialog box a modal view. Later in this chapter, you will see how to make nonmodal dialog boxes.

Now you can improve the stubbed version of your program by calling **SimpleBox** in the procedures that process the commands. The following listing shows a few examples for the flash card application:

```
Procedure AddCard;

Begin
SimpleBox('Add Card');
End;


Procedure ChangeCard;

Begin
SimpleBox('Change Card');
End;


Procedure SaveFile;

Begin
SimpleBox('Save File');
End;


Procedure OpenFile;
```

```
Begin
SimpleBox('Open File');
End;
```

The following illustrates a sample call to this procedure:

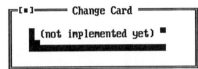

You will learn about dialog boxes in greater detail later in this chapter.

TDialog Object Summary   DIALOGS.TPU

Heritage

TDialog → TWindow → TGroup → TView → TObject

Primary Method

```
Constructor Init(Var Bounds : TRect;  ATitle : TTitleStr);
```

Creates a dialog box with the given dimensions and title.

Related Constants

```
cmOK = 10;
```

Event set when user presses the OK button or presses ENTER.

```
cmCancel = 11;
```

Event set when user presses the Cancel button or presses ESCAPE.

```
cmYes = 12;
```

Event set when user presses the Yes button, if there is one.

```
cmNo = 13;
```

Event set when user presses the No button, if applicable.

Primary Inherited Method

Inherited from **TGroup** (see **TGroup** summary):

```
Procedure Insert(P : PView);
```

Inherited from **TView** (see **TView** summary):

```
Procedure GetData(Var Rec); Virtual;
Procedure SetData(Var Rec); Virtual;
```

Other Methods

```
Procedure HandleEvent(Var Event : TEvent); Virtual;
```

Called internally to handle **cmOK, cmCancel, cmYes,** and **cmNo.** All other events are raised to the parent object.

```
Function GetPalette : PPalette; Virtual;
```

Can be overridden to change the dialog box colors.

```
Function Valid(Command : Word) : Boolean; Virtual;
```

Called internally to determine if the command is valid.

TView Object Summary   VIEWS.TPU

Heritage

TView → TObject

Primary Methods

```
Procedure GetData(Var Rec); Virtual;
```

Copies a number of bytes from its internal structure to the parameter, based on the size of the parameter.

```
Procedure GetExtent(Var Extent : TRect);
```

Returns a rectangle, with a (0, 0) origin, that matches the current size of the view.

```
Procedure SetData(Var Rec); Virtual;
```

Copies a number of bytes from the parameter to its internal structure, based on the size of the parameter.

Other Methods

View objects are almost never created explicitly, so their internal methods are of little value. See the methods for each descendant object type.

TObject Object Summary   OBJECTS.TPU

Heritage

None

Primary Methods

```
Constructor Init;
```

Allocates the space for an object and initializes all fields (sets them to zeros).

```
Procedure Free;
```

Disposes of an object.

Other Method

```
Destructor Done; Virtual;
```

Called internally by **Free** to handle memory cleanup for an object.

Writing Support Code

Until now you have watched the development of an application prototype that can support any Turbo Vision program. Once you are satisfied with the design and the interface, you must start on the implementation of the "meat" of the program. In this section, you will see the lowest level of the flash card application, an object that represents a single flash card. The next sections build on this object until the application is complete.

In the spirit of OOP, the rest of the design revolves around two objects: **TFlashCard**, which models a single flash card, and **TFlashCardSet**, which represents a group of flash cards. The implementation of **TFlashCard** is straightforward. As you can see by the **FLASHCRD** unit, the flash card object is similar in form to the **TPerson** object that you studied in Chapter 20:

```
Unit FLASHCRD;

Interface

Uses Objects;

Const
  QAMaxLen = 50;

Type
  FlashStr = String[QAMaxLen];
  PFlashCard = ^TFlashCard;
  TFlashCard = Object(TObject)
    Constructor Init;
    Function GetNumber : Integer;
    Function GetQuestion : FlashStr;
    Function GetAnswer : FlashStr;
    Procedure SetNumber(NewNumber : Integer);
    Procedure SetQuestion(NewQuestion : FlashStr);
    Procedure SetAnswer(NewAnswer : FlashStr);
  Private
    Number : Integer;
    Question : FlashStr;
    Answer : FlashStr;
    End;

Implementation

Constructor TFlashCard.Init;

Begin
Question := ' ';
Answer := ' ';
End;
```

```
(*********************************************)

Function TFlashCard.GetNumber : Integer;

Begin
GetNumber := Number;
End;

(*********************************************)

Function TFlashCard.GetQuestion : FlashStr;

Begin
GetQuestion := Question;
End;

(*********************************************)

Function TFlashCard.GetAnswer : FlashStr;

Begin
GetAnswer := Answer;
End;

(*********************************************)

Procedure TFlashCard.SetNumber(NewNumber : Integer);

Begin
Number := NewNumber;
End;

(*********************************************)

Procedure TFlashCard.SetQuestion(NewQuestion : FlashStr);

Begin
Question := NewQuestion;
End;

(*********************************************)

Procedure TFlashCard.SetAnswer(NewAnswer : FlashStr);

Begin
Answer := NewAnswer;
End;

End.
```

The implementation of **TFlashCard** further enforces the concept of encapsulation: including all possible functionality in the methods, with no access to the data fields.

Creating Collections

How many times have you written code to support arrays or linked lists? Every time you create a new record structure, you find yourself writing more code to support collections of that structure. With Turbo Vision, you may never have to write array support software again.

Turbo Vision includes an object type called **TCollection**, as well as a few descendant object types. These collection objects are independent of the user interface software, so they can be used easily in any application. Even more advantageous is that collections are polymorphic: Used properly, they can store different objects in the same set. If you want the collection to stay sorted at all times, use **TSortedCollection**. Be aware, however, that sorted collections do not support duplicate entries. If you need this ability, you must create your own descendant.

A Turbo Vision collection is a list of pointers. Therefore, to use a collection object, you do not need to create a descendant object type. For proper encapsulation, however, you will often create descendants anyway, to refine the functionality of the object type.

To make this clearer, look at the definition of the **TFlashCardSet** object in the FLASHSET unit:

```
Unit FLASHSET;

Interface

Uses Objects, FLASHCRD;

Type
  PFlashCardSet = ^TFlashCardSet;
  TFlashCardSet = Object(TCollection)
    Constructor Init;
    Function NewCard : PFlashCard;
    Procedure Replace(ACard : PFlashCard);
    Procedure Delete(ACard : PFlashCard);
    Function NextCard : PFlashCard;
    Function AnyCard : PFlashCard;
  Private
    CurrentCard : Integer;
    End;
```

This object definition provides complete functionality for a set of flash cards.

Now, examine each method of **TFlashCardSet** in more detail. The initialization is done primarily through a call to **TCollection.Init**:

```
Constructor TFlashCardSet.Init;

Begin
TCollection.Init(10, 5);
CurrentCard := -1;
Randomize;
End;
```

Init requires two parameters: the initial size of the collection and the amount the collection will grow when the initial size is exceeded. The growth process takes a relatively long time when the collections get large, so choose these numbers carefully. The call to **Randomize** is to support the ability to select flash cards at random.

Normally, when you want to add an object to a collection, you enter the data and then insert the pointer into the collection. From an object oriented sense, however, the flash card method works more like this: "Give me a new blank card, let me fill in both sides, and replace it in the set." Here is the **NewCard** method:

```
Function TFlashCardSet.NewCard : PFlashCard;

Var
  BlankCard : PFlashCard;

Begin
New(BlankCard, Init);
TCollection.Insert(BlankCard);
BlankCard^.SetNumber(Count);
NewCard := BlankCard;
End;
```

Collections number their entries from 0 to N-1, just like most computer science applications. Flash cards, however, are used by everyone, so it makes more sense to number them from 1 to N (where N is the number of cards). This number-shifting is evident in the **Replace** and **Delete** methods, shown here:

```
Procedure TFlashCardSet.Replace(ACard : PFlashCard);

Begin
TCollection.AtPut(ACard^.GetNumber - 1, ACard);
End;
```

```
(*********************************************)

Procedure TFlashCardSet.Delete(ACard : PFlashCard);

Begin
TCollection.AtDelete(ACard^.GetNumber - 1);
End;
```

The final two methods (actually, you'll see a few more later in the chapter) retrieve cards from the set, either in sequential order or in random order:

```
Function TFlashCardSet.NextCard : PFlashCard;

Var
  ACard : PFlashCard;

Begin
CurrentCard := CurrentCard + 1;
If CurrentCard = Count Then
  CurrentCard := 0;
ACard := TCollection.At(CurrentCard);
ACard^.SetNumber(CurrentCard+1);
NextCard := ACard;
End;


(*********************************************)

Function TFlashCardSet.AnyCard : PFlashCard;

Var
  ACard : PFlashCard;

Begin
CurrentCard := Random(Count);
ACard := TCollection.At(CurrentCard);
ACard^.SetNumber(CurrentCard + 1);
AnyCard := ACard;
End;
```

Notice that both of these methods set the number of a flash card, even though the number is stored in the collection. The reason is that, when the collection deletes an object, it doesn't know anything about numbering of the objects, so it can't make any updates. Therefore, the flash card numbers stored in the collection are not necessarily correct.

TCollection Object Summary   OBJECTS.TPU

Heritage

TCollection → TObject

Primary Field

```
Count : Integer;
```

The only way to determine current size of the collection is to access this data field.

Primary Methods

```
Constructor Init(ALimit, ADelta : Integer);
```

Creates a collection object with the desired initial size. When that size is exceeded, the collection will grow based on **ADelta**.

```
Function At(Index : Integer) : Pointer;
```

Gets a pointer to the *n*th entry in the collection.

```
Procedure AtDelete(Index : Integer);
```

Deletes the *n*th entry in the collection.

```
Function AtInsert(Index : Integer; Item : Pointer);
```

Inserts the new entry at the *n*th position. Entry positions beyond **Index** are incremented by one.

```
Function AtPut(Index : Integer; Item : Pointer);
```

Replaces the *n*th entry in the collection.

```
Procedure Delete(Item : Pointer);
```

Deletes a specific entry in the collection.

```
Procedure DeleteAll;
```

Deletes all entries in the collection.

```
Destructor Done; Virtual;
```

Disposes the entire collection.

```
Function FirstThat(Test : Pointer): Pointer;
```

Searches for a specific entry in the collection. **Test** is the address of the Boolean function that defines the condition. That function must be local to the subprogram that requires it and must be declared as a **Far** function.

```
Procedure ForEach(Action : Pointer);
```

Executes the specified procedure for every entry in the collection. **Action** is the address of a procedure that performs on a single entry. That procedure must be local to the subprogram that requires it and must be declared as a **Far** function.

```
Function IndexOf(Item : Pointer) : Integer; Virtual;
```

Determines the index of an entry in the collection.

```
Procedure Insert(Item : Pointer); Virtual;
```

Inserts an entry at the end of the collection.

```
Function LastThat(Test : Pointer) : Pointer;
```

Searches in reverse for a specific entry in the collection. **Test** is the address of the Boolean function that defines the condition. That function must be local to the subprogram that requires it and must be declared as a **Far** function.

Other Methods

```
Procedure Error(Code, Info : Integer); Virtual;
```

Called internally to handle errors. By default, the procedure causes a run-time error.

```
Function GetItem(Var S : TStream) : Pointer; Virtual;
```

Called internally to retrieve an entry from the stream. Must be overridden only if the entry type is not a descendant of **TObject**.

```
Constructor Load(Var S : TStream);
```

Called internally to load the collection from a stream.

```
Procedure Pack;
```

Removes all entries that point to **Nil**.

```
Procedure  PutItem(Var  S : TStream; Item  :  Pointer); Virtual;
```

Called internally to write an entry to the stream. Must be overridden only if the entry type is not a descendant of **TObject**.

```
Procedure SetLimit(ALimit : Integer); Virtual;
```

Changes the size of the collection. Although the collection will grow automatically, you may want this to shrink the collection after many entries have been deleted. It actually copies the collection into a smaller one, so it takes a long time.

```
Procedure Store(Var S : TStream);
```

Called internally to write the collection to the stream.

TSortedCollection Object Summary   OBJECTS.TPU

Heritage

TSortedCollection → TCollection → TObject

Primary Methods

```
Function  Compare(Key1,  Key2  :  Pointer)  :  Integer; Virtual;
```

Must be overridden with a function that compares the two keys, and returns −1, 0, or 1 based on the comparison.

```
Function IndexOf(Item : Pointer) : Integer; Virtual;
```

Searches for an entry and returns its index. If the entry is not in the collection, it returns the value −1.

```
Procedure Insert(Item : Pointer); Virtual;
```

Adds an entry to the collection in the proper place.

Primary Inherited Methods

From **TCollection** (see **TCollection** summary):

```
Count : Integer;    (a data field)
Constructor Init(ALimit, ADelta);
Function FirstThat(Test : Pointer): Pointer;
Procedure ForEach(Action : Pointer);
Function LastThat(Test : Pointer): Pointer;
```

Other Methods

```
Function KeyOf(Item : Pointer): Pointer; Virtual;
```

Can be overridden if the **Item** is not the entire key.

```
Function Search(Key : Pointer; Var Index: Integer) : Boolean;
         Virtual;
```

Called internally to search for a key in the collection.

TStringCollection Object Summary   **OBJECTS.TPU**

Heritage

TStringCollection → TSortedCollection → TCollection → TObject

Primary Inherited Methods

From **TSortedCollection** (see **TSortedCollection** summary):

```
Function IndexOf(Item : Pointer) : Integer; Virtual;
Procedure Insert(Item : Pointer); Virtual;
```

From **TCollection** (see **TCollection** summary):

```
Count : Integer;   (a data field)
Constructor Init(ALimit, ADelta);
Function FirstThat(Test : Pointer): Pointer;
Procedure ForEach(Action : Pointer);
Function LastThat(Test : Pointer);
```

Other Methods

```
Function Compare(Key1, Key2 : Pointer) : Integer;  Virtual;
```

A pure ASCII string comparison; may be overridden to sort using a different comparison.

```
Procedure FreeItem(Item : Pointer); Virtual;
```

Called internally to dispose of a string in the collection.

```
Function GetItem(Var S : TStream); Pointer; Virtual;
```

Called internally to read a string from the stream.

```
Procedure PutItem(Var S : TStream;  Item : Pointer); Virtual;
```

Called internally to write a string to the stream.

Creating More Complex Dialog Boxes

Until now, you have seen the skeleton user interface and the internal mechanisms for the flash card application. In this section, you will see how to put everything together to create a working program. Most of the commands involve the use of dialog boxes so you can see more examples of dialog box entries.

The first example is the **AddCard** procedure:

```
Procedure AddCard(Var ToSet : TFlashCardSet);

Type
  TEditData = Record
    Ans : FlashStr;
    Quest : FlashStr;
    End;

Var
  Dialog : PDialog;
  R : TRect;
  Control : Word;
  Q, A : PView;
  CardNumber : String;
  EditData : TEditData;
  ACard : PFlashCard;

Begin
(* repeat as long as the user wants to make additions *)
Repeat

  (* create the dialog box *)
  R.Assign(20, 6, 55, 20);
  Dialog := New(PDialog, Init(R, 'Add Card'));
  With Dialog^ Do
    Begin

    (* insert the card number as static text *)
    New(ACard, Init);
    ACard := ToSet.NewCard;
    Str(ACard^.GetNumber, CardNumber);
    R.Assign(3, 2, 29, 3);
    Insert(New(PStaticText,    Init(R,   'Card   Number  :     '+
CardNumber)));

    (* insert the answer InputLine with a label *)
    R.Assign(2, 8, 29, 9);
    A := New(PInputLine, Init(R, QAMaxLen));
    Insert(A);
    R.Assign(2, 7, 12, 8);
    Insert(New(PLabel, Init(R, 'Answer:', A)));

    (* insert the Ok command as a button *)
    R.Assign(5, 11, 15, 13);
    Insert(New(PButton, Init(R, '~O~K', cmOK, bfDefault)));

    (* insert the Cancel command as a button *)
    R.Assign(18, 11, 28, 13);
    Insert(New(PButton, Init(R, 'Cancel', cmCancel, bfNormal)));
```

```
      (* insert the question InputLine with a label *)
      R.Assign(2, 5, 29, 6);
      Q := New(PInputLine, Init(R, QAMaxLen));
      Insert(Q);
      R.Assign(2, 4, 12, 5);
      Insert(New(PLabel, Init(R, 'Question:', Q)));

      (* give values to the input lines *)
      EditData.Quest := ACard^.GetQuestion;
      EditData.Ans := ACard^.GetAnswer;
      SetData(EditData);
      End;

   (* execute the dialog box *)
   Control := DeskTop^.ExecView(Dialog);

   If Control <> cmCancel Then
     Begin

     (* save the information entered *)
     Dialog^.GetData(EditData);
     ACard^.SetQuestion(EditData.Quest);
     ACard^.SetAnswer(EditData.Ans);
     ToSet.Replace(ACard);
     End
   Else

     (* ignore the information entered and remove the card *)
     ToSet.Delete(ACard);
Until Control = cmCancel;
End;
```

This procedure starts by creating a dialog box. It then adds seven objects to the box. The first is the card number. Because this number cannot be changed by the user, the **PStaticText** object is used.

The last two objects actually go near the top of the dialog box. They are added last because they are the default items. These objects consist of a **TInputLine**, used to enter data, and a **TLabel**, which is a label for the input line. The label is linked to the input line object so that when the user tabs to that item, the label is highlighted. The rest of the objects are another input line and label pair, and two buttons.

Once you define a dialog box that requires data entry, you must assign initial values to entry areas. This process requires the definition of the **TEditData** record. After you assign values to the fields in this record, a call to the **SetData** method stores the data in the internal structures of the dialog box.

The **ExecView** method is called after the data values are set. This method does all of the I/O for the dialog box. It terminates only when the user presses one of the two buttons. The value of the button pressed is returned as the value of the function.

If the user presses the OK button, the **GetData** method is called to retrieve the values entered. Those values are then used in a call to the **Replace** method of the flash card set. The entire sequence is placed in a repeat loop to allow the user to enter multiple cards.

For the display of the flash cards, a different methodology was selected. Since there is one dialog box for the question and one for the answer, the two must work together. One way to accomplish this is to define global variables for the dialog boxes and process events outside the dialog boxes rather than within them. Here are the required global variables:

```
Var
  TheCard : PFlashCard;

Const
  QBox : PDialog = nil;
  ABox : PDialog = nil;
```

The first dialog box of the pair is the one that displays the question side of a flash card. Its dialog box looks like this:

```
Procedure ShowQuestion;

Var
  R : TRect;
  Control : Word;
  CardNumber : String;

Begin

(* create the dialog box *)
R.Assign(5, 2, 75, 11);
QBox := New(PDialog, Init(R, 'Question'));
With QBox^ Do
  Begin

  (* insert the question as static text *)
  R.Assign(4, 2, 63, 3);
  Insert(New(PStaticText, Init(R, TheCard^.GetQuestion)));

  (* include a Cancel button to allow the user to stop *)
  R.Assign(40, 5, 50, 7);
  Insert(New(PButton, Init(R, 'Cancel', cmCancel, bfNormal)));
```

```
(* include a Show Answer button for the ShowAnswer command *)
R.Assign(3, 5, 18, 7);
Insert(New(PButton, Init(R, 'Show ~A~nswer',
                         cmShowAnswer, bfDefault)));

(* insert the card number as static text *)
R.Assign(55, 5, 65, 6);
Str(TheCard^.GetNumber, CardNumber);
Insert(New(PStaticText, Init(R, 'Card: '+ CardNumber)));
End;

(* add the dialog box to the desktop (don't make it modal) *)
Desktop^.Insert(QBox);
End;
```

The dialog box itself has no new types of items—it has two static texts
and two buttons. The user cannot enter any data, so much of the code in
the previous dialog box is not required. You may have noticed a new
command constant: **cmShowAnswer**. There is no menu or status line
entry for this command, but it is required for the implementation.

Instead of calling **ExecView** to add the dialog box to the desktop,
this procedure calls **Insert**. The **Insert** method adds the dialog box, but
it allows events to occur outside of the box. This is the nonmodal form of
a dialog box. In this case, it was required because you don't want the
question box to be erased when the answer is displayed. Modal views
are closed before control is passed back to the caller.

If the user selects the Show Answer button, the program displays
the answer side of the flash card. The following procedure does this:

```
Procedure ShowAnswer;

Var
  R : TRect;
  Control : Word;

Begin

(* create the dialog box *)
R.Assign(5, 13, 75, 22);
ABox := New(PDialog, Init(R, 'Answer'));
With ABox^ Do
  Begin

  (* insert the answer as static text *)
  R.Assign(4, 2, 63, 3);
  Insert(New(PStaticText, Init(R, TheCard^.GetAnswer)));

  (* include a Next Question button *)
  R.Assign(25, 5, 42, 7);
```

```
      Insert(New(PButton, Init(R, '~N~ext Question',
                               cmNextCard, bfNormal)));

      (* include a Cancel button *)
      R.Assign(47, 5, 58, 7);
      Insert(New(PButton, Init(R, 'Cancel', cmCancel, bfNormal)));

      (* include a Random Question button *)
      R.Assign(3, 5, 23, 7);
      Insert(New(PButton, Init(R, '~R~andom Question',
                            cmRandomCard, bfDefault)));
      End;

(* add the dialog box to the desktop *)
DeskTop^.Insert(ABox);
End;
```

The dialog box itself presents nothing new. The logic is defined by the events that will occur when the user presses any of the various buttons.

Before examining that logic, study the last three command procedures:

```
Procedure NextCard(Var TheSet : TFlashCardSet);

Begin
TheCard := TheSet.NextCard;
RemoveBoxes;
ShowQuestion;
End;

(*********************************************)

Procedure RandomCard(Var TheSet : TFlashCardSet);

Begin
TheCard := TheSet.AnyCard;
RemoveBoxes;
ShowQuestion;
End;

(*********************************************)

Procedure RemoveBoxes;

Begin
Desktop^.Delete(ABox);
If ABox <> Nil Then
  Begin
  Dispose(ABox, Done);
  ABox := Nil;
  End;
```

```
Desktop^.Delete(QBox);
If QBox <> Nil Then
  Begin;
  Desktop^.Delete(QBox);
  Dispose(QBox, Done);
  QBox := Nil;
  End;
End;
```

The last procedure, **RemoveBoxes**, is also not part of the main menu, but it was added to support the nonmodal dialog boxes.

Here is how the commands work together:

1. The user starts by selecting **Random Card** or **Next Card**. Either of these clears the desktop and displays a question.

2. If the user wants to see the answer, that user presses the button, generating the **cmShowAnswer** event, which displays the answer.

3. If the user does not want to see the answer, the user can do one of three things:

• Press the **Cancel** button, which clears the desktop.

• Enter F8 or the **Random Card** menu command, which displays another question without showing the answer.

• Enter F9 or the **Next Card** menu command, which displays the next question without showing the answer. Presumably the user would use one of these last two options when the answer is obvious.

4. Once the answer side of the card is displayed, the user has the same three options, but these options are all included as buttons in the dialog box.

TButton Object Summary   **DIALOGS.TPU**

Heritage

TButton → TView → TObject

Primary Method

```
Constructor Init(Var Bounds : TRect; ATitle: TTitleStr;
        ACommand : Word; AFlags : Byte);
```

Creates a button object for insertion into a dialog box. Each button has a name and an event command (raised if the button is "pushed").

Related Constants

```
bfNormal = $00;
```

Flag for non-default, centered buttons.

```
bfDefault = $01;
```

Flag for default, centered buttons.

```
bfLeftJust = $02;
```

Flag for non-default, left-justified buttons.

```
bfDefault + bfLeftJust
```

Combination for default, left-justified buttons.

Other Methods

```
Destructor Done; Virtual;
```

Disposes of the fields for the button.

```
Procedure Draw; Virtual;
```

Called internally to display the button.

```
Function GetPalette: PPalette; Virtual;
```

Can be overridden to change the button's color scheme.

```
Procedure HandleEvent(Var Event : TEvent); Virtual;
```

Called internally to determine if the button was pressed.

```
Constructor Load(Var S : TStream);
```

Called internally to load a button from the stream.

```
Procedure MakeDefault(Enable : Boolean);
```

Can be called to make this button the default (or take away the default attribute).

```
Procedure  SetState(AState : Word; Enable : Boolean; Virtual;
```

Called internally to change the state of the button.

```
Procedure Store(Var S : TStream);
```

Called internally to send the button to the stream.

TInputLine Object Summary   DIALOGS.TPU

Heritage

TInputLine → TView → TObject

Primary Method

```
Constructor Init(Var Bounds : TRect; AMaxLen: Integer);
```

Creates an input line object that will allow input up to **AMaxLen** characters.

Other Methods

```
Function DataSize : Word; Virtual;
```

Called internally to get the maximum size of the input line. Can be overridden when creating a descendant object that handles other data types.

```
Destructor Done; Virtual;
```

Disposes of the input line object.

```
Procedure Draw; Virtual;
```

Called internally to display the input line. Can be overridden when creating a descendant object that handles other data types.

```
Procedure GetData(Var Rec); Virtual;
```

Can be used to convert a data type to a string suitable for editing.

```
Function GetPalette : PPalette; Virtual;
```

Can be used to change the input line's color scheme.

```
Procedure HandleEvent(Var Event : TEvent); Virtual;
```

Called internally to recognize events inside the input line.

```
Constructor Load(Var S : TStream);
```

Called internally to load an input line from the stream.

```
Procedure SelectAll(Enable : Boolean);
```

Highlights the entire input line, or unhighlights it.

```
Procedure SetData(Var Rec); Virtual;
```

Can be used to convert the input string into a user-defined data type.

```
Procedure  SetState(AState : Word; Enable  :  Boolean); Virtual;
```

Called internally to change the state of the input line.

```
Procedure Store(Var S : TStream);
```

Called internally to send an input line to the stream.

TLabel Object Summary   DIALOGS.TPU

Heritage

TLabel → TStaticText → TView → TObject

Primary Method

```
Constructor Init(Var Bounds : TRect; AText : String;
        ALink : PView);
```

Creates a label object that will be highlighted when the **ALink** view is selected.

Other Methods

```
Destructor Done; Virtual;
```

Disposes of the label object.

```
Procedure Draw; Virtual;
```

Called internally to display the label.

```
Function GetPalette : PPalette; Virtual;
```

Can be used to change the label's color scheme.

```
Procedure HandleEvent(Var Event : TEvent); Virtual;
```

Called internally to recognize events inside the label.

```
Constructor Load(Var S : TStream);
```

Called internally to load a label from the stream.

```
Procedure Store(Var S : TStream);
```

Called internally to send a label to the stream.

TStaticText Object Summary   DIALOGS.TPU

Heritage

TStaticText → TView → TObject

Primary Method

```
Constructor Init(Var Bounds : TRect; AMaxLen: Integer);
```

Creates a line of static (nonselectable, nonchangeable) text.

Other Methods

```
Destructor Done; Virtual;
```

Disposes of the static text object.

```
Procedure Draw; Virtual;
```

Called internally to display the static text.

```
Function GetPalette : PPalette; Virtual;
```

Can be used to change the input line's color scheme.

```
Procedure GetText(Var S : String); Virtual;
```

Called internally to obtain the stored string.

```
Constructor Load(Var S : TStream);
```

Called internally to load static text from the stream.

```
Procedure Store(Var S : TStream);
```

Called internally to send static text to the stream.

TCheckBoxes Object Summary   DIALOGS.TPU

Heritage
TCheckBoxes → TCluster → TView → TObject

Primary Inherited Method
Inherited from **TCluster** (see **TCluster** summary):

```
Constructor Init(Var Bounds : TRect;  AStrings : PSItem);
```

Other Methods

```
Procedure Draw; Virtual;
```

Called internally to display the check boxes.

```
Function Mark(Item : Integer) : Boolean; Virtual;
```

Called internally to see if an item is checked.

```
Procedure Press(Item : Integer); Virtual;
```

Called internally to toggle an item.

TRadioButtons Object Summary   DIALOGS.TPU

Heritage

TRadioButtons → TCluster → TView → TObject

Primary Inherited Method

Inherited from **TCluster** (see **TCluster** summary):

```
Constructor Init(Var Bounds : TRect;  AStrings : PSItem);
```

Other Methods

```
Procedure Draw; Virtual;
```

Called internally to display the radio buttons.

```
Function Mark(Item : Integer) : Boolean; Virtual;
```

Called internally to see if the *n*th item is selected.

```
Procedure MovedTo(Item : Integer); Virtual;
```

Called internally to tab over to the *n*th item.

```
Procedure Press(Item : Integer); Virtual;
```

Called internally when a button is pressed.

```
Procedure SetData(Var Rec); Virtual;
```

Called internally to copy button information into internal fields.

TCluster Object Summary   DIALOGS.TPU

Heritage

TCluster → TView → TObject

Primary Method

```
Constructor Init(Var Bounds : TRect;  AStrings : PSItem);
```

Creates a cluster object. Clusters are abstract objects used to define check boxes and radio buttons.

Related Data Types

```
PSItem = ^TSItem;
TSItem = Record
  Value : PString;              (* PString = ^String *)
  Next : PSItem;
  End;
```

Defines a linked list of strings for cluster objects.

Related Function

```
Function NewSItem(Str : String;  ANext : PSItem) : PSItem;
```

Allocates memory and assigns a string for inclusion into a **TSItem** record.

Other Methods

```
Function DataSize : Word; Virtual;
```

Called internally to get the number of items in the cluster.

```
Destructor Done; Virtual;
```

Disposes of the cluster object.

```
Procedure DrawBox; Virtual;
```

Called internally to display the box next to an item.

```
Procedure GetData(Var Rec); Virtual;
```

Called internally to copy cluster information from internal fields.

```
Function GetHelpCtx : Word; Virtual;
```

Allows for different help contexts based on which cluster item is selected.

```
Function GetPalette : PPalette; Virtual;
```

Can be used to change the cluster's color scheme.

```
Procedure HandleEvent(Var Event : TEvent); Virtual;
```

Called internally to recognize events inside the cluster.

```
Constructor Load(Var S : TStream);
```

Called internally to load a cluster from the stream.

```
Function Mark(Item : Integer): Boolean; Virtual;
```

Called internally to see which items are marked.

```
Procedure MovedTo(Item : Integer); Virtual;
```

Called internally to tab over to the nth item.

```
Procedure Press(Item : Integer); Virtual;
```

Called internally to select the nth item.

```
Procedure SetData(Var Rec); Virtual;
```

Called internally to copy cluster information into internal structures.

```
Procedure  SetState(AState : Word; Enable  :  Boolean); Virtual;
```

Called internally to change the state of the cluster.

```
Procedure Store(Var S : TStream);
```

Called internally to send a cluster to the stream.

TListBox Object Summary   DIALOGS.TPU

Heritage

TListBox → TListViewer → TView → TObject

Primary Methods

```
Constructor Init(Var Bounds : TRect; ANumCols : Word;
         VScrollBar : PScrollBar);
```

Creates a list box with a given size and number of columns. Can include an optional vertical scroll bar.

```
Procedure NewList(AList : PCollection); Virtual;
```

Assigns the items in a collection to the list box. See discussion of collections earlier in this chapter.

Other Methods

```
Function DataSize : Word; Virtual;
```

Called internally to get the current size of the list box.

```
Destructor Done; Virtual;
```

Disposes of the list box object.

```
Procedure GetData(Var Rec); Virtual;
```

Called internally to copy list items from internal structures.

```
Function  GetText(Item, : Integer;
          MaxLen : Integer) : String; Virtual;
```

Called internally to get the nth item in the list.

```
Constructor Load(Var S : TStream);
```

Called internally to load a list box from the stream.

```
Procedure SetData(Var Rec); Virtual;
```

Called internally to copy list items to internal structures.

```
Procedure Store(Var S : TStream);
```

Called internally to send a list box to the stream.

THistory Object Summary   DIALOGS.TPU

Heritage

THistory → TView → TObject

Primary Method

```
Constructor Init(Var Bounds : TRect;
          ALink : PInputLine; AHistoryID : Word);
```

Creates a pick-list associated with a given input line. The **AHistoryID** parameter allows multiple input lines to share the same history list. The list appears as a single icon (down arrow) until the icon is selected.

Other Methods

```
Procedure Draw; Virtual;
```

Called internally to display the history icon.

```
Function GetPalette : PPalette; Virtual;
```

Can be used to change the history icon's color scheme.

```
Constructor Load(Var S : TStream);
```

Called internally to load a history list from the stream.

```
Procedure Store(Var S : TStream);
```

Called internally to send a history list to the stream.

TFileDialog Object Summary   STDDLG.TPU

Heritage

TFileDialog → TDialog → TWindow → TGroup → TView → TObject

Primary Methods

```
Constructor Init(AWildCard : WildStr;
          ATitle : String;  InputName : String;
          Buttons : Word;  HistoryId : Byte);
```

Creates a dialog box with a list box for files, a history list, and one or more standard buttons.

```
Procedure GetFileName(Var S : PathStr);
```

Returns the name of the file chosen by the user.

Related Type

```
WildStr = Dos.PathStr;
```

Defines the initial value of the filename, which normally includes wildcard characters.

Related Constants

```
fdOkButton = 1;
```

Flag to include an **OK** button.

```
fdOpenButton = 2;
```

Flag to include an **Open** button.

```
fdReplaceButton = 4;
```

Flag to include a **Replace** button.

```
fdClearButton = 8;
```

Flag to include a **Clear** button.

Other Methods

```
Destructor Done; Virtual;
```

Disposes of the file dialog box.

```
Procedure GetData(Var Rec); Virtual;
```

Called internally to retrieve data from internal structures.

```
Procedure HandleEvent(Var Event : TEvent); Virtual;
```

Called internally to handle events within the file dialog box.

```
Constructor Load(Var S : TStream);
```

Called internally to read a file dialog box from the stream.

```
Procedure Store(Var S : TStream);
```

Called internally to write file dialog box data to the stream.

```
Function Valid(Command : Word) : Boolean; Virtual;
```

Called internally to determine which commands are valid.

Using Streams

The major commands remaining are those that save cards to a file and reload them. Turbo Vision provides an extremely powerful object, called a stream, to support this. A *stream* is a path that an object can follow to or from another location. The primary support for streams is for DOS files and EMS memory. Streams are as polymorphic as collections, allowing you to use the same stream for different object types.

The flash card application uses a buffered DOS file stream. This object type is called **TBufStream**. In order to use this stream in objects you create, you must register the objects into Turbo Vision. The first step in registration is to define a registration record. Here is the record for a flash card:

```
Const
(* for Stream registration *)
  RFlashCard : TStreamRec = (
    ObjType: 1050;
    VmtLink: Ofs(TypeOf(TFlashCard)^);
    Load: @TFlashCard.Load;
    Store: @TFlashCard.Store);
```

The first field of the registration record is a unique object ID. The valid values go from 1000 to 65,535. The second field points to the VMT of the object. The final two fields are the addresses of the procedures that access streams for this object type.

The implementation of the **Load** and **Store** procedures for this object type is shown here:

```
Constructor TFlashCard.Load(Var S : TStream);

Begin
S.Read(Number, SizeOf(Number));
S.Read(Question, SizeOf(Question));
S.Read(Answer, SizeOf(Answer));
End;

(*********************************************)

Procedure TFlashCard.Store(Var S : TStream);

Begin
S.Write(Number, SizeOf(Number));
S.Write(Question, SizeOf(Question));
S.Write(Answer, SizeOf(Answer));
End;
```

These procedures are implemented primarily by calling **TStream
.Read** and **TStream.Write** for each data field in the object type. If the
object is a descendant of another object, these overridden methods must
call the respective procedures of their ancestors.

The **TFlashCardSet** object type also requires stream registration
and support procedures:

```
Const
(* for Stream registration *)
  RFlashCardSet: TStreamRec = (
    ObjType: 140;
    VmtLink: Ofs(TypeOf(TFlashCardSet)^);
    Load: @TFlashCardSet.Load;
    Store: @TFlashCardSet.Store);

(*********************************************)

Constructor TFlashCardSet.Load(Var S : TStream);

Begin
TCollection.Load(S);
CurrentCard := -1;
Randomize;
End;

(*********************************************)

Procedure TFlashCardSet.Store(Var S : TStream);

Begin
TCollection.Store(S);
End;
```

Once you have set up each object in your application hierarchy, you must register the streams. This is often done in a single procedure at the start of the application. All object types that will be used in the stream must be registered. For the flash card application, registration is required for types **TFlashCard**, **TFlashCardSet**, and **TCollection**:

```
Procedure RegisterStreams;

Begin
RegisterType(RCollection);
RegisterType(RFlashCard);
RegisterType(RFlashCardSet);
End;
```

In the flash card program, streams are used for the **Save File** and **Open File** commands. Only files that were saved using the application can be read into the application.

Turbo Vision provides the entire dialog box used in the IDE for use in your own program. This object type, **TFileDialog**, was summarized earlier in the chapter. Writing a procedure to use this dialog box is fairly simple:

```
Procedure SaveFile(Var TheSet : TFlashCardSet);

Var
  SaveBox : PFileDialog;
  FCStream : TBufStream;
  Control : Word;

Begin

(* use the standard Save File dialog box *)
New(SaveBox, Init(TheFileName, 'Save File As',
     'Save File Name', fdOkButton, 1));
Control := DeskTop^.ExecView (SaveBox);
If Control <> cmCancel Then
  Begin

  (* save the set using a buffered stream *)
  SaveBox^.GetFileName(TheFileName);
  FCStream.Init(TheFileName, stCreate, 512);
  FCStream.Put(@TheSet);
  FCStream.Done;
  End;
End;
```

The dialog box created by this code is shown here:

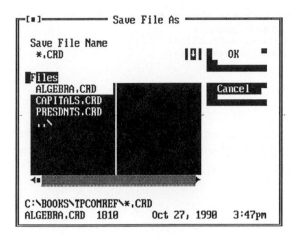

The **SaveFile** procedure starts by creating the dialog box. Required parameters for this initialization are the default filename, the title of the dialog box, a label for the filename, a list of buttons to be used, and a history list ID. The dialog box is then executed, and it returns an event based on the button pressed by the user.

Assuming the user wants to save the card set to the stream, the procedure gets the name of the file, opens the file as a stream, and calls **TBufStream.Put** with the address of the flash card set. The **Put** method calls the **Store** procedure for the **TFlashCardSet** object type, which in turn calls the **Store** procedure for each flash card.

Loading data from the stream follows a very similar process. First a dialog box obtains the filename. Second, a stream is created based on the filename. Finally, the data is loaded from the stream. Here is the code for opening a flash card file:

```
Procedure OpenFile(Var NewSet : TFlashCardSet);

Var
  OpenBox : PFileDialog;
  FCStream : TBufStream;
  Control : Word;
  PFCSet : PFlashCardSet;

Begin

(* use the standard Open File dialog box *)
New(OpenBox, Init('*.CRD', 'Open File', 'Card File Name',
     fdOkButton + fdOpenButton, 1));
Control := DeskTop^.ExecView (OpenBox);
If Control <> cmCancel Then
  Begin
```

```
(* read the file as a buffered stream *)
OpenBox^.GetFileName(TheFileName);
FCStream.Init(TheFileName, stOpenRead, 512);
PFCSet := PFlashCardSet(FCStream.Get);
NewSet := PFCSet^;
FCStream.Done;
End;
End;
```

The final step in making the entire flash card application work is to modify the main application methods to support the actual commands.

First you need a few variables:

```
Var
  FlashCardApp : TFlashCardApp;
  FlashCards : TFlashCardSet;
  OneCard : TFlashCard;
```

Next, you must add the required parameters to the event commands and add support for the new commands discussed earlier:

```
Procedure TFlashCardApp.HandleEvent(Var Event: TEvent);

Begin
TApplication.HandleEvent(Event);
If Event.What = evCommand Then
  Begin
  Case Event.Command Of
    cmFileOpen   : OpenFile(FlashCards);
    cmFileSave   : SaveFile(FlashCards);
    cmEditAdd    : AddCard(FlashCards);
    cmEditChange : ChangeCard;
    cmEditDelete : DeleteCard(FlashCards);
    cmNextCard   : NextCard(FlashCards);
    cmRandomCard : RandomCard(FlashCards);
    cmShowAnswer : ShowAnswer;
    cmCancel     : RemoveBoxes;
  Else
    Exit;
    End;
  ClearEvent(Event);
  End;
End;
```

Finally, you must add any other required initializations to the main program. The final program code will look like this:

```
Begin
FlashCards.Init;
RegisterStreams;
```

```
FlashCardApp.Init;
FlashCardApp.Run;
FlashCardApp.Done;
End.
```

You can now probably take any or all of this flash card application and use it to help you develop your own applications. Remember that many things (like error checking) were removed from the program to maintain simplicity. Also keep in mind that there are many other ways this same application could have been developed. Feel free to improve it in any way you wish.

TBufStream Object Summary   OBJECTS.TPU

Heritage

TBufStream → TDosStream → TStream → TObject

Primary Methods

```
Constructor Init(FileName : FNameStr;  Mode, Size : Word);
```

Creates or opens a file as a steam, using the given file mode and buffer size.

```
Destructor Done; Virtual;
```

Closes the file and flushes the buffer.

Primary Inherited Methods

Inherited from **TStream** (see **TStream** summary):

```
Function Get : PObject;
Procedure Put(P : PObject);
```

Related Constants

```
stCreate = $3C00;
```

Mode for creating or overwriting a file.

```
stOpenRead = $3D00;
```

Mode for opening a file as read-only.

```
stOpenWrite = $3D01;
```

Mode for opening a file as write-only.

```
stOpen = $3D02;
```

Mode for opening a file as read/write.

Related Types

```
FNameStr = String[79];
```

Limits filenames to 79 characters.

Other Methods

```
Procedure Flush; Virtual;
```

Called internally to flush the file buffer.

```
Function GetPos : Longint; Virtual;
```

Called internally to determine the file position.

```
Function GetSize : Longint; Virtual;
```

Called internally to determine the file size.

```
Procedure Read(Var Buf; Count : Word); Virtual;
```

Called internally to read bytes from the file.

```
Procedure Seek(Pos : Longint); Virtual;
```

Called internally to go to a file position.

```
Procedure Truncate; Virtual;
```

Called internally to delete to the end of the file.

```
Procedure Write(Var Buf; Count : Word); Virtual;
```

Called internally to write bytes to the file.

TEmsStream Object Summary   OBJECTS.TPU

Heritage

TEmsStream → TStream → TObject

Primary Methods

```
Constructor Init(MinSize : Longint);
```

Creates an EMS stream using the given number of bytes.

```
Destructor Done; Virtual;
```

Must be called to release EMS memory.

Primary Inherited Methods

Inherited from **TStream** (see **TStream** summary):

```
Function Get : PObject;
Procedure Put(P : PObject);
```

Other Methods

```
Function GetPos : Longint; Virtual;
```

Called internally to determine the current EMS address.

```
Function GetSize : Longint; Virtual;
```

Called internally to determine the size of the EMS stream.

```
Procedure Read(Var Buf; Count : Word); Virtual;
```

Called internally to read bytes from EMS memory.

```
Procedure Seek(Pos : Longint); Virtual;
```

Called internally to go to a specific address in EMS memory.

```
Procedure Truncate; Virtual;
```

Called internally to remove all data past the current EMS address.

```
Procedure Write(Var Buf; Count : Word); Virtual;
```

Called internally to write bytes to EMS memory.

TStream Object Summary   OBJECTS.TPU

Heritage

TStream → TObject

Primary Methods

```
Function Get : PObject;
```

Reads an object from the stream by calling the **Load** constructor for each part of the object.

```
Procedure Put(P : PObject);
```

Writes an object to the stream by calling the **Store** procedure for each part of the object.

```
Procedure Read(Var Buf; Count: Word); Virtual;
```

Reads a variable of a given size from the stream. Called by each **Load** procedure.

```
Procedure Write(Var Buf; Count : Word); Virtual;
```

Writes a variable of a given size to the stream. Called by each **Store** procedure.

Related Procedure

```
Procedure RegisterType(Var S: TStreamRec);
```

Allows an object type inherited from **TObject** to be loaded and saved using streams.

Related Types

```
PStreamRec = ^TStreamRec;
TStreamRec = Record
  ObjType : Word;               (* unique id (> 100) *)
  VmtLink : Word;        (* offset of the object type *)
  Load : Pointer;        (* address of the Load method *)
  Store : Pointer;      (* address of the Store method *)
  Next : Word;                      (* internal use *)
  End;
```

Defines the stream characteristics of an object.

Other Methods

Stream objects are almost never created explicitly, so their internal methods are of little value. See the methods for each descendant object type.

Other Turbo Vision Objects

The final four Turbo Vision major objects are useful for development of applications but were not used in the flash card program.

When you want to display a large amount of text or allow the user to enter a large amount of text, you should create a descendant of **TWindow**. Windows are special cases of groups: They are enclosed in a frame, numbered, and often have scroll bars to support traversal using a mouse. If the information in the window will not fit on the screen at once, a view object of type **TScroller** must be inserted into the window. The physical scroll bars are type **TScrollBar**. For an example of a scrollable window, study the **TVGUID08.PAS** program in the \TVISION subdirectory of your Turbo Pascal directory.

A resource is a special case of a buffered DOS stream. It is used to store and retrieve user-interface objects such as menus and dialog boxes. You can place the code that creates these objects into a separate program that also writes the objects to a resource file. Your main application program would then simply read the objects from the resource file. This makes your programs more modular and also decreases the size of your main executable program.

TWindow Object Summary   VIEWS.TPU

Heritage

TWindow → TGroup → TView → TObject

Primary Methods

```
Constructor Init(Var Bounds : TRect; ATitle: TTitleStr;
          ANumber : Integer);
```

Creates a window in the given location, with the given title and window number.

```
Function StandardScrollBar (AObjects : Word) : PScrollBar;
```

Creates and inserts a scroll bar in the window.

Related Constants

```
wfMove = 1;
```

Allows the window to be moved around the desktop.

```
wfGrow = 2;
```

Allows the window to be resized.

```
wfClose = 4;
```

Adds a close icon to the upper left corner of the window.

```
wfZoom = 8;
```

Adds a zoom icon to the upper right corner of the window.

Other Methods

```
Procedure Close; Virtual;
```

Called internally to close the window.

```
Descructor Done; Virtual;
```

Disposes of a window object.

```
Function GetPalette : PPalette; Virtual;
```

Can be overridden to change the window's colors.

```
Function GetTitle(MaxSize : Integer): TTitleStr; Virtual;
```

Called internally to get the window title.

```
Procedure HandleEvent(Var Event : TEvent); Virtual;
```

Called internally to handle events that occur within the window, such as moving, sizing, and zooming

```
Procedure InitFrame; Virtual;
```

Called internally to create a window frame.

```
Constructor Load(Var S : TStream);
```

Called internally to read a window from the stream.

```
Procedure SetState(AState : Word; Enable : Boolean); Virtual;
```

Called internally to change the state of the window.

```
Procedure SizeLimits(Var Min, Max : TPoint); Virtual;
```

Changes the size limits of the window.

```
Procedure Store(Var S : TStream);
```

Called internally to write a window to the stream.

```
Procedure Zoom; Virtual;
```

Called internally to zoom the window.

TScroller Object Summary   **VIEWS.TPU**

Heritage

TScroller → TView → TObject

Primary Methods

```
Constructor Init(Var Bounds : TRect; AHScrollBar,
        AVScrollBar : PScrollBar);
```

Creates a scroller within a window with optional scroll bars.

```
Procedure SetLimit(X, Y : Integer);
```

Sets the size of the data inside the scroll area (not the region of the
scroller itself).

Primary Inherited Methods

From **TView** (see **TView** summary):

```
Procedure Draw; Virtual;
```

Other Methods

```
Procedure ChangeBounds(Var Bounds : TRect); Virtual;
```

Called internally to change the size of the scroller.

```
Function GetPalette : PPalette; Virtual;
```

Can be overridden to change the scroller's colors.

```
Procedure HandleEvent(Var Event : TEvent); Virtual;
```

Called internally to handle scroller events.

```
Constructor Load(Var S : TStream);
```

Called internally to read a scroller object from the stream.

```
Procedure ScrollDraw; Virtual;
```

Called internally to redraw the scroller.

```
Procedure ScrollTo(X, Y : Integer);
```

Called internally to scroll to a different part of the view.

```
Procedure SetState(AState : Word; Enable : Boolean);
```

Called internally to change the state of the scroller.

```
Procedure Store(Var S : TStream);
```

Called internally to write a scroller to the stream.

TScrollBar Object Summary   *VIEWS.TPU*

Heritage
TScrollBar → TView → TObject

Related Constants
```
sbHorizontal = 0;
```

Allows a horizontal scroll bar to be included.

```
sbVertical = 1;
```

Allows a vertical scroll bar to be included.

```
sbHandleKeyboard = 2;
```

Allows support of keyboard commands for scrolling.

Other Methods
Objects of type **TScrollBar** are almost always created using the method **TWindow.StandardScrollBar**.

TResourceFile Object Summary   OBJECTS.TPU

Heritage

TResourceFile → TObject

Primary Methods

```
Constructor Init(AStream : PStream);
```

Initializes the resource file with a buffered DOS stream.

```
Function Get(Key : String): PObject;
```

Retrieves an object from the resource file.

```
Procedure Put(Item : PObject; Key : String);
```

Writes an object to a resource file, and assigns a key to the object.

Other Methods

```
Function Count : Integer;
```

Determines the number of objects in the resource file.

```
Procedure Delete(Key : String);
```

Deletes an object stored in a resource file.

```
Destructor Done; Virtual;
```

Disposes of a resource file after flushing the buffer.

```
Procedure Flush;
```

Flushes the buffer for the resource file if any changes were made.

```
Function KeyAt(I : Integer): String;
```

Can be used to determine the contents of a resource file.

```
Function SwitchTo(AStream : PStream; Pack : Boolean) : PStream;
```

Switches the resource file from one stream to another, packing the new file if desired.

Turbo Pascal Error Codes

Compiler Error Messages
Run-time Error Messages

Compiler Error Messages

Compiler error messages refer to problems in your code or programming environment that prevent Turbo Pascal from producing an executable file. In the integrated development environment, Turbo Pascal will attempt to locate the source-code location of the error.

1	Out of memory
2	Identifier expected
3	Unknown identifier
4	Duplicate identifier
5	Syntax error
6	Error in real constant
7	Error in integer constant
8	String constant exceeds line
9	Too many nested files
10	Unexpected end of file
11	Line too long
12	Type identifier expected
13	Too many open files
14	Invalid filename
15	File not found
16	Disk full
17	Invalid compiler directive
18	Too many files

19	Undefined type in pointer definition
20	Variable identifier expected
21	Error in type
22	Structure too large
23	Set base type out of range
24	File components may not be files or objects
25	Invalid string length
26	Type mismatch
27	Invalid subrange base type
28	Lower bound greater than upper bound
29	Ordinal type expected
30	Integer constant expected
31	Constant expected
32	Integer or real constant expected
33	Type identifier expected
34	Invalid function result type
35	Label identifier expected
36	Begin expected
37	End expected
38	Integer expression expected
39	Ordinal expression expected
40	Boolean expression expected
41	Operand types do not match operator
42	Error in expression
43	Illegal assignment
44	Field identifier expected
45	Object file too large
46	Undefined external
47	Invalid object-file record
48	Code segment too large
49	Data segment too large

50   Do expected
51   Invalid Public definition
52   Invalid Extrn definition
53   Too many Extrn definitions
54   Of expected
55   Interface expected
56   Invalid relocatable reference
57   Then expected
58   To or Downto expected
59   Undefined forward
60   Too many procedures
61   Invalid typecast
62   Division by zero
63   Invalid file type
64   Cannot read or write variables of this type
65   Pointer variable expected
66   String variable expected
67   String expression expected
68   Circular unit reference
69   Unit name mismatch
70   Unit version mismatch
71   Duplicate unit name
72   Unit file format error
73   Implementation expected
74   Constant and case types do not match
75   Record variable expected
76   Constant out of range
77   File variable expected
78   Pointer expression expected
79   Integer or real expression expected
80   Label not within current block

81	Label already defined
82	Undefined label in preceding statement part
83	Invalid @ argument
84	Unit expected
85	";" expected
86	":" expected
87	"," expected
88	"(" expected
89	")" expected
90	"=" expected
91	":=" expected
92	"[" or "(." expected
93	"]" or ".)" expected
94	"." expected
95	".." expected
96	Too many variables
97	Invalid For control variable
98	Integer variable expected
99	Files are not allowed here
100	String length mismatch
101	Invalid ordering of fields
102	String constant expected
103	Integer or Real variable expected
104	Ordinal variable expected
105	Inline error
106	Character expression expected
107	Too many relocation items
112	Case constant out of range
113	Error in statement
114	Cannot call an interrupt procedure

116	Must be in 8087 mode to compile this
117	Target address not found
118	Include files are not allowed here
120	Nil expected
121	Invalid qualifier
122	Invalid variable reference
123	Too many symbols
124	Statement part too long
126	Files must be Var parameters
127	Too many conditional symbols
128	Misplaced conditional directive
129	ENDIF directive missing
130	Error in initial conditional defines
131	Header does not match previous definition
132	Critical disk error
133	Cannot evaluate this expression
134	Expression incorrectly terminated
135	Invalid format specifier
136	Invalid indirect reference
137	Structured variables are not allowed here
138	Cannot evaluate without SYSTEM unit
139	Cannot access this symbol
140	Invalid floating-point operation
141	Cannot compile overlays to memory
142	Procedure or function variable expected
143	Invalid procedure or function reference
144	Cannot overlay this unit
147	Object type expected
148	Local object types are not allowed
149	VIRTUAL expected

150	Method identifier expected
151	Virtual constructors are not allowed
152	Constructor identifier expected
153	Destructor identifier expected
154	Fail only allowed within constructors
155	Invalid combination of opcode and operands
156	Memory reference expected
157	Cannot add or subtract relocatable symbols
158	Invalid register combination
159	286/287 Instructions are not enabled
160	Invalid symbol reference
161	Code generation error

Run-time Error Messages

A run-time error is an error condition that occurs while your program is running. When such an error occurs, Turbo Pascal displays this message:

Run-time error nnn at xxxx:yyyy

where **nnn** is the numeric code for the run-time error, **xxxx** is the program segment in which the error occurred, and **yyyy** is the offset of the location of the error.

DOS Errors

2	File not found
3	Path not found
4	Too many open files

5	File access denied
6	Invalid file handle
12	Invalid file access code
15	Invalid drive number
16	Cannot remove current directory
17	Cannot rename across drives

I/O Errors

100	Disk read error
101	Disk write error
102	File not assigned
103	File not open
104	File not open for input
105	File not open for output
106	Invalid numeric format

Critical Errors

150	Disk is write-protected
151	Unknown unit
152	Drive not ready
153	Unknown command
154	CRC error in data
155	Bad drive request structure length
156	Disk seek error
157	Unknown media type
158	Sector not found
159	Printer out of paper
160	Device write fault

161   Device read fault
162   Hardware failure

Fatal Errors

200   Division by zero
201   Range check error
202   Stack overflow error
203   Heap overflow error
204   Invalid pointer operation
205   Floating-point overflow
206   Floating-point underflow
207   Invalid floating-point operation
208   Overlay manager not installed
209   Overlay file read error
210   Object not initialized
211   Call to abstract method
212   Stream registration error
213   Collection index out of range
214   Collection overflow error

ASCII Codes for the PC

ASCII Value	Character	ASCII Value	Character
0	Null	12	Form-feed
1	☺	13	Carriage return
2	☻	14	♫
3	♥	15	☼
4	♦	16	►
5	♣	17	◄
6	♠	18	↕
7	Beep	19	‼
8	◘	20	π
9	Tab	21	§
10	Linefeed	22	▬
11	Cursor home	23	↨

Table B-1.   ASCII Codes for the PC

ASCII Value	Character	ASCII Value	Character
24	↑	58	:
25	↓	59	;
26	→	60	<
27	←	61	=
28	Cursor right	62	>
29	Cursor left	63	?
30	Cursor up	64	@
31	Cursor down	65	A
32	Space	66	B
33	!	67	C
34	"	68	D
35	#	69	E
36	$	70	F
37	%	71	G
38	&	72	H
39	'	73	I
40	(	74	J
41	)	75	K
42	*	76	L
43	+	77	M
44	,	78	N
45	-	79	O
46	.	80	P
47	/	81	Q
48	0	82	R
49	1	83	S
50	2	84	T
51	3	85	U
52	4	86	V
53	5	87	W
54	6	88	X
55	7	89	Y
56	8	90	Z
57	9	91	[

Table B-1. ASCII Codes for the PC *(continued)*

ASCII Value	Character	ASCII Value	Character
92	\	126	~
93	]	127	⌂
94	^	128	Ç
95	—	129	ü
96	'	130	é
97	a	131	â
98	b	132	ä
99	c	133	à
100	d	134	å
101	e	135	ç
102	f	136	ê
103	g	137	ë
104	h	138	è
105	i	139	ï
106	j	140	î
107	k	141	ì
108	l	142	Ä
109	m	143	Å
110	n	144	É
111	o	145	æ
112	p	146	Æ
113	q	147	ô
114	r	148	ö
115	s	149	ò
116	t	150	û
117	u	151	ù
118	v	152	ÿ
119	w	153	Ö
120	x	154	Ü
121	y	155	¢
122	z	156	£
123	{	157	¥
124	¦	158	Pt
125	}	159	f

Table B-1.   ASCII Codes for the PC (*continued*)

ASCII Value	Character	ASCII Value	Character
160	á	194	┬
161	í	195	├
162	ó	196	─
163	ú	197	┼
164	ñ	198	╞
165	Ñ	199	╟
166	a̲	200	╚
167	o̲	201	╔
168	¿	202	╩
169	⌐	203	╦
170	¬	204	╠
171	½	205	═
172	¼	206	╬
173	¡	207	╧
174	«	208	╨
175	»	209	╤
176	░	210	╥
177	▒	211	╙
178	▓	212	╘
179	│	213	╒
180	┤	214	╓
181	╡	215	╫
182	╢	216	╪
183	╖	217	┘
184	╕	218	┌
185	╣	219	█
186	║	220	▄
187	╗	221	▌
188	╝	222	▐
189	╜	223	▀
190	╛	224	α
191	┐	225	β
192	└	226	Γ
193	┴	227	π

Table B-1.   ASCII Codes for the PC (*continued*)

ASCII Value	Character	ASCII Value	Character
228	Σ	242	≥
229	σ	243	≤
230	μ	244	⌠
231	τ	245	⌡
232	φ	246	÷
233	θ	247	≈
234	Ω	248	°
235	δ	249	•
236	ϖ	250	·
237	∅	251	√
238	ε	252	^{n}
239	∩	253	^{2}
240	≡	254	■
241	±	255	(blank 'FF')

Table B-1.   ASCII Codes for the PC (*continued*)

The PC Keyboard

The computer keyboard produces codes that are associated with letters and symbols. One key, however, can produce a different set of codes when you press other keys at the same time. For example, the A key normally produces the letter "a" (ASCII code 97), but when pressed along with the SHIFT key, it produces the letter "A" (ASCII code 65). Two other keys—CTRL and ALT—produce even more codes.

Some keys, such as the function keys (F1 through F10), produce two codes: a scan code (#0) and another code that indicates the key pressed. To read keys that produce scan codes, use the following procedure:

```
Procedure Inkey(Var  ch : Char;
               Var fk : Boolean);
Begin
fk := False;
ch := ReadKey;
If ch = #0 Then
  Begin
  fk := True;
  ch := ReadKey;
  End;
End;
```

This procedure uses **ReadKey**, which is found in the CRT unit. When **fk** is TRUE, a scan-code key has been pressed and the ASCII code for that key is returned in **ch**. When **fk** is FALSE, a normal key has been pressed and the value is contained in **ch**.

The following table lists the keys on the PC keyboard and the codes they return.

Key	Normal		SHIFT		CTRL		ALT	
F1	0	59	0	84	0	94	0	104
F2	0	60	0	85	0	95	0	105
F3	0	61	0	86	0	96	0	106
F4	0	62	0	87	0	97	0	107
F5	0	63	0	88	0	98	0	108
F6	0	64	0	89	0	99	0	109
F7	0	65	0	90	0	100	0	110
F8	0	66	0	91	0	101	0	111
F9	0	67	0	92	0	102	0	112
F10	0	68	0	93	0	103	0	113
←	0	75		52	0	115		none
→	0	77		54	0	116		none
↑	0	72		56		none		none
↓	0	80		50		none		none
HOME	0	71		55	0	119		none
END	0	79		49	0	117		none
PGUP	0	73		57	0	132		none
PGDN	0	81		51	0	118		none
INS	0	82		48		none		none
DEL	0	83		46	0	255		none
ESC		27		27		27		none
BACKSPACE		8		8		127		none
TAB		9	0	15		none		none
ENTER		13		13		10		none
A		97		65		1	0	30
B		98		66		2	0	48
C		99		67		3	0	46
D		100		68		4	0	32
E		101		69		5	0	18
F		102		70		6	0	33
G		103		71		7	0	34
H		104		72		8	0	35
I		105		73		9	0	23
J		106		74		10	0	36
K		107		75		11	0	37

Key	Normal	SHIFT	CTRL		ALT	
L	108	76		12	0	38
M	109	77		13	0	50
N	110	78		14	0	49
O	111	79		15	0	24
P	112	80		16	0	25
Q	113	81		17	0	16
R	114	82		18	0	19
S	115	83		19	0	31
T	116	84		20	0	20
U	117	85		21	0	22
V	118	86		22	0	47
W	119	87		23	0	17
X	120	88		24	0	45
Y	121	89		25	0	21
Z	122	90		26	0	44
[	91	123		27	none	
\	92	124		28	none	
]	93	125		29	none	
'	96	126		none	none	
0	48	41		none	0	129
1	49	33		none	0	120
2	50	64	0	3	0	121
3	51	35		none	0	122
4	52	36		none	0	123
5	53	37		none	0	124
6	54	94		30	0	125
7	55	38		none	0	126
8	56	42		none	0	127
9	57	40		none	0	128
*	42	none	0	114	none	
Keypad +	43	43		none	none	
Keypad −	45	45		none	none	
=	61	43		none	0	131
/	47	63		none	none	
;	59	58		none	none	
−	45	95		31	0	130

Turbo Pascal Reserved Words

The following are Turbo Pascal reserved words.

Absolute   Declares a variable that resides at a specific memory location. For example:

```
Var
  R : Real;
  X : Integer Absolute R;         (* X shares memory with R *)
  Y : Integer Absolute 0000:0000; (* Y is located at segment 0
                                      at offset 0 *)
```

And   Combines two Boolean expressions such that both must be true for the entire expression to be true. For example:

```
If (A > B) And (C > D) Then ...
```

And also compares two bytes or integers and returns a third byte or integer. A bit in the resulting integer is turned on only if both bits in the same position are on in the first and second integers.

Array   Defines a data type that repeats its structure a specified number of times. For example:

```
Var
  i : Array [1..20] Of Integer;
```

defines a data item that consists of 20 integers.

Asm   Indicates that the code that follows is to be interpreted as assembly language instructions.

Begin   Indicates the beginning of a block of code.

Case   A control structure that branches conditionally based on the value of a scalar. For example:

```
Var
  i : Integer;

  Case I Of
  1 :
    Begin
    { Statements }
    End;

  2..3 :
    Begin
    { Statements }
    End;

  4 :
    Begin
    { Statements }
    End;

  Else
    Begin
    { Statements }
    End;

  End;
```

Const   Defines a data item as either a typed or untyped constant. For example:

```
Const
  i = 100;              (* Untyped constant *)
  j : Integer = 100; (* Typed constant *)
```

Constructor   Defines a method (in an object) that is used to initialize the virtual methods within an object.

Destructor   Defines a method (in an object) that is used to remove virtual methods from the virtual method table, usually before deallocating a dynamically allocated object.

Div   Performs integer division.

Do   Used with looping control structures. For example:

```
For i := 1 To 10 Do ...
```

```
While i < 11 Do ...
```

DownTo   Used in For-Do loops where the counter is decremented. For example:

```
For i := 100 DownTo 1 Do ...
```

Else   Executes a block of code when an **If-Then** statement is FALSE. For example:

```
If (A < B) Then
  Begin
  { Statements }
  End
Else
  Begin
  { Statements }
  End;
```

End   Denotes the end of a block of code, the end of a case statement, the end of a record definition, or the end of a program.

External   Tells Turbo Pascal to look in an object file for the executable code for a procedure. For example:

```
{$L ASM_PROC}
Procedure ExtProc; External;
```

File   A data type that stores data on a disk.

For   Used in For-Do loops. For example:

```
For i := 1 To 100 Do ...
```

Forward   Declares the heading of a procedure before the actual procedure is defined. The full heading is declared in the **Forward** statement. Later, when the body of the procedure is declared, only the procedure name is used. For example:

```
Procedure X(i,j : Integer) : Forward;

{ Statements }

Procedure X;
Begin
{ Statements }
End;
```

Function   Declares a subroutine to be a function. Functions return values of a specific data type. For example:

```
Function Add(a,b : Integer) : Integer;
Begin
Add := a + b;
End;
```

Goto   Transfers control to the location of the label contained in the **Goto** statement. For example:

```
Label
  EndProc; (* Label declaration *)

Begin
For i := 1 To 1000 Do
  Begin
  j := j + 1;
  If j > 1000 Then
    Goto EndProc;
  End;

EndProc;
End;
```

If   Used in **If-Then** statements. For example:

```
If (A < B) Then ...
```

Implementation   Indicates the beginning of the implementation section of a unit.

In   Tests for set inclusion. For example:

```
Var
  Ch : Char;

If Ch In ['A'..'Z'] Then ...
```

Inline   Tells Turbo Pascal to treat the code that follows as machine-language instructions. For example:

```
Inline($1E/$06/$07/$1F);
```

Interface   Defines the beginning of the interface section of a unit.

Interrupt   Defines a procedure as an interrupt procedure. Interrupt procedures are used for writing interrupt service routines.

Label   Declares labels used with **Goto** statements (see **Goto**).

Mod   Returns the remainder of integer division.

Nil   May be assigned to any pointer variable. Used in comparisons to test whether a pointer has a valid value. For example:

```
Type
  Aptr = ^Arecord;
  Arecord = Record
    i : Integer;
    Next : Aptr;
    End;
Var
  A : Aptr;

Begin
New(A);
If (A^.Next = Nil) Then ...
```

Not   Reverses the result of a Boolean expression. For example, if

```
(A > B)
```

is true, then

```
Not (A > B)
```

is false.

Object   Used to define an object consisting of data elements and methods.

Of   Used in the **Case** statement (see **Case**) and in declaration of a set or array data type.

Or   Combines Boolean expressions such that the entire expression is true if either condition is true. For example:

```
If (A > B) Or (C > D) Then ...
```

is true if either the first or the second comparison (or both) is true. **Or** also compares two bytes or integers and returns a third byte or integer.

A bit in the resulting integer is turned on if either or both bits in the same position are on in the first and second integers.

Packed   Declares arrays such that the arrays use less memory than they normally would. Turbo Pascal supports this reserved word, but it has no effect since all Turbo Pascal arrays are stored in packed format.

Procedure   Defines a block of code as belonging to a procedure.

Program   Defines a block of code as belonging to a program. This is the first statement in a program.

Record   Defines a complex data type that combines several simple or complex data types. For example:

```
Type
  Student = Record
    Name : String[20];
    Age : Integer;
    End;

  Class = Record
    Students : Array [1..30] Of Student;
    RoomNumber : Integer;
    End;
```

Repeat   Used in **Repeat-Until** control structures. For example:

```
i := 1;
  Repeat
  { Statements }
  i := i + 1;
  Until i > 100;
```

Set   Defines a set variable. For example:

```
Var
  Letters : Set Of Char;
```

Shl   Shifts the bits in a byte or integer one position to the left and sets the right-most bit to zero.

Shr   Shifts the bits in a byte or integer one position to the right and sets the left-most bit to zero.

String   Defines a **String** data type. A string can be defined from 1 to 255 characters long. If no length is specified, the length defaults to 255 characters. For example:

```
Var
  s : String; (* Maximum 255 characters *)
```

Then   Used in **If-Then** statements (see **If**).

To   Used in For-Do loops (see **For**).

Type   Defines data types that can then be used to define variables. For example:

```
Type
  PersonType = Record
    Name : String[20];
    Address : String[50];
    Income : Real;
    End;
Var
  Person1, Person2 : PersonType;
```

Unit   Declares the source file to be a Turbo Pascal unit.

Until   Used in Repeat-Until loops (see **Repeat**).

Uses   Declares the use of one or more units. For example:

```
Program Test;
Uses CRT, DOS;
```

Var   Defines variables. For example:

```
Var
  i : Integer;
  s : String;
```

Virtual   Used to define a method in an object as a virtual method.

While   Used in While-Do loops. For example:

```
i := 0;
While i < 100 Do
  Begin
  { Statements }
  i := i + 1;
  End;
```

With   Used for implicit reference to a record variable. For example:

```
Var
  Person : Record
    Name : String;
    Age : Integer;
    End;

Begin
With Person Do
  Begin
  ReadLn(Name);
  ReadLn(Age);
  End;
```

Xor   Combines Boolean expressions such that the entire expression is true if only one of two conditions is true. For example:

```
If (A > B) Xor (C > D) Then ...
```

is true if the first comparison is true or the second comparison is true, but not if both are true. **Xor** also compares two bytes or integers and returns a third byte or integer. A bit in the resulting integer is turned on if either, but not both, bits in the same position are on in the first and second integers.

Turbo Pascal Procedure and Function Reference

The following are Turbo Pascal standard procedures.

Abs

Syntax

Function Abs(r : Real) : Real;
Function Abs(i : Integer) : Integer;

Description   **Abs** returns the absolute value of the parameter passed to it. The function result is the same type (**Real** or **Integer**) as the parameter.

Addr

Syntax

Function Addr(Var Variable) : Pointer;

Description   **Addr** returns the address of a variable, typed constant, or procedure. The result is a **Pointer** type.

Append

Syntax

Procedure Append(Var F: Text);

Description   **Append** opens a text file for writing and positions the file pointer at the end of the file.

Arc   [GRAPH Unit]

Syntax

Procedure Arc(x, y : Integer;
            StAngle,
            EndAngle,
            Radius : Word);

Description   **Arc** draws a circle around coordinates **x:y** with a radius of **Radius**. The circle begins drawing clockwise from **StAngle** and stops at **EndAngle**.

ArcTan

Syntax

Function ArcTan(R: Real) : Real;

Description   **ArcTan** returns the arctangent of the parameter passed to it.

Assign

Syntax

Procedure Assign(Var F: File; Name : String);

Description   **Assign** links file variable **F** to the file named in **Name**.

AssignCrt   [CRT Unit]

Syntax

Procedure AssignCrt(Var F : Text);

Description   **AssignCrt** allows the user to send output to the video display by writing to file **F**.

Bar   [GRAPH Unit]

Syntax

Procedure Bar(x1, y1, x2, y2 : Integer);

Description   **Bar** draws a filled-in rectangular area of the screen.

Bar3D   [GRAPH Unit]

Syntax

Procedure Bar3D(x1, y1, x2, y2 : Integer;
                Depth : Word;
                Top : Boolean);

Description   **Bar3D** draws a filled-in three-dimensional rectangular area of the screen. The rectangle is drawn **Depth** pixels deep. If **Top** is TRUE, the procedure draws a three-dimensional top on the rectangle.

BlockRead

Syntax

Procedure BlockRead(Var F: File;
                    Var B: Type;
                    NumRecs: Integer;
                    Var RecsRead: Integer);

Description   **BlockRead** attempts to read **NumRecs** records from untyped file **F** into buffer **B**. **RecsRead** indicates the number of records actually read. Note that the **RecsRead** parameter is supported only in PC/MS-DOS versions.

BlockWrite

Syntax

Procedure BlockWrite(Var F: File;
                     Var B: Type;
                     NumRecs: Integer);

Description   **BlockWrite** writes **NumRecs** records from buffer **B** to untyped file **F**.

ChDir

Syntax

Procedure ChDir(S: String);

Description   **ChDir** changes the current directory to that in **S**.

Chr

Syntax

Function Chr(I: Integer);

Description   **Chr** returns the ASCII character that corresponds to **I**.

Circle   [GRAPH Unit]

Syntax

Procedure Circle(x, y : Integer;
                Radius : Word);

Description   **Circle** draws a circle with a radius of **Radius** around the coordinate **x:y**.

ClearDevice   [GRAPH Unit]

Syntax

Procedure ClearDevice;

Description   **ClearDevice** clears the graphics screen.

ClearViewPort   [GRAPH Unit]

Syntax

Procedure ClearViewPort;

Description   **ClearViewPort** clears the current viewport.

Close

Syntax

Procedure Close(Var F: File);

Description   **Close** flushes the buffer for file **F** and then closes the file.

CloseGraph   [GRAPH Unit]

Syntax

Procedure CloseGraph;

Description   **CloseGraph** restores the video display to the mode that existed prior to entering graphics mode. The procedure also frees memory used by the graphics system.

ClrEol   [CRT Unit]

Syntax

Procedure ClrEol;

Description   **ClrEol** clears the current screen line from the cursor position to the right edge of the screen.

ClrScr   [CRT Unit]

Syntax

Procedure ClrScr;

Description   ClrScr clears the screen and positions the cursor at location (1,1) on the screen.

Concat

Syntax

Function Concat(S1, S2, . . ., Sn) : String;

Description   Concat combines any number of strings and returns them as a single string. If the length of the concatenated string is greater than 255, Turbo Pascal generates a run-time error.

Copy

Syntax

Function Copy(S: String; P, L: Integer) : String;

Description   Copy returns a portion of string S, which starts at character number P and contains L characters.

Cos

Syntax

Function Cos(R: Real) : Real;

Description   Cos returns the cosine of R.

Cseg

Syntax

Function Cseg : Word;

Description   Cseg returns the segment address of the program's code segment.

Dec

Syntax

Procedure Dec(Var x : Scalar;
                    n : LongInt);

Description   Dec decrements variable **x** by **n**. If you omit **n**, **x** will be decremented by 1.

Delay   [CRT Unit]

Syntax

Procedure Delay(ms : Word);

Description   Delay halts program execution for **ms** milliseconds.

Delete

Syntax

Procedure Delete(S: String; P, L: Integer);

Description   **Delete** removes **L** characters from string **S** starting with character number **P**.

DelLine   [CRT Unit]

Syntax

Procedure DelLine;

Description   **DelLine** deletes the screen line on which the cursor is located. Lines below the deleted line scroll up one line.

DetectGraph   [GRAPH Unit]

Syntax

Procedure DetectGraph(Var GD, GM : Integer);

Description   **DetectGraph** returns the detected graph driver (**GD**) and graphics mode (**GM**) for the display adapter installed.

DiskFree   [DOS Unit]

Syntax

Function DiskFree(Drive : Word) : LongInt;

Description   **DiskFree** returns the amount of free disk space, in bytes, on drive **Drive** (1 = A, 2 = B, 0 = Default drive).

DiskSize   [DOS Unit]

Syntax

Function DiskSize(Drive : Word) : LongInt;

Description   **DiskSize** returns the size, in bytes, of drive **Drive** (1 = A, 2 = B, 0 = Default drive).

Dispose

Syntax

Procedure Dispose(P: Pointer);

Description   **Dispose** frees heap memory allocated to a **pointer** variable. **Dispose** is used in conjunction with the **New** command.

DosExitCode   [DOS Unit]

Syntax

Function DosExitCode : Word;

Description   **DosExitCode** returns the exit code of a subprocess (0 = normal termination, 1 = termination by CTRL-C, 2 = termination by device error, 3 = termination by **Keep** procedure).

DosVersion   [DOS Unit]

Syntax

Function DosVersion : Word;

Description   **DosVersion** returns the version of the operating system. The major release number is in the high-order byte, and the minor version number is in the low-order byte.

DrawPoly   [GRAPH Unit]

Syntax

Procedure DrawPoly(NumPoints : Word;
                    Var PolyPoints);

Description   **DrawPoly** draws a polygon defined by **NumPoints** points. The array **PolyPoints** contains the coordinates for the points of the polygon.

Dseg

Syntax

Function Dseg : Word;

Description   **Dseg** returns the segment address of the program's data segment.

EnvCount   [DOS Unit]

Syntax

Function EnvCount : Integer;

Description   **EnvCount** returns the number of strings defined in the DOS environment.

EnvStr   [DOS Unit]

Syntax

Function EnvStr(i : Integer) : String;

Description   **EnvStr** returns environment string number **i**.

Eof

Syntax

Function Eof(F: File) : Boolean;

Description   **Eof** returns TRUE when the file pointer in **F** reaches the end of the file.

Eoln

Syntax

Function Eoln(F: File) : Boolean;

Description   **Eoln** returns TRUE when the file pointer in **F** reaches either the end of a line (indicated by a carriage return and line feed) or the end of the file.

Erase

Syntax

Procedure Erase(F: File);

Description   **Erase** deletes disk file **F** and removes its information from the directory.

Exec   [DOS Unit]

Syntax

Procedure Exec(Path, CmdLine : String);

Description   **Exec** executes the file named in **Path** with command-line parameters defined in **CmdLine**. For example, in this program

```
{$M 2000,0,0}
Program TestExec;
Uses DOS;
Begin
Exec ('TESTPROG.EXE','A B C');
ReadLn;
Exec ('\COMMAND.COM','');
End.
```

the first **Exec** statement executes the program TESTPROG. EXE with command-line parameters A, B, C. The second **Exec** statement invokes the DOS COMMAND.COM file with no parameters; this creates a DOS shell from which you can run other programs. You can escape from the DOS shell by typing **EXIT** at the DOS prompt. Note that the program limits the amount of memory allocated to the heap in order to leave room for the program being executed.

Exit

Syntax

Procedure Exit;

Description   **Exit** causes a program to leave the block currently being executed.

Exp

Syntax

Function Exp(R: Real) : Real;

Description   **Exp** returns the exponential of **R**.

FExpand   [DOS Unit]

Syntax

Function FExpand(P : PathStr);

Description   **FExpand** accepts a filename **P** and returns the filename with its complete path structure, including drive.

FilePos

Syntax

Function FilePos(F: File) : Integer;

Description   **FilePos** returns the record number at which the file pointer in **F** is located.

FileSize

Syntax

Function FileSize(F: File) : Integer;

Description   **FileSize** returns the number of records currently contained in **F**.

FillChar

Syntax

Procedure FillChar(Variable: Type; I, Code: Scalar);

Description   **FillChar** fills **I** bytes of memory with the value **Code**, which may be of any scalar type, starting at the address of **Variable**.

FillEllipse   [GRAPH Unit]

Syntax

Procedure FillEllipse(x, y : Integer;
                    XRadius,
                    YRadius : Word);

Description   **FillEllipse** draws an ellipse centered at coordinates **x:y** with a vertical radius of **YRadius** and a horizontal radius of **XRadius**. The ellipse is filled with the current fill color and fill style, and the border is drawn with the current color.

FillPoly   [GRAPH Unit]

Syntax

Procedure FillPoly(NumPoints : Word
                 Var PolyPoints);

Description   FillPoly draws a polygon with **NumPoints** points. The array **PolyPoints** contains the coordinates for the points of the polygon.

FindFirst   [DOS Unit]

Syntax

```
Procedure FindFirst(Path : String;
                    Attr : Word;
                    Var S : SearchRec);
```

Description   FindFirst returns information on the first file found in directory **Path** whose attributes match **Attr**. The standard values of **Attr** are

```
Const
  ReadOnly    = $01;
  Hidden      = $02;
  SysFile     = $04;
  VolumeId    = $08;
  Directory   = $10;
  Archive     = $20;
  AnyFile     = $3F;
```

The **SearchRec** data type is defined as

```
Type
  SearchRec = Record
    Fill : Array [1..21] Of Byte;
    Attr : Byte;
    Time : LongInt;
    Size : LongInt;
    Name : String[12];
    End;
```

If the search is successful, the value of **DosError** will be zero.

FindNext   [DOS Unit]

Syntax

```
Procedure FindNext(Var S : SearchRec);
```

Description   **FindNext** returns information on the next file found in the directory **Path** defined in **FindFirst** whose attributes match those used in **FindFirst**. If the search is successful, the value of **DosError** will be zero.

FloodFill   [GRAPH Unit]

Syntax

Procedure FloodFill(x, y : Integer;
                    Border : Word);

Description   **FloodFill** fills an enclosed area of the graphics display with the current color and pattern. The area must be completely enclosed by the color **Border,** and the x:y coordinates must lie within the area to be filled.

Flush

Syntax

Procedure Flush(Var F : Text);

Description   **Flush** sends to disk all buffered output for file **F.**

Frac

Syntax

Function Frac(R: Real) : Real;

Description   **Frac** returns the noninteger portion of **R.**

FreeMem

Syntax

Procedure FreeMem(Var P: Pointer; I: Integer);

Description   **FreeMem** frees **I** bytes of heap memory associated with variable **P**, which must have been previously allocated by **GetMem**.

FSearch   [DOS Unit]

Syntax

Function FSearch(Path : PathStr;
                 DirList : String) : PathStr;

Description   **FSearch** searches in the list of directories included in **DirList** for a filename that matches **Path**. If the file is found, the result is returned as a string. If not found, the function returns an empty string.

FSplit   [DOS Unit]

Syntax

Procedure FSplit(Path : PathStr;
                 Var Dir : DirStr;
                 Var Name : NameStr;
                 Var Ext : ExtStr);

Description   **FSplit** accepts a filename **Path** and returns its components. The following types are used:

```
Type
  PathStr = String[79];
  DirStr  = String[67];
  NameStr = String[8];
  ExtStr  = String[4];
```

GetArcCoords   [GRAPH Unit]

Syntax

Procedure GetArcCoords(Var ArcCoords : ArcCoordsType);

Description   **GetArcCoords** returns the coordinates used by the most recently used **Arc** or **Ellipse** command. The structure of **ArcCoordsType** is as follows:

```
Type
  ArcCoordsType = Record
    x, y : Integer;
    Xstart, Ystart : Integer;
    Xend, Yend : Integer;
    End;
```

GetAspectRatio   [GRAPH Unit]

Syntax

Procedure GetAspectRatio(Var Xasp, Yasp : Word);

Description   **GetAspectRatio** returns in **Xasp** and **Yasp** the effective resolution of the graphics screen. The aspect ratio is computed as **Xasp** divided by **Yasp**.

GetBkColor   [GRAPH Unit]

Syntax

Function GetBkColor : Word;

Description   **GetBkColor** returns the index for the current palette of the current background color.

GetCBreak   [DOS Unit]

Syntax

Procedure GetCBreak(Var Break : Boolean);

Description   **GetCBreak** returns the current state of CTRL-BREAK checking in DOS. When **Break** is FALSE, DOS checks for CTRL-BREAK during console, printer, or serial I/O. When it is TRUE, DOS checks for CTRL-BREAK at every system call.

GetColor   [GRAPH Unit]

Syntax

Function GetColor : Word;

Description   **GetColor** returns the current drawing color in the graphics mode.

GetDate   [DOS Unit]

Syntax

Procedure GetDate(Var Year,
                      Month,
                      Day,
                      DayOfWeek : Word);

Description   **GetDate** returns the date as determined by the system clock.

GetDefaultPalette   [GRAPH Unit]

Syntax

Procedure GetDefaultPalette(Var Pal : PaletteType);

Description   **GetDefaultPalette** returns in **Pal** the default palette for the current graphics driver. The structure of **Palette Type** is as follows:

```
Type
  PaletteType = Record
    Size : Byte;
    Colors : Array [0..MaxColor] Of ShortInt;
    End;
```

GetDir

Syntax

Procedure GetDir(d: Byte; Var s: String);

Description   **GetDir** gets the directory for the drive specified by **d**. The directory is returned in **s**. If **d** is zero, **GetDir** searches the default drive.

GetDriverName   [GRAPH Unit]

Syntax

Function GetDriverName : String;

Description   **GetDriverName** returns the name of the current graphics driver.

GetEnv   [DOS Unit]

Syntax

Function GetEnv(EnvVar : String) : String;

Description   **GetEnv** returns the environment string for the environment variable specified in **EnvVar**.

GetFAttr   [DOS Unit]

Syntax

Procedure GetFAttr(Var F; Var Attr : Word);

Description   **GetFAttr** returns the file attribute for file **F**. Before calling this procedure, **F** must be assigned but not opened.

GetFillPattern   [GRAPH Unit]

Syntax

Procedure GetFillPattern(Var FP : FillPatternType);

Description   **GetFillPattern** returns in **FP** the definition of the current fill pattern. The structure of **FillPatternType** is

```
Type
  FillPatternType = Array [1..8] Of Byte;
```

GetFillSettings   [GRAPH Unit]

Syntax

Procedure GetFillSettings(Var FS : FillSettingsType);

Description   **GetFillSettings** returns in **FS** the current fill pattern and color. The structure of **FillSettingsType** is

```
Type
  FillSettingsType = Record
    Pattern : Word;
    Color : Word;
    End;
```

GetFTime   [DOS Unit]

Syntax

Procedure GetFTime(Var F; Var Time : LongInt);

Description   **GetFTime** returns in **Time** the time stamp for file **F**. File **F** must be assigned and opened before using this procedure. The variable **Time** is a packed value and must be unpacked with the **UnPackTime** procedure.

GetGraphMode   [GRAPH Unit]

Syntax

Function GetGraphMode : Integer;

Description   **GetGraphMode** returns the current graphics mode. The numeric value of the graphics mode must be interpreted in combination with the graphics driver.

GetImage   [GRAPH Unit]

Syntax

Procedure GetImage(x1, y1, x2, y2 : Integer;
                          Var BitMap);

Description   **GetImage** stores a rectangular portion of a graphics screen, defined by **x1:y1** and **x2:y2** in **BitMap**.

GetIntVec   [DOS Unit]

Syntax

Procedure GetIntVec(IntNo : Byte;
                          Var : Vector : Pointer);

Description   **GetIntVec** returns in **Vector** the current contents of interrupt vector number **IntNo**.

GetLineSettings   [GRAPH Unit]

Syntax

Procedure GetLineSettings(Var LST : LineSettingsType);

Description   **GetLineSettings** returns in **LST** the current settings for line style, pattern, and thickness. The **LineSettingsType** structure is

```
Type
  LineSettingsType = Record
    LineStyle : Word;
    Pattern : Word;
    Thickness : Word;
    End;
```

GetMaxColor   [GRAPH Unit]

Syntax

Function GetMaxColor : Word;

Description   **GetMaxColor** returns the highest value that represents a color in the current palette.

GetMaxMode   [GRAPH Unit]

Syntax

Function GetMaxMode : Word;

Description   **GetMaxMode** returns a value that indicates the highest-resolution graphics mode for the installed adapter.

GetMaxX   [GRAPH Unit]

Syntax

Function GetMaxX : Integer;

Description   **GetMaxX** returns the maximum horizontal coordinate for the current graphics mode.

GetMaxY

Syntax

Function GetMaxY : Integer;

Description   GetMaxY returns the maximum vertical coordinate for the current graphics mode.

GetMem

Syntax

Procedure GetMem(Var P: Pointer; I: Integer);

Description   GetMem reserves **I** bytes on the heap and stores the starting address in variable **P**.

GetModeName   [GRAPH Unit]

Syntax

Function GetModeName(ModeNumber : Word) : String;

Description   GetModeName returns a string describing the graphics mode denoted in **ModeNumber.**

GetModeRange   [GRAPH Unit]

Syntax

Procedure GetModeRange(GraphDriver : Integer;
                    Var LoMode,
                    HiMode : Integer);

Description   GetModeRange returns the highest (**HiMode**) and lowest (**LoMode**) resolution modes for the graphics driver denoted by **GraphDriver.**

GetPalette   [GRAPH Unit]

Syntax

Procedure GetPalette(Var P : PaletteType);

Description   **GetPalette** returns in **P** the current palette. The structure of **PaletteType** is

```
Const
  MaxColors = 15;
Type
  PaletteType = Record
    Size : Byte;
    Colors : Array [0..MaxColors] Of ShortInt;
    End;
```

GetPaletteSize   [GRAPH Unit]

Syntax

Function GetPaletteSize : Word;

Description   **GetPaletteSize** returns the maximum number of palette entries that the current graphics mode can support.

GetPixel   [GRAPH Unit]

Syntax

Function GetPixel(x, y : Integer);

Description   **GetPixel** returns the color of the pixel at coordinates x:y.

GetTextSettings [GRAPH Unit]

Syntax

Procedure GetTextSettings(Var TS : TextSettingsType);

Description **GetTextSettings** returns in **TS** the current text settings. The structure of **TextSettingsType** is

```
Type
  TextSettingsType = Record
    Font : Word;
    Direction : Word;
    CharSize : Word;
    Horiz : Word;
    Vert : Word;
    End;
```

GetTime [DOS Unit]

Syntax

Procedure GetTime(Var Hour,
                      Minute,
                      Second,
                      Sec100 : Word);

Description **GetTime** returns the time according to the system clock.

GetVerify [DOS Unit]

Syntax

Procedure GetVerify(Var Verify : Boolean);

Description   **GetVerify** returns the status of write-verification in DOS. When **Verify** is TRUE, DOS verifies all disk writes.

GetViewSettings   [GRAPH Unit]

Syntax

Procedure GetViewSettings(Var VP : ViewPortType);

Description   **GetViewSettings** returns in **VP** the current viewport settings. The structure of **ViewPortType** is

```
Type
  ViewPortType = Record
    x1, y1, x2, y2 : Integer;
    Clip : Boolean;
    End;
```

GetX   [GRAPH Unit]

Syntax

Function GetX : Integer;

Description   **GetX** returns the horizontal coordinate of the current position.

GetY   [GRAPH Unit]

Syntax

Function GetY : Integer;

Description   **GetY** returns the vertical coordinate of the current position.

GotoXY   [CRT Unit]

Syntax

Procedure GotoXY(x, y: Integer);

Description   **GotoXY** places the cursor at screen coordinates **X:Y**.

GraphDefaults   [GRAPH Unit]

Syntax

Procedure GraphDefaults;

Description   **GraphDefaults** resets the graphics settings to their default values.

GraphErrorMsg   [GRAPH Unit]

Syntax

Function GraphErrorMsg(Code : Integer) : String;

Description   **GraphErrorMsg** returns an error message corresponding to the error condition denoted by **Code**.

GraphResult   [GRAPH Unit]

Syntax

Function GraphResult : Integer;

Description   **GraphResult** returns an error code for the last graphics procedure.

Halt

Syntax

Procedure Halt;

Description   **Halt** terminates a program.

Hi

Syntax

Function Hi(I: Integer) : Byte;

Description   **Hi** returns the high-order byte from integer **I**.

HighVideo   [CRT Unit]

Syntax

Procedure HighVideo;

Description   **HighVideo** enables the high-intensity video display.

ImageSize   [GRAPH Unit]

Syntax

Function ImageSize(x1, y1, x2, y2 : Integer);

Description   ImageSize returns the number of bytes required to store the bit map for the portion of the screen defined by **x1:y1** and **x2:y2**.

Inc

Syntax

Procedure Inc(Var x; n : LongInt);

Description   Inc increments the value of scalar **x** by **n**. If **n** is omitted from the parameter list, **x** is incremented by 1.

InitGraph   [GRAPH Unit]

Syntax

Procedure InitGraph(Var GraphDriver : Integer;
                    Var GraphMode : Integer;
                    DriverPath : String);

Description   InitGraph initializes the graphics environment to the graphics driver **GraphDriver** and mode **GraphMode**. If **GraphDriver** is zero, the procedure automatically detects the display adapter and sets the mode to the highest resolution. The procedure will look for .BGI files in the path defined by **DriverPath**.

Insert

Syntax

Procedure Insert(Source : String;
                 Var Target : String;
                 Index : Integer);

Description   Insert inserts string **Source** into string **Target** at position **Index**.

InsLine   [CRT Unit]

Syntax

Procedure InsLine;

Description   **InsLine** inserts a blank line on the screen at the current cursor position.

InstallUserDriver   [GRAPH Unit]

Syntax

Function InstallUserDriver(Name : String;
                        AutoDetectPtr : Pointer) :
                        Integer;

Description   **InstallUserDriver** installs a non-Borland graphics driver. **Name** contains the name of the file that contains the driver, and **AutoDetectPtr** is a pointer to an optional autodetect function. The driver must be in .BGI format.

InstallUserFont   [GRAPH Unit]

Syntax

Function InstallUserFont(FontFileName : String) : Integer;

Description   **InstallUserFont** lets the user install a non-Borland font. The file named by **FontFileName** contains the font information.

Int

Syntax

Function Int(R: Real) : Integer;

Description   Int returns the integer portion of **R**.

Intr   [DOS Unit]

Syntax

Procedure Intr(Func : Byte; Var Regs : Registers);

Description   **Intr** calls BIOS interrupt **Func** with registers defined by **Regs**.

IOresult

Syntax

Function IOresult : Word;

Description   **IOresult** reports an error code when input/output operations are performed. If **IOresult** is not equal to zero, an error occurred.

Keep   [DOS Unit]

Syntax

Procedure Keep(ExitCode : Word);

Description   **Keep** terminates the program, but keeps it resident. The procedure passes **ExitCode** as a standard DOS error code.

KeyPressed   [CRT Unit]

Syntax

Function KeyPressed : Boolean;

Description   **KeyPressed** returns TRUE when a key has been pressed.

Length

Syntax

Function Length(S: String) : Integer;

Description   **Length** returns the length of string S.

Line   [GRAPH Unit]

Syntax

Procedure Line(x1, y1, x2, y2 : Integer);

Description   **Line** draws a line from **x1:y1** to **x2:y2**.

LineRel   [GRAPH Unit]

Syntax

Procedure LineRel(Dx, Dy : Integer);

Description   **LineRel** draws a line from the current pointer to a point defined by **Dx** and **Dy**. For example, if the current pointer is positioned at 1:2, then the command **LineRel(100,100)** will draw a line from 1:2 to 101:102.

LineTo   [GRAPH Unit]

Syntax

Procedure LineTo(x, y : Integer);

Description   **LineTo** draws a line from the current pointer to x:y.

Ln

Syntax

Function Ln(Var R: Real) : Real;

Description   **Ln** returns the natural logarithm of **R**.

Lo

Syntax

Function Lo(I: Integer) : Byte;

Description   **Lo** returns the low-order byte of integer **I**.

LowVideo   [CRT Unit]

Syntax

Procedure LowVideo;

Description   **LowVideo** sets the video display to low intensity.

Mark

Syntax

Procedure Mark(P: Pointer);

Description   **Mark** stores the top-of-heap address in pointer **P**.

MaxAvail

Syntax

Function MaxAvail: LongInt;

Description   **MaxAvail** returns the size of the largest block of unallocated memory on the heap.

MemAvail

Syntax

Function MemAvail: LongInt;

Description   **MemAvail** returns the total amount of unallocated memory on the heap.

MkDir

Syntax

Procedure MkDir(S: String);

Description   **MkDir** makes a directory with the name stored in string S.

Move

Syntax

Procedure Move(Var V1, V2; I: Integer);

Description   **Move** copies **I** bytes of memory from the location of variable **V1** to the location of variable **V2**.

MoveRel   [GRAPH Unit]

Syntax

Procedure MoveRel(Dx, Dy : Integer);

Description   **MoveRel** moves the current pointer to a position **Dx** pixels horizontally and **Dy** pixels vertically, relative to the current cursor position.

MoveTo   [GRAPH Unit]

Syntax

Procedure MoveTo(x, y : Integer);

Description   **MoveTo** positions the current pointer on pixel x:y.

MsDos   [DOS Unit]

Syntax

Procedure MsDos(Var Regs : Registers);

Description   **MsDos** executes DOS services using the values set in **Regs**.

New

Syntax

Procedure New(Var P: Pointer);

Description   **New** allocates memory on the heap for pointer **P**. After memory is allocated, the variable is referred to as **P^**.

NormVideo   [CRT Unit]

Syntax

Procedure NormVideo;

Description   **NormVideo** restores the default screen attributes to those that were present at the cursor position when the program started.

NoSound   [CRT Unit]

Syntax

Procedure NoSound;

Description   **NoSound** stops any tone currently being generated by the PC's speaker.

Odd

Syntax

Function Odd(I: Integer) : Boolean;

Description   **Odd** returns TRUE when **I** is odd and FALSE when **I** is even.

Ofs

Syntax

Function Ofs(<Variable, Procedure, or Function>) : Integer;

Description   **Ofs** returns the memory-address offset for any variable, procedure, or function.

Ord

Syntax

Function Ord(S: Scalar) : Integer;

Description   **Ord** returns the integer value of any scalar variable.

OutText   [GRAPH Unit]

Syntax

Procedure OutText(TextString : String);

Description   **OutText** displays the string **TextString** using the current settings for fonts, justification, height, and width.

OutTextXY   [GRAPH Unit]

Syntax

Procedure OutTextXY(x, y : Integer; TextString : String);

Description   **OutTextXY** displays the string **TextString** at position x:y using the current settings for fonts, justification, height, and width.

OvrClearBuf   [OVERLAY Unit]

Syntax

Procedure OvrClearBuf;

Description   **OvrClearBuf** empties the overlay buffer, requiring all overlays to be read from disk.

OvrGetBuf   [OVERLAY Unit]

Syntax

Function OvrGetBuf : LongInt;

Description   **OvrGetBuf** returns the size of the overlay buffer.

OvrInit   [OVERLAY Unit]

Syntax

Procedure OvrInit(FileName : String);

Description   **OvrInit** initializes the overlay manager. **File Name** contains the name of the overlay file.

OvrInitEMS   [OVERLAY Unit]

Syntax

Procedure OvrInitEMS;

Description   **OvrInitEMS** loads the overlay file into expanded memory if enough memory is available.

OvrSetBuf   [OVERLAY Unit]

Syntax

Procedure OvrSetBuf(BufSize : Integer);

Description   **OvrSetBuf** allocates **BufSize** bytes to the overlay buffer. **BufSize** must not be smaller than the default overlay buffer.

PackTime   [DOS Unit]

Syntax

Procedure PackTime(Var DT : DateTime;
                    Var Time : LongInt);

Description   **PackTime** accepts the variable **DT**, which contains date and time information, and returns **Time**, which contains the same information in packed form.

ParamCount

Syntax

Function ParamCount: Word;

Description   **ParamCount** returns the number of command-line parameters entered.

ParamStr

Syntax

Function ParamStr(I: Word: String);

Description   **ParamStr** returns parameters that were entered on the command line. For example, **ParamStr(1)** returns the first parameter. In DOS 3.x, **ParamStr(0)** returns the path and filename of the executed file.

Pi

Syntax

Function Pi : Real;

Description   **Pi** returns the value of the mathematical constant **Pi**. The precision of the number depends on whether 8087 mode is activated.

PieSlice   [GRAPH Unit]

Syntax

Procedure PieSlice(x, y : Integer;
                    StAngle, EndAngle, Radius : Word);

Description   **PieSlice** draws a slice of a pie chart centered at **x:y**, with radius **Radius**, starting at **StAngle** and ending at **EndAngle**.

Pos

Syntax

Function Pos(SubS, S : String) : Integer;

Description   **Pos** returns the position of SubS in S. If SubS is not found in **S**, **Pos** returns 0.

Pred

Syntax

Function Pred(Var S: Scalar): Integer;

Description   **Pred** decrements any scalar variable.

Ptr

Syntax

Function Ptr(Segment, Offset: Integer) : Pointer;

Description   **Ptr** accepts two integers that contain a segment and an offset and returns a single 32-bit pointer value.

PutImage   [GRAPH Unit]

Syntax

Procedure PutImage(x, y : Integer;
                   Var BitMap;
                   BitBlt : Word);

Description   **PutImage** displays the contents of **BitMap** starting at x:y. **BitBlt** specifies the process to use to display the bit map, and can take the following values:

```
Const
  CopyPut   = 0;
  XORPut    = 1;
  OrPut     = 2;
  AndPut    = 3;
  NotPut    = 4;
```

PutPixel   [GRAPH Unit]

Syntax

Procedure PutPixel(x, y : Integer; Pixel : Word);

Description   **PutPixel** plots a single point of color, defined by **Pixel**, at position x:y.

Random

Syntax

Function Random(I: Word): Word;
Function Random: Real;

Description   **Random** returns a number randomly generated by Turbo Pascal. If you pass an integer parameter, **Random** returns an integer greater than or equal to zero and less than the parameter. Without an integer, **Random** returns a real value greater than or equal to zero and less than 1.

Randomize

Syntax

Function Randomize;

Description   **Randomize** initializes the seed value of the random-number generator. The seed value is stored in a **LongInt** variable **RandSeed**.

Read (ReadLn)

Syntax

Procedure Read({Var F: File,} Parameters);
Procedure ReadLn({Var F: File,} Parameters);

Description   **Read** receives input from either the standard input device or the file specified by **F. ReadLn**, which can be used only on text files, receives input in the same way that **Read** does, but after reading in the data, **ReadLn** moves the file pointer forward to the next carriage return/line feed delimiter.

ReadKey   [CRT Unit]

Syntax

Function ReadKey : Char;

Description   **ReadKey** reads a character from the keyboard without echo. If the result is #0, then a special key has been pressed and you must call **ReadKey** again to capture the second part of the key code.

Rectangle   [GRAPH Unit]

Syntax

Procedure Rectangle(x1, y1, x2, y2 : Integer);

Description   **Rectangle** draws a rectangle with its upper-left corner at **x1:y1** and lower-right corner at **x2:y2**.

RegisterBGIdriver   [GRAPH Unit]

Syntax

Function RegisterBGIdriver(Driver : Pointer) : Integer;

Description   **RegisterBGIdriver** allows the user to load a .BGI driver file (read from disk onto the heap or linked into the program using BINOBJ) and register the driver with the graphics system. **Driver** is a pointer to the location of the .BGI driver. If an error occurs, the function returns a value less than zero; otherwise, it returns the assigned driver number.

RegisterBGIfont   [GRAPH Unit]

Syntax

Function RegisterBGIfont(Font : Pointer) : Integer;

Description   **RegisterBGIfont** allows the user to load a .BGI font driver file (read from disk onto the heap or linked into the program using BINOBJ) and register the font with the graphics system. **Font** is a pointer to the location of the .BGI driver. If an error occurs, the function returns a value less than zero; otherwise, it returns the assigned font number.

Release

Syntax

Procedure Release(Var P: Pointer);

Description   **Release** reclaims memory that has been since allocated since the **Mark** command. Used to store the top-of-heap address in **P**.

Rename

Syntax

Procedure Rename(Var F: File; S: String);

Description   **Rename** changes the name of file **F** to that contained in S.

Reset

Syntax

Procedure Reset(Var F: File {; I: Integer});

Description   **Reset** opens file **F** for reading. If the file is untyped, you can specify the record size in **I**.

RestoreCRTMode   [GRAPH Unit]

Syntax

Procedure RestoreCRTMode;

Description   **RestoreCRTMode** restores the video display to the mode that existed before graphics was initialized.

Rewrite

Syntax

Procedure Rewrite(Var F: File {; I: Integer});

Description   **Rewrite** prepares a file to be written. If the file does not exist, Turbo Pascal creates it. If the file does exist, its contents are destroyed. If the file is untyped, you can specify the record size in **I**.

RmDir

Syntax

Procedure RmDir(S: String);

Description   **RmDir** removes the directory specified in S.

Round

Syntax

Function Round(R : Real) : LongInt;

Description   **Round** returns the rounded integer value of **R**.

RunError

Syntax

Procedure RunError;
Procedure RunError(ErrorCode : Word);

Description   **RunError** halts program execution and generates a run-time error. If **ErrorCode** is included, Turbo Pascal will interpret this as the type of run-time error that occurred.

Sector   [GRAPH Unit]

Syntax

Procedure Sector(x, y : Integer;
                StAngle, EndAngle, XRadius, YRadius :
                Word);

Description   **Sector** draws a sector centered at **x:y**, starting at **StAngle**, ending at **EndAngle**, with horizontal radius **XRadius** and vertical radius **YRadius**.

Seek

Syntax

Procedure Seek(Var F: File; P: Integer);

Description   **Seek** moves the file pointer to the beginning of record number **P** in file **F**.

SeekEof

Syntax

Function SeekEof(Var F: File) Boolean;

Description   **SeekEof** is similar to EOF, except that it skips blanks, tabs, and end-of-line markers (CR/LF) sequences before it tests for an end-of-file marker. The type of result is Boolean.

SeekEoln

Syntax

Function SeekEoln(Var F: File): Boolean;

Description   **SeekEoln** is similar to **Eoln**, except that it skips blanks and tabs before it tests for an end-of-line marker. The type of the result is Boolean.

Seg

Syntax

Function Seg(Var Variable) : Word;
Function Seg(<Procedure or Function>) : Word;

Description   **Seg** returns the segment address of a variable, procedure, or function.

SetActivePage   [GRAPH Unit]

Syntax

Procedure SetActivePage(Page : Word);

Description   **SetActivePage** selects the graphics video display page to make active.

SetAllPalette   [GRAPH Unit]

Syntax

Procedure SetAllPalette(Var Palette);

Description   **SetAllPalette** changes all palettes to the definition contained in **Palette**.

SetAspectRatio   [GRAPH Unit]

Syntax

Procedure SetAspectRatio(Xasp, Yasp : Word);

Description   **SetAspectRatio** changes the aspect ratio used to display graphics to **Xasp** divided by **Yasp**.

SetBkColor   [GRAPH Unit]

Syntax

Procedure SetBkColor(Color : Word);

Description   **SetBkColor** sets the default background color for the graphics mode using entry **Color** of the current palette.

SetCBreak   [DOS Unit]

Syntax

Procedure SetCBreak(Break : Boolean);

Description   **SetCBreak** turns CTRL-BREAK on (when **Break** is TRUE) or off (when **Break** is FALSE).

SetColor   [GRAPH Unit]

Syntax

Procedure SetColor(Color : Word);

Description   **SetColor** sets the current drawing color to entry **Color** of the palette.

SetDate   [DOS Unit]

Syntax

Procedure SetDate(Year, Month, Day : Word);

Description   **SetDate** updates the system clock to the date passed as parameters. For example, the command **SetDate (1990,12,1)** sets the date to December 1, 1990.

SetFAttr   [DOS Unit]

Syntax

Procedure SetFAttr(Var F; Attr : Word);

Description   **SetFAttr** sets the attribute byte of file **F** to **Attr**. File **F** must be assigned but not opened before calling this procedure.

SetFillPattern   [GRAPH Unit]

Syntax

Procedure SetFillPattern(Pattern : FillPatternType;
                         Color : Word);

Description   **SetFillPattern** defines the graphic pattern used to fill portions of the screen with commands such as **FillPoly** and **FloodFill**.

SetFillStyle   [GRAPH Unit]

Syntax

Procedure SetFillStyle(Pattern : Word;
                       Color : Word);

Description   **SetFillStyle** sets the pattern used to fill areas of a graphic display.

SetFTime   [DOS Unit]

Syntax

Procedure SetFTime(Var f; Time : LongInt);

Description   **SetFTime** sets the time stamp of file **f** to the value of **Time**, which is a packed representation of the time and date. **Time** is created with the procedure **PackTime**.

SetGraphBufSize   [GRAPH Unit]

Syntax

Procedure SetGraphBufSize(BufSize : Word);

Description   **SetGraphBufSize** sets the size of the graphics buffer.

SetGraphMode   [GRAPH Unit]

Syntax

Procedure SetGraphMode(Mode : Integer);

Description   **SetGraphMode** sets the current graphics mode to that specified by **Mode**.

SetIntVec   [DOS Unit]

Syntax

Procedure SetIntVec(IntNo : Byte; Vector : Pointer);

Description   **SetIntVec** places the value of **Vector** at the interrupt **IntNo** in the interrupt vector table.

SetLineStyle   [GRAPH Unit]

Syntax

Procedure SetLineStyle(LineStyle : Word;
                       Pattern : Word;
                       Thickness : Word);

Description   **SetLineStyle** determines the style, pattern, and thickness of lines drawn in Graphics mode.

SetPalette   [GRAPH Unit]

Syntax

Procedure SetPalette(ColorNum : Word; Color : ShortInt);

Description   **SetPalette** sets color number **ColorNum** of the active palette to **Color**.

SetRGBPalette   [GRAPH Unit]

Syntax

Procedure SetRGBPalette(ColorNum,
                        RedValue,
                        GreenValue,
                        BlueValue : Integer);

Description   **SetRGBPalette** sets palette entry **ColorNum** to consist of any combination of red, green, and blue.

SetTextBuf

Syntax

Procedure SetTextBuf(Var f : Text; Var Buf);
Procedure SetTextBuf(Var f : Text; Var Buf; Size : Word);

Description   SetTextBuf assigns text file **f** to buffer **Buf**. If size is not specified, the buffer's size is that of **Buf**. **Size** can be used to override the default buffer size.

SetTextJustify   [GRAPH Unit]

Syntax

Procedure SetTextJustify(Horiz, Vert : Word);

Description   **SetTextJustify** defines the display format used by **OutText** and **OutTextXY**.

SetTextStyle   [GRAPH Unit]

Syntax

Procedure SetTextStyle(Font : Word;
                       Direction : Word;
                       CharSize : Word);

Description   **SetTextStyle** determines how characters will be displayed in Graphics mode. The characteristics include the font, the direction in which the writing takes place, and the size of the characters.

SetTime   [DOS Unit]

Syntax

Procedure SetTime(Hour, Minute, Second, Sec100 : Word);

Description   **SetTime** sets the system clock according to the values passed as parameters.

SetUserCharSize [GRAPH Unit]

Syntax

Procedure SetUserCharSize(MultX, DivX, MultY, DivY : Word);

Description **SetUserCharSize** changes the width and height proportions for stroked fonts. For example, if **MultX** is 1 and **DivX** is 2, then characters will be displayed with one-half the width they would normally have.

SetVerify [DOS Unit]

Syntax

Procedure SetVerify(Verify : Boolean);

Description **SetVerify** turns disk-write verification on (when **Verify** is TRUE) or off (when **Verify** is FALSE).

SetViewPort [GRAPH Unit]

Syntax

Procedure SetViewPort(x1, y1, x2, y2 : Integer;
                                  Clip : Boolean);

Description **SetViewPort** selects a rectangular portion of the graphics screen to use as the active screen. When clipping is TRUE, drawings are clipped at the borders of the viewport.

SetVisualPage   [GRAPH Unit]

Syntax

Procedure SetVisualPage(Page : Word);

Description   **SetVisualPage** selects the graphics page to display.

SetWriteMode   [GRAPH Unit]

Syntax

Procedure SetWriteMode(WriteMode : Integer);

Description   **SetWriteMode** selects one of two modes for drawing lines. In **CopyPut** mode (0) lines are drawn using the assembler MOV command. In **XORPut** mode (1) lines are drawn using the XOR command.

Sin

Syntax

Function Sin(R: Real) : Real;

Description   **Sin** returns the sine of **R**.

SizeOf

Syntax

Function SizeOf(Var Variable) : Word;

Description   SizeOf returns the number of bytes required by a variable or a data type.

Sound   [CRT Unit]

Syntax

Procedure Sound(Freq: Word);

Description   **Sound** generates a tone from the PC's speaker at a frequency specified by **Freq.** The tone continues until the **NoSound** command is issued.

SPtr

Syntax

Function SPtr : Word;

Description   **SPtr** returns the current value of the stack pointer (SP) register.

Sqr

Syntax

Function Sqr(R: Real) : Real;

Description   **Sqr** returns the square of **R.**

Sqrt

Syntax

Function Sqrt(R: Real) : Real;

Description   Sqrt returns the square root of **R**.

SSeg

Syntax

Function SSeg : Word;

Description   SSeg returns the current value of the stack segment (SS) register.

Str

Syntax

Procedure Str(I: Integer; [:Length,] Var S: String);
Procedure Str(R: Real; [:Length:Decimals,] Var S: String);

Description   Str converts a real or integer number into a string.

Succ

Syntax

Function Succ(S: Scalar): Integer;

Description   Succ advances by one the value of any scalar.

Swap

Syntax

Function Swap(I: Integer) : Integer;

Description   **Swap** reverses the positions of the low- and high-order bytes in an integer. For example, if **I** equals 00FFh, **Swap** returns FF00h.

SwapVectors   [DOS Unit]

Syntax

Procedure SwapVectors;

Description   **SwapVectors** exchanges the current values of the interrupt vector table with those that were saved when the program started executing.

TextBackground   [CRT Unit]

Syntax

Procedure TextBackground(Color: Byte);

Description   **TextBackground** changes the default background color to that specified by **Color**.

TextColor   [CRT Unit]

Syntax

Procedure TextColor(Color: Byte);

Description   **TextColor** changes the default foreground color to that specified by **Color**.

TextHeight   [GRAPH Unit]

Syntax

Function TextHeight(TextString : String) : Word;

Description   **TextHeight** determines how much vertical space **TextString** will require given the current font and multiplication factor.

TextMode   [CRT Unit]

Syntax

Procedure TextMode(Mode : Word);

Description   **TextMode** activates one of the text modes supported by Turbo Pascal. These include

```
Const
  BW40      =      0; (* 40 x 25 black & white / color adapter *)
  CO40      =      1; (* 40 x 25 color / color adapter *)
  C40       = CO40;  (* For 3.0 compatibility *)
  BW80      =      2; (* 80 x 25 black & white / color adapter *)
  CO80      =      3; (* 80 x 25 color / color adapter *)
  C80       = CO80;  (* For 3.0 compatibility *)
  MONO      =      7; (* 80 x 25 monochrome adapter *)
  Font8x8   =    256; (* EGA and VGA 43- and 50-line mode *)
```


TextWidth   [GRAPH Unit]

Syntax

Function TextWidth(TextString : String);

Description   **TextWidth** returns the width in pixels required to display **TextWidth** given the current font and multiplication factor.

Trunc

Syntax

Function Trunc(R: Real) : Integer;

Description   **Trunc** returns the integer portion of **R**. The result must be within the legal range of an integer.

Truncate

Syntax

Procedure Truncate(Var f);

Description   **Truncate** forces end of file at the current position of the file pointer. Contents of the file beyond the file pointer are lost.

TypeOf

Syntax

Function TypeOf(object) ; Pointer:

Description   **TypeOf** returns a pointer to an object type's virtual method table. The function takes a single parameter which can be either an object type identifier or an instance of an object. The primary use of **TypeOf** is to determine whether two objects (or an object type and an object instance) are the same type.

UnPackTime   [DOS Unit]

Syntax

Procedure UnPackTime(Time : LongInt;
                          Var DT : DateTime);

Description   **UnPackTime** decodes the variable **Time** and returns the results in **DT**. The structure of **DateTime** is

```
Type
  DateTime = Record
    Year, Month, Day, Hour, Min, Sec : Word;
    END;
```

Upcase

Syntax

Function Upcase(C : Char) : Char;

Description   **Upcase** returns the uppercase value of **C** if **C** is a lowercase letter.

Val

Syntax

Procedure Val(S: String; Var R: Real; Var Code: Integer);
Procedure Val(S: String; Var I: Integer; Var Code: Integer);

Description   **Val** attempts to convert **S** into a numerical value (**R** or **I**). If the conversion is successful, Turbo Pascal sets **Code** equal to zero. If unsuccessful, **Code** contains an integer that represents the character in the string at which the error occurred.

WhereX   [CRT Unit]

Syntax

Function WhereX: Byte;

Description   **WhereX** returns the column in the current window at which the cursor is located.

WhereY   [CRT Unit]

Syntax

Function WhereY : Byte;

Description   **WhereY** returns the row in the current window at which the cursor is located.

Window   [CRT Unit]

Syntax

Procedure Window(x1,y1,x2,y2 : Byte);

Description   **Window** restricts the active screen to the rectangle defined by coordinates **x1:y1** (upper left) and **x2:y2** (lower right). Turbo Pascal treats the upper-left corner of the window as coordinates 1:1.

Write   (WriteLn)

Syntax

Procedure Write({Var F: File,} Parameters);
Procedure WriteLn({Var F: File,} Parameters);

Description   **Write** accepts a list of parameters, which it writes to the default output device. When the first parameter is a file variable, output is directed to that file. **WriteLn**, which can be used only on text files, operates in the same way as **Write**, but it adds a carriage return and line feed at the end of the output.